Entrepreneurship, Innovation and Sustainable Growth

Entrepreneurship and innovation play a vital role in fostering sustainable development. Advances in technology and communications have both transformed the process of business as well as strengthened the role of entrepreneurship in developed and developing countries. This important book is the first to provide the fundamental concepts and applications for faculty and students in this field, and also serves as a professional reference for practicing entrepreneurs and policymakers.

Each chapter provides a clear guide to the conceptual and practical elements that characterize entrepreneurship and the process of new venture formation, including functional strategies in key areas such as marketing, information technology, human resources management, and accounting and finance.

Questions and exercises are presented throughout in order to encourage discussion and problem-solving. A quick summary of the important concepts and definitions are also provided. Keeping practicality as the book's core aim, all chapters include a long case study to set the scene and then draw upon shorter cases from both developing and developed countries to reinforce key learning objectives and the real-world application of the book's core concepts.

Nader H. Asgary is Professor of Management and Economics at Bentley University, USA, and founder and President of the CYRUS Institute of Knowledge.

Emerson A. Maccari is Professor and the Dean of Graduate School of Management at UNINOVE University, São Paulo, Brazil.

Entrepreneurship, Innovation and Sustainable Growth

Opportunities and Challenges

Nader H. Asgary and Emerson A. Maccari

Routledge
Taylor & Francis Group

LONDON AND NEW YORK

First published 2020
by Routledge
2 Park Square, Milton Park, Abingdon, Oxon OX14 4RN

and by Routledge
52 Vanderbilt Avenue, New York, NY 10017

Routledge is an imprint of the Taylor & Francis Group, an informa business

British Library Cataloguing-in-Publication Data
A catalogue record for this book is available from the British Library

Library of Congress Cataloging-in-Publication Data
Names: Asgary, Nader H., author. | Maccari, Emerson A., author.
Title: Entrepreneurship, innovation and sustainable growth /
Nader H. Asgary and Emerson A. Maccari.
Description: Abingdon, Oxon; New York, NY : Routledge, 2020. |
Includes bibliographical references and index. |
Identifiers: LCCN 2019033583 (print) | LCCN 2019033584 (ebook) |
ISBN 9780367204624 (hardback) | ISBN 9780367204631 (paperback) |
ISBN 9780429261640 (ebook) Subjects: LCSH: Entrepreneurship. |
Sustainable development. | Technological innovations–Economic aspects.
Classification: LCC HB615 .A84 2020 (print) |
LCC HB615 (ebook) | DDC 658.4/08–dc23
LC record available at https://lccn.loc.gov/2019033583
LC ebook record available at https://lccn.loc.gov/2019033584

ISBN: 978-0-367-20462-4 (hbk)
ISBN: 978-0-367-20463-1 (pbk)
ISBN: 978-0-429-26164-0 (ebk)

Typeset in Bembo
by Newgen Publishing UK

Visit the eResources: www.routledge.com/9780367204631

Dedicated to our family members!

Contents

Figures

Tables

Preface

Entrepreneurship, creativity, and innovation, amalgamated with the revolution in information technology and communications, are transforming the way businesses innovate and initiate processes around the world. This new approach, which is both creative and pioneering, is leading to significant economic efficiencies and improvements in the quality of life for billions of people globally. Many policymakers are initiating policies supporting entrepreneurial startups that result in job creation and economic development. The aim of this book is to contribute to the advancement of knowledge in the aforementioned areas and share experience with stakeholders, thus helping the advancement of economic development and growth.

This book has evolved over the past few years as the authors were involved in a few international entrepreneurial studies and projects. Both authors have been professional entrepreneurs prior to entering into academia. The content of the book has grown and been enriched through comments and suggestions from faculty, graduate, and Ph.D. students from institutions of higher education such as Bentley University, UNINOVE University, MIT, and other institutions. Contributions from Marcos Mazieri to the development of Chapters 3 and 5 of the book are acknowledged and greatly appreciated. Mazdak Asgary, Rajat Sharma Subedi, Diana Kontsevaia, Zlatina Aleksandrova, Ashley Acosta, Jairo Oliveira, Luis Zanin, Marcelo Meneghatti, Evelyn Bernardo, Jonathan Sales, Eugenio Briales, and Alf Walle who have assisted in the review of the content deserve special thanks. The enormous research contributions from Bhaskar Nandina, Pang Lien Hsu, and Neeka Asgary in content creation, editing, organization, formatting, and design is greatly appreciated and acknowledged. The support from the Bentley University and the CYRUS Institute of Knowledge is acknowledged.

This book is organized into four main parts: environment, individual characteristics, organizational setup, and processes. In the introductory chapter we provide an overview of the book. Each part individually influence entrepreneurship and collectively bring a holistic view of this process. Each part contains two to three chapters, totaling ten chapters. In a nutshell, this book provides a systematical, logical, and practical approach to scholars, students, and entrepreneurs who seek to enhance their knowledge as well as support entrepreneurial instigation. Each chapter provides basic definitions, theoretical background, real-world examples, applications, and implications of the concepts discussed. Each chapter begins with a brief abstract, the chapter's learning objectives, and ends with questions for discussions. Quick reviews summarizing the main topics are present within each chapter. Also, all the chapters have an opening case that highlights the key concepts, video clips, and questions for class discussion. Furthermore, the book displays more than 50 real-world examples from both the developing and the developed countries in the form of short case studies, containing elegant images about individuals, organizations, companies, and more.

About the authors

Dr. Nader H. Asgary, Professor of Management and Economics at Bentley University.

Dr. Nader Asgary is Professor of Management and Economics at Bentley University and founder and President of the CYRUS Institute of Knowledge (CIK). He also served as the Associate Provost for International Relations at Bentley, where he significantly expanded the global reach of the university. He has led several successful entrepreneurship and leadership-based development projects in Nicaragua, Brazil, Iran, the United States, etc. His extensive publication record coupled with his ample teaching and practical experiences in both public and private sectors enriches this textbook.

Dr. Asgary has published in numerous national and international journals, such as *Economic Inquiry, Journal of Business Ethics, Tourism Economics, Middle East Journal of Management*, and *Journal of Higher Education Policy and Management* and has participated in many international and national conference presentations and has been a guest speaker. He has taught courses in international business, global leadership, economics, and finance at the undergraduate and graduate levels and has been Ph.D students' advisor and the recipient of many educator awards.

CIK is a think-tank that focuses on research in business development, sustainability, and economic development. Some of CIK's (http://cyrusik.org/) activities include annual international conferences, executive training, and research/consulting services. As the president and founder of CIK, he has created an intellectual and networking environment for scholars, practitioners, and philanthropists to share their ideas and contribute to the advancement of knowledge and make a difference.

Dr. Emerson Antonio Maccari, Dean of Graduate School of Management and Professor at UNINOVE University in São Paulo, Brazil.

Dr. Maccari has led proposals in preparation for the development of new Masters and Doctorate programs in the fields of administration, accounting, economics, tourism, education, engineering, law, and health care. Since 1999, he has led and advanced Graduate, Masters, and Doctorate programs at the UNINOVE University and the University of São Paulo (USP).

In 2013 Dr. Maccari helped to create the first Master in Entrepreneurship in Brazil at the University of São Paulo. Additionally, he has assisted in the creation and development of scientific journals in the platform Open Journal System (OJS). He is a consultant to the CAPES, a Brazilian Agency that oversees developing and evaluating Graduate programs. Dr. Maccari has organized and led several international conferences, in particular SINGEP – International Symposium on Project Management, Innovation and Sustainability. He has developed international courses for graduate students in the United

States, Germany, France, Portugal, and China in the areas of Entrepreneurship, Innovation, Project Management, Strategy, Sustainability, Smart Cities, Sport Management, and Healthcare Management.

He is the co-founder of the Al Capizza Pizza with a unique concept called "Aquarium Concept (Fish-Bowl)". So far, Al Capizza has three owned companies (Flags Ship) and eight franchising and its strategy is to expand to 20 in São Paulo and other regions of Brazil by the end of 2019.

Introduction

Overview

Entrepreneurship and innovation play a vital role in fostering sustainable growth and development. Advances in technology and communications have transformed the process of business initiations and accelerated entrepreneurial operations in developed and developing countries. In this book, we examine the link between entrepreneurship and innovation from both a practitioner's and a scholar's perspective. We discuss entrepreneurship and innovation by placing entrepreneurial practice within broader contexts such as the economical, institutional, and technological circumstances.

In the introductory chapter we briefly describe thoughts, ideas, and processes that most entrepreneurs perform prior to moving forward to start a new venture. In the future chapters' topics of discussion include the characteristics of entrepreneurs, economic and technological environments, institutional and cultural infrastructure, and the process of new venture formation, which includes functional strategies in key areas such as marketing, information technology, human resources management, and accounting and finance. There are also broader strategic issues discussed, such as ethics, corporate social responsibility (CSR), strategy, institutions, and governance. We have provided questions that would encourage discussions and quick reviews that summarize topics within each chapter. Long and short case studies and videos of entrepreneurs, organizations, companies, etc. are incorporated within each chapter from both developing and developed countries. They help to reinforce key learning objectives and provide real-world examples.

Overall, we present a comprehensive perspective of the entrepreneurial ecosystem that are composed of interdependent players and factors that are coordinated and enable productive entrepreneurship. The six players in this ecosystem are government, corporations, non-governmental organizations (NGOs), foundations, academia, and investors. Their roles are essential and complementary to each other in the creation of an ecosystem in which entrepreneurship can flourish. In future chapters, we will discuss these issues in detail. These players can both complement and advance entrepreneurship by enabling, celebrating, training, and funding existing and upcoming entrepreneurs. And in this process – in the words of Adam Smith – serving their self-interests and society at large.[1]

This book is unique for its presentation of entrepreneurship and development within the institutional and technological context of developing regions. The role of entrepreneurship and innovation in the context of ongoing economic growth and development is discussed, taking into consideration the expanding globalization. Constraints and opportunities are discussed in a proactive manner. Each chapter contains lessons to be learned from successful entrepreneurs and firms. In addition, the book provides conceptual and practical guidance to entrepreneurs who seek greater knowledge and control over their careers and organizations, thus advancing sustainable development. The book provides an exceptional and lucrative contribution to economic growth and development literature.

Aims and contributions

In addition to the introductory chapter, the book consists of four parts: environment, individual characteristics, organization, and process. The introductory chapter provides an overview of the book and links the entrepreneurs' objectives and challenges to a roadmap that ultimately leads to the creation of a new venture. Chapter 3, entitled "Technology, communications, and entrepreneurship", has an overarching impact on all parts of the textbook. The summary of all chapters and parts are briefly described in the following. In a nutshell, the book provides a systematical, logical, and practical approach for scholars, students, and entrepreneurs who seek to enhance their knowledge and support entrepreneurial initiation.

Who should read this book?

This book is a vital resource for those concerned with the relations between entrepreneurship, innovation, and sustainable development. Its aim is to be a primary text that provides fundamental concepts and applications for faculty and students, and also serves as a professional reference for practicing entrepreneurs and policymakers. Professional jargon is kept to a minimum for the benefit of aspiring entrepreneurs and is suitable for both undergraduate and MBA courses geared towards topics such as entrepreneurship, business development, small and medium enterprises (SMEs), and economic development and growth.

Introductory chapter

The introductory chapter defines and describe the steps involved in the development of a business model. We will describe in brief the influence of an individual's personal and professional characteristics, and public circumstances on opportunity recognition. We will discuss frameworks about the processes of idea discovery to the development of a business model. Future chapters in the book will provide details of theoretical and empirical evidence on each section of the business model.

Part I: The environment and entrepreneurship

In this part, we discuss the entrepreneurial ecosystem in the context of developing economies. Chapter 1 provides explanation of the association between entrepreneurship, innovation, and development in an era of globalization with reference to both micro and macro variables. Chapter 2 focuses on both formal and informal institutional environments, with information on the government policies that support entrepreneurship and other related institutions. Chapter 3 focuses on the role of technology and communication and its overarching impact on all elements in the ecosystem.

Part II: Individual characteristics and training

In this part, we examine an individual's intent on pursuing entrepreneurial initiatives in developing economies. Chapter 4 discusses topics such as competencies, spirit, training, personality, and professional experience of entrepreneurs. Chapter 5 focuses on the entrepreneur's creativity and the ability to innovate. The ability to innovate and be creative is strongly associated with entrepreneurial opportunities. Creative ideas serve as the link between observing problems or needs and creating solutions to these needs. Entrepreneurs are the opportunists who search for answers and in this process, advance themselves and society.

Part III: The organization

This part is composed of Chapters 6 and 7 which present important information of building organization with good principles. We will discuss how to build institutions and governance, develop a viable roadmap to grow and be successful. Chapter 7 provides best practices, including social entrepreneurship, competitive advantage, and the triple bottom line.

Part IV: Process

In the final part, composed of Chapters 8, 9, and 10, we present the process for venture creation. To create a sustainable enterprise, the entrepreneur needs to educate themselves on aspects of business such as marketing, finance, and accounting. Understanding concepts in these chapters are vital for creating a functioning business.

A brief overview of each chapter

Introductory chapter: entrepreneurial discovery, creationary, and business model development

The introductory chapter provides concepts and techniques that entrepreneurs perform prior to the start of a new venture. The steps involved result in the development of a model that encompasses all concepts of the new business. Many factors influence the start of a venture, some of them are individuals' characteristics, personal and public circumstances, and market research, all of which influence the process of opportunity discovery and creationist and development of the model. We will set the stage for an in-depth presentation of theoretical and empirical corroborations in the areas of entrepreneurial environment, personal characteristics, organization structure, and process that is involved to succeed.

Part I: The environment and entrepreneurship

Chapter 1: Entrepreneurship and development in the era of globalization

In this chapter, the role that entrepreneurship plays in advancing sustainable development is analyzed, setting the stage to discuss distinctive skills, perceptions, orientations, and environmental challenges that impact entrepreneurship. Relevant theoretical principles are illustrated, using examples from both developing and developed economies. Fundamental economic theories of development are also presented while the positive and negative impacts of globalization on entrepreneurship are examined.

There are fundamental questions that scholars, policymakers, NGOs, and citizens ask about the impact of growing globalization on development and especially about entrepreneurship. Some questions include: Does globalization accelerate development by advancing entrepreneurship in developing countries? What is the impact of entrepreneurship on innovation in developing countries? What are the effects of entrepreneurship on employment and income? How has entrepreneurship in developing countries been impacted by the revolution of technology? In this chapter, we will provide an overview of these topics, which we will discuss in more detail over subsequent chapters.

Chapter 2: Cultural context, entrepreneurship, and development

This chapter introduces the concept of the entrepreneurial ecosystem and focuses on critical components of this ecosystem. Critical components include the national culture of entrepreneurship, formal and informal institutional framework, and government policies in support of entrepreneurship. The cultural context of entrepreneurial activities and traditions harmonize with innovation, motivations, and entrepreneurial endeavors. The concept of cultural convergence and its relation to both entrepreneurship and development is presented. By the help of models by Hofstede and other scholars, we examine the link between entrepreneurship and development. Numerous examples in the chapter identify ways policymakers in developing countries can enhance cultural traits to encourage and support entrepreneurial efforts. We consider it vital for growth-oriented entrepreneurship, as it is an important vessel for innovation and job creation. Therefore, governments should encourage entrepreneurship and help it grow and contribute to the country's economy.

Chapter 3: Technology and communications

This chapter presents the roles of technology and communications in an entrepreneurial ecosystem by analyzing their efficiency to create links for entrepreneurial activities. Technological advances and their applications are pervasive in world economics and are constantly changing. Technology has nurtured and advanced entrepreneurship since the dawn of the industrial revolution. The current digital revolution has exponentially expanded the impact of technology. Technological innovations have led to increased production and communication efficiency, allowing for better quality goods and services to be produced and delivered at lower costs. The production of new goods and services has become easier and more innovative, making it a catalyst for entrepreneurship in both developed and developing countries.

Technology is an overarching and constantly evolving phenomenon that changes the economic realm by transforming business and consumer demands. "Technology", in this context, refers to making, modifying, and using knowledge, tools, and operational systems in order to solve problems. This chapter focuses on the influence that technology and communications have had and continue to have on creating value and new opportunities.

Part II: Individual characteristics and training

Chapter 4: Personality, experience, and training

In this chapter, the nature of entrepreneurs and entrepreneurship, also called the entrepreneurial spirit, is discussed. We focus on personal characteristics, educational backgrounds, and prior experiences of entrepreneurs, while also dealing with ecological and social factors that influence entrepreneurial activities. The different perspectives surrounding entrepreneurs and entrepreneurship are discussed, from basic definitions to factors such as the education and experience that influence them. The chapter explores the importance of entrepreneurship and the role that experience, training, social and cultural connections, and networking play in shaping an entrepreneur's life. Most definitions of entrepreneurship agree on individuals' behaviors, such as taking initiative, continuous organization of social and economic mechanisms, turning resources and situations into something practical, and the acceptance of risk or failure.

Chapter 5: Creativity, innovation, and development

Creativity and the ability to innovate are strongly linked to entrepreneurship and economic development. Creativity and innovation are key factors that contribute to an enterprise's ability to thrive in an increasingly global marketplace. Creative ideas are connections between problems and solutions. A vital role of entrepreneurs is to find creative solutions to these problems. Innovation is not just about solving a problem, but the solution must also fit the customers' specific needs and desires. In this chapter, a deeper understanding of links between creativity, innovation, economic development, and entrepreneurship are discussed. The impacts of culture on creativity and innovation are examined and cultural influences on public policy are analyzed. The attitudes towards creativity and innovation vary widely from culture to culture, as does the access to and adoption of modern information and communication technology. Cultural attitudes towards creativity can facilitate or impede an enterprise's ability to bring an innovative product to market, thus affecting their economic success. The role of governments and public policy in offering incentives and creating rules, regulations, and rights are critical in this process.

Part III: The organization

Chapter 6: Institutions, governance, and strategy

In this chapter, we will present definitions of institutions, governance, and strategy, as well as their relationship to entrepreneurial activities and sustainable development. A strategic guide for the formation of a sustainable enterprise is presented. Understanding the role that institutions and governance play in articulating and implementing successful strategies are discussed in this chapter. Knowledge of these key concepts is necessary on both the micro and macro levels for building a sustainable and transparent organization with a credible system of governance. Good governance and relevant supporting institutions advance entrepreneurial activities in a society. When rules, regulations, and a clear and transparent roadmap for operations are designed and implemented, they will lead to a flourishing economy.

Chapter 7: Ethics and corporate social responsibility

The definitions are provided for the concepts of ethics and corporate social responsibility (CSR). The implications in the era of globalization on businesses and entrepreneurial activities are discussed. The chapter describes the stakeholders' theory with distinct emphasis on human resources management. It also addresses how ethical solutions to issues and adhering to CSR in developing countries create conditions for fairness and shared values, which will help the development of enterprises to create fair market conditions.

Part IV: Process

Chapter 8: Marketing, technology, and entrepreneurship

In the era of globalization and fierce competition, marketing is essential to the survival and success of an organization. Increase in the means for marketing in this era seems to have created "a flat world" to advertise products, services, and ideas. The focus of this chapter is on the knowhow and tools necessary for entrepreneurs, particularly those in developing countries, to market their products or services. Both the marketing concepts and their application help an entrepreneur advance his/her objectives. The role of marketing in the success of the business, the characteristics of marketing, and the essential application of technology in developing countries are described. Concepts such as the marketing mix (price, place, product, and promotion) and customer loyalty programs are explored. New means of communication provide a degree of competitive advantages for entrepreneurs and SMEs over large corporations.

Chapter 9: Financing opportunities and challenges

In this chapter, we take a detailed look at the opportunities and constraints facing entrepreneurs in their pursuit of financial resources. Emphasis is placed on the importance of obtaining appropriate and affordable streams of funding. Both direct and indirect constraints are discussed, from a global perspective, on both the micro and macro levels. The micro opportunities and constraints are the acquisition of funding opportunities in support of startups, while the macro opportunities and constraints concern generally with government policies. Comparing them in scale differentiation is made between startup entrepreneurs and large enterprises in their quest to secure financing.

Chapter 10: Essentials of bookkeeping

This chapter address two important questions related to bookkeeping for an entrepreneur: first, why must an entrepreneur keep financial records; and second, what are its important components? It is hard to acquire the necessary assistance for growth without knowledge of financial feasibility of the enterprise. The importance of both financial and managerial accounting from the entrepreneurial perspective are discussed. Precise record keeping is essential for tax purposes and for acquiring additional funding. The benefits of thorough accounting as well as the problems that arise from it are underlined in the chapter. It is very difficult to evaluate an idea or a business without being able to quantify its value in the marketplace. Therefore, a budget is one of the most important documents an entrepreneur must create which depends upon the detailed records of expenditures and revenues. In developing economies, entrepreneurs often operate in the informal sector, reducing the need to keep financial records for tax purposes.

Note

1 Adam Smith (1776) An Inquiry into the Nature and Causes of the Wealth of Nations.

Introductory chapter

Entrepreneurial discovery, creationary, and business model development

Learning objectives:

1. *Define a business opportunity*
2. *Discuss the indicator of the ease of doing business index*
3. *Differentiate internal and external stimulated opportunities*
4. *Analyze evaluation of the viability of an idea*
5. *Describe the business model and its essential role in building a viable business*

Introduction

The opening chapter will present an overview of the concepts and practices that entrepreneurs perform prior to the start of a business venture. It defines and describes all the steps involved from the formation of a business idea to the development of a business model. At each stage in the developmental journey, the entrepreneur discovers vital business concepts that govern the creation and substance of the new business venture. A brief discussion of the methods in starting entrepreneurial activities, discovery, and creation are highlighted. The chapter also discusses how an entrepreneur's individual characteristics, personal and public circumstances influence decisions that lead towards a successful opportunity recognition.

Each step of the creation process is an attempt by the entrepreneur to reach the goal of "enterprise formation". Each step is vital to the realization of a successful business model that has considered most aspects in business formation. Also, this chapter will provide a business model that combines the theoretical and applied knowledge discussed in the following sections. This chapter will end with a brief description of each section of the book. Future chapters will provide details on theoretical and empirical evidence in the areas of entrepreneurial environment, personal characteristics, organization, and process.

Defining a business opportunity

Scholars have used different terminologies such as recognition,[1] identification,[2] discovery,[3] and finding[4] to explain an opportunity. The business opportunity is defined as the process that leads to an end goal. The end goal depends on what each entrepreneur considers as a worthy achievement. According to De Bono,[5] a business opportunity is a "course of action" worth pursuing using non-linear creative thinking. De Bono's non-linear thinking characterizes a business opportunity as an effort to reach a solution(s) by expanding thinking in multiple directions, rather than in one direction. Based on the concept that there are multiple starting points from where one can apply logic to a business problem, you can ultimately end at multiple valid solutions. Kirzner[6] described a business opportunity as an entrepreneur's ability to recognize commercial value of products or services to be sold in new markets at a profit. Others scholars[7] see business opportunity as a detail plan to translate the "business concept into reality." In their search to understand an opportunity, Hulbert, Brown, and Adams[8] define it as the goal to "meet an unsatisfied need in a profitable manner." Ardichvili, Cardozo, and Ray[9] emphasized that the end goal is to deliver superior value to the end-user. While we observe that scholars have some degree of differences in their definition of the business opportunity, perhaps business discovery can be summarized as a process to achieve an expected positive outcome and gain.

Furthermore, the definition of business opportunity can be described as an end goal where a new functioning "business model" has been created. We achieve the end goal by following three consecutive processes, namely: discovery, development, and model-creation. In realizing the process we take into consideration the role of the entrepreneur both as a creative thinker and an acute businessman. Further, we also examine entrepreneurs' strategies in conjunction with his surrounding environment.[10] A functioning business concept can be developed to the following five outcomes:[11]

1. An invention looking to become a commercialized product,
2. Expanding products or services to new markets,
3. Commercializing an unmet market need,
4. Businesses trying to create differentiated products or services for an existing market,
5. Testing a novice business approach in the matured industry.

The process of opportunity recognition is considered an iterative process where each of the steps (discovery, development, and business model) are repeatedly tested as time progresses.[12] Iteration gives a greater advantage for fine tuning and staying relevant to the potentially changing market environment. While the model in this chapter is specified for the creation of new ventures, many aspects of the model apply to existing business strategies. As the recurring process of idea discovery and its development, the business model is further strengthened with newer concepts and approaches that become relevant to changing market dynamics (see Figure 0.1). Finally, the process of opportunity

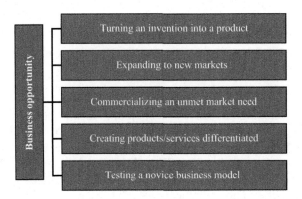

Figure 0.1 Defining opportunity

recognition favors improvement of business processes, the discovery of products, and recognition of trends and acknowledgment of changing market situations.

Environmental condition and entrepreneurship

The environment condition plays a significant role in the creation and the rate of success of entrepreneurial activities. Conditions that best suit venture creation is analyzed and presented using "the ease of doing business index." It is an index created by Simeon Djankov at the World Bank Group[13] and is widely regarded as an indicator that suggests entrepreneurial environment across countries around the world. Each country tries to improve its index rankings to portray itself as having business-friendly regulations. The indexes comprehensive use of 11 indicator sets measure aspects of business regulation that matter for entrepreneurship. An important finding is that better performance in doing business is associated with lower levels of unemployment and poverty.

Opportunity formation: discovery vs creation

Opportunities come in various forms. From a customer's point of view, it might mean unmet needs or changes in spending habits and preferences. From a market's perspective, they include the discovery of a new resource or scarcity of the existing resource, opening of new local/international markets, or expansion of market size. Opportunities in the macroeconomic perspective include a change in government policies such as regulation, privatization, employment objectives, etc. Therefore, public policy revisions, social and demographic changes, and technological evolution are events that can disrupt the existing competitive equilibrium in a marketplace. These revisions, changes, and evolution will provide opportunities for entrepreneurial acceleration. Some of the most recent inventions such as the iPhone/iPad have evolved from entrepreneurs who exploited technological advances to meet future customer needs. Thomas Friedman, in his book titled "Thank You for Being Late"[14] states that in 2007 several new and innovative businesses and companies such as Airbnb, Facebook, and Twitter took off when their founder understood business opportunities created.[15]

TED – talk

Maya Penn started her first company when she was 8 years old, and thinks deeply about how to be responsible both to her customers and to the planet.

Source: www.ted.com/talks/maya_penn_meet_a_young_entrepreneur_
cartoonist_designer_activist

Academics and researchers on entrepreneurship consider the formation of an opportunity as a function of two separate theories. It is widely accepted that entrepreneurial opportunities are formed by the application of either the discovery theory[16] or the creation theory.[17] However, both discovery and creationist theories[18] assume that the goal of entrepreneurs is to form an enterprise and exploit opportunities.[19] Some scholars have provided a historical perspective of entrepreneurship, growth, and development.[20]

The discovery theory interprets all opportunities as objective phenomena. The theory considers "change" as a constant in the market, therefore opportunities to be ever-present. Opportunity discovery theorists argue that opportunities are independent of entrepreneurs in the marketplace and are waiting to be discovered.[21] It is the task of ambitious entrepreneurs to discover these opportunities by using different sources of information. Entrepreneurs use data collection techniques to identify any/all changes that are currently happening in the market and develop strategies to then exploit them. By considering opportunities to be objective the entrepreneur can use a variety of techniques to understand the expected potential outcomes associated with an opportunity. Other conditions inherent in discovery theory include decision-making to be dependent on the credibility of the knowledge source, the importance of opportunity cost, and an exploitation strategy which is relatively complete and unchanging.

The discovery approach sometimes occurs when entrepreneurs stumble across existing problems which they attempt to find a solution to. They could be existing unmet customers' needs that require fulfilling or access to new resources that can build into a business or an efficient method to conduct business. These opportunities may be in the domain that the entrepreneur has prior experience in. With years of knowledge and understanding of an industry, the entrepreneur develops skills to recognize either growth in the customer segment, advancement of technology in the industry, gaps between cost and selling price, or gaps in the supply chain, which can lead to an efficient business model. Companies such as Airbnb and Uber are business opportunities where the founders identified an opportunity to create an entirely new and efficient business model around existing products/markets.

Most established businesses go through an external opportunity recognition process, being alert to changes in the market and actively analyzing opportunities to upsell or cross-sell to their customers. They gather information of markets and conduct tests by either creating new products or new subsidiaries around newer opportunities.[22] Companies also keep track of their own procedures by performing detailed observation and evaluation of their supply chain system, technology, government regulation, and their competition.

Creationists are those who believe that opportunities are endogenous and, therefore, are created by the actions, reactions, and enactment of entrepreneurs discovering ways to produce new products or services.[23] An entrepreneur's actions are the competitive imperfections in markets that generate opportunities. The theory applies the Schumpeterian perspective of opportunities as thoughtful efforts by an entrepreneur to create new combinations of ideas, knowledge, and resources.[24] Entrepreneurs act on exogenous shocks that create opportunities and form organizations to exploit it.[25]

Opportunities where entrepreneurs deliberately create ideas happen when they are engaged in creative thinking.[26] The techniques of creative thinking are a way of generating solutions to current and future foreseen problems through the use of unconventional creative thinking. Decision-making in creationist theory is an iterative, inductive, incremental method that uses the rule of thumb, educated guess, and common sense to find diverse solutions. The creative process of new business ideas formation follow four stages[27] of maturity (see Figure 0.2):

A. **Preparation:** The first stage involves gathering information. An entrepreneur tries to learn things using attention, reasoning, and planning to gather information.
B. **Incubation:** It is the unconscious recombination of information that results in novel ideas in the future. It is the unconscious part of a process whereby an intuition may become validated as an insight.

C. **Illumination**: As ideas begin to mature, entrepreneurs have an epiphany regarding how to piece their thoughts together in a manner that makes sense. The moment of illumination can happen unexpectedly.

D. **Verification:** Creative ideas are subjected to critical thinking in order to become polished and persuasive. This stage involves actively creating and testing diverse business ideas.

The fundamental differences in process of opportunity formation between discovery and creation theory are the actions taken by the entrepreneurs from the two groups of scholars who have articulated the theories. Management and construction of the business model have different contexts when considering both the approaches. Table 0.1 shows the different approaches that an entrepreneur might take depending on in which approach the opportunity is generated.[28]

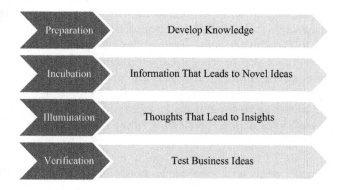

Figure 0.2 Creative approach

Table 0.1 Discovery and creation approach

	Discovery	*Creation*
Leadership	Based on expertise and experience	Based on charisma
Decision-making	Dependent on data; scientific; Values opportunity cost	Iterative, inductive, incremental decision-making
Human resource practices	Recruitment of specialized human capital	General and flexible human capital recruited from networking
Strategy	Relatively complete and set to move on	Emergent and changing
Finance	External capital sources such as banks and VC	"Bootstrapping", "friends, family"
Marketing	Changes in marketing mix as new information gets accumulated	Marketing mix fundamentally differs from existing channels
Sustaining competitive advantage	Speed, secrecy, and erecting barriers to entry may sustain advantages	Tacit learning is a path-dependent process which may sustain advantages

Role of information

While all entrepreneurs actively keep track of opportunities, experienced entrepreneurs develop greater pattern recognition skills of noticing connections between trends, changes, and events.[29] It is widely regarded by researchers[30] that entrepreneurs' superior intellectual skills and alertness are what makes them sensitive towards exploring new opportunities. Experienced entrepreneurs also quickly recognize the value in opportunities based on gut feeling rather than formal evaluation framework. This acquired skill set is the interaction of factors that combine individual characteristics, societal, cultural and institutional stimulation, which will be discussed in detail in future chapters. The aim of this book is to provide entrepreneurs with principles and frameworks for flourishing in the formation of the business.

Business ideas generated either through discovery or by creation are only as good as the information they are based on. Successful entrepreneurs have superior access to information that includes quality sources of search behavior, market gaps[31] which come from industry insiders, government connections, and financial institutions. Access to quality information depends on various factors, but the most important factor in emerging economies is an entrepreneur's status in the social ladder. Superior social ties and high-income groups have enhanced access to high-quality information about entrepreneurial opportunities.[32] However, entrepreneurs are alert to recognize the possibility of making money out of their existing business or new ventures by evolving their strategies through guesswork, analysis, and actions that test their initial findings. Entrepreneurs invest in building diverse social networks to improve the quantity and quality of information and to increase the speed of acquiring additional information.[33] Following either a deliberate search for a business idea or stumbling across an opportunity requires having credible knowledge, vigilance, and risk-taking.

In Table 0.2 is the summary of where ideas come from. Ideas can be broadly categorized into internally or externally stimulated by separating them on how deliberate the entrepreneur was in discovering the opportunity. Each of the two categories is divided

Table 0.2 Generating ideas

	Themes	*Illustrative key findings*
Internal stimulation	Personal desire and interest	Interest in the certain business sector and business idea from the beginning
	Family members	Encouragement and advice by parents and relatives
	A deliberate search of ideas	Series of activities to explore new business ideas and testing them
	New inventions/ discovery	Series of trial and error to find a market for a novice idea
External stimulation	Personal work experiences	Ideas generated observing current/past markets
	Personal experiences as customers	The desire to correct problems of products or services which were experienced as a consumer
	Evaluation	Growth in the product line, availability of new resources, new technology or gaps in the supply chain
	Market evaluations	New markets, government regulation, and challenging competition

into themes or techniques that contain recognized methods of idea generation. These techniques are highly influenced by the culture in which the individual lives or works. An individual's desire to create a venture can be influenced by both family members and his/her company's culture of innovation. Other techniques look at how a functioning venture creates ideas for new products and services by analyzing their market/customer needs. Each technique contains a series of activities that result in idea generation and have multiple factors (family, experience, reports) influencing the process.

Opportunity development and evaluation

Business opportunity can be realized by executing distinct processes of discovery, development, and creation (business model). Discovery is the process of creating or perceiving current and/or future market needs and/or underemployed resources. The customers' need previously discussed, the presence of resources, and new venture ideas arise from various channels ranging from personal expertise to deliberate research process. Opportunity development is the process where entrepreneurs perform "due diligence" by committing resources and investment for further development of an idea.[34] In this stage, entrepreneurs attempt to craft, shape, mold, and reconstruct the discovered opportunities by carrying out different fit and balance between resources and teams (human capital) to get the odds in their favor.[35] The important criteria are to consider the opportunity as moving targets where business strategies evolve through guesswork, analysis, and actions that the entrepreneur takes in an attempt to find a "fit".[36]

Development is the iterative process of "discovering fit" between particular market needs and specified resources, and in the process, the opportunity grows into a business model. The created business model compares market needs and resources until they match the entrepreneur's ambitions or objectives. In the following are evaluation methods that can be applied to an idea to discovering its business value.

An evaluation procedure known as feasibility analysis examines opportunities by stating the uniqueness/value of the discovery for prospective stakeholders. The method implies the existence of a business model, even one that might be basic in form. This basic business model contains the perceived market needs or resources that were discovered and conceptually create a business model that is feasible[37] in its abstract form. Feasibility analysis works in situations where business needs or underutilized resources are well-defined, easy to comprehend, and the knowledge of the market need is universally acknowledged.

However, for many opportunities, an entrepreneur discovers there is a need to define many of the aspects of a business model. Opportunities do not come with a defined market need, a fully functional product/service, or any prior evidence of its value to the stakeholders. Because the idea of the product/service is nascent, entrepreneurs face circumstances where the evaluation procedure has to define business concepts that make the business model. A popular procedure that may be adapted to a wide range of circumstances is the "stage-gate" procedure.[38] The procedure explicitly calls for evaluation of an opportunity at each of the several levels of its discovery where at each level the entrepreneur answers an integral business question. An opportunity to pass through each of the "gates" goes through a number of tests that aim to answer questions of its objective, problems it aims to solve, risks, technology/resource requirements, financials, the entrepreneur's responsibilities, and his/her personal objectives.

The entrepreneur is likely to conduct evaluations several times, and at every stage a piece of the business venture is realized. Evaluation of resources to market needs happen even

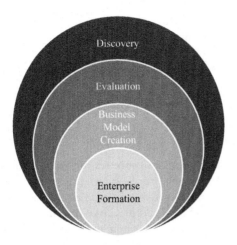

Figure 0.3 Evolution of opportunity

after the creation of a business venture and can often lead to useful revisions of business concepts or rethinking of business objectives for the venture to sustain. Additionally, the process also could lead to recognition of additional opportunities or adjustments to the initial vision of the business ideas. At the same time, it can result in the aborting of opportunities at any level of development. It is natural that the number of market needs and underemployed resources perceived greatly exceeds the number of successful businesses formed. Evolution of a business opportunity is summarized in Figure 0.3.

Business model

The business model is defined as "the architecture of a venture-soup to nuts-that lead to a financial outcome." [39,40] A business model contains viable and relatively reasonable financial details of the business opportunity. Formal cash flows, schedules of activities, and resource requirements are added to the continuously evolving venture creation process. Precision lays the foundation for cash flow statements and for identifying the major risk factors that could affect cash flow, all of these additions enable the business concept to transform into a full business plan. Figure 0.4 summarizes a business model.

Definitions[41]

Business Concept: An idea for a business that includes basic information about the service or product, the target demographic, and a unique selling proposition that gives a company an advantage over competitors. A business concept may involve a new product or simply a novel approach to marketing or delivering an existing product.

Business Model: A business model is a company's plan on how it will generate revenues and make a profit. It explains what products or services the business plans to manufacture and market, and how it plans to do so, including what expenses it will incur.

Figure 0.4 Business model

Financial Plan: A financial plan is a comprehensive evaluation of an investor's current and future financial state by using currently known variables to predict future cash flows, asset values, and withdrawal plans. These metrics are used along with estimates of venture growth to determine if the entrepreneur's financial goals can be met in the future.

A comprehensive business model includes not only a detailed report of the need, the resources, and the market size, but also a financial model estimates the value of the product or service that is being created and how that value might be distributed among stakeholders.[42] Financial reports can be considered as final steps of the development process as they require forecasting of cash flows which can be only determined by having detailed knowledge of all aspects of the business. The opportunity in financial terms is considered as investment thus is given a numerical value in currency denomination as all aspects of the business are standardized to financial terms.

Beyond the typical entrepreneurial process of venture formation, some new businesses are also formed through acquisitions, additional investment, or through loans. Methods of evaluating opportunities using financial terms/techniques such as payback, simple interest, discount or net present value (NPV), and internal rate of return (IRR) are widely used by venture capitalists, bankers, and financial experts.[43] An understanding of these methods of evaluation is important for the entrepreneur as they are the widely used medium of communication. Financial dimensions are covered in the future chapters.

Conclusion and future chapters

In this introductory chapter, we provide
entrepreneur will go through before he
new venture. These stages shall take place
individual's character, personal knowledg
cant impact on how an entrepreneur pro
provide theoretical and empirical presen
ment, personal characteristics, organizatio
important subjects.

We have developed questions that v
that summarize key subjects for each c
entrepreneurs, organizations, companie
to share experiences and advance discus
learning objectives of each chapter.

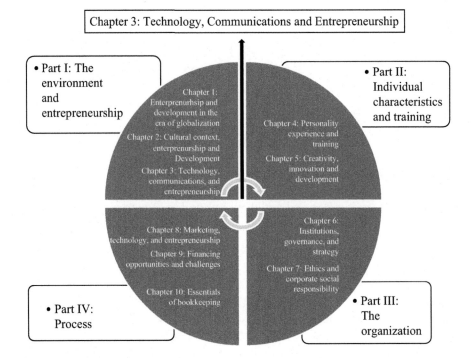

Figure 0.5 Textbook framework

Source: Adapted from Gartner, W. B. (1985). A conceptual framework for describing the phenomenon of new venture creation. Academy of Management Review, 10(4), 696–706.

The remaining of the book is summarized according to the Figure 0.5, showing an overarching impact on all sections of the textbook. The following shows each of the four parts of the book and the chapter titles. In summary, the book provides a systematic, logical, and practical approach for scholars, students, and entrepreneurs who seek to enhance their knowledge in the field and support entrepreneurial initiation.

Part I: The environment and entrepreneurship

This part discusses the entrepreneurial ecosystem in the context of developing economies. Chapter 1 provides an explanation of the association between entrepreneurship, innovation, and sustainable development in an era of globalization with reference to both micro and macro variables. Chapter 2 focuses on both formal and informal institutional environments, with information on government policies that support entrepreneurship and other related institutions. Chapter 3 focuses on the role of technology and communication and its overarching impact on all elements of the ecosystem.

Part II: Individual characteristics and training

This part is devoted to an individual's intent on pursuing entrepreneurial initiatives in developing economies. Chapter 4 discusses topics such as competencies, spirit, training, personality, and professional experience of entrepreneurs. Chapter 5 focuses on the entrepreneur's creativity and the ability to innovate. The ability to innovate and be creative is strongly associated with entrepreneurial opportunities. Creative ideas serve as the link between observing problems or needs and creating solutions to these needs. Entrepreneurs are the opportunists who search for answers and in this process advance themselves and society.

Part III: The organization

In this part, we explore the behavior of the organization as an economic participant and a corporate citizen. Chapter 6 describes institutions, governance, and strategy. It also provides an overview of key aspects of these factors in the context of developing countries with some learning lessons from developed countries. For most entrepreneurs in developing countries, knowledge of these issues remains new, therefore its discussion felt essential. Chapter 7, turns to the multiple business stakeholders and explores issues of ethics, CSR, and human resources management. Addressing the ethical issues appropriately and adhering to CSR in developing countries would create a condition for fairness which will help entrepreneurs building sustainable organizations. Having sustainable organizations in a society will lead to sustainable development.

Part IV: Process

In the final part, we investigate the process of new venture formation and the different activities that entrepreneurs engage in order to introduce the product in the market. We will discuss the financial opportunities and challenges, as well as the importance of accounting and bookkeeping in building financially viable enterprises in Chapter 8. Chapter 9 explores the fields of technological development and marketing. The focus is on the know-how, tools, and techniques required by entrepreneurs to communicate and reach out to the users of the products or services. The role, characteristics, and application of marketing to achieve a business's success in the developing countries is described. The marketing mix and customer loyalty programs suitable for entrepreneurs are also presented. Chapter 10 focuses on the key opportunities and challenges faced in acquiring financial and human capital. Chapter 10 provides the key essentials of bookkeeping and accounting. Methods to procure outside financing are discussed. In this part, we also will provide the benefits of proper accounting practices.

Supporting materials

This book offers an entrepreneurial approach for faculty and students in terms of teaching and learning. We provide essential content and supporting materials for presentation and discussion while leaving a significant degree of creativity and innovation for faculty and students to incorporate cases and content that they see best fits for their approach. In the following is the summary of supporting materials.

1. **Case Studies**: Each chapter has an opening case study that summarizes the essence of the chapter and follows with a few questions for discussion. We have included more than 50 international short case studies that display a real-life perspective of

important topics that are covered. The aim for including these cases is to stimulate discussion and debates in the class.

2. **Video Clips:** We have included about ten interesting TED Talks about important subjects of the book that will highlight fascinating perspectives for class discussion.
3. **Quick Reviews:** We have developed Quick Reviews within each chapter about important subjects of the chapter.
4. **PowerPoint Slides**: We have developed a comprehensive set of interesting and interactive PowerPoint slides for each chapter. Slides intend to assist instructors in their presentation of the materials and enable students to comprehend the concepts and their applications.
5. **Exam Questions**: About 15 thoughtful essay questions are developed for each chapter to facilitate class discussion and for usage by the instructor for quizzes and exams.

Notes

1   Tang, J., Kacmar, K. M., & Busenitz, L. (2012). Entrepreneurial alertness in the pursuit of new opportunities. Journal of Business Venturing, 27(1), 77–94. doi:10.1016/j.jbusvent.2010.07.001
2   Ardichvili, A. A., Cardozo, R., & Ray, S. (2003). A theory of entrepreneurial opportunity identification and development. Journal of Business Venturing, 18(1), 105–123. https://doi.org/10.1016/S0883-9026(01)00068-4
3   Alvarez, S. A., & Barney, J. B. (2010). Entrepreneurship and epistemology: the philosophical underpinnings of the study of entrepreneurial opportunities. The Academy of Management Annals, 4(1), 557–583. doi:10.1080/19416520.2010.495521
4   Venkataraman, S., Sarasvathy, S. D., Dew, N., & Forster, W. R. (2012). Reflections on the 2010 AMR Decade Award: whither the promise? Moving forward with entrepreneurship as a science of the artificial. Academy of Management Review, 37(1), 21–33. doi:10.5465/amr.2011.0079
5   De Bono, E. (1978). When opportunity knocks. Management Today, September, 102–105.
6   Kirzner, I. (1979). Perception, Opportunity and Profit. Chicago, IL: University of Chicago Press.
7   Long, W., & McMullean, W. (1984). Mapping the new venture opportunity identification process. Frontiers of Entrepreneurship Research (pp. 567–590). Wellesley, MA: Babson College.
8   Hulbert, B., Brown, R. B., & Adams, S. (1997). Towards an understanding of opportunity. Marketing Education Review, 7(3), 67.
9   Ardichvili, A., Cardozo, R., & Ray, S. (2003). A theory of entrepreneurial opportunity identification and development. Journal of Business Venturing, 18(1), 105–123.
10 Shane, S., & Venkataraman, S. (2000). The promise of entrepreneurship as a field of research. Academy of Management Review, 25, 217–226.
11 Kirchhoff, B. A. (1994). Entrepreneurship and Dynamic Capitalism: The Economics of Business Firm Formation and Growth. Westport, CT: Praeger.
12 Alvarez, S. A., & Barney, J. B. (2007). Discovery and creation: alternative theories of entrepreneurial action. Organizacoesem Context, 3(6), 123–152.
13 Doing Business. (2011). Retrieved May 20, 2013, from www.doingbusiness.org/.
14 Friedman, Thomas (2007). Thank You for Being Late: An Optimist's Guide to Thriving in the Age of Accelerations. New York: Farrar, Straus and Giroux.
15 Friedman, Thomas (2007). Thank You for Being Late: An Optimist's Guide to Thriving in the Age of Accelerations. New York: Farrar, Straus and Giroux.
16 Chandra, Y., Styles, C., & Wilkinson, I. F. (2009). The recognition of first time international entrepreneurial opportunities: evidence from firms in knowledge-based industries. International Marketing Review, 26(1), 30–61.

17 Alvarez, S. A., & Barney, J. B. (2007). Discovery and creation: alternative theories of entrepreneurial action. Organizacoesem Context, 3(6), 123–152.

18 Kirzner I. (1973). Competition and Entrepreneurship. Chicago, IL: University of Chicago Press.

19 Shane S. (2000). Prior knowledge and the discovery of entrepreneurial opportunities. Organization Science, 11(4), 448–470.

20 Walle, A. (2018). Beyond Heroic Paradigms: Expanded Models of Entrepreneurship. Cambridge, MA: Cyrus Institute of Knowledge.

21 McMullen, J., Plummer, L., & Acs, Z. (2007). What is an entrepreneurial opportunity? Small Business Economics, 28(4), 273–283. Retrieved from www.jstor.org/stable/40229532.

22 Louth, J. D. (1966). The changing face of marketing. McKinsey Quarterly.

23 Baker, T., & Nelson, R. E. (2005). Creating something from nothing: resource construction through entrepreneurial bricolage. Administrative Science Quarterly, 50(3), 329–366.

24 Dodgson, M. (2011). Exploring new combinations in innovation and entrepreneurship: social networks, Schumpeter, and the case of Josiah Wedgwood (1730–1795). Industrial and Corporate Change, 20(4), 1119–1151.

25 Sarasvathy, S. D. (2001). Causation and effectuation: toward a theoretical shift from economic inevitability to entrepreneurial contingency. Academy of Management Review, 26(2), 242–263.

26 THINKING Methods. (2018). Retrieved from www.ideaconnection.com/thinking-methods/.

27 Stillman, J. (2014, October 1). The 4 Stages of Creativity. Retrieved from www.inc.com/jessica-stillman/the-4-stages-of-creativity.html.

28 www.google.com/search?rlz=1C1GCEB_enUS815US815&q=discovery+and+creation+approaches+comparison&tbm=isch&source=univ&sa=X&ved=2ahUKEwjb7Lzm78HkAhVDu1kKHXMwDPUQsAR6BAgAEAE&biw=853&bih=406#.

29 Baron, R. A. (2007). Behavioral and cognitive factors in entrepreneurship: entrepreneurs as the active element in new venture creation. Strategic Entrepreneurship Journal, 1(1–2), 167–182.

30 Gaglio, C. M. (1997). Opportunity identification: review, critique and suggested research directions. In J. A. Katz, & R. H. Brockhaus (Eds.), Advances in Entrepreneurship, Firm Emergence and Growth (vol. 3). Greenwich, CT: JAI Press.

31 Kaish, S., & Gilad, B. (1991). Characteristics of opportunity search of entrepreneurs vs. executives: sources, interest and general alertness. Journal of Business Venturing, 6, 45–61.

32 Arenius, P., & De Clercq, D. (2005). A network-based approach on opportunity recognition. Small Business Economics, 24(3), 249–265.

33 Aldrich, H. E., & Zimmer, C. (1986). Entrepreneurship through social networks. In D. L. Sexton, & R. W. Smilor (Eds.), The Art and Science of Entrepreneurship (pp. 3–23). Cambridge, MA: Ballinger.

34 Venkataraman, S. (1997). The distinctive domain of entrepreneurship research: an editor's perspective. In J. Katz, & R. Brockhaus (Eds.), Advances in Entrepreneurship, Firm Emergence, and Growth (vol. 3, pp. 119–138). Greenwich, CT: JAI Press.

35 Timmon, J. A., & Spinelli, S. (2009). New Venture Creation: Entrepreneurship for the 21st Century (7th ed.). New Delhi, India: Tata McGraw-Hill Education Pvt. Ltd.

36 Bhide, A. (1994). How entrepreneurs craft strategies that work. Harvard Business Review, 72(2), March–April, 150–161.

37 Ardichvili, A., Cardozo, R., & Ray, S. (2003). A theory of entrepreneurial opportunity identification and development. Journal of Business Venturing, 18(1), 105–123. https://doi.org/10.1016/S0883-9026(01)00068-4.

38 Ardichvili, A., Cardozo, R., & Ray, S. (2003). A theory of entrepreneurial opportunity identification and development. Journal of Business Venturing, 18(1), 105–123. https://doi.org/10.1016/S0883-9026(01)00068-4.

39 FourWeekMBA. (n.d.). What Is a Business Model? 30 Successful Types of Business Models You Need to Know. Retrieved from https://fourweekmba.com/what-is-a-business-model/

40 Mayer, M., & Crane F. (2011). Entrepreneurship: An Innovator's Guide to Startups and Corporate Venture. Thousand Oaks, CA: SAGE.

41 What is business concept? Definition and meaning. (n.d.). Retrieved November 3, 2018, from www.businessdictionary.com/definition/business-concept.html.

42 Ardichvili, A., Cardozo, R., & Ray, S. (2003). A theory of entrepreneurial opportunity identification and development. Journal of Business Venturing, 18(1), 105–123. https://doi.org/10.1016/S0883-9026(01)00068-4.

43 Forrest, C. (n.d.). Glossary: Startup and Venture Capital terms you should know. Retrieved from www.techrepublic.com/article/glossary-startup-and-venture-capital-terms-you-should-know/.

Part I

The environment and entrepreneurship

1 Entrepreneurship and development in the era of globalization

Learning objectives:

1. *Understand definitions of entrepreneurship, development, and globalization*
2. *Comprehend the relationships between entrepreneurship, development, and globalization*
3. *Discuss the major theories of economic development*
4. *Evaluate entrepreneurship operations in developing countries*
5. *Examine the influences of globalization on entrepreneurship*

Figure 1.1 SEZ worldwide
Source: © iStock: Bingfengwu

Special economic zones and their impact on local economy

Special Economic Zones (SEZs) have been growing in the global economic land-scape. Special industrial privileges have been granted since centuries ago and helped guarantee free exchange along trade routes. The first "modern" SEZ is considered to be in Shannon Airport in Clare, Ireland.[1] Since then, from about the 1970s, many SEZs were established for labor-intensive manufacturing, mostly in Latin America and East Asia.[2] Indeed, we find that the building of SEZs in modern times has exploded since about 2005.

Why are SEZs attractive?

The word "Special Economic Zone" encompasses a broad range of special zones such as tax-exempt zones, free trade zones, export-processing zones, free ports, industrial parks, high-tech zones, economic and technology development zones, science and innovation parks, enterprise zones, and others. Special regions within a country are designated as SEZs where business and trade laws are different from the rest of the country with the purpose of attracting foreign investment and developing infrastructure and technology.

If implemented properly, SEZs can be an effective instrument to promote indus-trialization and development. In many developing countries, this strategy has paid off, particularly for countries in East Asia. Seeing results from this strategy, more countries implemented this tool as part of their development plans.

What is it about SEZs that enables countries to increase the pace of economic development of the country as a whole? SEZs generally include the following characteristics:

- It is a specifically separated area which is also mostly physically secured;
- It has its own separate management or administration than the rest of the country;
- It provides benefits for investors physically within the zone; and
- It has its own customs area (duty-free benefits) and own special procedures.[3]

Generally, SEZs are established to achieve one or more of the following policy objectives: (a) attract foreign direct investment (FDI); (b) help alleviate large-scale unemployment; (c) support economic reform strategies; and (d) serve as an experiment for new policies.[4] In this summary, we focus on the first objective, attraction of FDI, and use it as part of our basic definition for a "successful" SEZ.

Case continued at the end of the chapter...

Introduction

In this chapter we will describe the relationship between entrepreneurship, growth, and development as well as how globalization has influenced this relationship.

There are many fundamental questions scholars, policymakers, NGO activists, etc. are asking about the impact of globalization on the relationship between entrepreneurship and economic growth and development. Some examples include: Does globalization accelerate development by advancing entrepreneurship in developing countries? What is the impact of entrepreneurship on innovation in developing countries? What is creativity and how does it relate to innovation and development? What are the effects of entrepreneurship on employment and income in the era of globalization? How has entrepreneurship in developing countries been influenced by the revolution in technology? We will try to provide answers to these questions by applying relevant theories and discuss their practical entrepreneurial implications.

By the end of this chapter, you will be able to understand the profound link between entrepreneurship, globalization, and sustainable growth and development. Case studies, examples, and illustrations will help guide readers for a deeper understanding of the role of entrepreneurial business formation on growth and development.

Scholars, policymakers, and NGOs are examing the relationship between globalization, entrepreneurship, and sustainable development. More inquires are required.

Figure 1.2 Earth
Source: Image by valkrye131, Flickr

Defining entrepreneurship

There is a lack of agreement among stakeholders on what constitutes entrepreneurship. Some scholars view entrepreneurship as a process of new venture creation.[5] Others conceptualize it as the process of opportunity recognition, opportunity creation, and opportunity exploitation[6] or, more broadly, as "a dynamic interaction between entrepreneurial attitudes, entrepreneurial activity, and entrepreneurial aspiration that varies across stages of economic development."[7]

Still others define entrepreneurship, specifically strategic entrepreneurship, as a social process of mobilizing and orchestrating resources, creating value and generating wealth, etc. For the purposes of this textbook, we will follow a mid-range theoretical lens, and conceptualize entrepreneurship as a socially embedded and context-specific process of resource mobilization and opportunity exploitation, culminating in the creation of a new venture, whose purpose is to create value and generate wealth and other social enhancement benefits.[8] This approach provides a broad and theoretically robust framework with which we can critically review and integrate conceptual developments and empirical evidence that may highlight the unique characteristics of new venture creation when aligned with developing countries.

> Social and contextual aspects influence the fundamental way that entrepreneurship functions. For example, what works in India may not work in other countries.

The term "entrepreneur" was coined by French economist Jean-Baptist Say and was originally translated as "adventurer". In 1821 in his book, *A Treatise on Political Economy, or the Production, Distribution, and Consumption of Wealth*, Say described entrepreneurs as agents of change who seek opportunities for profit and, by doing so, create both new markets and fresh opportunities.[9]

Joseph A. Schumpeter, an Austrian-born American economist and political scientist, was perhaps the first scholar to theorize about entrepreneurship. In his 1911 book, *The Theory of Economic Development*, Schumpeter described entrepreneurs as being at the heart of a dynamic system of creative destruction, by which the economy as a whole is continuously reinvented. Another influential scholar in the study of entrepreneurship was Frank H. Knight. In his 1921 book, *Uncertainty and Profit*, Knight used the concepts of risk and uncertainty to explain the process by which entrepreneurs acquire resources.

Friedrich Hayek, in his 1945 book, *The Use of Knowledge in Society*, focused on the limited information available to individuals as the source of differential realization for entrepreneurial opportunities. Israel Kirzner, in his 1973 book, *Competition and Entrepreneurship*, posited that entrepreneurs are alert to profit opportunities and thus strive to help restore economic equilibrium rather than disturb it. The influential management and strategy scholar Peter F. Drucker also theorized on the importance of entrepreneurship. In his 1985 book, *Innovation and Entrepreneurship*, Drucker delved into classifications of entrepreneurial opportunities and provided practical advice to entrepreneurs, institutions, and the emerging entrepreneurial economy. William Baumol, in his 2002 book, *The Free-Market Innovation Machine*, described the key features of the free-market system that allowed for such incredible economic growth, including the important role played by independent entrepreneurs and the routinization of innovative activities by large corporations.

Defining economic development

The World Bank defines economic development as the "qualitative change and restructuring in a country's economy in connection with technological and social progress."[10] The main indicator of economic development is increasing Gross National Products (GNP) per capita or Gross Domestic Products (GDP) per capita, reflecting an increase in the economic productivity as well as average material well-being of a country's population. In the report, *Our Common Future*, written by the Brundtland Commission on Environment and Development, it was defined as "development that meets the needs of the present without compromising the ability of future generations to meet their own needs."[11]

Economic development is closely linked with economic growth. Economic growth is conventionally measured as the percentage increase in GNP or GDP for one year. Economic growth comes in two forms: an economy can either grow "extensively" by using more resources (such as physical, human, or natural capital) or "intensively" by using the same amount of resources more efficiently (productively). When economic growth is achieved through the use of greater labor, it does not result in the growth of per capita income.

But, when economic growth is achieved by more productive use of all resources, labor included, it results in higher per capita income and improvement in individuals' standard of living.[12] On the other hand, the 1998 Nobel Prize winner Professor Amartya Sen abandons the idea of measuring development through economic growth. Instead, he views "Development as Freedom".[13] His approach is mainly focused on "human flourishing" which he defines as the cornerstone of solving the problems of poverty and global inequality.[14]

He challenges the conventional understanding of development by changing the viewpoint of its meaning: "Development consists of the removal of various types of unfreedoms that leave people with little choice and little opportunity of exercising their reasoned agency".[15]

He further identifies the factors causing the "un-freedoms" as "poverty, tyranny, poor economic opportunities, systematic social deprivation, and neglect of public facilities and intolerance or overactivity of repressive states."[16] Some of the essential freedoms that he defines include: "economic opportunities, political freedoms, social facilities, transparency guarantees and protective security", which he argues need to be interconnected in order to function efficiently and effectively.

Sen's view of development was crucial for the twentieth century and played a significant role in redefining the concept of development to comprise human rights as a constitutive part.[17]

Amartya Sen is an Indian economist and philosopher, currently working at Harvard University. He made vast contributions to the studies of welfare economics, social choice theory, economic and social justice, economic theories of famines, and indexes of the measure of well-being of citizens in developing countries. These contributions awarded him a Nobel Memorial Prize in Economic Sciences in 1998.

Figure 1.3 Poverty and prosperity
Source: © iStock: tang90246

The World Bank Group has two goals: to end extreme poverty and promote shared prosperity in a sustainable way

With 189 member countries, staff from more than 170 countries, and offices in over 130 locations, the World Bank Group is a unique global partnership consisting of five institutions working for sustainable solutions that reduce poverty and build shared prosperity in developing countries.

Source: www.worldbank.org/

Major theories of economic development

Over the past century, several economists have articulated theories and relevant policies and practices to accelerate development. Understanding these theories and their applications will help recognize incentives that drive development at both micro and macro levels. Additionally, they will provide an understanding of the societal change that will emerge in developing countries.

Rostow's theory[18]

Rostow's theory is one of the major historical models of economic growth, which was developed by W. W. Rostow in 1960. The model proposes that economic growth occurs in five basic stages, of varying length:

1. Traditional society
2. Preconditions for take-off
3. Take-off
4. Drive to maturity
5. Age of high mass consumption

Each stage can only be reached through the completion of the previous stage. Rostow asserts that all developed countries have gone through these stages. These stages are as follows:

The traditional society: This is mostly societies with no access to science and technology where most of its resources are dedicated to agricultural use. Agricultural productivity is mostly at the subsistence level and there is limited market interaction.

Preparatory stage: There is an expansion in output which extends beyond agricultural produce to manufactured goods. This is the result of higher savings levels and investments in education. In this stage, there are lower levels of market specialization.

Take-off stage: At this stage, revolutionary changes occur in both agriculture and industry to attain a self-sustaining economic growth. There are greater urbanization and rise in human capital accumulation.

Drive to maturity: This stage takes place after a long period of time. The population involved in agriculture declines while industry becomes more diverse. Overall income per capita increases.

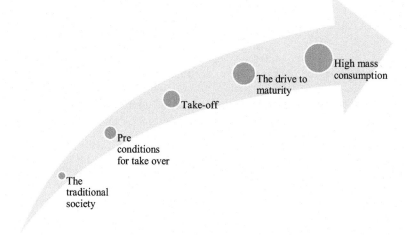

Figure 1.4 Rostow's theory

The rate of savings and investments is such that it can automatically sustain economic growth.

Stage of mass consumption: At this stage, a country's demand shifts from food, clothing, and other basic necessities to demand luxuries. To satisfy these needs, new industries involve themselves in mass production to match consumption.

Rostow's theory became one of the important concepts in the theory of modernization of America during J. F. Kennedy's leadership, but his thesis was criticized because it could not be replicated in places like Latin America or sub-Saharan Africa.

The Harrod-Domar model

The Harrod-Domar model is an early post-Keynesian model of economic growth that explains its growth rate in terms of the level of saving and productivity of capital. The implications are that growth depends on the quantity of labor and capital. More investment leads to higher capital accumulation which generates economic growth. The Harrod-Domar model was developed independently by Sir Roy Harrod in 1939 and Evsey Domar in 1946.

The future car

Innovation of Uber, Lyft, and many other similar car sharing models in developing countries will have significant impact on employment and the environment, which requires public policies in development and developing countries. Above all, incoming Autonomous Driving will have an enormous impact on several industries in developed countries and in the future of developing countries. These innovations, which are the practical application of innovation and technologies, will take societies to uncharted territories. Get ready and prepare yourself!

- There is a lack of agreement on what constitutes entrepreneurship among stakeholders.
- This book conceptualizes entrepreneurship as a socially embedded and context-specific process of resource mobilization and opportunity exploitation, culminating in the creation of a new venture, whose purpose is to create value and generate wealth and other social enhancement benefits.
- Economic growth comes in two forms: an economy can either grow "extensively" by using more resources (such as physical, human, or natural capital) or "intensively" by using the same amount of resources more efficiently (productively).
- "Development consists of the removal of various types of un-freedoms that leave people with little choice and little opportunity of exercising their reasoned agency".[19]

Lewis structural change

This model stresses the transformation from a traditional, agricultural economy to a modern, industrial economy. The Lewis model is attracting attention due to its linkages between traditional agriculture and modern industry through migration of workers from rural to urban areas. However, it is criticized for incorrectly assuming that real urban wages will not rise. Arthur Lewis believed that since the industrialized economy is run by capitalists, wages paid for labor are fixed instead of being paid according to the value imparted on the goods during production. He also believed that migration and modern sector employment grows proportionately to urban full employment.[20]

Chenery's patterns of development approach

Hollis Burnley Chenery's findings of the patterns of development are presented in an empirically styled visual and include the shift in production from agriculture to industry and services. It also shows the accumulation of physical and human capital, as well as the shift to material consumption, investment, and the growth of trade, which are presented as a share of GNP. See Figure 1.5.

Major theories of economic development

1. Rostow's theory
2. The Harrod–Domar model
3. Lewis structural change
4. Chenery's patterns of development approach
5. Dependency theory
6. Neoclassical theory

Figure 1.5 Chenery's patterns of development approach

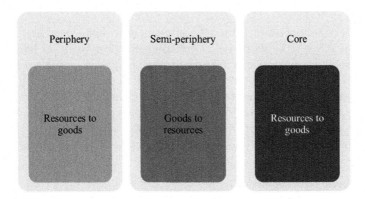

Figure 1.6 Andre Gunder Frank dependency theory

Dependency theory

This theory stipulates that resources flow from poor (periphery), underdeveloped states to wealthy (core) states and therefore, enrich the latter at the expense of the former. The central argument of this theory is that poor states are impoverished and rich ones enriched (see Figure 1.7).[21]

Neoclassical theory

The neoclassical-dependent school emphasizes unequal power relationships between the developed and less developed countries. It blames the reason for underdevelopment in a few countries (conscious or unconscious) on exploitation by the developed country. This is preserved by a small elite ruling class within such developing countries. Andre Gunder Frank, the leading dependency theorist, "suggests that lack of development is because Western nations have deliberately under-developed them." The international trading system and multinational companies practice is creating conditions that means less developed countries are dependent on western aids and markets.[22]

This theory of the 1980s is termed as neoclassical counterrevolution, and it emphasizes corruption, inefficiency, and a lack of economic incentives within developing countries as being responsible for the lack of development.

We can make a distinction between three approaches:

a.   The free market approach argues that markets are efficient and any government intervention is counterproductive.
b.   The public choice approach emphasizes inherent government failure and the self-interested behavior of public officials.
c.   The market-friendly approach, which was advocated by the World Bank, recognizes market imperfections, and hence a limited but important role for government through non-selective interventions such as infrastructure, education, and providing a climate for private enterprise.

Definition and classification of countries

According to the World Bank, developing economies are countries with low to mid-levels of GNP per capita, while five high-income developing economies – Hong Kong (China), Israel, Kuwait, Singapore, and the United Arab Emirates – also fall into this category. These five economies are classified as developing, despite their high per capita income because of their economic structure or the official opinion of their governments. Several countries that are currently in transition from a centrally planned economy to a market economy are sometimes grouped with developing countries because of their low to mid-levels of per capita income. In a few cases, they sometimes are grouped among the developed countries because of their high level of industrialization. Higher than 80 percent of the world's population lives in the 100+ developing countries.[23]

The World Bank classifies all the developing countries into heavily indebted poor countries (HIPCs), low-income, lower-middle-income, and middle-income economies.[24,25] Figure 1.7 shows the classifications.[26]

What is a living wage? How it compares to the minimum wage

The living wage is the amount of income needed to provide the cost of living in any location for anyone who works full-time, which is adjusted to compensate for inflation.

The purpose of a living wage is to make sure that anyone who works full-time should have enough money to live above the federal poverty level and avoid homelessness.

Source: Definition from thebalance.com

The World Economic Forum, which is recognized by the Swiss authorities as an international body, provides a similar classification of countries at different levels of economic development. This classification places a country at three major stages of economic development: factor-driven economies, efficiency-driven economies, and innovation-driven economies. There also exist two transition stages, the transition from factor-driven to efficiency-driven, and transition from efficiency-driven to innovation-driven. See Figure 1.8.

Table 1.1 presents the countries/economies at each stage of development, based on the World Economic Forum's 2015–2016 Global Competitiveness Index.[27]

Entrepreneurship in the developing countries

The link between entrepreneurship and economic development is complex. On one hand, the level of a country's economic development determines the nature of entrepreneurial initiatives available to its aspiring entrepreneurs. On the other hand, the entrepreneurial activity itself is seen by many as a major vessel for self-employment, empowerment, poverty alleviation, economic growth, and social progress. In the following, we discuss both aspects of the relationship.

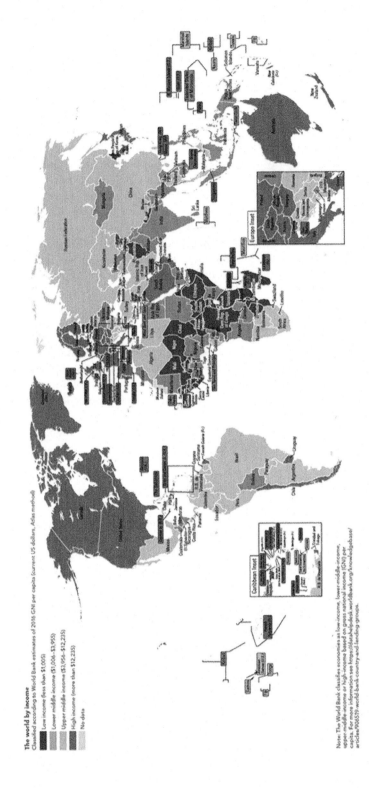

The world by income
Classified according to World Bank estimates of 2016 GNI per capita (current US dollars, Atlas method)

Low income (less than $1,005)
Lower middle income ($1,006–$3,955)
Upper middle income ($3,956–$12,235)
High income (more than $12,235)
No data

Note: The World Bank classifies economies as low-income, lower-middle-income, upper-middle-income or high-income based on gross national income (GNI) per capita. For more information see https://datahelpdesk.worldbank.org/knowledgebase/articles/906519-world-bank-country-and-lending-groups.

Figure 1.7 WB classification

Source: © 2018 The World Bank Group. The world by income (FY 2018). (n.d.). Retrieved from http://datatopics.worldbank.org/sdgatlas/the-world-by-income.html

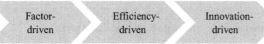

Factor to efficiency ||| Efficiency to innovation

Figure 1.8 Development classification factors

Table 1.1 Countries/economies at each stage of economic development

Stage 1: Factor-driven (35 economies)	Transition from stage 1 to stage 2 (16 economies)	Stage 2: Efficiency-driven (31 economies)	Transition from stage 2 to stage 3 (20 economies)	Stage 3: Innovation-driven (38 economies)
Bangladesh	Algeria	Albania	Argentina	Australia
Benin	Azerbaijan	Armenia	Brazil	Austria
Burundi	Bhutan	Bolivia	Chile	Bahrain
Cambodia	Botswana	Bosnia and Herzegovina	Costa Rica	Belgium
Cameroon	Gabon	Bulgaria	Croatia	Canada
Chad	Honduras	Cape Verde	Hungary	Cyprus
Cote d'Ivoire	Iran	China	Latvia	Czech Republic
Ethiopia	Kazakhstan	Colombia	Lebanon	Denmark
Gambia	Kuwait	Dominican Republic	Lithuania	Estonia
Ghana	Moldova	Ecuador	Malaysia	Finland
Guinea	Mongolia	Egypt	Mauritius	France
Haiti	Nigeria	El Salvador	Mexico	Germany
India	Philippines	Georgia	Oman	Greece
Kenya	Saudi Arabia	Guatemala	Panama	Hong Kong SAR
Kyrgyz Republic	Venezuela	Guyana	Poland	Iceland
Lao PDR	Vietnam	Indonesia	Romania	Israel
Lesotho		Jamaica	Russian Federation	Italy
Liberia		Jordan	Seychelles	Japan
Madagascar		Macedonia, FYR	Turkey	Korea. Rep.
Malawi		Montenegro	Uruguay	Luxembourg
Mauritania		Morocco		Malta
Mozambique		Namibia		Netherlands
Myanmar		Paraguay		New Zealand
Nepal		Peru		Norway
Nicaragua		Serbia		Portugal
Pakistan		South Africa		Qatar
Rwanda		Sri Lanka		Singapore
Senegal		Swaziland		Slovak Republic
Sierra Leone		Thailand		Slovenia
Tajikistan		Tunisia		Spain
Tanzania		Ukraine		Sweden
Uganda				Switzerland
Zambia				Taiwan, China
Zimbabwe				Trinidad and Tobago
				U.A.E
				U.K
				U.S.A

Stage of economic development and entrepreneurial activity

The stage of a country's economic development determines, to a large extent, the scope of its entrepreneurial activity, as well as the nature of feasible entrepreneurial initiatives. As mentioned earlier, countries can be classified into five stages of economic development, namely: factor-driven; in the transition from factor-driven to efficiency-driven; efficiency-driven; in the transition from efficiency-driven to innovation-driven; and innovation-driven. Companies present in countries that are in the first stage of economic development compete on the basis of price. They sell basic products or commodities with low productivity, which reflects their lower prices. As business becomes more competitive, the countries move into the efficiency-driven stage of development. Companies begin to develop more efficient production processes and also improve their product quality. The wages rise due to the requirement of a skilled workforce, but yet they do not see any increase in prices. Finally, as countries move into the innovation-driven stage, wages will have risen so much that they reach an equilibrium, thus improving the standard of living. Businesses that are able to produce new and unique products survive. At this stage, companies have to compete by producing new and different goods and services using the most sophisticated production processes and invention methods.

In terms of scope, the entrepreneurial activity in an economy follows a curvilinear, "U"-shaped relationship with GDP, as shown in Figure 1.9. At low levels of per capita GDP, the entrepreneurial sector provides job opportunities and potential for the creation of new markets. The per capita income increases and the emergence of new technologies and economies of scale allow larger and more established firms to satisfy the increasing demand for growing markets. Therefore, increase their relative role in the economy and the role of smaller and newer firms may decline.

Finally, in the third stage, the role played by the entrepreneurial sector in countries with higher GDP increases again, as more individuals have the resources to go into business in an economic environment that may present high-potential opportunities.[28]

Uber operation in developing countries

Catherine Cheney (August 2016) in the devex.com wrote a piece entitled "What is driving Uber's global impact?" She discusses the evolution of Uber, shared cars, accelerating expansion and employment, etc. She stated that "Uber Nigeria is a locally incorporated company that hires employees, runs support services, and adapts the platform to meet the demands of local consumers." While Uber riders in most markets pay via credit card through the app, riders in Nigeria and across sub-Saharan Africa have the option to pay in cash, which means adjusting to local market conditions. The most populous cities in the world cannot afford a future in which ridesharing and carpooling are not available.

Source: Cheney (2016)[29]

Thus, in terms of the nature of entrepreneurial initiatives, at lower levels of economic development, entrepreneurship is predominantly necessity-driven.

Necessity-based entrepreneurship occurs when individuals participate in entrepreneurial activities because all other employment options are either absent or unsatisfactory.[30]

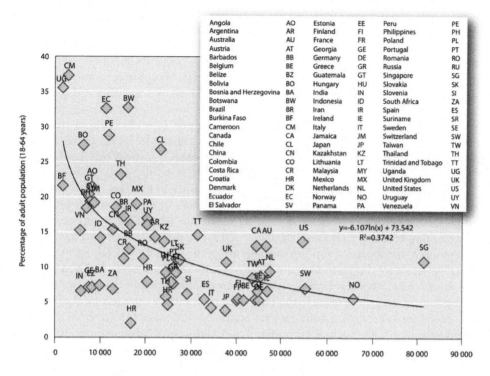

Figure 1.9 GDP per capita and Total Entrepreneurial Activity (TEA) rate, 2014

Source: Global Entrepreneurship Monitor, 2014. GEM 2014 Global Report. (2015, March 27). Retrieved from www.gemconsortium.org/report/49079

The relationship between the level of economic development and level of entrepreneurial activity is presented in Figure 1.9. At higher levels of economic development, technological and institutional sophistication (i.e., the United States) gives rise to opportunity entrepreneurs, e.g. those who are driven by the achievement of success through exploiting an opportunity for some form of gain often believed to be economic.[31]

Opportunity-driven entrepreneurship is more desirable because it is more likely to be both technology and innovation-based with high growth orientation, thus contributing to economic growth and development. As the level of economic development of the country increases, the ratio of necessity-to-opportunity entrepreneurship goes down.

Entrepreneurial activity and economic development

Entrepreneurship in emerging markets is much different than its presence in developed countries. Of particular interest is the growth-oriented entrepreneurship, which has a greater capacity to create sustainable economic growth than microenterprises.[32] Entrepreneurship has played an important role in economic growth and innovation while increased competitiveness has also played a key role in poverty alleviation over time.

Opportunities for entrepreneurs in developing countries are broader in scope than in developed countries because entrepreneurs in developing markets face different sets of environmental restrictions than those in developed economies. These differences are rooted in the underlying fundamental economic differences, cultural characteristics, and the role of governments. Most developing countries lack stable and clearly defined market mechanism rules, regulations, ownership rights, and enforcement instruments. Thus, the opportunity for entrepreneurship is not only broader, but also more challenging in the building of successful and sustainable organizations. It is broader due to higher demand for better quality of goods and services and the availability of certain factors of input. It is challenging due to the scarcity of resources, regulations, and enforcement capabilities. Of course, the level of educational completion of the population also plays a critical role in the extent of challenges.

From an economic development point of view, entrepreneurship raises two major issues: one is economic development and growth and the other is the progress of nations. The mechanism of development has been the subject of a continuing lively debate among scholars.[33] The validity of any economic policy is measured by its impact on economic development and growth. The progress of a nation is taking place when there is a need for improvement in social conditions, citizenship rights, and political transparency. Many developing countries are trying to implement prescriptions of development theories or replicate the process that most developed economies pursued. Of course, most developing countries are trying to find ways to expedite the process by applying new tools such as technology and educational advancement in order to accelerate economic development.

Figure 1.10 Globalization good or bad
Source: ©iStock: syahrir maulana

When globalization meets entrepreneurship it can be a force for good

Entrepreneurship is described as the pursuit of opportunities and often seen as a hero of the global economy. On the other hand, globalization is criticized. Entrepreneurship and globalization go hand in hand in three ways. First globalization facilitates technology because it fosters the innovation of ecosystems. Second, it also facilitates transnational entrepreneurship when corporations use what they know to create new businesses. Lastly, it facilitates social entrepreneurship by addressing societal problems. Many multinationals have concluded globalization as a powerful tool to gain new ventures.

Source: Prashantham (2018)[34]

Sustainable economic development leads to diminishing illiteracy, reduction of unemployment, a higher standard of living, and overall better quality of life for current and future generations. An important factor that can lead to sustainable economic development is the degree of entrepreneurial activity. Most developing countries aspire to boost the enriching environment for entrepreneurship by enacting entrepreneur-friendly policies. In turn, entrepreneurs spur economic development through a constant process of economic experimentation and efficiency. Startup companies can engage in economic experimentation because they are not constrained by the limits of old technologies, the traditional ways of organizing production, or the need to serve established markets. Instead, entrepreneurs can be more aggressive than established organizations in pursuing radical approaches to the creation of economic value. Globalization provides opportunities for such economic experimentation. Digital startups, for example, require far less capital than, say, building a factory, and a brilliant piece of software can be distributed to millions at a minimal cost. Digital technologies have allowed young Russian entrepreneurs to set up a virtual talent agency for models (castweek.ru); Asian-American electric cellists to teach people how to make new sounds using a laptop (danaleong.com); and young Nigerians to start a new publishing house for African romantic novelists (ankarapress.com).[35] The value of startup activity is not limited to the substantial value created by new businesses, but also includes the benefits from increased competitive pressure on established firms.

- World Bank classifies the developing countries into countries with low or middle levels of GNP per capita.
- World Bank further classifies developing countries into heavily indebted poor countries (HIPC), low-income, lower-middle-income, and middle-income.
- The World Economic Forum provides a similar classification of countries at two transition stages, transition from factor-driven to efficiency-driven, and transition from efficiency-driven to innovation-driven.
- The stage of a country's economic development determines, to a large extent, the scope of entrepreneurial activity in an economy, as well as the nature of feasible entrepreneurial initiatives.

Table 1.2 Major types of economic experiments

Technological experiments	Market experiments	Organizational experiments
Attempts to exploit a scientific discovery of engineering opportunity for economic gain.	Attempts to identify and exploit the market applications where the technology may be most valuable.	Attempts to link together individuals and organizations in the pursuit of exploiting the interaction between market and technical opportunities.

We can differentiate between three major types of economic experiments in Table 1.2.

To sum up, by playing a fundamental role in the process of economic experimentation, entrepreneurship contributes decisively to the range and diversity of economically useful knowledge, which is at the base of economic prosperity. Some scholars have suggested that it does not change among existing businesses and entities that generate the greatest transformations, but rather the creation of new firms and competition that does.[36]

Entrepreneurial activity contributes to a country's economic development through innovative products, services, and ideas, increased competition leading to productivity gains, consumer benefits, and increased learning capacity.[37] Entrepreneurship is credited for being the "engines of growth" and for "providing catalyst" for economic development in both developed and developing countries.[38] In fact, according to Ernst & Young CEO Jim Turley, some statisticians show that "100% of the net job growth over many years came from entrepreneurs."[39]

Key factors of entrepreneurship and development

The value of entrepreneurship to the contributions of a nation's wealth is becoming increasingly significant. In an era of globalization, countries are leaning on entrepreneurship as a sustainable way to improve their economy. Culture affects how individuals in a society view entrepreneurship, which is a key influencer of the likelihood of a person becoming an entrepreneur. The culture of a country also helps to explain why certain countries have an environment that fosters entrepreneurship, while others rely on partnerships, corporations, or state-run institutions.

The role of government is significant when shaping the future of entrepreneurship in a country. Leaders must examine the type of culture that exists before making regulatory changes that will impact entrepreneurs. For example, in an individualistic culture, governments attempt to reform by strengthening institutions, engaging with private sector, and legitimizing small informal businesses. This is typically well-received and can result in new ventures and economic development. Encouraging innovation through competition and monetary incentives have proven successful as well.

Entrepreneurship has different definitions depending on which part of the world you are. For the western countries, it might mean a lavish lifestyle and money, while for other countries it is a tool for survival. Starting a business involves taking financial risk, which most countries cannot afford. Even though people believe that the United States leads in entrepreneurship, it's actually Uganda that is the most entrepreneurial. Uganda has a 28 percent, coming second is Thailand with 16 percent, growth in entrepreneurial startups each year. Even though a large percent of young adults are unemployed, Uganda still manages to have great entrepreneurial success, largely due to training and support from the government and other non-government organizations.

For most people in the west, starting a new business is based upon an existing job or good finances. But for developing countries it means earning the essential income for family needs and also challenges of poor economic conditions.

Source: Rajna (2015)[40]

However, a more incremental approach may be necessary for collectivist cultures – particularly in areas where society is apprehensive towards government regulation. Encouraging new ventures to be created as formal businesses, for example, is a more indirect, hands-off approach that will likely have more success. By identifying a society's cultural values, the government can provide monetary and non-monetary motivators that enable entrepreneurship and innovation. Entrepreneurship has become one of the primary mechanisms in the transformation of many economies. Developing countries have begun to examine the role of entrepreneurship in their potential development.

With this shift in developmental policy, a greater focus on the role of the private sector as a vital engine for economic growth in emerging economies and a de-emphasis on the role of government is becoming evident. Entrepreneurship in emerging markets is much different from that in developed nations. Of particular interest are new and growth-oriented entrepreneurship, which has a greater capacity to create sustainable economic growth.

Entrepreneurship has played an important role in economic growth, innovation, and competitiveness and it will also play a role over time in poverty alleviation. The focus has been on describing the attributes of entrepreneurship in developing countries, but rather it has to be on providing a framework in which entrepreneurs and policymakers can plan and execute innovative business models. Existing models of entrepreneurship are based largely on research conducted in the United States and other developed countries and do not adequately describe how entrepreneurship is carried out in developing countries. Opportunities for entrepreneurs in developing countries are broader in scope than in developed markets because entrepreneurs in developing countries face a different set of circumstances than their counterparts in developed economies. These differences are rooted in the underlying political, economic, cultural, and social environments that they operate.

For example, Mexico has made a commitment to transform itself into a competitive nation by privatizing state-owned industries, reducing tariffs, making it easier for foreign investment, and setting up free-trade agreements (NAFTA) with neighbors such as the United States and Canada.

How women in rural India turned courage into capital: Chetna Gala Sinha

When bankers refused to serve her neighbors in rural India, Chetna Gala Sinha did the next best thing: she opened a bank of her own, the first ever for and by women in the country. In this inspiring talk, she shares stories of the women who encouraged her and continue to push her to come up with solutions for those denied traditional financial backing.

You can check in more details the full TED Talk in this link: www.ted.com/ talks/chetna_gala_sinha_how_women_in_rural_india_turned_courage_into_cap- ital/details

However, to sustain the changes and expand them, there needs to be a thriving private sector, where new entrepreneurs are needed. The informal sector in some developing countries is an important source of entrepreneurial and economic activity. Brazil, for example, has a substantial share – about 60 percent by some measures – of its employees working without a labor registry. In addition, 58 percent of the country's population below the poverty line live in families headed by informal workers. In Brazil, formal employment usually implies that the worker is an employee with a signed employment booklet (card). Informal employment in Brazil is understood to imply that the worker is an employee without a signed employment booklet (no card), which means that these employees are not registered with the Ministry of Labor and therefore, not legally covered by labor codes (meaning that the worker probably does not receive certain benefits and protections). These are mostly Mom or Pop enterprises, which is generally more common in most developing countries. Most developing countries have certain provisions to provide free primary school education to children. Training students through an initiative-driven learning and teaching environment inspires the discovery of new ideas, problem-solving, creative thinking, experimentation, and collaborative student projects, which will prepare students to think in entrepreneurial manners in their daily learning processes.

The two dimensions of developing entrepreneurs are through the educational system and through the creation of incentives and reduction of costs in starting the business.

There are entrepreneurs who have not been to school or college, yet are extremely successful in their endeavors, such as setting up a small roadside business, working with street vendors, and many other forms of enterprise. This is the most prevalent mode of entrepreneurship in India and many other developing countries. The scope of such a business in terms of revenues is limited but is sufficient to support or contribute to the livelihood of such entrepreneurs and their families on a day to day basis. These entrepreneurs operate in rural as well as urban areas. Entrepreneurship is required in all facets of society and economy such as education, research, agriculture, and business.

Cambridge incubator

Cambridge Innovation Center (CIC)'s flagship location was founded in Cambridge, Massachusetts in 1999 in Kendall Square, and has since become an established critical mass of thriving innovative companies. More than 800 startups are housed in the CIC. Dozens of successful companies have grown to prominence while housed at CIC, including Hubspot, MassChallenge, GreatPoint Energy, and Android. CIC Cambridge's One Broadway location is home to more than $7 billion of venture capital, putting this single CIC location ahead of many nations in terms of total venture capital.

Defining globalization

The Merriam-Webster dictionary defines globalization as "the development of an increasingly integrated global economy marked especially by free trade, free flow of capital, and the tapping of cheaper foreign labor markets."

Stiglitz (2007) defines globalization as "the expanding scale, growing magnitude, speeding up and deepening impact of transcontinental flows and patterns of social interaction."[41]

In other words, globalization can be observed as the increased freedom for movement of goods (or the visible trade), services (or the invisible trade), capital (investment flows), and people (migration). Globalization has been spurred by developments in the world-wide political situation, reduction in the barriers to trade, advancement in communication and transportation, the establishment of global institutions such as the World Bank, the International Monetary Fund, World Trade, etc.

Entrepreneurship without a formal education is common, especially in developing countries, such as roadside business shown here.

Figure 1.11 Fruit seller in India

Source: Image by Carol Ermany, Flickr. iStock.com/Pjhpix

- Most developing countries aspire to boost the environment for entrepreneurship by enacting entrepreneur-friendly policies.
- Entrepreneurs can be more aggressive than established organizations in pursuing radical approaches to the creation of economic value.
- According to Ernst & Young CEO Jim Turley, some statisticians show that "100% of the net job growth over many years came from entrepreneurs."
- Information technology enhancements affect customer relationships.
- Cloud computing and globalization have created virtual teams that must focus on continuous innovation.

These organizations and their relevant domestic and international institutions facilitate globalization. Reduction in trade barriers has led to an improvement in the overall standards of living. A major boost to globalization is provided by the improved communications and transportation technology. In the following, we provide two examples of the rapid pace of globalization.

Figure 1.12 illustrates the accelerated growth of world trade as a percentage of GDP between 1960 and 2015. Figure 1.12 reports the percentage of people in different areas of the world who would consider emigrating from their home country in search of better opportunities.

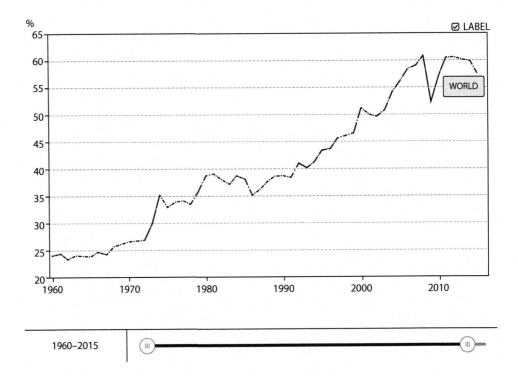

Figure 1.12 World trade as a percentage of world GDP: 1960–2015

Source: © 2019 The World Bank Group. Trade (% of GDP). (n.d.). Retrieved from https://data.worldbank.org/indicator/NE.TRD.GNFS.ZS.

Table 1.3 Global desire to migrate rebounds in some areas

	Desire to migrate, 2010–2012 %	Desire to migrate, 2013–2016 %	Change Pct. Pts.
Sub-Saharan Africa	30	31	+1
Europe (outside European Union)	21	27	+6★
Latin America and Caribbean	18	23	+5★
Middle East and North Africa	19	22	+3★
European Union	20	21	+1★
Commonwealth of Independent States	15	14	-1
Australia/New Zealand/Oceania	9	10	+1
Northern America	10	10	0
South Asia	8	8	0
East Asia	8	7	-1
Southeast Asia	7	7	0
Global	13	14	+1★

Source: Esipova, Ray & Pugliese (2017)[42]

Globalization and entrepreneurship

The rapid transformation of the economic landscape across the globe has had a significant impact on economic, political, cultural, and social issues both within and among countries. Globalization, which started with the economic theories of efficient allocation of resources by reducing and eliminating barriers to trade, has led to various economic opportunities and created challenges for citizens and their governments (see Table 1.3).

The reduction and elimination of barriers of movement of capital, goods, and services, and in some instances (i.e., European Union) labor, provided opportunities for businesses to establish themselves throughout the world.

Innovations in communications, transportation, and technology have brought millions of citizens of the world closer to one another. Multinational enterprises (MNEs) are tapping into workforces and consumers around the globe. This rapid movement has brought its own economic, cultural, and social challenges that require careful attention. Throughout this process, the role of national governments and international organizations are being redefined.

Across the globe, entrepreneurs exchange ideas, collaborate, and compete. Entrepreneurs and entrepreneurship are getting prizes from policymakers and are rewarded by both the public and private sectors. Rising pressure and the desire of citizens in developing countries to attain the quality and living standards of developed nations have forced a major transformation in most developing governments. As a result, institutions and other non-state actors have come to fill the governance void. In developed countries, institutions and private organizations are generally powerful and integrated into society, while in developing countries they are slowly evolving.

> Globalization makes our world seem smaller, increasing the pace that ideas, goods, services, and people move around the globe.

Globalization and entrepreneurship interact in multifaceted ways. In Table 1.4, we present both the positive and the negative effects of globalization on entrepreneurship.[43]

Table 1.4 Positive and negative effect of globalization on entrepreneurship

Positive impacts of globalization on entrepreneurship	Negative impacts of globalization on entrepreneurship
Reduction of trade barriers act as strong incentive for innovation to flourish in attempts to meet demand.	Competition from cheaper imported products and against companies that have access to lower cost infrastructures and resources makes it more challenging for entrepreneurs in developing countries.
Continuous innovation to meet demand and quality of the global markets	Late globalization might lead to insufficient time for innovate domestically. Thus losing to competitors from the developed countries
In terms of large-scale production, jobs are created domestically.	Technical and managerial difficulties of producing standardized goods by entrepreneurs for markets and being differentiated to meet the needs of any specific costumer simultaneously.
Globalization facilitates the flow of technology between nations by increasing the mobility of production factors. Consequently, the borrowing process of ideas and methods for entrepreneurs gets easier.	It prepares an opportunity for developed countries to dump goods that are substandard to developing countries. It makes the competition hard for entrepreneurs.
The mobility of most of the production factors as well as reduction of trade boundaries would provide incentives for entrepreneurs to operate globally.	Globalization depletes the production resources (such as brain drain, raw material, and etc....) of developing countries by providing them with a way out from their home country.
The window of communication opened by globalization led to the collaboration of entrepreneurs with foreign investors or other entrepreneurs by joint venture contracts. Getting managerial and technical consultations got easier.	

Source: (Akpor-Robaro & Mamuzo, 2012)[44]

Concluding remarks

The definitions, theories, and concepts of economic development, entrepreneurship, and globalization were described and the relationship between entrepreneurship and development was analyzed. Additionally, the role of globalization in this process was discussed.

In the opening case of the chapter, SEZ, we provided an overview of entrepreneurial policies with objectives of creating jobs and development. Additionally, several short cases about different countries and issues are presented to enhance our understanding of the concepts and their applications. In the history of humanity, every generation has been unique in its own ways, learning, achieving, and experiencing life shaped by global occurrences and trends. Each generation has had a storehouse of "human experiences", values, attitudes, skills, and practical knowledge passed on to them through seasoned intellectual minds such as their parents, grandparents, teachers, mentors, coaches, etc.

From a microscopic view, each youth's "human experiences" become learned aspects of his or her personality. The youth today, primarily the millennial generation, have grown up in a globalized and dynamically interconnected world, where it is, for example, possible for a student at a University in India to virtually connect with peers, professors, and experts at a university in the USA without very little cost.[45]

Table 1.5 Key terms

Entrepreneurship	Chenery's patterns of development approach
Economic development	Dependency and neoclassical theory
Gross National Products (GNP)	Heavily indebted poor countries (HIPCs)
Rostow's theory	Factor-driven economies and efficiency-driven economies
The Harrod-Domar model	Sustainable economic growth
Lewis structural change	Globalization

Discussion questions

1. What were the main points of this chapter?
2. What has been the influence of globalization on entrepreneurship in developing countries?
3. Are there differences in entrepreneurial initiation in developed versus developing countries?
4. Analyze the impact of entrepreneurial activity on sustainable development.
5. Discuss positive and negative impacts of globalization on entrepreneurship.

Case study – continued

Special Economic Zones and their impact on local economy

Despite initial investment and development, most SEZs take 5–10 years to become effective. While some countries have exhibited rapid growth, many SEZs, especially in Africa, failed to develop local economies, even after 10 years of operation (although it is still too early to tell for some).[46]

Questions for discussion

1. Analyze the role of SEZs on the development of communities and countries.
2. Are there any drawbacks for having SEZs in the long-run?
3. Why do SEZs have different outcomes in different regions of the world?

Notes

1 Zeng, D. Z. (2015). Global experiences with special economic zones: focus on China and Africa. World Bank. Retrieved from http://documents.worldbank.org/curated/en/810281468186872492/pdf/WPS7240.pdf
2 Boyenge, J. (2007). ILO database on export processing zones. International Labour Office.
3 FIAS. (2008). Special Economic Zones: Performance, Lessons Learned, and Implications for Zone Development. Washington, DC: World Bank.
4 Cling, J. P., & Letilly, G. (2001). Export Processing Zones: A Threatened Instrument for Global Economy Insertion? DIAL/Unite de Recherche CIPRE Document de Travail DT/2001/17; Madani, D. (1999). A review of the role and impact of export processing zones. World Bank Policy Research Working Paper 2238; Zeng, D. Z. (2010). Building Engines for Growth and Competitiveness in China: Experience with Special Economic Zones & Industrial Clusters.

Washington, DC: World Bank; FIAS. (2008). Special Economic Zones: Performance, Lessons Learned, and Implications for Zone Development. Washington, DC: World Bank; Fuller, B., & Romer, P. (2012). Success and the city: how chartered cities could transform the developing world? A McDonald-Laurier Institute publication (April); Farole, T., & Akinci, G. (Eds.). (2011). Special Economic Zones: Progress, Emerging Challenges, and Future Directions. World Bank.

5 Gartner, W. B. (1985). A conceptual framework for describing the phenomenon of new venture creation. Academy of Management Review, 10(4), 696–706.

6 Alvarez, S. A., & Barney, J. B. (2010). Entrepreneurship and epistemology: the philosophical underpinnings of the study of entrepreneurial opportunities. The Academy of Management Annals, 4, 557–577; Shane, S., & Venkataraman, S. (2000). The promise of entrepreneurship as a field of research. Academy of Management Review, 25(1), 217–226.

7 Acs, Z. J., & Szerb, L. (2009). The global entrepreneurship index (GEINDEX). Jena Economic Research Papers No 2009–028. Available online at https://ideas.repec.org/p/jrp/jrpwrp/2009-028.html

8 Hitt, M. A., Ireland, R. D., Sirmon, D. G., & Trahms, C. A. (2011). Strategic entrepreneurship: creating value for individuals, organizations and society. Academy of Management Perspectives, 25(2), 57–75.

9 Beattie, A. (2018, May 17). Who coined the term "entrepreneur"? Retrieved December 14, 2018, from www.investopedia.com/ask/answers/08/origin-of-entrepreneur.asp.

10 Retrieved from www.worldbank.org/.

11 Sustainable Development. (2018, November 29). Retrieved December 14, 2018, from www.iisd.org/topic/sustainable-development.

12 www.worldbank.org/.

13 Sen, A. K. (1999). Development as Freedom. Oxford: Oxford University Press.

14 Clifton, H. (2013). Amartya Sen on development. Retrieved from WordPress.com.

15 Sen, A. K. (1999). Development as Freedom. Oxford: Oxford University Press.

16 Sen, A. K. (1999). Development as Freedom. Oxford: Oxford University Press.

17 Uvin, P. (2010). From the right to development to the rights-based approach: how human rights entered development. In A. Cornwall and D. Eade (Eds.), Deconstructing Development Discourse. Buzzwords and Fuzzwords (pp. 163–174). Oxford: Practical Action Publishing Ltd.

18 Rostow's Model. (2015, April 30). Retrieved from www.emaze.com/@ALRQOZWQ/Rostow's-Model.

19 Sen, A. K. (1999). Development as Freedom. Oxford: Oxford University Press, p. xii.

20 Structural Changes Models. (2011, January 12). Retrieved December 14, 2018, from https://erikkrantz.wordpress.com/2011/01/12/structural-changes-models/.

21 Unit 2 People and the Planet – Linear. (2013, December 12). Retrieved December 14, 2018, from https://geogyourmemory.wordpress.com/unit-2/.

22 Kiely, R. (2010). Dependency and world-systems perspectives on development. International Studies, March 2010 (online November 2017). DOI 10.1093/acrefore/9780190846626.013.142

23 www.worldbank.org/.

24 Retrieved February 20, 2016, from www.worldbank.org/depweb/english/beyond/global/glossary.html.

25 Countries and Economies. (n.d.). Retrieved from https://data.worldbank.org/country.

26 World Economic Forum, 2016. Global Competitiveness Index 2015-2016. https://reports.weforum.org/global-competitiveness-report-2015-2016/appendix-methodology-and-computation-of-the-global-competitiveness-index-2015-2016/, accessed February 20, 2016. https://devex.com/news/what-is-driving-uber-s-global-impact-88419.

27 The Global Competitiveness Report 2015–2016. (n.d.). Retrieved February 20, 2016, from http://reports.weforum.org/global-competitiveness-report-2015-2016.

28 Audretsch, D. (2007). Entrepreneurship capital and economic growth. Oxford Review of Economic Policy, 23(1), 63–78; Acs, Z. J., & Szerb, L. (2009). The global entrepreneurship

index (GEINDEX). Jena Economic Research Papers No 2009–028. Available online at wwwjeneconde; Wennekers, S., Van Stel, A., Thurik, A. R., & Reynolds, P. (2005). Nascent entrepreneurship and the level of economic development. Small Business Economics, 24(3), 293–309.

29 Cheney, C. (2016, August 05). What is driving Uber's global impact? Retrieved December 14, 2018, from www.devex.com/news/what-is-driving-uber-s-global-impact-88419.

30 Acs, Z. J. (2006). How is entrepreneurship good for economic growth? Innovations, 1(1), 97–107.

31 Kelley, D. J., Bosma, N., & Amorós, J. E. (2011). Global Entrepreneurship Monitor: 2010 Global Report. Wellesley, MA: Babson College and Santiago Chile: Universidad Del Desarrollo. Retrieved from www.av-asesores.com/upload/479.PDF.

32 Acs, Z. J., Desai, S., & Hessels, J. (2008). Entrepreneurship, economic development and institutions. Small Business Economics, 31(3), 219–234.

33 Todaro, M. P., & Smith, S. (2011). Economic Development, 11th Edition, Prentice Hall.

34 Prashantham, S. (2018, September 19). When globalisation meets entrepreneurship it can be a force for good. Retrieved December 14, 2018, from http://theconversation.com/when-globalisation-meets-entrepreneurship-it-can-be-a-force-for-good-64415

35 The Economist. (2016). The walled world of work.

36 Jackson, J., & Rodkey, G. (1994). The attitudinal climate for entrepreneurial activity. The Public Opinion Quarterly, 58(3), 358–380.

37 Eunni, R. V., & Manolova, T. S. (2012). Are the Bric economies entrepreneur-friendly? An institutional perspective. Journal of Enterprising Culture, 20(2), 171–202. https://doi.org/10.1142/S0218495812500082

38 Steenhuis, H.-J., & Gray, D. O. (2006). The university as the engine of growth: an analysis of how universities can contribute to the economy. International journal of technology transfer and commercialization, 5(4), 421–432.

39 http://business.slu.edu/news-and-events/events/event/2016/04/21/vasquez-wuller-accounting-lecture-presents-james-turley-former-chairman-and-ceo-of-ernst-young/.

40 Rajna, T. (2015, August 06). Uganda named the world's most entrepreneurial country. Retrieved December 14, 2018, from www.virgin.com/entrepreneur/uganda-named-worlds-most-entrepreneurial-country.

41 Stiglitz, J. E. (2007). Making Globalization Work. WW Norton & Company.

42 Esipova, Neli, Ray, Julie, & Pugliese, Anita. (2017, June 8). Number of potential migrants worldwide tops 700 million. Gallup. Retrieved from https://news.gallup.com/poll/211883/number-potential-migrants-worldwide-tops-700-million.aspx

43 Asgary, N., Frutos, D., & Samii, M. (2015). Introduction to Foundations of Global Business. IAP – Information Age Publishing Inc. Asgary N., Frutos D., Samii, M., & Varamini, H. (2019). Global Business: Economic, Social and Environmental Approach, Second edition, Information Age Publishing Inc.

44 Akpor-Robaro, M. O. M. (2012). The impact of globalization on entrepreneurship development in developing economies: a theoretical analysis of the Nigerian experience in the manufacturing industry. Journal of Management Science and Engineering, 6(2), 1–10.

45 In the knowledge economy that we are currently moving towards, it is critical to develop entrepreneurial characteristics at all levels of educational process. Entrepreneurship education in most countries is limited to university level education. In the United States, according to a survey conducted by the Gallup Organization, it was discovered that 70 percent of the high school students in the sample wanted to start their own business, and yet only 44 percent had basic knowledge about entrepreneurship.

46 Farole, T., & Akinci, G. (Eds.). (2011). Special Economic Zones: Progress, Emerging Challenges, and Future Directions. World Bank.

2 Cultural context, entrepreneurship, and development

Learning objectives:

1. *Learn the definition of culture*
2. *Understand the relationship between culture and entrepreneurship*
3. *Examine the relationship between innovation, motivations, and culture in relation to entrepreneurial activities*
4. *Examine the influence of technology on culture*
5. *Comprehend the role of government in shaping entrepreneurial culture*
6. *Study the role of culture on development*

Figure 2.1 Culture of entrepreneurship at MIT
Source: © iStock: peterspiro

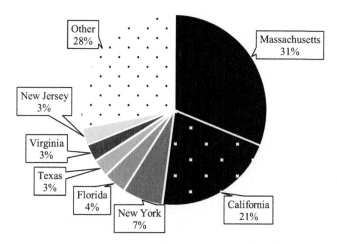

Figure 2.2 Percentage of total ventures

Entrepreneurial culture in an institution of higher education

Massachusetts Institute of Technology (MIT) is one of the most well-known higher education institutions in the world where the entrepreneurial culture has led to significant worldwide development and advancement. In the following is a summary of some of these activities. Analyze the different activities of MIT and draw conclusions for higher education institutions in other countries.

Alumni-founded companies have created 4.6 million jobs, generating nearly $2 trillion in annual revenues ~ MIT News (2017), http://web.mit.edu/

Martin Trust Center for MIT Entrepreneurship is one of the largest research and teaching centers at the MIT Sloan School of Management. It nurtures many student-run startups inside the campus. Most MIT ventures get initial funding and mentoring services. California, with its experienced IT and technology environment, is another favorite destination. Both Boston and California locations contain skilled workforce and intelligent minds.

Introduction

This chapter explores how diverse cultures influence the outcome of a country's/region's entrepreneurship, and economic development. The means and policies will be discussed that culture can be influenced (e.g., government policies and interventions) in ways that cannot only encourage and reduce entrepreneurial barriers, thus contributing to the growth of a country. Overcoming and encouraging entrepreneurial and risking taking cultural barriers is a serious question to be answered.

The chapter discusses traits and traditions that complement innovation, motivation, and entrepreneurial endeavors. The concept of cultural convergence and its relationship to entrepreneurship are presented. The application of Geert Hofstede's model of cultural variation largely connects the chapter's concepts and conclusions.

3 levels of culture

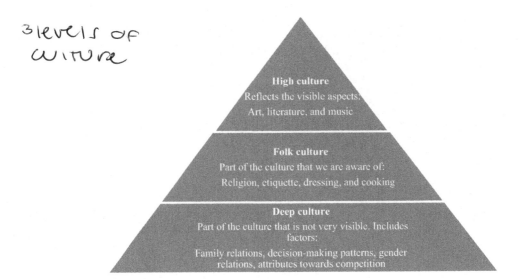

Figure 2.3 Cultural pyramid

Culture definition

National culture can be separated into three levels (see Figure 2.3).

The cultural attitude varies to a great extent among various countries and societies. Geert Hofstede developed a model for cultural analysis intended for business purposes. The Hofstede's model is discussed in the next section.

Business or organizational culture is the set of values and beliefs that exist within an organization. These include, among others, the relationship between managers and workers, the degree of formality of an organization, the degree of risk-taking, and the attitude towards social responsibility. Organizations with a strong social culture have an alignment between the value system and the belief of the employees, while organizations with a weak social culture have little alignment between the two.

Both the culture of the organization and the overall culture of a country influence and affect each other. The organization's culture initially takes to a great extent the form of the home country value system. The degree of this influence obviously varies from organization to organization. For example, if a society is characterized by entrepreneurship and risk-taking, it is inevitable that such an attitude would not be reflected in the enterprises operating in that country. Obviously, the degree of entrepreneurial tendency varies and depends on a number of factors that are firm specific.

Aristotle said, "We are what we repeatedly do." This view elevates repeated behavior or habits as the core of culture and deemphasizes what people feel, think or believe. It also focuses our attention on the forces that shape behavior in organizations, and so highlights an important question: are all those forces (including structure, processes, and incentives) "culture" or is culture simply the behavioral outputs?[1]

Figure 2.4 Aristotle

Source: Image by Martin aka Maha on Flickr. www.famous-mathematicians.com/images/aristotle.jpg

Anthropologist Edward Hall, in his 1976 book, *Beyond Culture*, defines culture as "the way of life of a people, the sum of their learned behavior patterns, attitudes and material things" and articulates the following "ideas and metaphors":[2]

1. Culture = models, templates.
2. Culture is the medium we live in; like the air, we breathe.
3. Culture is innate but learned (i.e. we are born with the physical necessity and capacity to specialize our bodies, brains, hearts in line with cultural patterns).
4. Culture is living, the interlocking system(s) – touch one part, the rest moves.

5. Culture is shared; it is created and maintained through relationships.
6. Culture is used to differentiate one group from another. (In other words, division into groups comes first; deliberate differentiation via cultural symbols comes second.)

Therefore, Hall's ideas of cultures are systems that "extend" the abilities of the human being.

Kluckhohn and Strodtbeck (1961) define culture as "a shared, commonly held body of beliefs and values that define the 'should' and 'ought' of life."[3] James Spradley et al. (2015) defined culture as "the acquired knowledge people use to interpret experience and generate behavior."[4] Hofstede et al. (2010) defines culture as "the collective programming of the mind distinguishing the members of one group or category of people from others."[5] Culture is seen in groups and can be defined as a pattern of basic assumptions shared and learned by the group that works well enough to be considered valid and therefore taught to new members.[6]

We can draw the conclusion that culture is the accepted values and norms that influence the way in which people think, feel, and behave in their everyday life. Every society has its own culture that affects the spirit of its people. It is transferred from one generation to another, thus it can be difficult to change or influence. However, evaluation of globalization and, therefore, a higher level of cultural interactions among different cultures shall lead to cultural conversion.

Table 2.1 summarizes a cultural map from the perspectives of four teams of scholars in four related areas: cultural elements (Hall), value patterns (Hofstede),[7] sociological and anthropological framework (Trompenaars), and variations in value orientations (Kluckhohn & Strodtbeck).[8]

Culture, entrepreneurship, and development

Culture has a critical impact on entrepreneurial activities. Therefore, cultural characteristics of a developing country or community shall be carefully studied in order to identify its degree of openness to entrepreneurship. Table 2.1 shows Hofstede's six cultural differences that influence entrepreneurial activities. Holding everything else constant, we can draw the conclusion that some cultures are less open and familiar to entrepreneurial activities than others. Therefore, public policies can begin to influence entrepreneurial activities in a developing country that has interest.

Table 2.1 Cultural maps

Culture elements (Hall)	Value patterns (Hofstede)	Sociological and anthropological FW (Trompenaars)	Variations in value orientation (Kluckhohn & Strodtbeck)
• Time • Space • Things • Friendships • Agreement • Interpersonal behavior	• Power • Risk • Individualism • Masculinity • Time • Management theories – practice	• Universalism vs Particularism • Collectivism vs Individualism • Affective vs neutral relationships • Achievement vs ascription • Orientation towards time • Internal vs external control	• Relation to nature • Orientation to time • Belief about human nature • Mode of human activity • Relationships • Space • International business practice

"No culture can live if it attempts to be exclusive." Mahatma Gandhi.
  We need:

• Partnership between people of north and south (of India)
• Ownership by marginalized people at the grassroots level
• Participation of people with disabilities so that no groups are at risk of being
  left behind.

Does Gandhi's ideology apply to organizations as well?

Figure 2.5 Gandhi
Source: Photo by Bryce Edwards on flickr

Table 2.2 The Hofstede model

Trait	Description
Power distance	Refers to the distance between social classes and groups in the society.
Individualism/collective	Level of interdependence among members of society
Masculine/feminine	Masculinity versus femininity: Motivation by competition vs motivation by interest.
Uncertainty avoidance	Extent to which society is tolerant of unknown situations and attempts to avoid them.
Long-term orientation	Societal long-term, future-oriented perspective rather than a short-term outlook.
Indulgence/Restraint	How freely one can fulfill their needs and desires.

The effects that culture has upon entrepreneurship can be highlighted using various examples that often refer back Hofstede's attributes (see Table 2.2). A useful general theory advanced by Nguyen et al. (2009) provides comparative analyzes which enable entrepreneurship activities.[9]

The logic for such a theory embraces the following chain of thought: (1) countries such as the United States that show high levels of individualism are motivated by competition and personal achievement; (2) these traits tend to support higher individual contributions, innovation, and new ideas; (3) this, and the other traits listed earlier, tend to both support and create a fertile environment for entrepreneurship.

Cultures that have low uncertainty avoidance, furthermore, are more comfortable with ambiguous situations such as those that involve risk-taking. Thus, some cultures encourage risk-taking while others do not. As a result, cultures in which risk-avoidance is the norm may have difficulty developing a tradition of strong and vital entrepreneurship because people hesitate to take the risks that fuel entrepreneurial efforts. Thus, those who choose to reduce risk taking (by, for example, choosing job security) cease to be candidates for entrepreneurial enterprises.[10] This type of response can dampen the economic development and growth that entrepreneurial activity could trigger. Ernst & Young CEO Jim Turley, for example, suggests that South Korea's "fear of failure" is the first thing that must change if the country is to maintain its economic momentum and attract entrepreneurs and innovators.[11,12]

Low power distance

Cultures that have a low power distance have lesser distinctive social classes and partake in more intimate social interactions. This environment may provide a greater degree of freedom for people throughout society, therefore, shall foster more entrepreneurial activities. Many developed western countries are characterized by a low power distance. Established democracies in which officials are elected rather than appointed tend to have cultural, social, and legal environments that nurture a relatively low power distance.

High masculinity

Cultures that are defined as high in masculinity promote competition and recognition. These cultures place a higher value on success and innovation than cultures that tend

Table 2.3 Organizational cultural traits

Masculine	Feminine
Connect compensation with power	Encourage equity with parity
Maintain rigid control of staffing	Provide equal opportunity for all
Focus on material rewards	Focus on relationships

to be more feminine and value their personal interests and rank quality of life higher than individual "success" or "achievement". The more masculine, developed countries in Western Europe and North America, for example, tend to be more motivated by monetary incentives and competition than most developing countries. A country high in masculinity not only promotes an environment of competition but also can foster a culture of selfishness. Of course, this could be for selfish reasons as well. Countries where feminine cultural values are dominant should have more partnerships and alliances. A country's culture is often intimately linked to its heritage, traditions, and historical foundation. Table 2.3 summarize organizational cultural traits.

History and culture is more important than profits

A small business artist in Rio de Janeiro, Brazil, Marta's values, for example, are symbolic of her country's deep-rooted passion for displaying and maintaining one's history and culture, and putting this before profits. As a Brazilian, Marta is proud of her heritage and is willing to make business decisions to preserve this heritage at the risk of failure. This is an example of having low masculinity – following passion and interests rather than money or competition. This helps to explain why Brazil tends to lean towards the feminine end of Hofstede's masculinity index (Hofstede et al., 2010).[13] Marta receives a lot of respect in Rio de Janeiro for not only being a successful entrepreneur, but for being a successful Afro-Brazilian female entrepreneur. While many countries would also praise this, there are developing countries that would not give Marta the respect she finds in Brazil. It seems there is significantly less praise for entrepreneurs in Russia than in Brazil. The contrast between Russia and Brazil illustrates how culture and government can breed an environment that favors or hinders entrepreneurship. Compounding the lack of respect for entrepreneurs in Russia, the uncertainty index is also very high, resulting in a strong fear of failure. Russia's entrepreneurial activity is thus less favorable than a society that praises successful ventures.[14]

Sweden, as an example, is a developed country with a history of cooperation and strong interpersonal skills among its traders and seafarers.[15] This history has shaped its culture, as it is considered one of the most feminine cultures in the world, according to Hofstede's country analysis.[16] This tradition helps to explain why intrapreneurship – behaving like an entrepreneur within a large company – drives innovation in Sweden rather than entrepreneurship that presupposes a greater degree of independence.[17] Braunerhjelm (2012) defines intrapreneurship as the act of "behaving like an entrepreneur while working within a large organization."

Figure 2.6 Marta's value
Source: Image by laverrue on flickr

In 1998, recipient of the Nobel Memorial Prize in Economic Sciences, Professor Amartya Sen observed that culture has wrongfully been understated for its role in economic development. Instead, the dominant paradigm of neoclassical economists has focused on the rational thought and the maximization of self-interest.

Sen reminds us that culture exerts a strong influence because it reflects and guides the way people live their lives. As a result, it can exert a significant influence upon economic development. Policymakers of any country that would like to boost its entrepreneurial activities shall identify its cultural characteristics and articulate relevant policies. There is no question that policymakers shall highlight the positive impact of entrepreneurship for the well-being of society and create a relevant atmosphere. They can have an influence on educational institutions, from elementary to college, and support the creation of other institutions that support entrepreneurship. For example, in the United States there are Small Business Development Offices in towns and cities whose roles are to provide professional, and in some cases financial, support to entrepreneurs.

Extended Stay America's CEO, Jim Donald, gave employees "Get Out of Jail Free" cards that they could use when they wanted to take a big risk for the company.

Toyota and other Japanese companies ask and expect employees to look for "small problems" and take responsibility for fixing them on their own.

Ericsson's "Light It Up" campaign invites employees to submit "game-changing" ideas.

Source: Everwise (2016)[18]

Jackson and Rodkey state that besides parents, educators and institution are most influential in forming children's attitudes and culture.[19] Between parents, school, society, and the government, it is a very difficult and arduous process to change the culture of a region. An alternative vision also exists: a United Nations' "systems task team" agrees that "culture can be a powerful driver for development, with community-wide social, economic and environmental impacts."[20]

In congruence with the Millennium Development Goals, this team at the United Nations is focused on the social and economic development of weak, developing countries. Instead of identifying ways to change the culture of society like prior researchers, this team is identifying ways that countries can harvest their own cultural background into a plan for further development. Developing countries often have both a large labor force and a culture-rich heritage. Using their unique culture and labor force to promote tourism, cultural infrastructure, or promoting their cultural heritage, countries can create sustainable revenue growth. Cultural tourism will revive cultural heritage and generate employment in the segment of the economy. Of course, it will revive entrepreneurial initiation in this domain. There are many success stories in countries such as Brazil, China, Iran, Turkey, etc. In the following is an example of how culture and development are linked. More effective development policy interventions that lead to an increase in entrepreneurship development could have economic benefits in terms of employment and wealth creation for entrepreneurs who are engaged. However, problems could also arise, such as inclusiveness, equity, and diversity. Therefore, policymakers shall address these issues over time through appropriate policies to maximize the benefits for larger segments of the society and to minimize its negative impacts.[21]

In the past, governments have often tried to influence entrepreneurial attitudes (even if only indirectly) through cultural intervention. Various examples of this sort are discussed in order to identify ways in which the leaders of developing countries can use and enhance cultural traits in ways that encourage and support entrepreneurial efforts (see Table 2.3). Doing so can be vital because entrepreneurship is an important economic engine in many contemporary societies. Although many experts believe that globalization is leading to greater cultural homogeneity, some nations and cultures appear to have cultures and traditions that embrace innovation and entrepreneurship.

The evolution of globalization has reduced barriers to cross-cultural interactions and understanding and therefore the advancement of entrepreneurship. The role that culture plays in the advancement or discouragement of entrepreneurship and economic development can have serious social and economic ramifications upon a developing country or region. This results because the heritage and traditions of a people can influence innovation, motivations, and the incentives for entrepreneurs.[22] The continuous growth of entrepreneurship can culminate in a material impact on the economic development of a country. There are various measurements of culture and evidence suggests that certain cultural tendencies affect the entrepreneurial potential for a culture, region, and/or country. It is therefore important to study which cultural behaviors, tendencies, and traits influence entrepreneurial potentials. Building this understanding can help societies to leverage their cultural traits in ways that encourage entrepreneurship.

Believing in entrepreneurship can encourage economic growth; public policies often strive to encourage entrepreneurial behavior. Worries about social engineering aside, governments often play an important role in affecting cultural and social change. How intervention of this type can both foster and deter entrepreneurial activities requires studies. The analysis of culture is not only used to examine the entrepreneurial potential of a country, but entrepreneurial behavior can be viewed as an artifact or expression of it.

Stories of local eco-entrepreneurship

How is entrepreneurship affecting local communities and thus culture? "The future of green is local. Majora Carter tells three inspiring stories of people who are saving their own communities while saving the planet."

You can check in more details in the full TED Talk in this link: www.ted.com/talks/majora_carter_3_stories_of_local_ecoactivism/discussion?language=en

Drawing upon an individual's or a region's cultural heritage can provide a sustainable means by which an entrepreneur in a developing country can contribute to economic development.

Scholars have shown that the prevalence of entrepreneurial activity is closely related to cultural and social considerations.[23] The United States, often seen as a classic example of an entrepreneurial culture, exhibits a long tradition of valuing hard work and individual achievement, which is the most important precondition for entrepreneurial cultures.[24] They state that two basic positions exist regarding the relationship between culture and entrepreneurship:

A. culture as a precursor to entrepreneurship;
B. the other discounted culture's affect altogether.

The role of females in entrepreneurship is varied among cultures and religions.

Debate, how has your community and the government encouraged female entrepreneurs?

Figure 2.7 Female entrepreneurs

Source: © iStock: jeffbergen. Global Entrepreneurship and Development Institute. (n.d.). Retrieved December 14, 2018, from www.thegedi.org/

The lack of adequate and appropriate entrepreneurial activities is one of the most important obstacles for sustainable development and growth in most developing countries. It appears that the relatively small entrepreneurial group in developing countries is engaged. Focus and sustainable public policies that provide financial and educational incentives for entrepreneurial activities and influence cultural perceptions can impact positively on startups growth.

It is important to notice that, before the industrial revolution, economic development and growth was slow and basically non-existent. Robert Lucas (2004) reported that annual growth rates "…of 1 percent for the entire 19th century, of one-third of 1 percent for the 18th century."[25] In some cultures, hard work and the workers themselves were looked down upon by the elite. However, with the advancement of capitalism and globalization, this view has been changing. Due to the revolution in technology and communication, societies are becoming more interconnected. Additionally, countries that have been more entrepreneurial have had a higher rate of growth and standard of living. In this process, the perspectives of elites are changing. The Global Entrepreneurship Monitor (GEM) survey shows these advances in recent years.[26]

A respect for the value of work, however, is not enough to fuel a robust embrace of entrepreneurship. Other aspects that are at least partially related to culture exert impacts, including the society's view on individual achievement and the ability for commercial activities to have sufficient freedom in which to operate. Such cultural aspects are often reflected in the legal and regulatory environment of a country.

Figure 2.8 History of opportunity
Source: © iStock: chaofann. www.fundersandfounders.com

The conclusion that follows from these observations is that, from a cultural perspective, the preconditions for entrepreneurial activity include placing a high value on hard work, a generally positive attitude towards those who function as an entrepreneur, and the freedom to experiment and innovate.

Since the beginning of time, entrepreneurs have always found ways to innovate. Debate what is the most important trait of an entrepreneur from your perspective?

Culture and innovation

Country culture

Country culture is like our immune system: woven into all aspects of life. Country culture, in its broadest sense, is cultivated behavior, or the totality of what a person has accumulated in experience through social learning. Thus, different cultural groups may think, feel, and act differently towards topical issues such as innovation.

Hofstede (1991, cited in Marcus and Gould, 2000)[27] defined a schema for describing a culture using four key dimensions:

Power distance

The degree to which less-empowered members accept the power distribution within a culture.

Individualism/collectivism

c.) The degree to which a member of a culture is oriented towards the needs of the individual vs the needs of the group.

a.) we decide what the members of a culture

b.) the needs of the group are + important than the individual.

Masculinity

The degree to which the culture places value on masculine (assertiveness, competition) vs feminine (home, people) concerns.

Uncertainty avoidance

The degree to which a culture tolerates ambiguity and creates strategies to manage it.

Each of these dimensions has possible ramifications towards innovation. Power distance, for instance, can affect how comfortable employees feel communicating new ideas with their employers. Collectivism over individualism would indicate a culture in which design is done by committee and therefore possibly does not generate as many unique ideas as a culture that supports individualism. A masculine culture would be more competitive than a feminine culture and would thereby foster creativity and innovation through such competition. A risk-averse culture would avoid making creative, but risky, decisions that would foster innovation.

Thirty-eight countries were surveyed and ranked against each other along these dimensions (Hofstede, 1991, cited in Marcus and Gould, 2000).[28] By analyzing the scores for each country, we can predict the impact of cultural attitudes on innovation through each element's effect on creativity.

2017 Nobel Prize in Economic Science for Human Behavior

Richard H. Thaler from the Booth School of Business at the University of Chicago was awarded the Nobel Memorial Prize in Economic Science for his contributions to behavioral economics who concluded that it is important for policymakers to consider human behavior as an important factor. Professor Thaler stated that the basic premise of his theories was that, "In order to do good economics you have to

keep in mind that people are human." He named this phenomenon an "endowment effect". Humans may act irrationally. Please read more…
www.nytimes.com/2017/10/09/business/nobel-economics-richard-thaler.html

For example, Spain can be characterized as having a culture with dimensions of low power distance. The factors that work well for Spanish innovation are low power distance and high individualism. Low power distance indicates that subordinates and supervisors work closely together as equals, and organizational structures may be flatter hierarchies. This has a positive impact on the innovation in an organization, as employees may feel comfortable to share ideas freely with their supervisors and work together on implementation (See Figure 2.9).

High individualism also predicts positively towards innovation, indicating that the society places higher relative value on freedom of personal self-expression, which is crucial for the generation of ideas.

The cultural factor that could negatively affect innovation is high uncertainty avoidance. In this type of culture, formal structure is preferred to ambiguity, and familiarity is preferred to what is different. This is problematic towards the development of a culture of innovation, where failure and experimentation are encouraged, and innovators should take risks.

According to a recent study of creativity and design in European countries, Spain is ranked 13 of 27 countries overall and is consistently ranked slightly higher than the median in each dimension taken into account for the scoring.[29] Self-expression is one of the lower-ranked areas, ranked at 17, suggesting that cultural factors could be obstructing the generation of ideas.

Morocco, as a developing country, can be characterized as a culture with high power distance (see Figure 2.10). These characteristics predict that Morocco may have cultural barriers conducive of a less innovative environment in comparison to Spain. Firstly, high power distance suggests a high inequality of power between employees and employers. The primary attitude is that knowledge resides in the hands of those who are empowered or esteemed, such as teachers or supervisors, and obedience is expected from employees (Hofstede, 1991, cited in Marcus & Gould, 2000).[30]

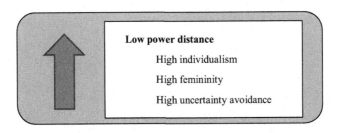

Figure 2.9 Low power distance

Source: Hofstede (1991, cited in Marcus, A., & Gould, E. W. (2000). Crosscurrents: cultural dimensions and global web user-interface design. Interactions ACM, 7(4), 32–46. https://doi.org/10.1145/345190.345238

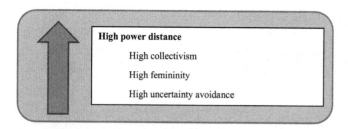

Figure 2.10 High power distance

Source: Veltri, N. F., & Elgarah, W. (2009). The role of national cultural differences in user adoption of social networking. In Southern Association for Information Systems Conference, Charleston, SC.

A culture holding collectivism highly values the needs of the group over the individual and places low emphasis on personal autonomy or challenges. Individuals raised within these cultural settings tend to be less assertive and competitive in a business setting, as compared to other societies (Hofstede, 1991, cited in Marcus & Gould, 2000).[31] Generally speaking, highly collectivist societies are less likely to be innovative.[32]

As a country with relatively high uncertainty avoidance, Morocco would tend to prefer the "tried and true path" versus taking risks.

Similar to Spain, experimentation would be discouraged, and rules and policies are geared towards managing uncertainty rather than encouraging creativity.[33] Innovation and permissiveness to experiment could even be viewed as an attack on the culture's traditions, morals, and values. Therefore, culture, especially national culture, is a crucial factor in the process of innovating.

Working together

Valve is a gaming company responsible for classics such as Half-Life, Counter-Strike, Portal, and many others. At Valve there are no job titles and nobody tells you what to work on. Instead, all the employees at Valve can see what projects are being worked on and can join whichever project they want. If an employee wants to start their own project then they are responsible for securing funding and building their team. For some, this sounds like a dream; for others, their worst nightmare.

Country culture is like our immune system; its job is to kill intruders before they can harm the body. Unless the country culturally honors ideas and supports risk-taking, innovation will be suppressed before it even has a chance to commence. Therefore, the knowledge of cultural factors that promote or constrain innovation will have an important impact on the development of a country.

Culture demission and innovation

The relationships between cultural dimension and innovation have been discussed previously.[34,35] There is a negative relationship between power distance and innovation.

Figure 2.11 Flat organizations

Source: Image by Long Zheng on flickr – Forbes article. Morgan, J. (2015, July 20). The 5 Types of Organizational Structures: Part 3, Flat Organizations. Retrieved December 14, 2018, from www.forbes. com/sites/jacobmorgan/2015/07/13/the-5-types-of-organizational-structures-part-3-flat-organizations/ #7553a8316caa

Holding everything else constant, it seems that higher levels of innovation are positively correlated with higher levels of the spread of information.

This social culture is also accepted by companies. There is a process of validation of the culture that individuals acquire in the external environment. The leadership of an organization and the culture that is built can transmit its culture, such as a culture of innovation.[36]

In low power distance societies, communication across functional or hierarchical boundaries is easier and more common, which makes it possible to connect different thoughts and creative ideas which lead to breakthroughs.[37] However, given a large power distance, the sharing of information can be constrained by the hierarchy.[38]

There is a positive relationship between individualism and innovation. The process of initiating innovation is often regarded as the act of an individual. The initial ideas emerge in the head of an individual, while the group can only be supportive or not. Since individualistic cultures value freedom more than collectivistic cultures, people in individualistic societies have more opportunities to try something new.[39] There is a negative relationship between masculinity and innovation. In feminine societies, people focus on humanity and relationships that can lead to a more supportive climate. A warm and kind environment, with mutual trust, low conflict, and socio-emotional support helps employees cope with uncertainty in relation to new ideas.[40]

- Holding everything else constant, we can draw the conclusion that some cultures are less entrepreneurial than others.
- Cultures that have a low power distance are in more intimate contact in social encounters, government interactions, and business.
- A country high in masculinity not only promotes an environment of competition, but also can foster a culture of selfishness.
- More feminine countries will tend to have partnerships and alliances.
- Lawrence Harrison and Samuel Huntington's ten traits that represent advanced, developed economies can serve as a blueprint for developing countries in their quest for economic and social development.
- Jackson and Rodkey state that besides parents, educators and institution are the most influential in forming children's attitudes and culture.
- Governments have often tried to influence entrepreneurial attitudes.

There is a negative relationship between uncertainty avoidance and innovation. Innovations are always associated with some risk and uncertainty. As a result, cultures with strong uncertainty avoidance are more resistant to innovations.[41] To avoid changes, these cultures adopt rules to minimize ambiguity, and rules in return constrain the opportunities to develop new solutions. There is a strong correlation between innovation and entrepreneurial activities and creativity. Therefore, we can conclude that the previous arguments are also applicable to cultural characteristics and entrepreneurial behavior and will influence development.

Based on the relationship between cultural dimension and innovation mentioned earlier, we can conclude that innovation will flourish in a creative environment. It seems horizontal organizations are more conducive to innovation. Low power distance index and high individualism are positive in the way of treating others in the first stages of innovation. Creative people should be comfortable volunteering their opinions and motivated to exploring new ideas. Some examples show China and Morocco to have high power distance and low individualism. It means that people in China and Morocco do not feel comfortable speaking up when it comes to idea creation relative to people in the United States.

Although generally having a low power distance and high individualism are better for innovation, it does not mean each country does not innovate only in accordance with these gauges. Low uncertainty avoidance is also an important factor that affects innovation. It indicates that, for example, in China, employees prefer to search for solutions for unstructured situations. Unstructured situations are unknown, surprising, and different from the "norm" situations. In Spain, employees, on average, have a high uncertainty avoidance compared to China and Morocco. Spanish citizens seem to prefer to plan everything carefully to avoid uncertainty.

Innovation faces cultural constraints for various reasons, such as shaping the mentality and patterns people deal with, as well as human behaviors concerning risks and opportunities.

Figure 2.12 Afghan women
Source: © iStock: DMEphotography

In Afghanistan an entrepreneur thrives

Edward Girardet (2009) highlights micro, macro, and cultural challenges that exist in the country, especially for women.[42] One of these brave entrepreneur's stories is that of Ms. Hassina Syed, who is an outspoken 30-year-old former refugee and mother of two. Giradet states that, "Despite numerous obstacles, including threats by warlords, government officials and rival male interests who deeply resent a female in their presence, Hassina now ranks as one of the most successful entrepreneurs in Afghanistan."

He reports that she has created several companies and is the founder of the nonprofit Afghan National Women's Organization (NOW). NOW's aim is to help women develop their own livelihoods. Above all, she is the only female member of the powerful Afghan Chamber of Commerce and Industry (ACCI) who has taken official trade delegations overseas with President Hamid Karzai.

Figure 2.13 Corporate innovation framework

Source: © iStock: NicoElNino). www.innovationmanagement.se/2014/01/27/seven-steps-to-creating-a-successful-innovation-framework/

The key issue is to what extent and in what ways culture influences individual and group phenomena in organizations.[43] Figure 2.13 demonstrates the importance of corporate frameworks in building an innovational culture.[44]

Figure 2.13 shows the link between creativity, design, and innovation, and its influence on culture. Creativity and design are important strategic resources for an enterprise and a key differentiator for a business. A creative climate in a country or a business organization leads to the generation of ideas, which can be turned into innovative products or services. Swann and Birke argued that a creative climate in an organization is an important selling point for the organization.[45] The application of creativity and design to innovation is well-defined and should be well-managed. Organizations that have a clear roadmap for this process will have a competitive advantage over their competitors. In the global economy, creativity and design as drivers of innovation are important for handling economic uncertainty and can help ensure global acceptance of a product.[46] Creativity and design are not only important enablers of innovation in the context of an organization, but are also important features of a knowledge economy, and necessary for a society to be economically competitive.[47] Creativity, design, innovation, and entrepreneurial activities are positively linked and can play a critical role in the development of an economy.

Entrepreneurship, culture, and government

The government can play a large role in shaping the attitudes in an entrepreneurial environment. The regulatory framework and establishment of policies and institutions can encourage the process of creating new businesses as well as helping to ensure property rights, intellectual property, and so forth are protected.[48] Governments at all levels can create incentives for entrepreneurship, doing so in ways that are designed to reflect the culture and its society.

Vietnam provides a good example of this possibility. Vietnam's culture, as a whole, is similar to African, Latin-American, and Middle-Eastern cultures in the sense that it possesses collectivist tendencies. A strong individual approach is atypical and the country tends to be quite low on the masculinity index.[49]

These two characteristics seemingly indicate that Vietnamese culture would not produce many entrepreneurs. However, there are two reasons why the Vietnamese culture has become a stronghold for entrepreneurship. Based on Hofstede's assessment, the country scores very low for "uncertainty avoidance" or fear of failure. The culture views uncertainty as an opportunity, whereas Latin culture tends to view it as a risk. The government's current "socialist-oriented market economy", furthermore, has created institutions, regulations, and infrastructure to support the private sector and entrepreneurial activity.[50] Although the government once discouraged private enterprises, strategic changes in governmental policies have created a vibrant entrepreneurial spirit. It could be possible that during the French colonial period from the eighteenth century until 1954, many aspects of capitalism and entrepreneurial culture were introduced there and influenced the culture characteristics of Vietnam.

AUC Venture Lab is Egypt's first university-based incubator and accelerator at The American University in Cairo (AUC). The lab enables startups to capitalize on AUC's intellectual capital, world-class facilities, and research capacities. It connects innovative startups with AUC's network that includes alumni, faculty, mentors, and investors. Through this, it fosters a thriving ecosystem of innovation, education, and responsible business.

The mission of the AUC Venture Lab is twofold: to help Egyptian startups commercialize their innovative technologies and business models into viable ventures that contribute to economic growth, competitiveness, and job creation; and to provide a learning and research platform for the AUC community to connect with entrepreneurs.

As the government of Vietnam once did, nations can develop laws and regulations that act as a deterrent to entrepreneurship. The long-standing socialistic culture of the former Eastern Bloc, for example, tends not to nurture entrepreneurial activity. In some regions of the world, profiting from private enterprises is considered unfavorable and is viewed as being selfish.[51] This notion can inhibit private innovation and entrepreneurship.

Russia, for example, has a strong developing economy, supported by substantial energy resources, but relatively few have significantly benefited. The high power distance, going all the way back to Czarist times and continued through the socialist era, resulted in a society generally not prone to taking risks. This helps to explain why uncertainty avoidance is very high in Russia and, as a result, why, as a society, they do not encourage entrepreneurship and bottom-up development.[52]

In the case of Brazil, the government has fostered an unfavorable business market through its regulatory system, or lack thereof. Many entrepreneurs and small businesses are considered "informal" and do not report themselves in any way to the government. This results in less tax revenue for the government and creates an environment where formal tax abiding businesses must compete with smaller, informal businesses on an uneven playing field. Currently, a reported 50 percent of the Brazilian economy is operating informally so as to avoid the high tax rates of formal businesses.[53]

This may be an additional reason why a small business leader does not want his or her business to grow. When we asked a few informal entrepreneurs in Brazil about their organizational and operational strategies, they did not feel as though they were doing anything wrong, observing "it's simply the way it is." Brazil has created an environment where being an informal entrepreneur or small business is the norm rather than the exception.

All of these informal entrepreneurial activities create jobs and generate income that is good for a developing economy. Because self-interest and needs are combined to improve the quality of life, governments should support this outcome. If governments have the ability to clamp-down on the informal sector to collect taxes, then the unemployment rate may increase which could be a bigger challenge for the government.

- From a cultural perspective, the preconditions for entrepreneurial activity include placing a high value on hard work, a generally positive attitude towards entrepreneurship, and the freedom to experiment and innovate.
- Hofstede (1991, cited in Marcus & Gould 2000)[54] defined a schema for describing a culture using four key dimensions: Power Distance, Individualism/Collectivism, Masculinity, Uncertainty Avoidance.
- High Individualism also predicts positively towards innovation.
- High Uncertainty Avoidance could impact innovation negatively.
- Generally speaking, high collectivist societies are less likely to be innovative.
- Unless the country culture honors ideas and supports risk-taking, innovation will be stifled before it begins.
- There is a negative relationship between masculinity and innovation.
- There is a strong correlation between innovation and entrepreneurial activities and creativity.
- Culture affects innovation because it shapes the mentality and patterns people deal with novelty, as well as human behaviors in regards to risks and opportunities.
- Creativity and design are important strategic resources for an enterprise and a key differentiator for a business.

This is a period of development in some developing countries. The institutions of government are not developed adequately and are not able to collect taxes to build infrastructure and provide basic services. Therefore, the informal economy and government may co-exist in the short-run for the purpose of growth and employment.

However, by transcending an informal status, entrepreneurs and small businesses should theoretically benefit. Evidence from countries such as Uruguay and Argentina furthermore legitimize the claim that informal micro-enterprises and entrepreneurs can jumpstart an economy. In 1989, Uruguay and Argentina were two economically and culturally similar countries. Argentina reformed its policies to legitimize its informal entrepreneurs and small businesses, while Uruguay did not.[55] As a result, Uruguay's economy fell behind while Argentina's flourished.[56] The growth proved that legitimization of micro-enterprises could have a much more significant effect on the large Brazilian economy today. In addition to regulatory action, governments of developing countries can also benefit from the experiences of developed countries when seeking to provide relevant incentives for entrepreneurship.[57]

Conclusions

The influence of culture on entrepreneurship and development was discussed in this chapter. We presented perspectives of scholars and practitioners regarding the relationship between culture, entrepreneurship, and development. We can draw conclusions that government policies can impact behavior by enacting policies which will provide incentives to accept and accelerate entrepreneurial activities.

We examined cultural traditions that are more or less complementary entrepreneurship activities. Additionally, the concept of cultural convergence and its relationship to entrepreneurship and development were discussed.

Figure 2.14 Cultural tourism

Source: Image by Julia Maudlin on flickr

We provided several cases from different countries to showcase these relationships, including the opening case about MIT – a higher education institution with a strong entrepreneurial culture.

Cultural tourism and entrepreneurship

The owner of the Instituto de Pesquisa E Memoria Pretos Novos in Rio de Janeiro is just one example of an entrepreneur capitalizing on Brazil's rich culture. After identifying the site as a burial ground of African slaves, the owner uncovered buried artifacts and turned the house into a museum to display the rich history of the region. Many of Brazil's entrepreneurs exhibit their history and traditions in the products they make or services they render. One woman sells her acarajé, a traditional snack with black-eyed peas and shrimp, in Rio de Janeiro as a tribute to her cultural traditions in northern Brazil. Not only is it something she knows very well, but it allows her to make money while expressing her culture. These "cultural and creative industries" are generating strong growth in most developing regions. By incorporating culture into a national development plan can work towards economic and human rights purposes while making the plan more relevant to the needs of the people and linking to their heritage and self-interest.

Discussion questions

1. What is the definition of a culture?
2. What is the relationship between culture and entrepreneurship, and is it relevant?
3. Provide examples of cultures that are open to innovation, motivational techniques, and entrepreneurial happenings.
4. Conduct a case study of two different cultures whose response to entrepreneurship is different. Provide public policies that may alter their entrepreneurial behavior.
5. What is cultural convergence? Is it good or bad? Make your arguments.
6. Is technology altering cultural behavior? How has it influenced you?
7. Does the government have a role in shaping entrepreneurial cultures?

Table 2.4 Key terms

Culture	Uncertainty avoidance
Cultural map	Long term orientation
Power distance	Indulgence/restraint
Individualism/collectivism	U.N. Millennium Development Goals
Masculine/feminine	

Figure 2.15 Women in business

Source: © iStock: fizkes. Women in business facts and statistics. (n.d.). Retrieved December 14, 2018, from www.prowess.org.uk/facts; Huntley, J. (2014, August 28). Are Women In Business Making Advancements? Retrieved December 14, 2018, from https://sheownsit.com/women-business-making-advancements/; McElhaney, K. (2013, November 12). More Women in Business Makes For Better Business Overall. Retrieved December 14, 2018, from www.theguardian.com/sustainable-business/blog/women-better-for-business?CMP=twt_gu; Institute for Small Business and Entrepreneurship. (n.d.). Retrieved December 14, 2018, from https://isbe.org.uk/.

Case study

Women and entrepreneurship case

According to a survey conducted by IIT-Delhi, in developed countries like the United States and Canada, in recent years one-third of women owned small businesses. Women in Asian countries led 40 percentage of the total workforce. In Britain and China the women workforce preceded dramatically from men. In a 15-year period, 1980–1995, Japanese women entrepreneurs increased 2.4 percentages. Women entrepreneurship has a significant role in developing countries. However, in the same developing countries, women encounter many obstacles at the initial stages of commencement of their own business. The majority of top-management positions are held by men; and even the most professional female entrepreneurs have the least chance to make it through the commercial market. Traditionally it is believed that only men could have an entrepreneurship role in society, while women's part is limited to paid-employees. Presuming that a woman deviates from the norm of society and initiates their own business, in the running process of her business she would be suppressed by other male competitors or if not, society would do it. Lack of experiments in entrepreneurship for women would be another hassle. Some women involve themselves in training programs without having sufficient entrepreneurial aptitude. Predominance in financial markets, gaining financial resources, complicated loan procedures, and managing working capital in business are financial issues that, to some extent, perhaps men would be structured to perform better than females. Severe competition in the marketplace would be a repellent for vulnerable genders. The main hinder is the female double role: first motherhood in family then business women in society. Balancing between these roles is too demanding. Sometimes women spend too much time on their former role that their inability to attend the workplace would add conflicts. It seems women are less risk-takers than men, therefore the capital structure they are making would involve less risky capital. They rarely accept credit from bankers for the simple reason of a lack of collateral security.

Questions for discussion

1. Take multiple examples of major companies across industries and evaluate the role/number of females in top-management.
2. Explain why do these numbers differ across cultures, countries, and industries?

Notes

1 Watkins, M. (2013). The First 90 Days. Boston, MA: Harvard Business Review Press.
2 Hall, E. T. (1976). Beyond Culture. Garden City, NY: Anchor Press.
3 Kluckhohn, F. R., & Strodtbeck, F. L. (1961). Variations in Value Orientations. Evanston, IL: Row, Peterson.
4 Spradley, J. W., McCurdy, D. W., & Shandy, D. (2015). Conformity and Conflict: Readings in Cultural Anthropology (15th ed.). Pearson.
5 Hofstede, G., Hofstede, G. J., & Minkov, M. (2010). Cultures and Organizations: Software of the Mind (3rd ed.). New York: McGraw-Hill Education.
6 Schein, E. H. (2010). Organizational Culture and Leadership (Vol. 2). John Wiley & Sons.
7 Hofstede, G., Hofstede, G. J., & Minkov, M. (2010). Cultures and Organizations: Software of the Mind (3rd ed.). New York: McGraw-Hill Education.
8 Lane, H. W., Maznevski, M., DiStefano, J., & Deetz, J. (2009). International Management Behavior: Leading with a Global Mindset. Wiley Publishing.
9 Nguyen, T. V., Bryant, S. E., Rose, J., Tseng, C.-H., & Kapasuwan, S. (2009). Cultural values, market institutions, and entrepreneurship potential: a comparative study of the United States, Taiwan, and Vietnam. Journal of Developmental Entrepreneurship, 14(01), 21–37. https://doi.org/10.1142/S1084946709001120
10 Jackson, J., & Rodkey, G. (1994). The attitudinal climate for entrepreneurial activity. The Public Opinion Quarterly, 58(3), 358–380.
11 Da-ye, K. (2012). Entrepreneurial culture begins with a tolerance for failure. Korea Times.
12 Smit, C. (2016, October 21). What is Uncertainty Avoidance? Retrieved December 14, 2018, from https://culturematters.com/what-is-uncertainty-avoidance/. Noort, M. C., Reader, T. W., Shorrock, S., & and Kirwan, B. (2015). The relationship between national culture and

safety culture: implications for international safety culture assessments. Journal of Occupational and Organizational Psychology, 89(3), Version of Record online: December 12, 2015.

13   Hofstede, G., Hofstede, G. J., & Minkov, M. (2010). Cultures and Organizations: Software of the Mind (3rd ed.). New York: McGraw-Hill Education.

14   Eunni, R. V., & Manolova, T. S. (2012). Are the Bric economies entrepreneur-friendly? An institutional perspective. Journal of Enterprising Culture, 20(2), 171–202. https://doi.org/10.1142/S0218495812500082

15   Steensma, H. K., Marino, L., & Weaver, K. M. (2000). The influence of national culture on the formation of technology alliances by entrepreneurial firms. The Academy of Management Journal, 43(5), 951–973.

16   Hofstede, G., Hofstede, G. J., & Minkov, M. (2010). Cultures and Organizations: Software of the Mind (3rd ed.). New York: McGraw-Hill Education.

17   Braunerhjelm, P. (2012). Swedish Entrepreneurs Prefer to be Employed. Global Entrepreneurship Monitor.

18   Everwise. (2016, March 15). Encouraging Smart Risks in the Workplace. Retrieved December 14, 2018, from www.geteverwise.com/leadership/encouraging-smart-risks-in-the-workplace/.

19   Jackson, J., & Rodkey, G. (1994). The attitudinal climate for entrepreneurial activity. The Public Opinion Quarterly, 58(3), 358–380.

20   UN System Task Team. (2012). Culture: A Driver and an Enabler of Sustainable Development. UNESCO.

21   UN System Task Team. (2012). Culture: A Driver and an Enabler of Sustainable Development. UNESCO.

22   La Porta, R., Lopez-de-Silanes, F., & Shleifer, A. (2008). The economic consequences of legal origins. Journal of Economic Literature, 46(2), 285–332.

23   Ondracek, J., Bertsch, A., & Saeed, M. (2011). Entrepreneurship education: culture's rise, fall, and unresolved role. Interdisciplinary Journal of Contemporary Research in Business, 3(5), 15–28.

24   Ondracek, J., Bertsch, A., & Saeed, M. (2011). Entrepreneurship education: culture's rise, fall, and unresolved role. Interdisciplinary Journal of Contemporary Research in Business, 3(5), 15–28.

25   Robert Lucas (2004) reported that "The striking thing about postwar economic growth is how recent such growth is. I have said that total world production has been growing at over 4 percent since 1960. Compare this to annual growth rates of 2.4 percent for the first 60 years of the 20th century, of 1 percent for the entire 19th century, of one-third of 1 percent for the 18th century. For these years, the growth in both population and production was far lower than in modern times. Moreover, it is clear that up to 1800 or maybe 1750, no society had experienced sustained growth in per capita income. (Eighteenth century population growth also averaged one-third of 1 percent, the same as production growth.) That is, up to about two centuries ago, per capita incomes in all societies were stagnated at around $400 to $800 per year. But how do we know this? After all, the Penn World Tables do not cover the Roman Empire or the Han Dynasty. But there are many other sources of information" (Lucas, R. E. (2004, May 1). The Industrial Revolution: Past and Future, 2003 Annual Report Essay (Chapter 5 of his Lectures on Economic Growth). Cambridge: Harvard University Press, 2002).

26   "GEM is a trusted resource on entrepreneurship for key international organisations like the United Nations, World Economic Forum, World Bank, and the Organisation for Economic Co-operation and Development (OECD), providing custom datasets, special reports and expert opinion" (Global Entrepreneurship Monitor. (n.d.). Retrieved from www.gemconsortium.org/).

27   Marcus, A., & Gould, E. W. (2000). Crosscurrents: cultural dimensions and global web user-interface design. Interactions ACM, 7(4), 32–46. https://doi.org/10.1145/345190.345238

28 Marcus, A., & Gould, E. W. (2000). Crosscurrents: cultural dimensions and global web user-interface design. Interactions ACM, 7(4), 32–46. https://doi.org/10.1145/345190.345238

29 Hollanders, H., & van Cruysen, A., (2009). Design, Creativity and Innovation: A Scoreboard Approach. Pro Inno Europe, Inno Metrics.

30 Marcus, A., & Gould, E. W. (2000). Crosscurrents: cultural dimensions and global web user-interface design. Interactions ACM, 7(4), 32–46. https://doi.org/10.1145/345190.345238

31 Marcus, A., & Gould, E. W. (2000). Crosscurrents: cultural dimensions and global web user-interface design. Interactions ACM, 7(4), 32–46. https://doi.org/10.1145/345190.345238

32 Veltri, N. F., & Elgarah, W. (2009). The role of national cultural differences in user adoption of social networking. In Southern Association for Information Systems Conference, Charleston, SC.

33 Veltri, N. F., & Elgarah, W. (2009). The role of national cultural differences in user adoption of social networking. In Southern Association for Information Systems Conference, Charleston, SC.

34 Shane, S. (1993). Cultural influences on national rates of innovation. Journal of Business Venturing, 8, 59–73.

35 van Everdingen, Y. M., & Waarts, E. (2003). The effect of national culture on the adoption of innovations. Marketing Letters, 14(3): 217–232. doi:10.1023/A:1027452919403.

36 Schein, E. H. (2010). Organizational Culture and Leadership (Vol. 2). John Wiley & Sons.

37 Shane, S. (1993). Cultural influences on national rates of innovation. Journal of Business Venturing, 8, 59–73.

38 van Everdingen, Y. M., & Waarts, E. (2003). The effect of national culture on the adoption of innovations. Marketing Letters, 14(3): 217–232. doi:10.1023/A:1027452919403.

39 Waarts, E., & van Everdingen, Y. (2005). The influence of national culture on the adoption status of innovations: an empirical study of firms across Europe. European Management Journal, 23(6), 601–610.

40 Nakata, C., & Sivakumar, K. (1996). National culture and new product development: an integrative review. Journal of Marketing, 60(1), 61–72.

41 Waarts, E., & van Everdingen, Y. (2005). The influence of national culture on the adoption status of innovations: an empirical study of firms across Europe. European Management Journal, 23(6), 601–610.

42 Girardet, E. (2009). In Afghanistan, an entrepreneur thrives. Forbes, Oct. 12. Retrieved from www.forbes.com/2009/10/12/afghanistan-women-hassina-syed-forbes-woman-entrepreneurs-mega-finance.html#6ee83b1824a7.

43 Aycan, Z. (2000). Cross-cultural industrial and organizational psychology. Contributions, past developments, and future directions. Journal of Cross-Cultural Psychology, 31, 116–128.

44 Swann, P., & Birke, D. (2005). How do Creativity and Design Enhance Business Performance? A Framework for Interpreting the Evidence. UK Department of Trade and Industry.

45 Swann, P., & Birke, D. (2005). How do creativity enhance business performance? A framework for interpreting the evidence. Think piece for DTI Strategy Unit.

46 Swan, K. S., Kotabe, M., & Allred, B. B. (2005). Exploring robust design capabilities, their role in creating global products, and their relationship to firm performance. Journal of Product Innovation Management, 22(2), 144–164.

47 Djeflat, A. (2005). Innovation Systems and Knowledge Economy in North Africa: New Opportunity for Innovation Take Off? Third GLOBELICS Conference. Pretoria: South Africa: October–November.

48 Nguyen, T. V., Bryant, S. E., Rose, J., Tseng, C.-H., & Kapasuwan, S. (2009). Cultural values, market institutions, and entrepreneurship potential: a comparative study of the United States, Taiwan, and Vietnam. Journal of Developmental Entrepreneurship, 14(01), 21–37. https://doi.org/10.1142/S1084946709001120

49 Hofstede, G., Hofstede, G. J., & Minkov, M. (2010). Cultures and Organizations: Software of the Mind (3rd ed.). New York: McGraw-Hill Education.

50 Nguyen, T. V., Bryant, S. E., Rose, J., Tseng, C.-H., & Kapasuwan, S. (2009). Cultural values, market institutions, and entrepreneurship potential: a comparative study of the United States, Taiwan, and Vietnam. Journal of Developmental Entrepreneurship, 14(01), 21–37. https://doi.org/10.1142/S1084946709001120

51 Eunni, R., & Manolova, T. (2012). Are the BRIC economies entrepreneur-friendly? An institutional perspective. Journal of Enterprising Culture, 20(2), 171–202.

52 Nguyen, T. V., Bryant, S. E., Rose, J., Tseng, C.-H., & Kapasuwan, S. (2009). Cultural values, market institutions, and entrepreneurship potential: a comparative study of the United States, Taiwan, and Vietnam. Journal of Developmental Entrepreneurship, 14(01), 21–37. https://doi.org/10.1142/S1084946709001120

53 Eunni, R., & Manolova, T. (2012). Are the BRIC economies entrepreneur-friendly? An institutional perspective. Journal of Enterprising Culture, 20(2), 171–202.

54 Marcus, A., & Gould, E. W. (2000). Crosscurrents: cultural dimensions and global web user-interface design. Interactions ACM, 7(4), 32–46. https://doi.org/10.1145/345190.345238

55 "Although Uruguay has natural resources similar to those of Argentina, innovative entrepreneurs and economic development have been seriously stunted by excessive government intervention as well as by high inflation" (University of Canterbury. (n.d.). Retrieved December 14, 2018, from www.canterbury.ac.nz/).

56 Nguyen, T. V., Bryant, S. E., Rose, J., Tseng, C.-H., & Kapasuwan, S. (2009). Cultural values, market institutions, and entrepreneurship potential: a comparative study of the United States, Taiwan, and Vietnam. Journal of Developmental Entrepreneurship, 14(01), 21–37. https://doi.org/10.1142/S1084946709001120

57 Instituto de Pesquisa Econômica Aplicada. (2010). Brasil em Desenvolvimento: Estado, planejamento e políticas pública. 00 p. 3 v.: gráfs., mapas, tabs. (Brasil: o Estado de uma Nação). Retrieved from www.ipea.gov.br/bd/pdf/Livro_BD_vol2.pdf

3 Technology, communications, and entrepreneurship

Learning objectives:

1. *Understand the relationship between entrepreneurship, technology, and communications*
2. *Comprehend the role of technology on entrepreneurship in developed and developing countries*
3. *Understand the different platforms of IT*
4. *Examine the relationship between technology and the knowledge economy*
5. *Study the valuation of IT in a business*
6. *Explain the role of technology for startups*

Figure 3.1 Hmizate team logo

Entrepreneurship and technology: the case of Hmizate in Morocco

Differentiation, Customer Service, Networking, and Surviving the Competition

Hmizate.ma is Morocco's first online site that has, to date, successfully imitated Groupon's business model before evolving into the country's first internet shopping mall. The founder and CEO, Mr. Kamal Reggad, sees his "self-funded" venture as the start of e-commerce in Morocco and as an illustration to new business owners. Launched in January of 2011, Hmizate.ma is Morocco's first daily deals site offering its users deep discounts of up to 80 percent on travel, hotels, electronics, and apparel. To get started, the founder decided not to go through the commonly used African One-Stop Shop Investment Centre (OSSIC), but chose to do everything himself through the network of people he met during his time in the United States.

Building on the early success of Hmizate.ma, in the spring of 2012 Kamal created Hmall.ma – an Amazon-like online shopping site that offers value discounts on the world's well-known brands in clothing, beauty, sports, and other direct-to-consumer categories (the discounts, however, are not as deep compared to Hmizate.ma).

In 2013, to fuel its growth the company raised funding of $2 million from two reputable venture capitalists (VCs) in Europe and the Middle East (Hummingbird Venture & MenaVenture Investments).

Within a few short months of the companies being launched, as many as 20 similar businesses surfaced in the area. To differentiate itself from this quick wave of imitators, the website offered its customers a point-based loyalty program that offers redemption options towards future purchases. The company also keeps a commitment of high customer value and an impeccable level of service. Hmall.ma ensures delivery within 48 hours of placing an order. Also, once the customer places his or her order, a Hmall.ma Customer Service representative calls the customer to confirm order details. According to Mr. Reggad, this kind of hands-on approach is the only way he can ensure the highest standard of service and also survive in the industry.

Case continued at the end of the chapter…

Introduction

In this chapter, we will examine the impact of technology on entrepreneurship and development and its relationship with globalization. A brief background on the evolution of technology is provided. We will present different platforms of IT that entrepreneurs can take advantage of to advance their objectives.

Globalization was largely made possible by a radical innovation that occurred about 300 thousand years ago which was by the daily use of fire. In the book *Sapiens: A Brief History of Humankind*, by Yuval Noah Harari, the main events that may explain about how the domestication of fire led Homo sapiens to the top of the food chain is discussed.[1] For us, the fire can be thought of as one of the first radical innovations that is known that made it possible to cook. Cooking was the technology developed from the radical innovation "domain of fire" that allowed us to introduce non-digestible foods through the intestine of the human organism. For humans, two capacities were developed: we spend less time per day preparing food to feed ourselves and increase the chances of survival by ingesting food. While a chimpanzee took 5 hours to eat raw food, a Homo sapien took a single hour to eat cooked food. The energy involved in the digestion of food eaten by chimpanzees, obviously, was far greater than the energy involved in the digestion of food eaten by a human. When cooking food, many other ingredients were introduced into the diet of humans, which would not be if they had not achieved this technology (cooking). As we know chimpanzees did not achieve cooking.

Approximately 230,000 years after the start of the daily use of fire, humans began to migrate to Europe and Australia from Africa; perhaps a kind of entrepreneurship that led to a first globalization, keeping the specificities of the time. Entrepreneurship can be seen as a multidimensional phenomenon involving economic, technological, political, and cultural aspects, among others. Thus, the world is configured by regions according to their level of economic development: developing, emerging, and developed. There is certainly much discussion around the criteria for levels of development. However, there is some consensus that these three blocs make some sense to understand the world from an economic point of view. What we can understand is that the footprint of entrepreneurship intrinsically presents economic development as part of the characteristics of its trajectory. We can also infer that when developing solutions for needs or desires, technologies are designed (high, intermediate, or low technology) and these technologies are elements to support entrepreneurial activities. By technologies, we understand here that they are the practices and the tools that solve or facilitate addressing many problems; just as 300,000 years ago, a radical innovation (fire domain) may have made possible the rise of Homo sapiens to the top of the food chain and its prominence as a dominant species (expansion of Homo sapiens from Africa to Europe and Australia). In 1947, another radical innovation developed that defined the contours of technology and entrepreneurship of the twenty-first century: the invention of the transistor, which we will examine next.

Transistor: the father of the digital age

Before the transistor, the processing and communication equipment operated by means of valves. The problems were mainly the cost of each valve, the heating, the consequent consumption of energy, and the space that the equipment occupied. We can imagine without much exaggeration that for a single smartphone in 1940, it would require a building of some floors to process all the data and the communication. In other words, without transistors, without microchips, without computers, without mobile phones, and without internet, it would not be easy to operate.

The fact is that the transistor is a radical innovation. Professor Fitzgerald (2011) from MIT published a book entitled *Inside Real Innovation*.[2] He describes the invention of the X-ray and the transistor as the two fundamental innovations (radicals) in the strictest sense. From this point of view, all these applications you use on your smartphone, or perhaps the Electronic Reader you're using to read this book, were only possible after we invented the transistor, in particular.

To invent the transistor, it was necessary to learn to master the transmission of electric current through a material different from the conductors; of the semiconductor type (germanium and silicon). In 1947, scientists Bardeen, Brattain, and Shockley invented the transistor while working for Bell Telephone Laboratories.

Making paper from stone – innovation and caring for environment

"Stonepaper" (also known as rock paper, lime paper, or mineral paper) is a new generation of paper that was first developed by Taiwan Lung Meng Tech Co. in Taiwan during the late 1990s. The primary material of this paper is calcium carbonate powder, which replaces the use of wood for the production of paper. Its properties are waterproof, tear resistance, its magic effect of colors on it, and finally its reversibility to the soil. BS Group in Iran is the fourth company in the world which is making papers from stone (Figure 3.2).

Figure 3.2 Eco paper
Source: © iStock: kyoshino

The relationship between entrepreneurship and technology is complementary, one supporting the other and vice versa. Still, in analyzing technologies that originate from a radical innovation such as the domestication of fire 300,000 years ago or the invention of the transistor 70 years ago, we can infer that these technologies begin to delineate the contours of both entrepreneurship and economic development. By inventing the transistor to advance to data-processing devices (integrated circuit and then microprocessors), we came to transistor-powered computers in 1950. Soon after, in 1960, developments began in the United States, the United Kingdom, and France of the communication protocols called the Advanced Research Projects Agency Network (ARPANET). This system used packet switching to allow multiple computers to communicate on a single network. The way we are doing this chronological description is to explain from another perspective of entrepreneurship, innovation, and development.

In just 20 years, starting with the invention of the transistor, it was possible to get to computers in 1950 (Hardware), to begin to processing data (Software), and to make feasible the principles of data transmission in 1960 (Telecommunications). The Internet Protocol Suite (TCP/IP) was introduced (1982) as ARPANET's standard communication protocol, almost at the same time as the Swiss Tim Berners-Lee developed the concept of the world wide web (www) that consisted of the inclusion of documents based on hypertext within an information system that was accessible to any node of this network. In the late 1980s and early 1990s, the internet became available to society and not only to universities and research centers. This mass diffusion of a low-cost communication technology (internet) can be considered as one of the essential benefits for entrepreneurship. Society responds when more information is at its disposal. The phenomenon of dissemination of information, initiated with the availability of a network (internet), drastically reduces information asymmetry, provoking impacts on society, on companies, on governments, and consequently influencing the way in which economic development has taken place.

- Entrepreneurship, technology, and globalization are directly and intimately related, beginning with the use of fire and leading to the first case of entrepreneurship and globalization – the migration to Europe and Australia from Africa.
- Entrepreneurship can be seen as a multidimensional phenomenon involving economic, technological, political, and cultural aspects, among other phenomenon.
- The world is configured by regions according to their level of economic development: developing, emerging, and developed.
- The relationship between entrepreneurship and technology is complementary, one supporting the other and vice versa.
- The culmination and mass diffusion of a low-cost communication technology (internet) can be considered as one of the most essential benefits for entrepreneurship.

This explains why technology nurtures entrepreneurship after the industrial revolution. The main aspects that demonstrate the "replacement" of the industrial revolution by the technological revolution has been an inducer of entrepreneurship. By understanding the relationship between information, communication technology, and entrepreneurship, we can explain the ramifications of entrepreneurship in the context of developed and developing countries, which seem to have different nuances.

Thomas Friedman, *The New York Times* columnist and the author of several bestselling books including *Thank You for Being Late*, presented data that in 2007 many new innovations evolved. However, due to the 2008 financial crises it did not get the attention it deserved. During 2007, 15 Revolutionary Inventions such as the iPhone and the Kindle, etc. were unveiled. Most of these innovations have revolutionized our means of communications (i.e., iPhone) and ways of our lives.[3] Figure 3.3 shows Apple's new campus.

Social and contextual aspects influence the fundamental way that entrepreneurship functions. For example, what works in India may not work in other countries.

Figure 3.3 Apple campus
Source: © iStock: Dronandy

Entrepreneurship in developed and developing countries

Since the dawn of the industrial revolution, technology has nurtured entrepreneurship. The current digital revolution seems to expand it exponentially. Through technological innovations, the efficiency of communication has increased. The production of goods and services is now cheaper and broader as compared to the previous decades. The production of new products and services has become easier and more innovative. No wonder it is a catalyst for entrepreneurship in the developed as well as in the developing countries.

Technological advances and applications are becoming ubiquitous because they are constantly evolving at an increased speed. Even the definition of technology is being modified in the process. This chapter focuses on traditional views such as production, modification, usage, and knowledge of tools and systems that solve problems in a systematic manner. Technology is shaping and transforming all aspects of life. It is creating newer dimensions for expansion of entrepreneurship as an actor and also as a class of leaders and innovators.

Business dictionary (BusinessDictionary.com) describes that technology can be divided into five categories as demonstrated in Table 3.1.

This table highlights the different aspects of technology valuation and usages. Different segments of society use technology to serve their basic needs for communication to advance projects. What is clear is that more and more of the world citizens are finding that it is an amazing tool to use and gain knowledge.

Table 3.1 The range of technology

Aspect	Discussion
Tangible	Blueprints, models, operating manuals, prototypes
Intangible	Consultancy, problem-solving, and training methods
High	Fully or semi-automated and intelligent technology that manipulates ever finer matter and ever powerful forces
Intermediate	Semi-automated partially intelligent technology that manipulates refined matter and medium level forces
Low	Labor-intensive technology that manipulates only coarse or gross matter and weaker forces

Information Technology (IT)

The contemporary digital age is changing the way business is being conducted. It is universally understood that all types of information and transactions pass through the internet at great speeds. In addition, IT plays various roles in business and entrepreneurship. For example, computers, equipment, software, and other technologies have found their way into all areas of business including finance, marketing, sales, distribution, and others. IT plays an indispensable role in making a company successful during uncertain and turbulent economic conditions.[4]

IT is used to encompass a range of new technologies and their applications including in all aspects of the use of computers, microelectronic devices, satellites, and communication technology. IT can affect a firm's products, services, markets, producing costs, and product differentiation. Hence, the success of innovative firms critically depends on the implementation and creative use of IT. The rapid evolution of Artificial Intelligence and its application to all aspects of human life will be drastic.

As it was discussed in previous chapters, entrepreneurs are risk-takers who develop new ideas, organizations, products, and services. Novelty and innovativeness is the outcome of entrepreneurship while uncertainty is always present during the process of achieving such milestones. Success requires opportunity, timing, hard work, and perhaps some luck. Entrepreneurs tend to embody several traits such as being proactive innovators and risk-takers, who are willing to do what is necessary in order to bring their ideas to fruition.[5] In the contemporary world as in the past, technology provides the emerging tools that allow entrepreneurs to achieve their goals by gaining a competitive edge at a reduced cost. It is widely recognized that any new business venture creates jobs in the economy and improves the general economic conditions in both developing and developed countries. Moreover, these organizations generate new ideas, new business models, and new ways of selling goods and services, and technology has been the essential factor in all of them.

Although many obstacles pose as challenges for entrepreneurs, most of them can be mitigated through the effective use of IT. IT plays a significant positive role in firms' performance.[6] They highlight that through dynamic capabilities of the organization (i.e., agility, digital options, and entrepreneurship), alertness and strategic processes are derived from IT. Enterprises will improve their course of strategic actions, which in turn impact the firms' performance.

Modern day IT offers a wealth of tools, which entrepreneurs can use to lower the risks, reduce costs, and serve their customers and clients better. Information technologies are significantly changing the global economy and conventional businesses are becoming more and more dependent on technology for their continued success.

Careers of the future

In the article called "Career in Information Technology: Future Prospects", Jason Wong writes that we humans have included the use of operating systems from mobile phones to automated company tasks.[7] He expects a growth of 32 percent by 2018 for jobs in computer software engineering, according to the Bureau of Labor Statistics (Figure 3.4). And with change in the US economy, a greater number of opportunities and wealth are available for experts in computer science and technology. Currently, more students are interested in an IT or Computer Science degree, but still the industry grows at a faster pace. He explains that in the field of IT and CS, you do not have to be a tech person to get involved in the industry. Like many other skills, technology skills can be learned on the job.

He lists five most trending jobs in IT, which are IT consultant, Mobile/Web application developer, system administrator, network architect, and lastly data/business analyst.

IT, particularly the internet, is having a significant impact on the operations of all organizations, especially for entrepreneurs and SMEs.

IT has become essential for economic growth in general and for the success of enterprises because they provide the tools for communication. Compared to the conventional way of doing business, new technologies facilitate and increase interactivity,

Figure 3.4 Future career

Source: © iStock: gorodenkoff. Wong, J. (2015, April 02). Career in Information Technology: Future Prospects. Retrieved December 14, 2018, from https://info.focustsi.com/it-services-boston/topic/managed-services/career-in-information-technology-future-prospects.

flexibility, lowers cost, and also improves the linkage between customers/clients and suppliers.[8] IT is having a significant positive impact on entrepreneurial activities by improving linkages between stakeholders in both Business to Business (BTB) and Business to Consumer (BTC) companies.

Knowledge economy

The digital age has had a great impact on the global society/economy by changing the process and the speed of communication, and also on how organizations conduct business. In the last two decades of the twentieth century, globalization of the world economy, as well as technological developments, transformed the majority of the wealth-creating methods from physically based to knowledge-based.[9] These days, the economic environment is increasingly dependent on new technologies and, therefore, making knowledge and information essential is the key factor of production.[10] In this knowledge-based economy, ideas, processes, and information are the foundation of trade and the catalyst triggering improvements in the quality of life experienced by the people. This transformation (that continues to broaden and deepen) has greatly enhanced the value of information to business organizations by offering new opportunities and solutions to problems. Business organizations, of course, revolve around two factors of production: labor and capital. Although this may still be true, however, an evolution is occurring where information and knowledge have altered the labor market significantly. Especially in developed countries, technology is replacing many "low skilled" jobs with positions requiring specialization and skill.

A basic principle for entrepreneurs is the ability to effectively use knowledge and information to advance their power. An entrepreneur who can attain rapid and relevant information will have a great competitive advantage over those who cannot. IT plays a critical role in delivering this information. Entrepreneurs should be able to tap into this information and create a competitive advantage. Therefore, technologies that support decision-making, which provides an effective interface between users and computer technology and other advantages to entrepreneurs, will be better off. The new technologies, especially the internet, are changing the business environment in trade, investment, and the competitive advantage of industries.[11] These changes, combined with the need for information, are requiring all enterprises, no matter their size, to invest in new technology. Not only are entrepreneurs to adopt these technologies, but also their business sustainability and survival depends on it. With the successful integration of IT, enterprises enhance the availability of information in ways that improve the quality, effectiveness, and efficiency of their operations.

Therefore, many entrepreneurs in the age of IT work to produce high-quality goods and services by using communication and technology tools. These entrepreneurs use the fruit of IT to transform knowledge and their assets into products and services that meet customer/client needs. In this knowledge society, businesses require high-quality information so that they can gain a competitive edge in quality, price, and service.[12]

IT as resources

There are various resources such as the internet, e-commerce, wireless/mobile technology, and social media that can facilitate the advancement of a firm.[13] They state what drives a firm's performance is their processes, which in turn influences their earnings. Linna and

Figure 3.5 Budget
Source: Image by GotCredit on flickr

Richter (2011) examined the use of technology as a potential engine for economic and social transformation in Kenya.[14] They concluded that young Kenyan tech entrepreneurs are using mobile technologies to overcome challenges at the Bottom of the Pyramid. While most of the studies have focused on mobile service, the business models are from the developed economy.[15,16] There are few studies that have examined the opportunities and challenges in emerging markets.[17,18]

The conclusion is that the approach and applications tend to be different between the developed and the developing countries because each faces a different set of opportunities and constraints. In a developing country's setting, "benefits of mobile services may not only include profits but also less tangible societal benefits such as the empowerment of users, improving access to the use of information, improving coordination among agents and increasing market efficiency."[19,20]

Strategizing IT expenditure

Schilke (2015) discusses key components to answer before investing the budget on Information Technology in one's business (Figure 3.5).[21] Most people see expenditure on technology taking higher importance than other factors, but fall behind and look at the big picture outcome.

Most businesses spend between ½ percent and 10 percent of their revenue on technology. If the company is not spending enough on technology, it probably means they are not taking advantage of all the benefits available. On the other hand, businesses may be spending more than they need to on proprietary solutions. Thus the author is using her experience with various businesses to come up with questions every business should ask before budgeting money or time on technology, questions such as "Is there a core business benefit to be gained?"; "why do it in the first place?" and others.

Deciding on which area to spend resources is also an important question. Infrastructure is one of the main areas where businesses spend their budgets, from computers, to networking equipment, to internet service providers. It is important to know when a business should make the changes because it will affect employees and customers. Finally, she advises on adapting to small things little by little over changing everything at once. Read the full article to learn more: http://teamstrength. com/information-technology-in-business-the-big-picture/

By providing the tools and information for innovation in a distributed and accessible way, there has been a great revolution in the models of innovation in terms of cost and format. One of the responses to an Observable Restrictive Context (ORC) is the Frugal Innovation. Frugal Innovation is the response to an observable restrictive context, with drastic resource savings that focus on the inclusion of the unattended demographic masses.[22]

Some regions have attracted special interest in Frugal Innovation since these countries (regions) still have the presence of significant restrictions on both financial and human resources. It seemed, in fact, that in this new scenario, these countries would have access to other ways to innovate.[23,24] These regions or countries are the so-called emerging countries, those that have severe restrictions to access innovation or to produce innovation in a structured innovation model. The structured innovation model requires consistent financial investments, offering resources on a long-term, but in these regions, financial resources are not available.

Changes in the flow of capital between regions of the world have reordered economies by raising the block of emerging markets, those with a strong GDP growth and market economy orientation.[25]

Mobile technology is a way to reduce the effects of some constraints. On one hand, mobile technologies are enablers of information for people. On the other hand, mobile technology represents a relevant platform for entrepreneurs developing a new business model, for instance.

The world is demanding many applications that run on a mobile platform to solve quotidian problems of society. Some entrepreneurs could observe problems locally and create a new big software solution on a mobile platform. The dissemination of a mobile application is fast and unlimited because they use the internet structure to do so.

Finally, it is important to verify that mobile technology is different when we compare it in developed countries and developing countries. In developed countries, mobile technology is not only a platform for entrepreneurial activities but also a way to address lifestyle and attend to the desires of the people. In developing countries, normally, the mobile platform is used as a platform for entrepreneurial activities by focusing on problem-solving. Despite the different visions, the catalytic effect on entrepreneurial activities is relevant for both countries, developed and developing, and it plays an important role in entrepreneurial behavior and in entrepreneurship.

- Technology is a catalyst for entrepreneurship in the developed, as well as in the developing, countries.
- Technology can be categorized into five types based on their aspects: Tangible, Intangible, High, Intermediate, and Low
- Information Technology (IT) plays various roles in business and entrepreneurship.
- IT encompasses a range of new technologies and their applications. IT affects a firm's products, services, markets, producing costs, and product differentiation.
- IT is having a significant positive impact on entrepreneurial activities and improved the linkages between stakeholders in both Business to Businesses (BTB) and Business to Consumer (BTC) companies.
- The majority of wealth creating methods shifted from physically based to knowledge based.
- Entrepreneurs use IT to transform knowledge and their assets into products and services that meet customer/client needs.

Internet

Most of us know what the internet is and what it does. Perhaps we may find it very hard to operate without it. The internet is a global system that connects computer networks together through wireless and electronic means. The internet serves as a key component and point of access for a wealth of IT resources and applications. It has grown from being a tool for military communication into a digital web, serving over 3 billion users: a number that continues to grow, as shown in Table 3.2.[26] A tool of this magnitude is obviously of vital importance and its power continues to grow. Table 3.2 provides information usage of different regions of the world in 2017 and 2000. The usage in all regions from December of 2000 to March 2017 has increased by 924 percent, which is a significant increase. For all developing countries, the growth has been very high and still is increasing. The increase in internet usages from 2000 to March of 2017 for regions of Africa, Middle East, and Asia has been 7331 percent, 4207 percent, and 1524 percent respectively, which is the highest increase. The same regions have the highest potential for growth.

This kind of increase in internet usage has great economic, political, and social impacts.

The reach of the internet coupled with its low cost allows smaller firms to reduce their transactional costs and levels the playing field against larger organizations. Common benefits of the internet include expanding the scope of marketing, wider and richer communication, reaching new markets, and partnering with suppliers and collaborators. It is evident that the adoption of the internet can help entrepreneurs tremendously by giving them resources that in the past only the larger business organizations could attain. Yet, many SMEs and entrepreneurs, especially in developing countries, fail to realize the benefits of adopting the internet. The degree of usage of the internet can be organized as per Table 3.3.

Table 3.2 World internet usage

WORLD INTERNET USAGE AND POPULATION STATISTICS
JUNE 30, 2017 – Update

World Regions	Population (2017 Est.)	Population% of World	Internet Users 30 June 2017	Penetration Rate (% Pop.)	Growth 2000– 2017	Internet Users %
Africa	1,246,504,865	16.6%	388,376,491	31.2%	8,503.1%	10.0%
Asia	4,148,177,672	55.2%	1,938,075,631	46.7%	1,595.5%	49.7%
Europe	822,710,362	10.9%	659,634,487	80.2%	527.6%	17.0%
Latin America / Caribbean	647,604,645	8.6%	404,269,163	62.4%	2,137.4%	10.4%
Middle East	250,327,574	3.3%	146,972,123	58.7%	4,374.3%	3.8%
North America	363,224,006	4.8%	320,059,368	88.1%	196.1%	8.2%
Oceania / Australia	40,479,846	0.5%	28,180,356	69.6%	269.8%	0.7%
WORLD TOTAL	7,519,028,970	100.0%	3,885,567,619	51.7%	976.4%	100.0%

Source: Internet World Statistics[27]

Table 3.3 Levels of internet penetration

Level	Definition	Descriptions
Level 0	The firm only has an email account but no website	The firms have an email account that they use to establish connectivity with customers and business partners.
Level 1	The firm has a web presence	Though web presence exists, it remains underutilized. Websites at this stage only have the capacity to provide information and brochures and normally tend to be non-strategic in nature.
Level 2	Prospecting websites exist within the firm's structure at this level	At this stage, firms use websites to provide information regarding product specifications, news, and interactive content to customers. The firms using a website at this stage do not relate it in business strategy.
Level 3	Firms at this level incorporate web applications in business strategies	The firm uses website and internet to establish a cross-functional link with its customers and suppliers. The firm also integrates web strategy in their business plan.
Level 4	The level represents the application of web adoption in business transformation	This level represents the highest level of web adoption with the ability to transform business model throughout the organization. The focus is on building relationships and seeking new business opportunities.

E-commerce

Electronic commerce (e-commerce) facilitates the buying and selling of products and services over the internet. Doing so can provide substantial benefits to entrepreneurs and SMEs largely by improving efficiencies and raising revenue.[28] It can also create new business opportunities and serve as a vital tool for new businesses. E-commerce enables electronic transactions to occur, and can also help to transform internal systems management, control, data mining, and research in ways that can help build relationships with customers and other stakeholders. E-commerce can cheaply facilitate buying and selling by reducing barriers such as time and place. Despite these benefits, many entrepreneurs have not been able to take full advantage. It is quite important for entrepreneurs to realize the importance of e-commerce for their growth and success. E-commerce allows entrepreneurs to sell their products and services from their home decreasing infrastructure and other costs. Through its low cost, low-risk features, e-commerce creates tremendous opportunities for entrepreneurs to start-up, expand, and sustain the growth of their businesses.

Wireless/mobile technology

Mobile communication devices offer entrepreneurs a way to overcome the challenges of doing business because it will create linkages.[29] The mobile phone offers more flexibility and efficiency but has its own constraints compared to other means of communication. It will also improve access to capital and market information, facilitate mobile payments, and help to reach new customers. Mobile phones can help entrepreneurs communicate with one another, access market information, sell products across geographic areas, reach new consumers, and enter mobile payment systems. Furthermore, researchers have found

Figure 3.6 Developing countries operation challenges
Source: Image by Marco Verch on flickr

that each "one percent increase in mobile penetration is associated with 0.5–0.6 rate of FDI/GDP growth."[30] Mobile technology is a key part of IT and is playing a critical role in improving opportunities for entrepreneurs throughout the world.[31]

Technological inertia

The company "Sepahan", which produces "disposable plastic containers" in Iran, is facing multiple challenges to grow (Figure 3.6). While the imposition of sanctions on the country has negatively impacted the price of raw materials, there also exists the difficulty in incorporating technology in the company's sales and distribution activities. The focus in this short case is to analyze benefits and challenges in opening a direct online channel of sales to the final users.

Sepahan is a small partnership company which has been in operation for about 15 years. It currently (2015) has 30 employees who work three shifts seven days of the week. The management constitutes three key personal, the director of marketing, the director of operations, and the director of human resources. The hardware consists of three imported machines from China, which in a relatively short process turns the powder of raw materials to useable containers.

Since inception, the output has been sold to middlemen, who in turn sell them to final users who are mostly Yogurt producers. The company in this process makes about 20 percent of profit. Their marketing and sales processes remain old fashioned, having no real contact with end-users. Therefore, the company is considering a strategic shift that aims at eliminating its dependence on middlemen. By setting up their website and sales teams, the company aims to reach the final user(s) via the promise of lower prices and better services. Evaluate the company's case by considering opportunity and challenges that it might face during this process.

Figure 3.7 shows the role of wireless technology (WT) in advancing entrepreneurial activities in certain countries. It indicates that WT plays a bigger role in entrepreneurship in the developing countries (i.e., Indonesia, India, and China) rather than the developed countries.

It appears that WT is the primary means for conducting most aspects of a business (i.e., communication, marketing, etc.) in developing countries. There are more choices for communication in developed countries and it does require more professional networking, fundraising, marketing, and communications.

A Time's Mobility Poll, conducted in cooperation with Qualcomm, which surveyed 4,250 entrepreneurs in eight countries, shows the following results: 93 percent believe that wireless/mobile technology is very or somewhat important for entrepreneurship. The survey revealed that 81 percent of those interviewed reported that mobile technology helped them search for the lowest available price for something they wanted to buy; 78 percent felt it gave them access to a larger group of potential customers; 78 percent believed it helped them follow up with their customers; 77 percent thought it granted access to financial service information; 74 percent believed it allowed them to find where they could sell goods for the best price; and 63 percent believed it strengthened the economy in their home country.[32]

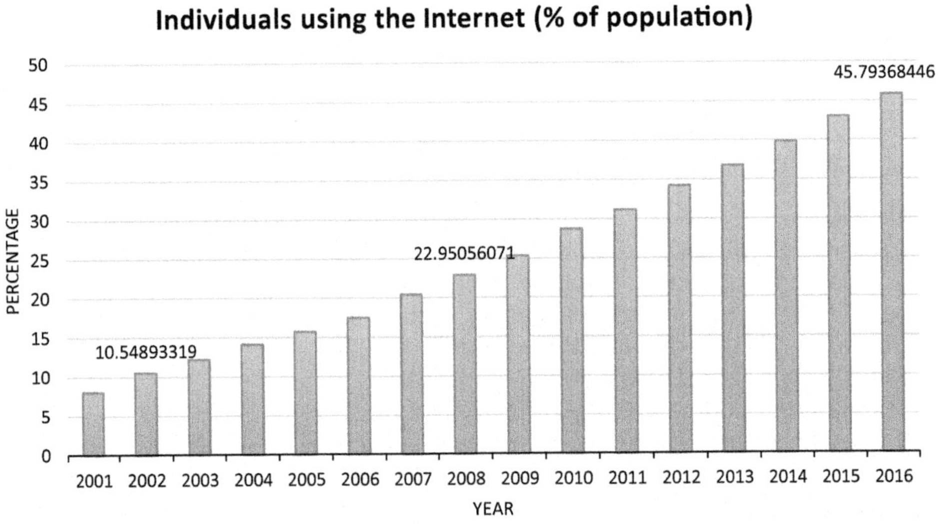

Individuals using the Internet (% of population)

Figure 3.7 Wireless tech

Source: © 2019 The World Bank Group. www.worldbank.org/en/research/brief/world-bank-policy-research-working-papers

Social media

For many entrepreneurs across the globe, one of the biggest challenges is mass marketing. Large corporations have immense marketing budgets and the manpower to conduct marketing campaigns. So how can a small enterprise start and compete?

The answer lies in social media. Social media technology, which is a platform based on the internet, allows people to create, share, and exchange information with other people. Social media facilitates the exchange of information as well as more effective interaction between businesses and their customers. Examples of social media include Facebook, Twitter, and weblogs. Social media has billions of users worldwide and these users are highly interactive.

Social media can be used by businesses for a range of functions, including but not limited to marketing and customer relationship management. It is particularly suitable for entrepreneurs and SMEs because of its minimal costs, low barriers to participation, and low level of IT skill set required for usage.

IT and its business valuation

The positive role of IT on entrepreneurship development is clear because it will allow easy access to all relevant information, suppliers, and consumers. It does so by adding immense business value to any organization, no matter what the size or the economic condition.

In many developing countries, it is a major challenge to gain access to information that could be relevant to improving a business. IT will solve some of these challenges by providing tools such as the internet which houses trillions of bytes of information on everything and anything that could be fathomed. Furthermore, IT allows a business to portray its information to billions of users over the web at an extremely low cost.

Thank you for being late

Thomas Friedman, author of the book *Thank You for Being Late* and the well-known columnist of *The New York Times*, discusses the thriving age of innovation accelerations. He points out that 2007 was the year Facebook and Twitter really took off; when Hadoop emerged as a software framework for processing very large data sets; when Airbnb was dreamed up; the Amazon Kindle was launched; and IBM started work on building the Watson computer system and other evolutions (Figure 3.8). These are critical advances that mostly happened in one year and have led to accelerations of more innovations which are drastically impacting our way of living. Friedman highlights that these technological innovations are moving in such a rapid speed that they are outrunning society's ability to adapt. Combining globalization and climate change has led to an unchartered domain that people find threatening and sometimes frightening.

Figure 3.8 Era of revolution in knowledge
Source: Image by cometstarmoon on flickr

IT helps entrepreneurs serve broader geographic areas and reach new consumers. It does so by reducing the barriers of physical boundaries. Because of the nature of IT, one does not need to be physically present to share information and conduct transactions as all of this is now facilitated over the web. This expands their opportunities and helps them grow their businesses. We can summarize the value of IT as:

1. Access to IT is essential for entrepreneurship, which will have a positive impact on economic development
2. Some of the resources IT provides are the internet, e-commerce, wireless/mobile technology, and social media
3. IT is facilitating the flow of knowledge and information which is replacing many conventional jobs
4. Entrepreneurs utilize IT resources to stay competitive in their industry at a very low cost
5. With the correct usage of these IT resources, entrepreneurs can add tremendous value to their business.

The rapid growth of technological innovations and the fusion of IT have drastically changed the way companies compete. Entrepreneurs and SMEs are widely recognized as a critical aspect of the developed/developing economies. Hence, it is vital that entrepreneurship continues to thrive. One way to gain a competitive advantage is by utilizing (efficiently and effectively) IT and all the resources it provides. As new technologies are introduced in businesses, they have to be mutually adaptive for them to generate profitability and survivability, otherwise these businesses could face collapse brought by changes of the newly introduced technologies.[33] Through the appropriate usage and combination of these resources, entrepreneurs can create value for their customers and prosper as a result. Doing so can help pave the way for future growth and sustainability.

- There are various resources such as the internet, e-commerce, wireless/mobile technology, and social media that can facilitate the advancement of a firm.[34]
- Frugal Innovation is the response to an observable restrictive context, with drastic resource savings and focuses on the inclusion of the unattended demographic masses.
- Mobile technology is the way to reduce the effects of some constraints and serves as a catalyst on entrepreneurial activities for both developed and developing countries, and it plays an important role in entrepreneurial behavior and in entrepreneurship.
- The usage of the internet in all regions from December of 2000 to March 2017 has increased by 924 percent.

Technology and culture

As internet penetration rates in the developing economies increase, so does the ability to be linked with the developed countries. Through this process, exposure to foster innovation is enhanced in developing countries. In 2006, just 18 percent of the world's population was online. According to the United Nations' Millennium Development Goals Report of 2012, by 2011, this number had increased to 35 percent. While there was certainly growth in developed countries, the developing countries have experienced a tremendous rise in internet penetration. In 2006, the developing countries accounted for 44 percent of all internet users, and by 2011 this had grown to 63 percent (United Nations).[35] The internet can foster innovation by connecting merchants, educating entrepreneurs, and establishing a global marketplace. The growing success of eBay and Amazon globally is an indication of the role of technology. As the world becomes a global marketplace, citizens of developed and individualistic countries overlook the entrepreneurs in the developing and collectivist countries that value their lifestyle and relationships.

Holding everything else constant, actually, there are higher desires for entrepreneurial activities in developing countries for the purpose of improving the quality of life. And as they migrate to developed countries, they are determined to make it. Many Laos Hmong war refugees resettled in the United States following the communist takeover of Laos in 1975. When they were relocated, the government spread them throughout the country to avoid concentrations of this group in one place. The Hmong, however, used the internet to get in touch and moved to where other Hmong lived. There are now large Hmong communities in cities such as East Lansing, Michigan.

The role of technology for startups

Startups are initiatives of certain groups of people aiming at building untested business models (new business models). Such a definition helps us to achieve some of the key features of a startup, such as high risk, high potential for return on investment, and often in contexts of great uncertainty. Since the 2000s the term startup has ceased to be just one of the initial phases of a business or enterprise and has become a term that self-describes as being companies that use technology intensely. Each startup is unique, as well as in a company with a traditional business model, which denotes the complexity derived from this idiosyncrasy.

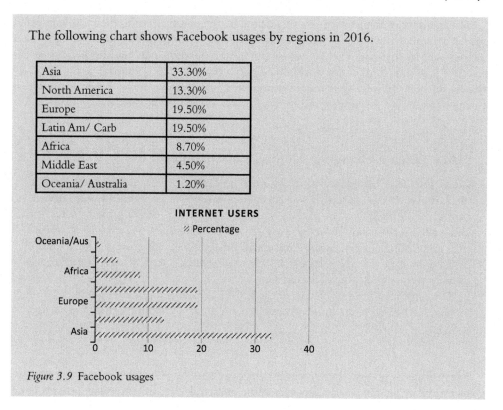

The following chart shows Facebook usages by regions in 2016.

Asia	33.30%
North America	13.30%
Europe	19.50%
Latin Am/ Carb	19.50%
Africa	8.70%
Middle East	4.50%
Oceania/ Australia	1.20%

INTERNET USERS

% Percentage

Figure 3.9 Facebook usages

What is common among startups is the strong propensity to use technology. In a startup company, technology provides support for both the middle activities and the final activities. These are therefore technology-intensive initiatives, whether for the design of the business or for the operation and management process itself, as well as for the design of the product or service that the startups intend to deliver to the market. Perhaps there are still arguments that a company that exploits a more traditional sector can use some innovations and therefore claim for themselves the title of startups.

As time passes (and goes by fast) we can see that the definition of startups is: those involved with technology in their final product, being nanotechnology, biotechnology or information, and communication technology most often found in incubators and accelerators. Thus, we have observed the tendency for the definition of startup to evolve more and more to describe business initiatives intensely related to technology.[36]

Of course, the movement that made mass-accessible hardware, software, and communication (internet) outlined many of the opportunities sought by startups. These opportunities are enabled on the one hand by the use of IT and communication to work in the startup itself (processing of office tasks, such as email, electronic workflow, low-cost websites, and smartphones), and, on the other hand, the massive democratization of access to information. Another aspect related to the role of technology in startups is the software market, whether in the client-server, web, or app architecture. Virtually anyone with internet access, anywhere in the world, can learn some programming language and develop the next big billion-dollar application. Initial investments to develop web or app software have become almost zero, reducing the entry barrier, producing real armies of young and not-so-young entrepreneurs in the field of information and communication technology.

The mobility of information access, favored by the cheap access to the mobile internet and smartphones, not only enabled the emergence of startups that offer their new products and services to the market: they also outlined new markets. Mobile internet access has placed at least one-third of the world on a single network, with potentially accessible consumers instantly generating and consuming products, services, and content using digital channels. Yes, today we are generating information seven days a week and 24 hours a day.

"How China is changing the future of Shopping"

China is a huge laboratory of innovation, says retail expert Angela Wang, and in this lab, everything takes place on people's phones. Five hundred million Chinese consumers – the equivalent of the combined populations of the United States, the United Kingdom, and Germany – regularly make purchases via mobile platforms, even in brick-and-mortar stores. What will this transformation mean for the future of shopping? Learn more about the new business-as-usual, where everything is ultra-convenient, ultra-flexible, and ultra-social.

You can check in more details in the full TED Talk in the following link:
www.ted.com/talks/angela_wang_how_china_is_changing_the_future_of_shopping#t-806182

Every place we go, every restaurant in which we have lunch or dinner, or every time we go to university, we provide our position, time of arrival, etc.… By carrying a smartphone connected to the internet, we form a network of 3 billion people who generate and consume information.

Startups have been working hard to fill this network with service offerings that solve the problems of people connected with entertainment and lifestyle proposals. Social networks for all interests are available, but also applications that can be installed according to the interest of each user. Smartphone applications can be especially understood as a disruption in distribution channels. By developing "virtual" products like apps and making them available in an app store, billions of people will be able to "consume" it right away. Of course, this possibility changes the entire cost structure related to the distribution of a new product.

The startups, therefore, have the information and communication technology and the elementary parts (information, market access, and automation of office routines and communication) to start a potential company. The platform to develop the business model, generate the product (which is also technological), and distribute the channel itself is available to new entrepreneurs, with virtually no entry barriers related to cost. From this point of view, technology plays a central role in startups. Let us take a moment to look at the technological aspects of one of the most valuable companies in the world: Google. It is very difficult to discuss entrepreneurship and technology without involving any case related to Google. This is due to two main factors. First, most of us use almost any product from Google, especially the search engine. Second, because of the company's example of economic success, challenging companies from both the media and other powerful industries. What we are saying is that Google has more market value than oil companies. Google is worth $558 billion in 2017. Apple, Amazon, Facebook, Alibaba, eBay, Microsoft, etc., in terms of users reach, services, and capitalization, show the revolution in technology and its influence in the economic, political, and social issues.

Failure is the foundation of successful innovation

"Success is not final, failure is not fatal." – Winston Churchill

In 2012, a group of friends in Mexico City got together to talk about why their business ventures had gone awry. It was a strange thing to do, as entrepreneurs were usually asked to share how they succeeded, not how they failed. Each speaker shared their major business failure – or fuckup as they called it – and the lessons learned. And so Fuckup Nights was born.

Since 2012, Fuckup Nights has turned into a worldwide phenomenon, where entrepreneurs of all walks of life share how they failed. There are monthly events in cities all over the world that invite startup founders to share their failures – and their eventual way to success. The event was deemed as a way to "reveal the honest side of entrepreneurship".[37] Indeed, the curious thing is, no one had to explain why it was important to talk about failure. In fact, most speakers and attendees wondered why this hasn't started sooner, especially given the fact that 50 percent of startups fail in their first five years, and 70 percent fail in the first ten years.[38]

Continued at the end…

Figure 3.10 Startup fails
Source: © iStock: gustavofrazao

Furthermore, there are about 220 startups called "unicorns". Unicorns are the startups with the market value from $1 billion.[39] In the Table 3.4, we can observe that of the ten listed unicorn startups, five (4, 6, 8, 9, and 10) provide services with IT and communication in the final product, four (1, 2, 5, and 7) provide services on-demand, using information and communication technology as a means to transact its services and one (3) manufactures smartphones, therefore, offers mobile internet access infrastructure. We also noticed that both the United States (six startups) and China (four startups) dominate the list, in these top 11 positions.

Technology and economic growth

Technology is defined by the Merriam-Webster Dictionary as "the practical application of knowledge in a particular area." The modern era, named the "information age", is marked by technological advancements. Therefore, success is based on knowledge, which in turn leads to efficient production methodologies. To compete in this framework and the new era marketplace, businesses need communicative networks, an educated workforce, and management support of technology.

Technology is an important component of economic growth. Labor, capital, and technology combine to form the production function. Robert Solow, the Economic Sciences Nobel Prize winner, theorizes that:

$$Q=A (t) f(K/L)$$

where Q is the output, A(t) is an index of technology, K is capital, and L is labor in total hours worked. Thus, the index of technology combines with the ratio of capital and labor to account for a significant percentage of the production output.[40] In addition to increasing productivity, technology improves the quality of products and operational efficiency.

Table 3.4 Startup valuations

Startup	Valuation	Date joined	Country	Industry	Select investments
Uber	$68	8/23/2013	United States	On-Demand	Lowercase Capital, Benchmark Capital, Google Ventures
Didi Chuxing	$50	12/31/2014	China	On-Demand	Matrix Partners, Tiger Global Management, Softbank Corp.
Xiaomi	$46	12/21/2011	China	Hardware	Digital Sky Technologies, QiMing Venture Partners, Qualcomm Ventures
Airbnb	$29.3	7/26/2011	United States	Commerce/ Marketplace	General Catalyst Partners, Andreessen Horowitz, ENIAC Ventures
SpaceX	$21.2	12/1/2012	United States	Other Transportation	Founders Fund, Draper Fisher Jurvetson, Rothenberg Ventures
Palantir Technologies	$20	5/5/2011	United States	Big Data	RRE Ventures, Founders Fund, In-Q-Tel
WeWork	$20	2/3/2014	United States	Facilities	T. Rowe Price, Benchmark Capital, SoftBank Group
Lu.com	$18.5	12/26/2014	China	Fintech	Ping An Insurance CDH Investments, Bank of China
China Internet Plus Holding	$18	12/22/2015	China	eCommerce/ Marketplace	DST Global, Trustbridge Partners, Capital Today
Pinterest	$12.3	5/19/2012	United States	Social	Andreessen Horowitz, Bessemer Venture Partners, Firstmark Capital
Flipkart	$11.6	8/6/2012	India	eCommerce/ Marketplace	Accel Partners, SoftBank Group, Iconiq Capital

Source: Unicorn Club[41]

Financially, IT systems help companies produce goods at a lower cost, through efficiency and the incorporation of robotic systems in production. Operational improvements, such as identifying new organizational structures or processes that decrease costs and provide efficiencies, lead to competitive advantages through low costs and improved quality. IT enhancements affect customer relationships when they identify new segments for direct marketers or provide cutting-edge experiences to purchasers. Moreover, IT is a gateway to new markets. New value propositions and newly created products for information innovation can be very profitable. If competitors also have access to information, it leads to an information-driven culture that results in the fight to obtain first-mover advantage and patents.

Technology can provide incremental improvements or transformational innovation, thus making international expansion easier to access and more reliable, increasing real-time data communications. Technology has become increasingly portable. Mobile phones and remote desktop setups have provided flexible work options for most stakeholders. Moreover, cloud computing and a globalized workforce have created virtual teams that focus on continuous innovation. Technology also opened up constant feedback funnels, connecting consumers to the company through social media channels. Employees are now asked to solve trans-discipline problems using vast amounts of information. It is evident that good quality education is needed to manage this kind of large cognitive load. This connectivity also allows companies to gather the opinions of multiple stakeholders before making decisions and create clear expectations for consumers. Customers have become continuously informed about how companies operate and expect ethical conduct from them.

This creates a need for companies to manage their brand reputation worldwide.[42]

Technologies are helping to reshape our economies by bringing significant improvements in communication and efficiencies.

- Entrepreneurs and SMEs are widely recognized as a critical aspect of developed/developing economies.
- There are about 220 startups called "unicorns". Unicorns are the startups with market value above $1 billion.
- Technology is an important component of economic growth. Labor, capital, and technology combine to form the production function.
- Technology improves the quality of products and operational efficiency. It helps companies to produce goods at a lower cost, through efficiency and the incorporation of robotic systems in production.
- Growth will continue in the areas of information and communication technology, development of e-businesses, manufacturing, and technological design. These will help businesses to compete effectively in the global market.

Future IT developments will be measured by their quality, usability, ergonomics, and ultimately, user satisfaction. Processes are becoming increasingly automated, yet also are successful in providing a personalized service to their customers. Value is being placed on the human experience.

Growth will continue in the areas of information and communication technology, development of e-businesses, manufacturing, and technological design. These improvements will help businesses compete effectively in the global market, which will directly influence economic growth. Technology mediates productivity, but it takes technology and innovation to raise the economy to its desired level.

Concluding remarks

In the recent past, technology has nurtured and advanced entrepreneurship through a significant evolution in technology. It has been the most important tool in building bridges, repairing them, and perhaps questioning their values. The digital revolution is expanding exponentially and leading to new innovations and higher efficiencies. The production of new products and services has become easier and more innovative, thus expediting entrepreneurship in developed as well as developing countries.

Discussion questions

1. How has technology impacted entrepreneurship and development?
2. What is the relationship between IT and globalization?
3. What are the different platforms of IT? What do you think would be the future platforms?
4. How would you do a valuation of IT in a business?
5. Are you planning to start a business that applies technology?

Case study – continued

Entrepreneurship and technology: the case of Hmizate in Morocco

Today, the site has close to 700,000 members, of whom 169,000 have made at least one purchase. The company now employs 50 full-time staff members, many of whom are women. The company's office space is distinct with a wide-open concept, vibrant colors, glass walls, and sun-filled common workspaces which shout innovation, collaboration, and equality.

In addition to billboard ads, the company is very active on Facebook and Twitter. The use of ads on social media and email remains the main customer acquisition and retention channels. Hmizate.ma accepts the Moroccan card as the main form of payment, while Hmall.ma site users can choose to pay "cash on delivery" or by cash through their local bank

Questions

1. List the reasons for the survival of Hmizate.ma.
2. How were customers in Morocco different from those in the United States and other European countries?
3. What were the reasons for a European VC to consider funding Kamal over other similar ventures?

Table 3.5 Key terms

Transistor	Internet
Advanced Research Projects Agency Network (ARPANET)	Levels of internet penetration
Internet Protocol Suite (TCP/IP)	E-commerce
The range of technology	Wireless technology
Frugal Innovation	Technology

Failure is the foundation of successful innovation

These founders realized that failure is much more instructive than success. In fact, success and failure can be much more similar, and greatly depends on how each is being measured and defined to truly distinguish between the two.[43] Yet, how do you recognize or define which one is which? And how do you change people's mindset: that failure can also be success?

Entrepreneurs start their businesses because of their desire for change and innovation. On their journey, they frequently hear from the people who were successful, and then they learn about all the reasons why a startup may fail. A good number of studies have analyzed the reasons behind startup failure. For example, top reasons according to Statistic Brain are things such as lack of focus, lack of motivation, too much pride, and taking the wrong advice.[44] In another study, CB Insights mentions the more economic reasons behind failure, such as no market need, running out of cash, and not having the right team.[45] These are all aggregated reasons that a founder might take to heart – but ultimately, they are vague, hard to relate to, and even harder to apply to avoid the problems in the entrepreneurs' own unique situations. What has thus far been missing is how everyday people dealt with the challenges. And most importantly, how they have redefined failure in order to move on.

While acceptance of failure has grown in recent years, there is still much work to do to make it an acceptable, educational part of entrepreneurship. It's not that entrepreneurs should be encouraged to fail, rather they should be encouraged to create in the best way possible without being ashamed or scared of failure.[46] Popular business outlets have started to suggest that failure is a vital component of innovation, but none have gone deep enough to study the positive effects of failure.

Following the success of Fuckup Nights, the team behind the worldwide phenomenon founded the Failure Institute in recognition of the educational value of failure. The Institute is dedicated to studying why and how failure affects businesses. In 2017, they launched the "Global Failure Index", which will help gather more ground level information about why businesses fail, what ideas work and which ones do not, and what do to about it. Most importantly, they're on a mission to redefine what it means to be successful – by ensuring failure is seen as the foundation and the best teacher of success.

Notes

1 Harari, Y. N., & Perkins, D. (2014). Sapiens: A Brief History of Humankind. London: Harvill Secker.

2 Fitzgerald, E., Wankerl, A., & Schramm, C. J. (2011). Inside Real Innovation: How the Right Approach Can Move Ideas from R&D to Market – and Get the Economy Moving. World Scientific.

3 15 Revolutionary Inventions of 2007. (2008, August 19). Retrieved December 14, 2018, from www.entrepreneur.com/slideshow/188038.

4 Deans, P. C., & Kane, M. J. (1992). Information Systems and Technology. Boston, MA: PWS-Kent Publishing.

5 Morris, M. H., & Sexton, D. (1996). The concept of entrepreneurial intensity: implications for company performance. Journal of Business Research, 36(1), 5–13.

6 Sambamurthy, V., Bharadwaj, A., & Grover, V. (2003). Shaping agility through digital options: reconceptualizing the role of Information Technology in contemporary firms. MIS Quarterly, 27(2), 237–263.

7 Wong, J. (2015, April 02). Career in Information Technology: future prospects. Retrieved December 14, 2018, from https://info.focustsi.com/it-services-boston/topic/managed-services/career-in-information-technology-future-prospects.

8 Beley, S. D., & Bhatarkar, P. S. (2013). The role of Information Technology in small and medium sized business. International Journal of Scientific and Research, 3(2).

9 Berisha-Namani, D. M. (2009). The role of Information Technology in small and medium sized enterprises in Kosova. Small Places Can Change the World, 1–8.

10 Berisha-Namani, D. M. (2009). The role of Information Technology in small and medium sized enterprises in Kosova. Small Places Can Change the World, 1–8.

11 Lucey, T. (2005). Management Information Systems (9th ed.). London: Thomson Learning; Miles, R. E., & Snow, C. C. (1978). Organizational Strategy, Structure, and Process. New York: McGraw-Hill.

12 Pollard, D. (2006). Promoting Learning Transfer, Developing SME Marketing Knowledge in the Dnipropetrovsk Oblast, Ukraine.

13 Teece, D. J., Pisano, G., & Shuen, A. (1997). Dynamic capabilities and strategic management. Strategic Management Journal, 18(March), 509–533.

14 Linna, P., & Richter, U. (2011). Technology entrepreneurship-potential for social innovation? The case of Kenyan mobile industry companies. International Journal of Business and Public Management, 1(1), 42–50.

15 Hedman, J., & Kalling, T. (2003). The business model concept: theoretical underpinnings and empirical illustrations. European Journal of Information Systems, 12 (1), 49–59.

16 Pateli, A., & Giaglis, G. (2004). A research framework for analysing business models. European Journal of Information Systems, 13, 302–314.

17 Anderson, J. (2006). A structured approach for bringing mobile telecommunications to the world's poor. The Journal of Information Systems in Developing Markets, 27, 1–9.

18 Ivatury, G., & Pickens, M. (2006). Mobile phone banking and low income consumers: evidence from South Africa, CGAP, UN Foundation, Vodafone Group Foundation, available via www.cgap.org/publications/mobilephonebanking.pdf.

19 Aker, J. C., & Mbiti, I. M. (2010). Mobile phones and economic development in Africa. Journal of Economic Perspectives, 24(3), 207–232.

20 Howard, P. N., & Mazaheri, Nimah. (2009). Telecommunications reform, internet use and mobile phone adoption in the developing world. World Development, 37(7), 1159–1169.

21   Schilke, S. (July 24, 2015). Information Technology in Business: The Big Picture, website. Retrieved from https://teamstrength.com/information-technology-in-business-the-big-picture/

22   Mashelkar, R. A., & Prahalad, C. K. (2010). Innovation's Holy Grail. Harvard Business Review, 116–126

23   Tiwari, R., & Herstatt, C. (2012). Assessing India's lead market potential for cost-effective innovations. Journal of Indian Business Research, 4(2), 97–115.

24   Tiwari, R., & Herstatt, C. (2014). Emergence of India as a lead market for frugal innovation. Hamburg: Consulate General of India.

25   UNCTAD. (n.d.). Retrieved December 14, 2018, from https://unctad.org/en/pages/home.aspx.

26   Internet World Statistics. (n.d.). Retrieved December 14, 2018, from www.internetworldstats.com/stats.htm.

27   Internet World Statistics. (n.d.). Retrieved December 14, 2018, from www.internetworldstats.com/stats.htm.

28   Pease, W., & Rowe, M. (2003). E-commerce and small and medium enterprises (SMEs) in regional communities. The Future of Marketing with Particular Reference to Asia and the Antipodes.

29   Andjelkovic, M. (2010). The future is mobile: why developing country entrepreneurs can drive internet innovation. SAIS Review, 30(2), Summer–Fall.

30   Vodafone Group. (2005). Africa: the impact of mobile phones. Vodafone Policy Paper Series.

31   West, D. M. (2014). Going Mobile: How Wireless Technology is Reshaping Our Lives. https://books.google.com/books?isbn=0815726260.

32   Time (2012). How Has Wireless Technology Changed How You Live Your Life? August 27, pp. 34–39. The Time Mobility Poll was undertaken in cooperation with Qualcomm.

33   Linton, J. D., & Solomon, G. T. (2017). Technology, innovation, entrepreneurship and the small business – technology and innovation in small business. Journal of Small Business Management, 55(2).

34   Teece, D. J., Pisano, G., & Shuen, A. (1997). Dynamic capabilities and strategic management. Strategic Management Journal, 18(March), 509–533.

35   www.un.org/millenniumgoals/reports.shtml.

36   Blank, S. (2012). The Startup Owner's Manual: The Step-by-Step Guide For Building a Great Company. BookBaby.

37   Narvey, Jonathon. (2016, October 7). Fuckup Nights Reveal the Honest Side of Entrepreneurship, Betakit. Available at betakit.com/fuckup-nights-reveal-the-honest-side-of-entrepreneurship/.

38   Henry, Patrick. (2017, February 18). Why Some Startups Succeed (and Why Most Fail), Entrepreneur. Available at www.entrepreneur.com/article/288769.

39   Rungi, M., Saks, E., & Tuisk, K. (2016). Financial and strategic impact of VCs on start-up development: Silicon Valley decacorns vs. Northern-European experience. Industrial Engineering and Engineering Management (IEEM), 2016 IEEE International Conference on (pp. 452–456). IEEE.

40   McCombie, J. S. L. (2001). What does the aggregate production function show? Further thoughts on Solow's "Second Thoughts on Growth Theory". Journal of Post Keynesian Economics, 23(4), 589–615.

41   The Global Unicorn Club. (n.d.). Retrieved December 14, 2018, from www.cbinsights.com/research-unicorn-companies.

42   Asgary, Nader, & Li, Gang (2015). Corporate social responsibility: its economic impact and link to the bullwhip effect. Journal of Business Ethics, 81(1), 223–234.

43 Farson, Richard, & Keyes, Ralph. (2003, July). The Innovation Paradox: The Success of Failure, the Failure of Success. Simon and Shuster.

44 Statistic Brain (2017, May 5). Startup Business Failure Rate By Industry. Available at www.statisticbrain.com/startup-failure-by-industry.

45 CB Insights. (2017, September 27). The 20 Reasons Startups Fail. Available at www.cbinsights.com/research/startup-failure-reasons-top/.

46 Harvard Business Review. (2015, October 19). To Encourage Innovation, Stop Punishing Failure. Available at hbr.org/tip/2015/10/to-encourage-innovation-stop-punishing-failure.

Part II

Individual characteristics and training

4   Personality, experience, and training

Learning objectives:

1. *Understand the definition of entrepreneurship and personal characteristics impact*
2. *Studying the classification of entrepreneurs*
3. *Examine the role of the big five personal characteristics of an entrepreneur*
4. *Analyze the role of academic education and job experience on entrepreneurship*
5. *Comprehend the role of financial, environmental, and cultural infrastructure on entrepreneurship*

Figure 4.1 Story of an Indian entrepreneur
Source: Image by offbit2010 on flickr

Story of a young, dedicated entrepreneur

Entrepreneurship does not necessarily involve building a brand or a firm from scratch. For example, the franchise business model essentially constitutes an entrepreneur purchasing a branch of a preexisting, successful brand. This is the story of the Quality Group of brands in India. Tharun Rao, the founder and managing director of the Quality Group, proudly assembled an eclectic portfolio of franchises composed of different brands competing in diverse industries.

Tharun describes his style of entrepreneur who considers association with brands as essential. It is based upon acquiring franchises with the plan of introducing these preexisting brands into new markets. His understanding of entrepreneurship is derived from his graduate education in business at the Royal Holloway University. During his time in England, Tharun studied foundational business disciplines such as marketing and financing, branding, accounting, networking, management, and situational analysis. However, he also learned skills essential to entrepreneurship, including how to identify business opportunities, ideas, and planning; strategic and organizational models behind new venture innovation and strategic renewal; finance and marketing of both small and large organizations. These studies taught Tharun the dispositive influence that a firm's culture can have on a firm, and how to adapt an international franchise's culture when introducing the concept in India.

Tharun graduated in 2014 with a degree in Entrepreneurship. Since that time, he has successfully grown the Quality Group into six diverse brands, including clothing, automobiles, and agricultural products. Together, the Quality Group franchises gross more than $9 million annually.

Despite the Quality Group's early success, startup funding was not easy. Tharun was unable to secure funding for his early ventures from conventional financial institutions. This was based on his lack of an established track record as an entrepreneur. Accordingly, the Quality Group was forced to derive its early capital from Tharun's family and friends. Today, these circumstances have changed. The Quality Group's planed growth is supported by banks.

Continued at the end of the chapter...

Introduction

In this chapter, we will consider the nature of entrepreneurship with a focus on personal characteristics, educational backgrounds, and prior experiences of entrepreneurs. We will also consider the ecological and social factors that impact entrepreneurial activities. It is essential to understand evolving definitions of entrepreneurship and the impact of experience and training in shaping an entrepreneur.

Definitions of entrepreneurship

The definition of entrepreneurship has been debated for centuries. Early eighteenth century definitions present entrepreneurship as an economic concept describing the process of bearing the risk of buying at certain prices and selling at uncertain prices.

At the beginning of the nineteenth century, French economist J. B. Say provided that entrepreneurship, "shifts economic resources out of an area of lower into an area of higher productivity and greater yield."[1] Others broadened the definition to include the concept of bringing together the factors of production.[2]

These definitions led others to question whether entrepreneurship was a unique organizational form of business, or whether it was simply a management philosophy.

In recent decades, the innovation has become a prominent component of the definition of entrepreneurship. Conceptually, the scope of the innovation concept encompasses process innovation, market innovation, product innovation, factor innovation, and organizational innovation. As we will consider later in this book, even the business model itself may represent significant innovation and constitute the source of sustainable competitive advantage.

> A father told his sons to go out daily and try to generate some value and bring it back home; if you could not make it, bring in a small piece of rock so you feel you have achievement.
>
> Ramezon – Iran

The symbiosis of innovation and entrepreneurship are a central characteristic of most contemporary definitions of entrepreneurship. In this regard, these definitions focus on the creation of new enterprises and describe the founders as entrepreneurs. Virtually all of the definitions include the following common concepts: initiative taking, risk-taking or the possibility of failure, and the process of value creation (which is derived from organizing and reorganizing of social and economic mechanisms, resources, and situations).[3] Each of the foregoing definitions views entrepreneurs from a slightly different perspective. However, they all contain similar notions, such as newness, organizing, creation, wealth, and risk-taking.

Entrepreneurs are not an exclusive group of extreme economic risk-takers. Rather, they are a diverse group from all walks of life. Additionally, their entrepreneurial endeavors are not confined to conventional for-profit firms. Instead, they are found in all professions, including medicine, research, law, architecture, engineering, social work, distribution, and government – and even in not-for-profit enterprises.

In sum, a contemporary definition must capture the notion that entrepreneurship is the process of creating new or different value by devoting the necessary time and effort, assuming the accompanying financial, intellectual, and social risks, and receiving any resulting benefits, whether monetary, in-kind, tangible, or intangible rewards (including personal satisfaction and independence).[4] Figures 4.2 and 4.3 are qualities that make a successful entrepreneur.

Schumpeter distinguishes between inventor and innovator. An inventor conceives of new products and services. In contrast, an innovator exploits inventions in new combinations that provide and create new value. Moreover, according to Schumpeter, a person functions as an entrepreneur only when he [or she] actually carries out new combinations and loses that character as soon as he has built up his business and later settles down to running it as other people run their business.

The bearing of risk and managing uncertainty are additional essential components of entrepreneurship. Richard Cantillon, a seventeenth-century economist, provided that an "entrepreneur is an agent who buys means of production at certain prices and sells them at uncertain prices."[5] Entrepreneurs must balance potential losses against potential gain under circumstances of uncertainty.

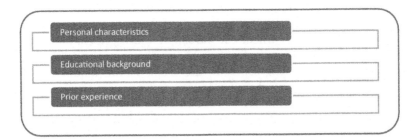

Figure 4.2 Entrepreneur qualities

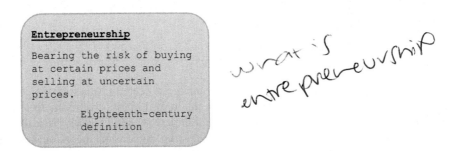

Figure 4.3 Risk-taking

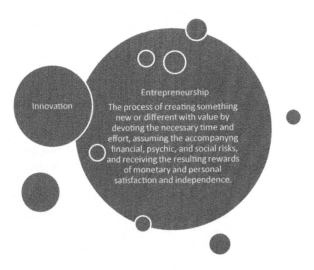

Figure 4.4 Definition

Peter Drucker stated that "maximization of opportunities" is a meaningful, indeed a precise, definition of the entrepreneurial job.[6] It implies that effectiveness rather than efficiency is essential in business. The pertinent question is not how to do things right, but how to find the right things to do and to concentrate resources and efforts on them.

An entrepreneur should be a person who determines objectives and is expected to make decisions on the type of business and the most efficient way of doing it. They must see the upcoming opportunities and make decisions in given situations. The previous sections describe the historical evolution of the definition of entrepreneurship, which is clearer and is becoming more concise.

Figure 4.5 Apple HQ
Source: Image by chris-mueller on flickr

Steve Jobs is known for creating a company under the assumption that his Apple products and services would revolutionize the world. Since the beginning, he had an unbelievable imagination; he always envisioned that his company would change how people communicated, worked, and lived.

The ability that Steve Jobs had to develop and design products was incredible, unlike anyone else. He can be recognized as a legend in innovation and interactive design. The certainty that he had of believing that having the perfect design was the most important factor in the evolution of a new generation of products such as the iPhone.

He was known for being passionate and fearless in regards to developing what is known today as Apple. The decisions and actions that he took and made could have been risky in the development of the company, but that did not stop him. Every employer must find a way to push his or her company and employees without crossing any unnecessary boundaries.

The dedication for perfection that Steve Jobs had regarding his company and design shows you that each individual has some traits that if used in the right direction can lead to success. To complete our goals it is important to believe and trust ourselves in the same way that Steve Jobs believed in perfection.[7]

Classifications of entrepreneurs

The following is Galindo and Ribeiro's (2012) entrepreneur classification summary, which highlights who is and who is not considered to be an entrepreneur:[8]

1. An entrepreneur innovates on a regular basis and consistently introduces new products, organizations, or processes. In this class, entrepreneurship is seen as a characteristic which could appear or disappear in any individual. The key point is understanding the difference between an inventor and an entrepreneur; that's the structure destroying and creating simultaneously by the entrepreneur on the organizational (firm) level.
2. An entrepreneur is a speculator or an opportunist. Their role is to keep the economic system in equilibrium. Institutions facilitate the competitiveness and incentives that entrepreneurs need.
3. An entrepreneur is not a risk manager, instead, he manages uncertainty; this differs from risk by being insurable or not. While there is no frequency related to recent events, the entrepreneur (uncertainty manager) tries to ensure the success of his subjects. Profit is a reward for managing uncertainty.
4. Entrepreneurs are environmentally oriented and have to be productive or non-productive depending on the environmental opportunities that are available to them. This point of view could be applicable to developing countries because there are fewer entrepreneurs per capita than in developed countries. Overall, in developing countries, there are more environmental challenges compared with most developed countries. However, developing countries need more economic and social entrepreneurs to develop.
5. An entrepreneur possesses charismatic, Protestant, and bureaucratic or non-bureaucratic characteristics. This point of view combines interpersonal skills, religious, and knowledge aspects of the personality of an entrepreneur.

Therefore, entrepreneurship could be seen from an individual or organizational perspective. At the individual level, entrepreneurs have the unusual ability and belief to articulate innovative ideas. At the organizational level, decision-making and policy implementation will lead to creative production, marketing, etc. It should be feasible to expand further classifications of entrepreneurs.

Balachandran and Sakthivelan define Netpreneurship as a person who runs his or her business on the internet.[9] The primary requirement for this kind of entrepreneur is "Connectivity" and "Intellectual Capital" as the main variable factors of input and the "Connectivity Infrastructure" as the only physical input. It is clear that the internet has created the greatest revolution in science and technology with so many benefits. The Netpreneur provides service to the community in all aspects of life and employment.

Figure 4.6 presents a graphical presentation of this discussion.

A social entrepreneur is driven to improve and transform economic, social, environmental, and educational conditions. Their main traits and characteristics are the ambition to change for the better and rejection of accepting the world "as it is". For example, issues such as reduction and elimination of poverty are one of their objectives. They seek to develop innovative solutions to global problems that can be replicated.

They are also driven to create social and caring values for the community. Zahra et al. said that "social entrepreneurs make significant and diverse contributions to their communities and societies, adopting business models to offer creative solutions to complex

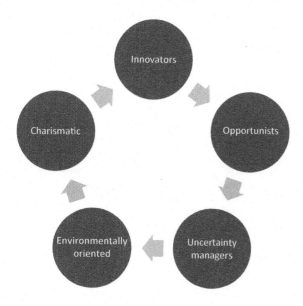

Figure 4.6 Circle of innovation

and persistent social problems."[10] They offer a typology of entrepreneurs' search processes that lead to creating opportunities for social ventures and highlight ethical concerns in the societies. Table 4.1 shows some statistics regarding social entrepreneurship from around the world.

A serial entrepreneur is a person who continuously generates new ideas and starts a new business. These individuals have a high propensity for risk-taking and are innovative and drivers for achievement and change. A typical entrepreneur will often come up with an idea and build on it to make it successful and functional as a new company. Most of these typical entrepreneurs hold leadership positions in the organization. However, a serial entrepreneur will often articulate an idea and get things started; thereafter, they will give responsibility to others to move it forward. A person who places passion ahead of other factors and combines personal interests and talent to earn a living is defined as "lifestyle entrepreneur".

They may become self-employed because they can have higher personal freedom and work on projects that inspire them. It can be a combination of hobby and profession that will bring satisfaction and financial means. They also may like a good work/life balance and owning a business without shareholders.

Personal characteristics

Another common debate in literature is whether the entrepreneurial personality is something a human is inherently born with or something that can be learned. Fisher and Koch (2008) have studied both genetic evidence and survey data and concluded that a considerable share of entrepreneurial behavior is genetically inherited.[11] They cite the characteristics of risk-taking, innovation, optimism, extroversion, high energy levels, self-confidence, competitiveness, and a motivating vision of an entrepreneur.

Table 4.1 Country statistics[a]

Country	Statistics
Australia	• 20,000 social enterprises • 37% growth over the past 5 years • 2–3% of GDP[b]
Belgium	• 63% self-generated • over 50% of their revenues through fees or sales (2014)[c]
Canada	• 57% are less than three years old (2015) • 45% operate to achieve a cultural purpose • 26% work towards employment development • 27% focus on the environment (2016)
European Union	• 1 out of 4 new enterprises set-up every year are social enterprises
India	• More than 89% less than 10 years old • 88% in the pilot, start-up, or growth stage (2012)
Indonesia	• 80% are small-scale enterprises (2012)
Malaysia	• 21% lack adequate funding (2015)
Middle East	• 75% of universities teaching social entrepreneurship (2009) • Estimated 78 globally recognized social entrepreneurs operating in the region (2010) • 20–30% of business plan competition submissions are social enterprises (2013)
Philippines	• 25% are 'multi-organizational systems' – amalgamation of for-profit and non-profit organizations (2015)
Scotland	• 42% formed in the last 10 years • 54% generated half or more of their income from trading • 60% are led by a woman (2015)
Senegal	• 18.1% of the population are pursuing social entrepreneurial activity (2015)
Vietnam	• 68% are working towards poverty reduction and 48% have environmental objectives (2012)
United Kingdom	• 73% earn more than 75% of their income from trade • 27% have the public sector as their main source of income (2015)
United States	• 22% have over $2 million in revenue • 89% were created since 2006 • 90% focus on solving problems at home (2012)

[a] Boolkin, J. (2016). Social Enterprise: Statistics from Around the World – Social Good Stuff. Retrieved from http://socialgoodstuff.com/2016/08/statistics-from-around-the-world/.
[b] Social Enterprise in Australia. (2016). Retrieved from www.socialtraders.com.au/about-social-enterprise/fases-and-other-research/social-enterprise-in-australia/.
[c] Ip, M. (2014). 5 Facts About Social Enterprise in Belgium. Retrieved from www.socialenterprisebuzz.com/2014/05/06/5-facts-about-social-enterprise-in-belgium/.

The authors also explained that certain entrepreneurship characteristics will enhance the probability of entrepreneurial success but are not the sole determinants of success. Research also has shown the entrepreneurship personality. Most characteristics have centered around three of the "Big Five" personality traits.

Comparing entrepreneurship in Europe and in the United States

Writer and entrepreneur Babs Carryer claims that Europe is falling behind in entrepreneurship. She writes that after the 1950s, only seven new big companies have been founded compared to 52 in the United States. She gives five main reasons for this phenomenon:

1. European strong labor and union laws
2. Bankruptcy being harshly punished in Europe
3. Europe's fragmented markets making it difficult to reach a substantial number of customers
4. Absence of startup hubs around the European Union compared to the United States
5. Lower venture capital investment due to bubble burst in year of 2000.

The article concludes with an opinion that Europe has to think hard about this problem and try to fix it now; otherwise there will be serious consequences for the economy in the future.

Source: Carryer (2014)[12]

The "Big Five" are the five broad factors (dimensions) of personality that are based on empirical research. Figure 4.8 shows what they include.

Neuroticism, Openness to Experience, and Extroversion traits are strongly related to entrepreneurial behavior.

Figure 4.7 EU and USA
Source: © iStock: mediaphotos

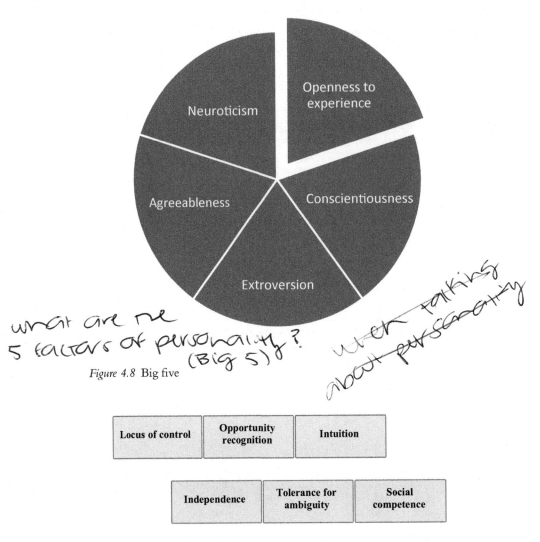

Figure 4.8 Big five

what are the
5 factors of personality?
(Big 5)

when talking
about personality

Locus of control	Opportunity recognition	Intuition

Independence	Tolerance for ambiguity	Social competence

Figure 4.9 Locus of control

Additional traits have also been added to this list

People with an internal locus of control believe they are in control of their destiny (see Figure 4.9). By contrast, people with an external locus of control believe that fate is the form of chance that events outside their control have a dominating influence on their lives.

While it is advisable for an entrepreneur to be aware of how other forces may affect their business, it seems entrepreneurs encompass more of an internal locus of control, which would work in cooperation with their need for achievement and desire to be independent.

In Table 4.2, common characteristics of entrepreneurs, their definition, and a brief analysis are provided.

Table 4.2 Characteristics of an entrepreneur

Characteristics	Definition	Analysis
Risk-taking	A personal attribute where individuals seek to achieve results when there is a high degree of uncertainty in the outcome.	An individual who is a risk-taker is willing to explore new opportunities even though he/she is facing many uncertainties; willing to accept financial risk and look for efficiency.
Innovative	Generation of new ideas leading to the formation of new products, services, organizations, etc.	Innovators think outside of the box and look for new and different ways of solving problems. The innovative individual is vital for the creation and formulation of new products, services, and organizations.
Creativity	Creativity means thinking outside of the box and the imagination that leads to the generation of new ideas and solutions.	Creativity is an important individual characteristic which leads to finding solutions to questions that have not previously been thought of.
Optimism	Ability to be hopeful even without a clear path to success.	The expectation for a positive outcome; cheerfulness. An indication of being hopeful amidst uncertainties.
Extroversion	Friendliness, the sense of being preoccupied with an external locus.	It enables growth based on changing market dynamics.
Self-confidence	Being confident in one's thoughts and actions.	It is a feature to possess because it creates a sense of assurance in the completion of tasks.
Competitiveness	The ability to perform competitively in a large setting.	Being competitive gives an individual or organization the impetus to perform better.
Persistent problem-solving	Being resilient in seeking ways to achieve the outcome.	The need for persistent problem-solving is an important component for entrepreneurs seeking to define their standing in a new endeavor within the market.
Goal-directed behavior	It is a characteristic of focusing on achieving goals.	Portray certain behavioral properties that mark the consistency of processes to achieve a particular goal.
Emotional stability	The ability to make logical decisions without emotional influence.	A moderation buffer where the individual or organization is capable to manage smoothly during critical times.
Passion	A serious commitment to a particular idea, event, or entity.	A serious commitment to an idea or belief. Love and have an inherent zeal to achieve.
Vision	Formation of a clear agenda aimed at a goal.	A visionary entrepreneur can clearly articulate the current status of an idea or organization to point to the direction where it wishes to be.
Ability to communicate	Ability to convey information in a clear and convincing manner.	Ability to communicate well and clearly the goal and/or the objective is critical to success.

Training for entrepreneurship

This section will provide descriptions and examples for training and learning how to become an entrepreneur. Many will identify their passion and belief to succeed in entrepreneurial activities while they may have had very little education or training on starting an enterprise. There has been increasing skepticism in the United States about whether or not college is necessary to succeed in the entrepreneurial world. Granted, some of the United States' greatest entrepreneurs (such as Steve Jobs, Mark Zuckerberg, and Bill Gates) are not college graduates. The examples of mentioned college dropouts have good economic reasons for their decisions. It is the concept of economic opportunity cost and choices that individual is making at the given time. Either one of the previously mentioned entrepreneur's gained knowledge from continued education would be significantly lower compared to them dropping-out and implementing their ideas.[13]

Lesonsky discusses the non-academic skills learned in school and emphasizes that the social and networking skills that are gained in college are actually more important than the academic lessons that may be learned.[14]

In addition, we must also realize that in order to start a business you should have some skills sets, especially business functioning. For example, if Steve Jobs knew nothing about computers, it would have been rather difficult for him to develop a computer business. So while going to school to earn a degree in entrepreneurship may not be the most accepted path to running your own business, learning skills at college are vitally important to the running of a new business. That is not to say that people without a college degree cannot succeed in the business; it is evident that they can. While in fact:

> the entrepreneurship activity rate among the least-educated group (high school dropouts) decreased from 0.59 percent in 2010 to 0.57 percent in 2011 but remains significantly higher than for groups with other educational levels. The largest decrease in entrepreneurial activity occurred for college graduates.[15]

We can see that high school dropouts are still more likely to begin an entrepreneurial venture as opposed to college graduates. This may be due to the knowledge gained in college and the risk of uncertainty. Students who have completed college are most likely going to have a better view of the startups and the risks associated with starting a new business. Additionally, high school dropouts have less choice to be employed because of lower skill sets and therefore have lower risk-premium.

There are numerous people that have started businesses and do not hold a degree in entrepreneurship (they may or may not hold a degree in another field), and scholars are split on whether or not a business education can actually help entrepreneurs. At the Tuck Business School at Dartmouth College, only a "small percentage" of recent graduates start their own businesses, but about half of the school's alumni are entrepreneurs two decades after graduation. "We have entrepreneurship, but it comes a little later in life when they have more experience, more money, and more networks."[16] So while a business degree may not inspire someone to start their own business right after graduation, it does give them the skills to get the experience, money, and networks that they need in order to build a business later on in life.

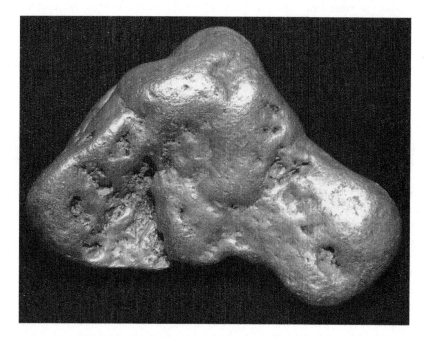

Figure 4.10 Choosing a different path
Source: Image by James St. John on Flickr

Patrice Motsepe learned at a young age that he must choose a career that would keep him away from his family business of selling liquor. He went on to earn a BA from Swaziland University and a LLB from Wits University, and in 1994 he became the first black lawyer to be made a partner at the law firm Bowman Gilfillan. At Wits he specialized in mining and business law, which led him to shift into the mining industry where he started his own business. Today, Patrice Tlhopane Motsepe is Executive Chairman of African Rainbow Minerals Limited, ARM; a leading, niche-diversified mining and minerals company, based in Johannesburg, South Africa.

Forbes magazine ranked him as the 642nd richest man and the first African-American billionaire. Patrice is an example of how even at a young age we can set our goals and work hard to achieve them. He also shows us that sometimes we must make our own paths and not follow what our family wants for us, but instead do what makes you happy.

There are strong indications [that] exist that an entrepreneurial education will produce more and better entrepreneurs than were produced in the past. Tomorrow's educated entrepreneurs will know better when, how, and where to start their new ventures. They will know how to better pursue their careers as entrepreneurs, and how to maximize their goals as entrepreneurs, not just for themselves, but also for the betterment of society.[17]

While a business education does not automatically translate into entrepreneurial success, it does give graduates the necessary skills to better improve their chances of starting their own successful business.

- Entrepreneurial innovation could be process innovation, market innovation, product innovation, factor innovation, and even organizational innovation.
- An entrepreneur sees profitable opportunities and exploits them.
- An innovator uses inventions to make a new combination, which gives him/her more profit.
- An entrepreneur innovates on a regular basis and consistently introduces new products, organizations, or processes.
- An entrepreneur is a speculator or an opportunist.
- An entrepreneur manages uncertainty.
- Entrepreneurs are environmentally oriented and have to be productive or non-productive depending on the environmental opportunities that are available to them.
- Entrepreneurs possess charismatic, protestant, and bureaucratic or non-bureaucratic characteristics.
- Netpreneurship is a person who runs their business on the internet.
- Social entrepreneurs adopt business models to offer creative solutions to complex and persistent social problems.

Colleges and universities also have the advantage of having the resources to promote entrepreneurship to their own staff as well. College professors have the advantages of experience and strong networks which can help them build their own businesses with the skills and capital gained from a university. Colleges have a large stake in the success of many entrepreneurial ventures as well. In 2009, The Economist reported that:

> America's universities are economic engines rather than ivory towers, with pro-liferating science parks, technology offices, business incubators, and venture funds. Stanford University gained around $200m in stock when Google went public. It is so keen on promoting entrepreneurship that it has created a monopoly-like game to teach its professors how to become entrepreneurs. About half of the startups in Silicon Valley have their roots in the university.[18]

Colleges and universities have a lot to gain from educating the next group of entrepreneurs. Not only do well-known alumni provide schools with credit and higher prestige, but they also give the colleges opportunities to invest and benefit from their alumni's success through investments and donations. Higher education institutions are not the only organizations jumping on the entrepreneurship bandwagon; many other organizations are promoting entrepreneurship and education as well:

> The Kauffman Foundation spends about $90m a year, from assets of about $2.1 billion, to make the case for entrepreneurialism, supporting academic research,

training would-be entrepreneurs and sponsoring 'Global Entrepreneurship Week', which last year involved 75 countries. Goldman Sachs is spending $100m over the next five years to promote entrepreneurialism among women in the developing world, particularly through management education.[19]

This shows that while a college education is the most traditional way to gain knowledge about entrepreneurship and other fields, there are other options for people who are interested in starting their own businesses. In addition to private organizations encouraging entrepreneurship through their own form of education, public organizations are now becoming involved as well.

The Federal Deposit Insurance Corporation (FDIC) and Small Business Administration (SBA) have developed a program called 'Money Smart for Small Businesses', which is "10-step instructional guide for financial institutions and other stakeholders to teach budding entrepreneurs the basics of running a business." This instructor-led program is designed to be taught to financial institutions and small business development centers which in turn give the training to entrepreneurs.[20]

In Table 4.3, Heinonen and Poikkijoki summarize the relationship between individual characteristics, process, and behavior for entrepreneurial activities.

While there are different opinions on the best ways to "teach" or "train" entrepreneurs, one thing they all have in common is that there are skills that can be gained from receiving an education, whether it be in entrepreneurship or another field. This education can be learned at a formal institution, in a community program, or even through life experience, but an education of some sort is necessary to succeed.

Figure 4.11 Entrepreneur relation
Source: © iStock: gustavofrazao

Education, innovation, and creativity

Education influences innovation from early ages throughout college and within organizations. Education that employees receive prior to employment and how the company continues to educate employees after hire play a big role in creating and continuing innovative culture. Many from developing countries come to the United States to acquire education and exposure to innovation. For example, the founder of Hmizate an e-commerce business was educated in the United States and was exposed to innovative culture. He returned to Morocco, where he applied the concepts and behaviors that he learned from experience abroad.

The way in which companies educate their employees after hire also influences the innovation abilities of the companies. For example, Intel brand provides workshops and classes for its employees in order to keep them fresh and current. In an industry such as marketing, companies, brands, and trends change on a daily basis; keeping employees educated on a constant basis is the only way to maintain their knowledge base and inspire innovation.

Experience

The experience of an individual is seen to have an important influence on that person's performance in new endeavors. Normally educational and job experience are common requirements for finding a job in general as they are designed to standardize the performance of individuals. However, the backgrounds of business owners are heterogeneous, which has led to the suggestion that differences in the experiences of owners might explain variance in the performance of their enterprises. Entrepreneurs could use their experience to identify possible innovations and how to capitalize on the experience they have, such as entering certain industries. In addition, previous industry experience will help entrepreneurs build relationships, network, identify new products and markets, and acquire funding (see Figure 4.12).

Training of entrepreneurs' competencies in higher education – Brazil

The teaching project in entrepreneurship was created for undergraduate students of Pharmacy from the State University of the West of Paraná – UNIOESTE, located in the city of Cascavel, Brazil in 2013. The objective of this entrepreneurship consisted of teaching, extension, and research activities, which were: (1) creation of the discipline "Entrepreneurship in Pharmaceutical Sciences"; (2) implementation of the teaching project "Entrepreneurial Experiences in Pharmaceutical Sciences"; and (3) conducting surveys to evaluate the profile of students and undergraduate alumni of the Pharmacy course. The purpose of this project is to contribute to the higher education courses for the training of entrepreneurial skills of its academics, and to the formation of an entrepreneurial culture that has reflexes in the external environments to the institutions promoting the regional development.

Figure 4.12 Company success

Surveys and research of investors in the developed countries who invest in new companies consistently reveal that industry experience for startup companies are among the most important determinants of new company success.

This suggests that experience enhances the performance and sustainability of new ventures. Therefore, we can draw conclusions that experience is a good education for entrepreneurs.

However, industry experience remains a controversial topic in aiding entrepreneurial success. One can argue that industry experience can lead entrepreneurs to run their firms better, as suggested earlier, but it is also possible that industry experience has no impact at all. If entrepreneurial performance is driven by the value of available opportunities and not by an entrepreneur's abilities, then industry experience can be seen in a different view. By taking this view, people with industry experience may have a greater ability to identify opportunities which will help them to succeed, but they may not perform better than other entrepreneurs with less experience; they are just making better-informed risks. This reasoning would also help break down the myth that experience is key to performing better for entrepreneurs.

Environmental infrastructure

Economic factors

Competition is central to the entrepreneurial spirit and the driving force of economies. Since the early history of economics, entrepreneurship has been regarded as the critical success factor for economic performance. In a developed market economy, entrepreneurial knowledge is transmitted as a part of the open culture. Successful entrepreneurs are praised in the mass media and there are countless examples of role models. Under capitalism (the basis of many developed nations' economies), innovative activity becomes somewhat given.

This is one of the reasons that market economies have been recommended for developing nations. For example, one of the issues that Central and Eastern European countries faced in the transformation from centrally planned into market economies was the need to develop a private business sector which allows entrepreneurs to create their own businesses. The transformation occurred in three ways. First, on the firm level, there needs to be a shift from public ownership to the private owner which can be done through the direct privatization of formerly state-owned companies or through the creation of a completely new business, thereby lowering the barriers for entrepreneurship. The second is the liberalization of markets, which increases market opportunities as well as in the level of competition. The third involves the creation of market institutions, such as banks, other financial intermediaries, and business and training support services, which are an integral part of the external environment for business development in mature market economies.[21]

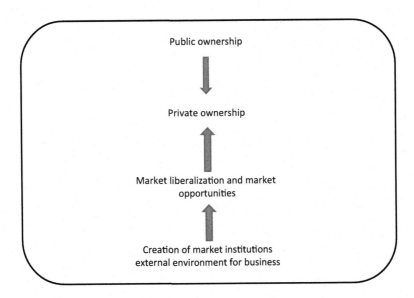

Public ownership

Private ownership

Market liberalization and market opportunities

Creation of market institutions external environment for business

Figure 4.13 Environmental infrastructure

Of course, there are many lessons that need to be learned from the privatization of the former Soviet Union and Eastern Europe. Many public industries were given away for the sake of market economy and did not necessarily create a fair and balanced market economy. The growth of oligarchy in the Russian Federation is an indication of the inappropriate privatization process.

While innovation and entrepreneurship are the drivers for economic growth, in developing countries, there are also ways where entrepreneurship can actually hinder economic development due to the misallocation of entrepreneurial talent. This misallocation arises from the absence of good institutions (see Figure 4.13).

Financial structure

Obtaining adequate access to capital is one of the biggest hurdles to start and grow a new business. Entrepreneurs may not be aware of the financial loan products available to them. If they are aware of financial institutions, entrepreneurs also need to provide sufficient collateral and meet interest obligations which might be difficult. In addition, financial institutions may be reluctant to lend to entrepreneurs or SMEs due to a lack of reliable credit information and limited capacity to appropriately assess credit risks. In the future chapters, we will discuss this subject in detail.

- Education prior to employment and during employment in the company plays a big role in creating and continuing innovative culture.
- Previous industry experience will help entrepreneurs build relationships, network, identify new products and markets, and acquire funding.

- In a developed market economy, entrepreneurial knowledge is transmitted as a part of the open culture.
- Misallocation of entrepreneurial talent arises from the absence of good institutions.
- Financial institutions may be reluctant to lend to entrepreneurs or SMEs due to a lack of reliable credit information and limited capacity to appropriately assess credit risks.

Greater bank competition due to market economies is thought to have allowed capital to flow more freely towards projects yielding the highest returns. When banks are not available, entrepreneurs in developed countries can turn to small business associations, crowdfunding, venture capital, angel investors, bond markets, and other alternative financing methods to get capital. In addition, most entrepreneurs use their family wealth and income to finance their businesses. It is this plentiful access to financial capital that has fueled developed nations to promote entrepreneurship. In Chapter 10, we will discuss funding sources and challenges that entrepreneurs are facing in developing countries. While there are different sources of funds available for entrepreneurs in developed countries, that is not the case for most developing countries.

Social structure

Culture

Despite the considerable progress some countries have achieved in developing their economies, entrepreneurial activity remains relatively limited in many of these nations. For example, Russia has yet to be entrepreneurially successful despite the presence of a new economic system.[22] This is because Russia has yet to fully experience a cultural shift that supports entrepreneurial behavior.

As such, a national culture that supports and encourages entrepreneurial activity is needed. Borozan and Barkovic described the rules of the games that developed nations have established as important for creating an entrepreneurial environment. They include adequate knowledge, adequate human resources, appropriate institutional organization, appropriate entrepreneurial infrastructure, and a value system and social norms suitable to entrepreneurship (see Figure 1.3). Adequate knowledge refers to the training and education that is offered in a country that would aid in competitiveness.[23] Education needs to be flexible to the demands of the current business environment in order to continue to provide development and sustainability of competitive advantage. A lack of education will lead to a lack of prepared human resources. Having satisfactory human resources are vital in entrepreneurship. An entrepreneurship culture also needs to have the appropriate institutional infrastructure such as legal and government institutions in order to prevent corruption and create competition.

Why Germany is so much better at training its workers

Apprenticeship is different in the United States and Europe. Today in the United States, only 5 percent train as an apprentice, while in Germany it is closer to 60 percent. Many companies in Europe use dual training to ensure that students learn the work habits and responsibilities necessary to succeed in the workplace. Germans see this training as useful for everyone, not only for struggling students. You can also see that both the employers and employees benefit better by an apprenticeship than a short-term training.

One of the reasons that it might be hard for the United States to transition is the cost. In Germany the range of cost per apprentice is between $25,000–$80,000. Other reasons are the differences in centralization in both countries. It's hard to imagine the level of state control that Germany has compared to the United States. The last difference is also how Americans see education and training in comparison to how Germans do.

Source: Jacoby (2014)[24]

Entrepreneurs need to be confident that regulations will be abided by, especially in regards to contracts and intellectual property. A lack of faith in these intuitions creates business uncertainty, which undermines entrepreneurship. An appropriate entrepreneurial infrastructure also includes a support system for entrepreneurs such as business incubators, technological parks, and development centers. These segments need to work together to provide services that aid in entrepreneurship development.

In Table 4.3, Heinonen and Poikkijoki summarize the relationship between individual characteristics, process, and behavior for entrepreneurial activities. There is the consensus that a framework for creating an entrepreneurship culture should include the variables described in the Table.

Table 4.3 Framework for culture

Characteristic	Definition	Analysis
Education	Acquiring knowhow and processes with new ideas.	Investment in education is critical because it encourages critical thinking and helps address the challenges faced in the process.
Entrepreneurial knowledge	The possession of relevant information related to entrepreneurship.	Entrepreneurial knowledge is critical because it fosters experience and good practices. Building networking among entrepreneurs, institutions, organizations, and universities.
Self-achievement	Ability to realize personal goals.	Being independent; confident in solving problems.
Entrepreneurial climate	A nurturing and rewarding atmosphere.	Needs to cater to which self-achievement and social responsibility will be nurtured, rewarded, and promoted; government policies and regulations and culture play a significant role.
Legal ramifications	Consequences faced when guilty of business irregularities.	This helps monitor activity in the business environment including corrupt activities, entry regulations, and obstacles faced when seeking finances.

Source: Heinonen, Jarna, & Poikkijoki, Sari-Anne. (2006) An entrepreneurial-directed approach to entrepreneurship education: mission impossible? Journal of Management Development, 25(1), 80–94.

Creative problem-solving in the face of extreme limits

Navi Radjou has spent years studying "jugaad", also known as Frugal Innovation. Pioneered by entrepreneurs in emerging markets who figured out how to get spectacular value from limited resources, the practice has now caught on globally.

You can check in more details in the full TED Talk in this link: www.ted.com/talks/navi_radjou_creative_problem_solving_in_the_face_of_extreme_limits

Social connections   *what are networks?*

Networks are often defined as relationships between individuals, groups, or organizations. Networks may take many forms including strategic alliances, joint ventures, licensing arrangements, subcontracting, etc.

An organizational network is a voluntary arrangement between two or more firms that involves an exchange, sharing, or co-development of new products and technologies.[25]

An example of a network for entrepreneurs is a trade organization in which many entrepreneurs are a member. To meet challenges, an entrepreneur has to develop a network, which results in connections to resource providers (clients, partners, consultants, governments, etc.). Entrepreneurs require information, capital, skills, and labor in order to start their new business. While they hold some of these resources themselves, they often complement their resources by accessing their contacts. These contacts are often informal work and non-work connections. These relations may extend across professional networks, reaching friends and colleagues from earlier collaborations. Research has shown that networks are very useful for entrepreneurs. The first is size. Entrepreneurs can enlarge their networks to get crucial information and other resources from knowledgeable others. The next is positioning. Entrepreneurs position themselves within a social network to shorten the path to get what they need. Over time, entrepreneurs accumulate social capital, which is crucial for starting a new business.

The role of the family in networking and entrepreneurship is to acquire resources and/or information. But the role of the family in aiding entrepreneurs has a long history and it seems to have a mixed outcome. Generally, entrepreneurs draw on their family and friends for input and in many cases as a role model (i.e., SMEs) or to acquire financial support. Entrepreneurial parents provide emotional encouragements and unique skills to their children's initiations and are an easily accessible resource.[26,27] Some scholars have explored the factors associated with the scope of startup activities among young emerging entrepreneurs. They have found that the effects of family support on "young nascent entrepreneurs' start-up activity are complex and multi-faceted."[28]

Type of business most common to entrepreneurship

With the current technology boom, it would be thought that the most common entrepreneurial ventures would take place in technological fields.

The recent report about the United States stated that:

> By industry, construction had the highest entrepreneurial activity rate at 1.68 percent, continuing an upward trend over the past several years, followed by the services industry at 0.42 percent. The manufacturing startup rate was the lowest among all industries, with only 0.11 percent of non-business owners starting businesses per month during 2011.[29]

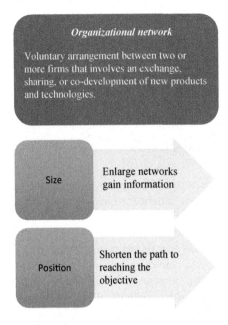

Figure 4.14 Organizational networks

Table 4.4 High growth industries

Internet services (data processing)	Science
Computer systems	Technical consulting
Software	Home health care
Employment services	Personal Financial Advisory
Management	Childcare services, Arts and Entertainment

Therefore, in the recent past construction businesses are the most prominent businesses for entrepreneurs in the United States. However, it would not be unlikely for this to change in the coming years. Using the Bureau of Labor Statistics'[30] job-growth projections for 2002 to 2012, Inc.com came up with a list of the ten industries "that are projected to have enormous growth-and opportunities."[31]

From this list, we can see that technology companies are going to be more prominent in the coming years, although we cannot say for sure that they will be the most lucrative entrepreneurial business. However, we can see from the success of Silicon Valley that technology is likely to be the field with the most growth in the coming years, and therefore the best industry in which to start a new company. We can see already the success that technology-driven entrepreneurs have had with companies such as Apple, Google, and Facebook. One interesting factor to consider when determining the growth of an industry is to look more closely at who these entrepreneurs are and where they have received their training.

There is no question that technology and communications are influencing most, if not all, businesses in developed and developing countries. Technology as a tool is continually reinventing itself through entrepreneurial work. This is influencing developing countries in many ways that we will discuss in future chapters.

Concluding remarks

In this chapter, we discussed entrepreneurs' traits and characteristics. Many traits and characteristics are common globally. Factors such as education, government regulations and policies, and cultural characteristics have significant influences on entrepreneurial initiation. The need for experience is also important because it emerges after acquiring certain levels of knowledge and training has occurred. Characteristics such as innovation are important because they influence an entrepreneurial agenda. An innovative and curious mind explores various areas in the development of an organization such as production processes, marketing, and product design. Other features related to entrepreneurial attributes are acting as market speculators and exhibiting abilities to manage risks. For entrepreneurs, the need to understand the basic is important because it reinforces the need for consistency once certain characteristics are integrated. The importance of formal education is emphasized for the development of critical thinking and specialization. Various support avenues should be sought with particular emphasis on capital acquirement.

Discussion questions

1. Define entrepreneur and entrepreneurship.
2. What are the different classifications of entrepreneurship? Do they make sense to you? In which classifications might you be in?
3. What are your thoughts in terms of the role of education and experiences in relation to entrepreneurship?
4. Which one of the personal characteristics do you think you have?
5. Write a short case about an entrepreneur that you admire.

Case study – continued

Story of a young, dedicated entrepreneur

There is no scarcity of people aspiring to become an entrepreneur by applying the franchise business model. However, Tharun successfully differentiates himself by learning everything about the franchisor's brand, including the Customer Value Proposition (CVP) of the brand (i.e., the problem it solves for the consumer) and how consumers perceive the brand. This comprehensive understanding of the brand and the franchise forms a strong foundation for Tharun's business proposals. Tharun's approach towards entrepreneurship is influenced by his education, which distinguishes him from virtually all competitors.

Questions for discussion

1. What were the unique challenges faced during his initial stages of establishing the Quality Group?
2. How would skills acquired by an entrepreneur differentiate him from the competition?
3. Discuss all the advantages and disadvantages of starting a venture without prior experience.
4. Construct a set of pre-requisites that each entrepreneur should possess and discuss each skill's influence in advancing his/her cause.

Table 4.5 Key terms

Entrepreneurship	Lifestyle entrepreneur
Classifications of entrepreneurs	Characteristics of an entrepreneur
Serial entrepreneur	Money smart for small businesses

Notes

1 Say, J. B. (1997). An Economist in Troubled Times. New Jersey: Princeton University Press. Selected and translated by Robert Palmer.
2 Hisrich, R. D., Peters, M. P., & Shepherd, D. A. (2005) Entrepreneurship (6th ed., paperback). McGraw Hill.
3 Hisrich, R. D., Peters, M. P. & Shepherd, D. A. (2005). Entrepreneurship (6th ed., paperback). McGraw Hill.
4 Hisrich, R. D., Peters, M. P., & Shepherd, D. A. (2005). Entrepreneurship (6th ed., paperback). McGraw Hill.
5 Mises Institute. (2010). Richard Cantillon: founder of political economy. Mises Institute. Retrieved from https://mises.org/library/richard-cantillon-founder-political-economy.
6 Himmel, R. (2013). What Personality Traits Made Steve Jobs Successful? Entrepreneur.com. Retrieved from www.entrepreneur.com/answer/226410.
7 Himmel, R. (2013). What Personality Traits Made Steve Jobs Successful? Entrepreneur.com. Retrieved from www.entrepreneur.com/answer/226410.
8 Galindo, M.-Á., & Ribeiro, D. (2012). Women's Entrepreneurship and Economics: New Perspectives, Practices, and Policies. Springer, Edited book.
9 Balachandran, V., & Sakthivelan, M. S. (2013). Impact of Information Technology on entrepreneurship. Journal of Business Management & Social Sciences Research, 2(2), 50–56.
10 Zahra, S. A., Gedajlovic, E., Neubaum, D. O., & Shulman, J. M. (2009). A typology of social entrepreneurs: motives, search processes and ethical challenges. Journal of Business Venturing, 24(5), 519–532. https://doi.org/10.1016/J.JBUSVENT.2008.04.007
11 Fisher, James Lee, & Koch, James V. (2008). Born, Not Made: The Entrepreneurial Personality. Greenwood Publishing Group.
12 Carryer, B. (2014, November 14). Comparing Entrepreneurship in Europe and in the US. Retrieved December 15, 2018, from http://newventurist.com/2012/11/comparing-entrepreneurship-in-europe-and-in-the-us/.
13 Krugman, P., & Wells, R. (2013). Microeconomics (3rd ed.). Worth Publishers.

14 Lesonsky, R. (n.d.). Is College Necessary for Young Entrepreneurs? Retrieved June 23, 2012, from MSN: Business on Main: http://businessonmain.msn.com/browseresources/articles/smallbusinesstrends.aspx?cp-documentid=29202016#fbid=ZXwbJs0Clh8.

15 Pruitt, B. (2012, March 19). New Business Startups Declined in 2011, Annual Kauffman Study Shows. Retrieved June 16, 2012, from Ewing Marion Kauffman Foundation: www.kauffman.org/newsroom/new-business-startups-declined-in-2011-annual-kauffman-study-shows.aspx.

16 Wecker, M. (2012, June 12). Skip Business School, MBA Entrepreneurs Say. Retrieved June 16, 2012, from US News- Education: www.usnews.com/education/best-graduate-schools/top-business-schools/articles/2012/06/12/skip-business-school-mba-entrepreneurs-say.

17 Kent, C. A. (1990). Entrepreneurship Education. Westport, CT: Quorum Books.

18 The Economist. (2009, March 12). The United States of Entrepreneurs. Retrieved June 16, 2012, from The Economist: www.economist.com/node/13216037.

19 The Economist. (2009, March 12). The United States of Entrepreneurs. Retrieved June 16, 2012, from The Economist: www.economist.com/node/13216037.

20 Adler, J. (2012). FDIC, SBA take on small-business training. American Banker, 177(64).

21 Smallbone, D., & Welter, F. (2001). The distinctiveness of entrepreneurship in transition economies. Small Business Economics, 16(4), 249–262. https://doi.org/10.1023/A:1011159216578

22 Lee, S. M., & Peterson, S. J. (2000). Culture, entrepreneurial orientation, and global competitiveness. Journal of World Business, 35(4), 401–416. https://doi.org/10.1016/S1090-9516(00)00045-6

23 Borozan, D., & Barkovic, I. (2005). Creating entrepreneurial environment for SME's development: the case of Croatia. Silicon Valley Review of Global Entrepreneurship Research, 1, 44 – 55.

24 Jacoby, T. (2014, October 20). Why Germany Is So Much Better at Training Its Workers. Retrieved December 16, 2018, from www.theatlantic.com/business/archive/2014/10/why-germany-is-so-much-better-at-training-its-workers/381550/.

25 Groen, A. J. (2005). Knowledge intensive entrepreneurship in networks: towards a multi-level/multi dimensional approach. Journal of Enterprising Culture, 13(01), 69–88. https://doi.org/10.1142/S0218495805000069

26 Greve, A., & Salaff, J. W. (2003). Social networks and entrepreneurship. Entrepreneurship Theory and Practice, 28(1), 1–22. https://doi.org/10.1111/1540–8520.00029

27 El Jadidi, J., Asgary, N., & Weiss, J. (2017). Cultural and institutional barriers for western educated Entrepreneurs in Morocco, Cyrus Chronicle Journal: Contemporary Economic and Management Studies in Asia and Africa, 2, 61–75.

28 Edelman, L. F., Manolova, T. S., Shirokova, G., & Tsukanova, T. (2016). The impact of family support on young nascent entrepreneurs' start-up activities. Journal of Business Venturing, 31(4), 365–484.

29 Pruitt, B. (2012, March 19). New Business Startups Declined in 2011, Annual Kauffman Study Shows. Retrieved June 16, 2012, from Ewing Marion Kauffman Foundation: www.kauffman.org/newsroom/new-business-startups-declined-in-2011-annual-kauffman-study-shows.aspx.

30 United States Department of Labor. (n.d.). Business Employment Dynamics: Entrepreneurship and the U.S. Economy. Retrieved June 10, 2012, from Bureau of Labor Statistics: www.bls.gov/bdm/entrepreneurship/entrepreneurship.htm.

31 Steiman, J. (2005, April 6). Top 10 Industries to Start and Grow a Business. Retrieved June 23, 2012, from Inc.com: www.inc.com/articles/2005/04/top10.html.

5   Creativity, innovation, and development

Learning objectives:

1. *Define and analyze creativity and innovation*
2. *Examining the role of culture on creativity and innovation*
3. *Describe the predominant types of innovation*
4. *Discuss the 4P's of innovation*
5. *Understanding the role of human resources on creativity*
6. *Examining the five Factors of Stagnation*

Figure 5.1 Fish Bowl Pizza
Source: Al Capizza, Brazil/2017

Al Capizza: a creative and unique pizza restaurant, São Paulo, Brazil

Everybody likes a hot fresh pizza, but nobody wants an order; not as before!

Background

It was the year 2000 when Mr. Corleone decided to open a pizzeria in Blumenau, a southern city of Brazil. Having paternal roots from Italy and a childhood love for Italian food inspired him to find recipes for the first pizzas. Mr. Corleone took great care of every detail, starting from the purchase of the ingredients to the preparation of pizzas. His customers soon arrived and thus began the Don Corleone pizzeria. The pizzeria started to serve its Blumenau customers, through services like home delivery and customer pick up. Though Don Corleone had a few tables where customers could eat the pizza on the spot, it was not the focus of the business. His two children, Sony and Michael, soon acquired their father's love for pizza and promptly joined the family pizza business. A few years later, the two brothers saved enough money from their work at Don Corleone and with $3,000 in initial funds opened a second Don Corleone pizzeria, also in Blumenau. While Michael runs the business, Sony went to study abroad in the United States.

Growth and current challenges

Building on the initial success, by 2016 the family owned five Don Corleone Pizzerias. One is run by Mr. Corleone and the other four by his son Michael. As of 2016, the sales from all five pizzerias amounted to 10 million pizzas. Their delivery process starts with the customer making the call to choose the flavor and the crust. The pizzeria always prepares the pizza with fresh ingredients and delivers on time to the customer's address. This model has been successfully implemented for the last 17 years. However, the Corleone family have identified customer preference changes, especially from the new generations who ask for much better use of information and communication technologies (mobiles, apps, tracking, etc.). Also, the arrival of brands of multinational pizzerias in Brazil are new challenges and concerns for the Corleone family.

Case continues at the end of this chapter…

Introduction

Creativity and innovation are essential components of an organization and a culture for economic development. However, both creativity and innovation can be constrained by cultural factors, in turn, inhibiting a country's ability to live up to its potential. These cultural factors run deep, and they are expressed in the inner workings of an office, in the innovation processes that a company has chosen to foster, and even in the development of a business model itself, as discussed in earlier chapters. There are many questions regarding the relationship and impact of creativity and innovation on economic development which will be addressed in this chapter.

Economic development is dependent upon many factors, which include creativity and innovation. These are the focus of this chapter. As we discussed in the earlier chapters, the most significant determinants of economic development are human capital, capital stock, and technology. To ensure economic development, countries should nurture creativity and innovation. We examine the role of creativity and its relationship with innovation and culture. We examine its impact on entrepreneurial activities and economic development. Creativity and the ability to innovate are closely linked to entrepreneurial activities and therefore to economic development.

Creativity design and innovative technology are important factors that contribute to an enterprise's ability to succeed in an increasingly global marketplace. However, attitudes towards creativity and innovation are culturally constructed and vary widely from country to country, as is the access to and adoption of modern information and communication technology. Cultural attitudes towards creativity can facilitate or impede an enterprise's ability to bring an innovative product to market, thus directly impacting their economic success, as discussed in Chapter 2.

Creativity is often described as technological, economic, and artistic innovation, but fundamentally it is the desire to express oneself, which can only take place in an open environment that is oriented towards the exchange of ideas.

The degree of creativity in a culture is difficult to measure for lack of quantifiable evidence, but attempts have been made to assess cultural attitudes towards creativity and to infer a composite creativity score based on other measurable and related markers.[1,2]

Hollander's and Van Cruysen's study shows that creative education is linked most closely to a country's ability to innovate. This being the case, it's important to understand further how culture impacts innovation. Creative ideas are connections between problems and solutions for the first time. When working on understanding the voice of the customer, producers have to identify customers' needs. People typically ask for an idea or solution to problems. However, it is the role of entrepreneurs to be creative and find the solution. Innovation aims to answer a question or solve a problem; it is best if it fits customers' needs.

Creativity can be defined as the inherent ability of all human individuals to generate novel ideas.[3] Creativity could be defined as the human mind conceiving new ideas and bringing them into being. The new Oxford Dictionary of English defines innovation as "Making changes to something established by introducing something new." This definition does not suggest that innovation is only related to a "thing." It has a broader definition and implications.

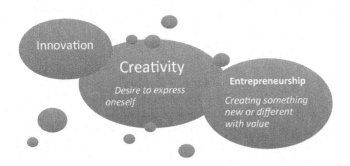

Figure 5.2 Creativity definition

Figure 5.3 Creativity

Source: netsnake, via Flickr. https://search.creativecommons.org/photos/38107c31-a156-4758-8e88-2c2982ae0180

When Alexander the Great visited Diogenes and asked whether he could do anything for the famed teacher, Diogenes replied: "Only stand out of my light." Perhaps some day we shall know how to heighten creativity. Until then, one of the best things we can do for creative men and women is to stand out of their light.
What did Diogenes mean by "Only stand out of their light"?

John W. Gardner

Definition of creativity

To explain the concept of creativity, it is important to consider the most common objects of analysis in the literature of creativity.[4] Usually creativity as an object of analysis can be associated with an individual, a group, and an organization.[5] This scope of study has been designed especially because the individual, the group of individuals, and the organization are interdependent constituent parts, when creativity is thought of as a system.[6]

The focus at this stage will be on organizational creativity and its proximity to the concept of economic development, which is the focus of this textbook. However, the presence of an individual's or a group's creativity is found for better understanding of the overall creativity of the organization. Organizational creativity can be understood as the creation of a new product, service, idea, procedure, or process that is valuable and useful, and is developed by individuals working together in a complex social system.[7] The article by Puccio and Cabra has the general objective that contributes to understanding the formation of the individual components of creativity through a systemic approach, basing itself from the works of other authors such as Woodman and his colleagues.[8] The definition of creativity has strong proximity to the concepts of innovation. Innovation is what was done previously on various issues such as product, process, marketing, or organizational arrangement and it generates an economic value.[9] Creativity and innovation can be understood as integrated skills which apparently have different cutoff points as argued by Anderson et al (2014).[10] Creativity does not have to generate economic value necessarily, but should be considered useful.[11] They claim innovation necessarily has to generate economic value to be considered as such. Puccio et al. (2010) discuss fostering creativity and creating demand and economic value.[12] In fact, it seems that generating economic value is not a condition for the existence of creativity, but rather the generation of a useful idea. The distance of a more objective definition of the term "useful idea" seems to highlight the challenge or the distance between the two concepts, useful and idea in practice. A useful idea can be understood as the idea that generates economic value, concluding that creativity is in fact innovation.

This conclusion was obviously incorrect, since these are concepts of a different nature and essence and this could be the dominant opinion. On the other hand, considering that innovation creates economic value in the form of interest income (income) while creativity does not generate any economic value will result in creativity to be viewed as a spillover effect. Therefore, we can distinguish them in terms of their ultimate goal, which is not discussed permanently in any of the cited articles, although the three articles have workings of the two concepts in the same context of discussion. The arguments in this textbook consider that innovation has its ultimate aim of income (i.e., financial income), while creativity has its ultimate goal as the outcome, or as they say in economics, the spillover effects.

The spillover can occur in the form of social impact, the environment, improving the organizational climate, or other outcomes that may not be financial.

Promoting organizational creativity

Organizational behavior specialists have deemed that creativity, lateral thinking, and communication are the key skills to innovation and success in the business world. Thus various companies conduct creative building events throughout the year: Manchester Metropolitan University has an annual "Engage Week", Cognizant Business Consulting hosts "Insight Days", and every year Virgin Management asks their employees for suggestions on how to improve the workplace, of which one to three suggestions are implemented. Companies believe the best way to earn employee loyalty and engagement is to give them a voice and show them that their ideas matter.

For more information see Manchester Metropolitan University (2017)[13]

Figure 5.4 Metropolitan university
Source: © iStock: VTT Studio

In this line of reasoning, one can seek to evaluate the organizational creativity from the results obtained and these will be analyzed from the recognition and measurement of generated spillovers. In this context, ambidextrous is the ability to adapt, bring together, and manage complex and conflicting demands, in order to promote engagement between fundamentally different activities. Despite many approaches and visions of creativity, we can show in Figure 5.4 the Amabile's approach, defining the components of individual creativity or for small groups.

Definition of innovation

It is clear that innovation plays an important role around the globe, but it looks very different when it occurs in developing countries compared to advanced economies such as the United States. The realities of developing countries can render innovation much less likely to occur, more difficult to bring to market, and limited to only modest success. We will explore these specific factors later in this chapter. Despite these challenges, innovation is essential to the advancement of our world. Not only can it cure diseases and save lives, it can combat climate change, and also has an undeniable impact on economic growth. Even with limited resources, technological advancements have the ability to improve efficiency.

Technological innovations (such as low-cost tablet computers) can lead to increased access to education, greater employment rates, and solutions to everyday problems. Most importantly through the economic perspective, innovation is a creator of wealth and of jobs, with the potential to escalate national economies to higher levels of growth.

Table 5.1 Prominent theories

Amabile's theory	Highlights the influence of working environment on creativity. The elements of working environment include knowledge, creative thinking skills, and intrinsic motivation.
Interactionist perspective	Proposes that creativity is a complex relationship between the individual and their work situation at different levels: individual, team, and organizational configurations.
Individual's model of creative action	Explained with the individual as the starting point of creativity, influenced by processes that make sense, motivation, knowledge, and skill.
Fourth prominent theory	Describes creativity with a construct explained by cultural differences, including listing the differences between the Western and Eastern regions.
Fifth prominent theory	Describes four factors (vision, participative safety, guidance, and support innovation task) related to the climate for the innovation team. The most relevant issue of this theoretical perspective is in the care of the process of criticism and judgment among the team members.
Sixth theory	Deals with the ambidextrous related mediation and conflict management at multiple organizational levels and as a factor that explains the innovative success.

"Thus, it has been claimed that entrepreneurship is the main vehicle of economic development"[14]…the more entrepreneurs there are in an economy, the faster it will grow; the engine of this economic growth is the entrepreneur.[15,16,17] Innovation is defined as "the act of inventing new processes, products, services, or solutions that can be brought to market, implemented within an existing organization, or used to contribute value to society."[18] In this chapter we argue that innovation should be promoted in all countries, especially in the developing countries who are desperately in need of advancement, as it is our most powerful tool for achieving a higher global standard of living. Entrepreneurship and innovation have not been addressed in an integrated way, however, since 1911 and, especially from the perspective of Schumpeter, it can be seen that it is related to large overlapping themes.

In this section, we intend to address more aspects related predominantly to innovation, and later in the final section of this chapter, perform the integrated approach to innovation and entrepreneurship.

Schumpeter identified the value of the migration phenomenon between the traditional factors of production to a new emerging production factor called "knowledge". The new logic showed that land or capital – financial resources – would not be enough to sustain the growth of the economic world in the future. The economy, however, is the result of social changes carried out at different times in the past.[19] When we look at rates or economic factors, we are actually checking what has already happened (past). The logic proposed by Schumpeter, which is based on economic concepts, demonstrated the need to consider "knowledge", and classified it as a new form of power and as an input for economic development.

Therefore, Schumpeter epitomized that "new things" or "differentiation" would result from recombination of skills and competencies of the companies. These recombinations would be a history of a kind of creative destruction.[20] The definition of innovation

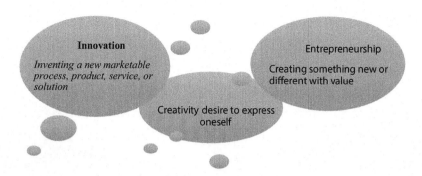

Figure 5.5 Innovation definition

has evolved over time. Innovation is a modification of any previous inventions and methods, whether it be product, marketing, organization, or arrangement process. An invention becomes an innovation through diffusion processes – ways in which innovation spreads and becomes available for usage (see Figure 5.5). The adoption and valuation of the invention by users who are willing to pay for it are the determinants of success.[21] When the value of innovation is recognized, people decide to pay for it and they make up the market. Market in this particular case is the set of people who have their problems solved by this innovation. By this definition, considering the principles set out in the Oslo manual, to be called innovation, the goal is to generate economic value. Some classifications of innovation have been developed in a very useful way to help your understanding.

Identified in the literature are four predominant types of innovation described as incremental innovation, radical innovation, modular innovation, and architectural innovation, whose differences lie in the combination of knowledge and skills of the innovator – current or future knowledge – and the locus of change – if the central or peripheral concept.[22] Widely studied by Christensen, disruptive innovation is the innovation that comes from unmet needs in already established markets that are not addressed by large corporations and therefore exposes them to risks when they are overcome by smaller companies which take advantage of the identified opportunity.[23,24,25,26,27,28] Through the models of Henderson, his colleagues and Christensen have not been compared by the authors at the time; other later studies of the authors have identified some complementarities between them, or both appear to argue that their theories are complementary and in a convergent way. It can be seen in the case of disruptive innovation that the emergence of opportunities related to market shares are not satisfied.

Such dissatisfaction, according to Christensen, is related to the logic of the development of products and services in the enterprise. This logic is to constantly increase the amount of features of products and services to add value and raise the price the market will pay for them, thus increasing profit margins by increasing the surplus (surplus is the term for perception of consumer value and is the reason why the consumer pays the price charged by the manufacturer or supplier of a product or service).

Figure 5.6 Hydroponics
Source: © iStock: VTT Studio

Developing country wide solution

Droughts or floods are widely known to completely destroy farms in Kenya, leaving the country unsure how to repair the land. Peter Chege, a Kenyan man, wanted to design a solution that could lead to more productive, resilient farming and potentially boost the entire economy.

Hydroponics Kenya company (2011) developed a method of hydroponic farming, which uses water containing mineral solutions to grow crops. This method uses ten times less water than traditional farming, leaving more water for other needs such as drinking and bathing.[29] It also gives the farmer much more control over their crops, since they grow in trays inside sheds or greenhouses. The crops also grow significantly faster and are higher quality. Chege used his findings to develop entire systems he could sell to farmers, including humidity-controlled greenhouses, hydroponic sheds, trays, mineral solutions, seeds, and the associated training.

Chege caught the attention of the Kenyan CIC (Climate Innovation Center), an aid program funded by the World Bank that gave $10 million per year in the form of private donations. The CIC provided Chege with the funding he needed in addition to office space, business guidance, assistance with tax registration, legal support to protect his intellectual property, and a computer to do research, budget, and create a website.

Source: Company's website[30]

Disruptive innovation and ambidextrous organization

As the value of innovation continues to grow and organizations begin to invest in more initiatives to attain a competitive advantage over their competitors, leaders must be wary of disruptive innovations. Disruptive innovation is a development that helps to form a new market and value network. These advancements eventually begin to disrupt the existing markets and displace older technologies, rendering them obsolete.

Clayton Christensen, who coined the term disruptive innovation, explains that today, many organizations are innovating "faster than their customers' needs evolve."[31] This causes them to produce products that can be considered too sophisticated, too expensive, or even too complicated for the customers in their market. Christensen continues to explain that companies who try to monetize these innovations by selling them to the higher tiers in their markets can leave them susceptible to "disruptive innovations". As corporations begin to focus their innovation efforts on market segments where they can maximize profitability, leaders often lose sight of the developments in the external environment. It is important for future leaders in innovative firms to understand how to balance the challenges of "dualism".[32]

Dualism is the ability to function efficiently in the present to sustain the success and bottom line of their organizations while preparing for the long term by investing in innovation and, at the same time, developing their own forms of disruptive innovation. "Not only must business organizations be concerned with the financial success and market penetration of their current mix of products and services, but they must also focus on their long-term capabilities to develop or commercialize…"[33]

- Creativity and innovation can be constrained by cultural factors, in turn, inhibiting a country's ability to live up to its potential.
- To ensure economic development, countries should nurture creativity and innovation.
- Creativity is often described as technological, economic, and artistic innovation, but fundamentally it is the desire to express oneself.
- Creativity could be defined as the human mind conceiving new ideas and bringing them into being; there are six most prominent theories that define creativity.
- Innovation is defined as "the act of inventing new processes, products, services, or solutions that can be brought to market, implemented within an existing organization, or used to contribute value to society."[34]

Regardless of how an organization is structured, leadership with the help of Human Resources must find ways to manage both operations at the same time. Still on the dualism, O'Reilly and Tushman presented the concept of ambidextrous organization.[35] The vision of ambidextrous organization discusses the managerial challenge of looking at almost the same time to the past, depleting products, processes, organizational arrangements, and developed marketing (Exploitation) and for the future, exploring market opportunities and demands of consumers that are not yet met by the organization. On the one hand, it is needed to pay diligent attention to issues related to efficiency, such as reducing costs and

Figure 5.7 Disruptive innovation
Source: © iStock: Peshkova

incremental improvement of the quality of the mix of current products and services; on the other hand, managers need to identify threats to the business considered by O'Reilly as "emerging business". Looking at the bias of strategic planning in a more superficial way, one might think that this is macro-environment mapping, considering the matrix SWOT a possible threat. The point is that the SWOT matrix mapping could identify possible threats that were not detailed.

The vision of ambidextrous organization brings the understanding of the need to develop integrated management structures in exploitation (past) and exploration (future). It is considered, therefore, that ambidextrous organizations are those with organizational structures that address in an integrated way these two views that can be antagonistic. The ambidextrous organization was defined as one that has organizational structure with culture and resources with the focus on exploitation and exploration whose integration is the management.

It can be noticed that there is no sharing between structures, manufacturing, sales, and R&D. This is shown in Figure 5.8.

Creativity and innovation

The personal characteristics and ability of exploring and identifying ideas is defined as creativity.[36] Design can be described as the application of creativity in the relevant context of an issue. Knight defines innovation as "the adoption of a change, which is new to an organization and to the relevant environment."[37]

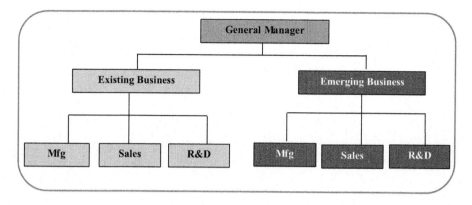

Figure 5.8 Ambidextrous organization

O'Reilly, C. A., & Tushman, M. L. (2004). The ambidextrous organization. Harvard Business Review, 82(4), 74–81, 140. Retrieved from www.ncbi.nlm.nih.gov/pubmed/15077368

All innovations aren't necessarily positive, however. We will focus on innovation as defined by Whyte, Bessant, and Neely: "the successful application of new ideas."[38] Design leads to innovation by bringing together user needs, form, and function in a new way. Innovation does not necessarily have to be technological; it can be in the realm of aesthetics, function, sustainability, reliability, or manufacturability. However, technology plays a key role in the modern design process. The computer and other tools are not only the medium in which many design activities are carried out, but also enable simulation and testing of concepts prior to production, thus speeding up the time to market for a product.

"Creativity and design can thus be linked to innovation as the first contributes to the expansion of available ideas and the second to increased chances of successfully commercializing these ideas."[39] The main difference between creativity and innovation is the outcome. Creativity is about the human mind conceiving new ideas. These ideas could show themselves in the form of something we can imagine, observe, hear, smell, touch, taste, and feel. It is not easy to measure creativity because it is a subjective matter; however, innovation is measurable and output oriented. Innovation is about making changes that lead to revised and different outcomes. It also deals with the work required to make an idea into a viable outcome. By identifying either an unrecognized, unmet, or prospective need, an individual or organization can innovate and use resources to design an appropriate practical solution and gain from its investment. Innovation is the applied knowledge that is preceded by invention and creation of a new product or approach of delivery. Innovation is required to keep the discovery relevant in light of changing times. However, not all inventive progress referred to as innovations end up succeeding.[40] Innovations do not happen in isolation.

Dubina, Carayannis, and Campbell (2012) state that mediums or intermediaries need to account for associated risks and offer distribution platforms to ensure that these novelties get the exposure in the marketplace; and, therefore, influence changes and make their contributions towards economic growth.[41] Innovations require market exposure to public and private institutions and their agents to become relevant and therefore influence economic development. These institutions serve to distribute risks associated with innovation and provide the necessary financial support in a manner that makes sustainable innovation

Figure 5.9 Design thinking

Source: © iStock: Radiokukka. George Kembels' (Co-Founder and Executive Director, Stanford) model from his discussion with Oliviero Toscani at the d.confestival in Potsdam 2012. NOVIS. (n.d.). Creativity, Design and Design Thinking. Retrieved December 16, 2018, from www.inovis.cc/innovation/ 68-creativity-design-and-design-thinking.

possible.[42] They are the intermediaries in facilitating active participation of innovations, an outcome that spurs economic growth.[43] Governance has a direct effect on the level of risks that a particular innovation encounters in its formation and implementation. Economic and environmental factors are associated with launching innovations and will impact its outcome.[44] Risk mitigation measures are characterized by economic policies and government protection measures that ensure the launching of innovations is met with minimal resistance in the marketplace.

For decades, innovation has been a key driver of competitiveness between the major cities in the United States. It is considered one of the most important factors underlying economic growth in today's global economy and is an important source of new technologies, products and services, industries, jobs, and income. Often people consider that innovation begins with a creative idea or the introduction of new technologies or methodologies, for example, the internet or Apple's iPhone and iPad. However, this is a common misconception as innovation does not actually begin with an idea of creating something new. A simple idea is nothing more than connecting two pieces of already known information together. A creative idea, however, is slightly different as it takes these existing elements and combines them in a new way. This may seem like the construction of a solution to a current need, but it cannot be considered innovation. One relevant vision of Amabile is the integrative vision between organizational innovation and individual creativity, shown in Figure 5.10.

Figure 5.10 Innovation
Source: © iStock: MF3d

It is important that a leader who is looking to promote improvement in an organization understands that innovation does not come from creative ideas, but rather proper information. In an organization, when a customer is faced with a specific need, the company will match that need to a technology that adequately addresses the problem. However, if that technology does not exist then innovation is required.

A leader who asks their team to brainstorm and come up with innovative ideas to satisfy the customer's need is operating inefficiently and does not understand the true concept of innovation. This is a common problem for many organizations. To be an innovative leader, they must stress to their employees to learn as much information about the problem as possible and to continuously ask questions. Asking questions forces individuals to think deeper and harder. Often times if organizations can figure out the true source of a need, they can effectively concentrate their research and development efforts to appropriately satisfy the customer.

To illustrate the process of innovation, let's review an example. Dr. Paap discussed that a person approached a company and asked them to find a way to reduce the wrinkles on their face. If one were to stop and think about what the true need of this request was, responses such as "to look younger" or "to feel more attractive" would probably come to mind. This was a great start to solving the problem because it gave the company information to work with. However, they needed more, so the employees began to ask more questions, digging deeper into what the root cause of the problem might be.

Costa Rican entrepreneur wins prize in global competition for clean energy

Citrus 3.0 is a Costa Rican project in which a system was created with aerobic bacteria that is capable of creating biodiesel from whey. This project started with a group of eight colleagues from the University of Costa Rica and the National University. It won first place in competitions like the Clean Tech Open held in California.

> David Garcia is one of the eight colleagues that created such innovative tech-
> nology. When asked about this project Garcia said,
>
> > the most important thing is to have perseverance and to believe in it. If the
> > idea is good and the test have already validated the performance, then you
> > must believe so other people will believe in you and your idea.
>
> This project and hard work of the group of individuals promotes and encourages
> us to never stop believing in ourselves. No matter what others say, if you believe in
> what you can do, others will support you and help you achieve your goals.
>
> Source: Costa Rica News (2013)[45]

Ultimately, the company found that the true problem was not actually to reduce the
size of their wrinkles, but simply the appearance of them. Wrinkles are visible because
of shadows caused by direct light on a particular area on the body. After the company
gathered this information, they were able to come together as a team and brainstorm
ideas for a new technology that reduced the appearance of wrinkles rather than the physical size. They ultimately created a form of makeup with microscopic mirrors imbedded
within it to reflect the pathways of light, reducing the presence of shadows. This is true
innovation. The solution came from a team who gathered as much information about the
problem as possible and came together focusing their efforts on the defined need. This
method is significantly more efficient than investing time and money into multiple ideas
hoping somebody comes up with a creative idea.

Innovation has become a global idea and many people, companies, and governments
are exploring it. Innovation is present in most, if not all, industries. Most people around
the world are beginning to understand the effects of innovation on their daily life. The
true meaning of international innovation is shown when governments display how their
innovation made the lives of people better. Strong and effective risk management policies serve to promote the implementation of innovation considering intellectual property
rights. Competition is a key factor for successful innovations because it will ensure that the
best ideas are given the chance to succeed. Open trade and investment for business and/or
financial environments ensures that innovations get the necessary support and guarantee
of success. Research and development infrastructure and resources will advance innovation
and therefore will have a positive influence on economic growth. Of course, government
and institutional commitment through funding and policy formulation are necessary.

Education is the cornerstone of creativity and innovation, and its role in sustainable
economic growth has been documented. Advancements in science and innovation will
create and nurture constant flow of ideas and technological knowledge to promote sustainable growth.[46] Transparent and efficient regulatory systems are needed to ensure the
implementation of innovations that adhere to the rule of law and are ethical.

Innovation has become the primary source of competitive advantage for companies
in all industries, driving efficiency and productivity. Recent history shows innovative
entrepreneurs who have created new products and services and therefore have changed
the economic, political, and social landscapes.

With the exponential growth of technology, its role in innovation has become increasingly important as a powerful driving force in innovative capacity. This is true in both the
evolution of innovation, as well as the way these innovations proliferate. Economic theory
revealed that labor, capital, and technology are the main drivers of production process.[47]

Assessing and understanding how to foster innovation are essential in defining the trajectory of a country's economic development (see Figure 5.11).

Innovation is the development of values through developing solutions that meet new requirements or needs. This is accomplished through the construction of better products, services, processes, technologies, or ideas. As we discussed, innovation differs from invention in that innovation refers to the use of a better, novel idea or method, whereas invention refers more directly to the creation of the idea or method itself (see Figure 5.12).

Innovation also differs from improvement in that innovation refers to the notion of doing something different rather than doing the same thing better. Tidd and Bessant

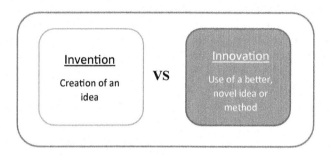

Figure 5.11 Invention vs innovation

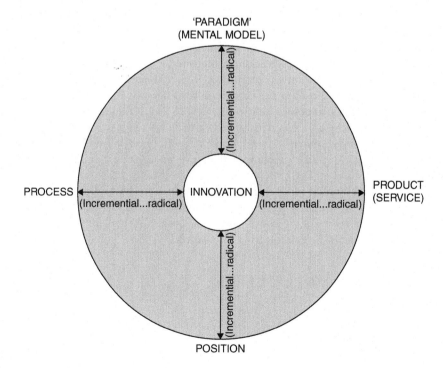

Figure 5.12 The 4Ps

discuss the 4Ps of innovation which are paradigm, process, products, and position.[48] Figure 5.12 describes the relationship between the 4Ps: paradigm, process, products, and position.

The importance of the human side is clear in both definitions of creativity and the different dimensions observed in innovation. It was decided to succinct the role of human resources in this next section, understanding that it is one of the connection points between creativity innovation and entrepreneurship.

Creative use of "Prime" model by Amazon

Despite Amazon's sigma-six tough workplace reputation, the company is a pioneer when it comes to creativity and innovation. The open secret to Amazon's success is the expansion upon their "Prime" model. CEO Jeff Bezos believes that the only way Amazon builds customer loyalty is by always offering the best deal, which the company made possible through Amazon Prime. Amazon's creativity in expansion of Amazon Prime and brand innovation in new industries has earned the company $100 billion in annual sales and stock that has skyrocketed over 300 percent over the past five years. There are 40–50 million Prime members in the United States alone. Although Amazon has a strict corporate work environment, there is no lack of creativity that has led to superior innovation within the company.

Source: Robischon (2017)[49]

Human Resources and innovation

The Human Resources departments within organizations play a significant role in fostering innovation. Over the last decade in business, the value of a well-functioning Human Resources department has significantly increased.

Along with organizing initiatives, recruiting high caliber talent, and structuring employee compensation, to list a few, the department has become responsible for aligning organizations appropriately to ensure long-term success. Promoting innovation has been a proven methodology to gain a competitive advantage. This process has since become a responsibility of Human Resources. "…HR leaders should strive to build and strengthen the unique set of organizational capabilities that give an organization its competitive advantage."[50]

A survey conducted by IBM for global Human Resource leaders indicates that driving creativity and innovation is one of the greatest challenges for businesses. The survey also pointed out that of a majority of the people surveyed, close to 70 percent felt that Human Resources play a significant role in fostering innovation.

Figure 5.13 Innovation and competitive advantage

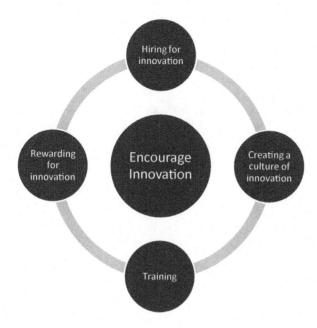

Figure 5.14 Encourage innovation

However, "71 percent said they don't use any screening tools designed to bring in creative and innovative candidates."[51] Additionally, it was shown that nearly 53 percent do not tie performance-management systems to even help promote or drive innovation. What this information is doing is showing leaders in Human Resources that the topic of innovation is an issue that truly matters to too many people, but initiatives are not taking place to do anything about it. Promoting innovation is much easier said than done.

There are three initiatives Human Resources professionals can adopt to help encourage continuous innovation within their organizations; hiring for innovation, creating a culture of innovation and training, and rewarding for innovation (see Figure 5.14).

One of the most crucial operations that Human Resources is responsible for is the recruitment and acquisition of talent for their firms. Innovation is created by people who have the ability to look at problems differently than others. If an organization has aspirations to become more pioneering, then efforts on recruiting individuals who carry the capabilities of innovation must be a top priority. They should recruit employees who ask questions, welcome coworkers' points of view, and are open-minded to new ideas. If Human Resources departments focus efforts on recruiting individuals who have these capabilities, then they will have built a solid foundation on which their companies can foster innovation.

Developing countries: structured for stagnation

In contrast to developed countries, the rest of the world must overcome both the inherent risk of innovation as well as significant obstacles posed by the local environment. Not

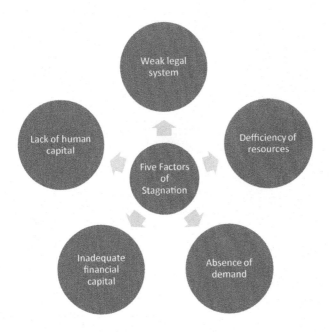

Figure 5.15 Factors of Stagnation

considering the issues of international trade, we have identified five Factors of Stagnation which create these barriers (Figure 5.15). They are: (1) a deficiency of resources, (2) absence of demand, (3) inadequate financial capital, (4) a lack of human capital, and (5) weak legal systems.

1. Deficiency of resources and infrastructure

Developing countries are often unable to innovate due to a lack of resources or infrastructure to bring their ideas to fruition. As mentioned earlier, developing countries typically lack modern technology or access to the internet. High-tech manufacturing centers, climate-controlled warehouses, or even modern office spaces can be entirely inaccessible. Many times, raw materials cannot be sourced locally and innovators do not have the network to overcome these obstacles. Due to natural disasters and extreme poverty, even finding clean drinking water can be a challenge. According to the UN News Centre, "Some 70 to 83 percentage of countries are reportedly falling significantly behind the trends required to meet their national targets for access to sanitation and drinking water, respectively."[52]

Further, certain innovations can never be effectively brought to market because there is an absence of complementary industries. For example, the country of Chad has one of the worst shortages of health care workers in the world, with only one doctor for every 20,000 people and four hospital beds for every 10,000 people. Because the health care industry is so underdeveloped, certain types of innovation which thrive in developed countries are unthinkable. There is no value in innovating new batteries for medical devices, because medical devices are so rarely purchased by hospitals. It's not feasible to create a software to manage medical records, because most doctor's offices don't have computers. Even inventing a new vaccine could be futile given a weak supply of syringes. Without complementary industries and resources, many types of innovation become nearly impossible to successfully create.

In addition, there is often a lack of infrastructure to support transportation. This can affect consumers' ability to travel to buy a product, an innovator's ability to coordinate an efficient supply chain, and the possibility of trading internationally. Latin America has struggled with this issue for decades.

> Until recently, investment in infrastructure actually had been declining as a percentage of GDP, from 4 percent of South America's GDP in 1980–85 to 2.3 percent of its GDP in 2007–08. The region's weak infrastructure has hurt its competitiveness in various respects, including productivity, international trade volume and foreign direct investment.[53]

- An invention becomes an innovation through: diffusion processes and adoption so that when the value of innovation is recognized, people decide to pay for it and so they make up the market.
- Disruptive innovation is a development that helps to form a new market and value network.
- The vision of ambidextrous organization brings the understanding of the need to develop integrated management structures, in exploitation (past) and exploration (future).
- "Creativity and design can thus be linked to innovation as the first contributes to the expansion of available ideas and the second to increased chances of successfully commercializing these ideas."[54]
- Innovation is the applied knowledge that is preceded by invention and creation of a new product or approach of delivery.
- Integrative vision between organizational innovation and individual creativity by Amabile shows the Organizational Innovation Model and Individual Creativity.

As a result, South America has the lowest proportion of paved roads out of any region in the world.

Kotschwar writes, "Latin America's greatest disadvantage, by far, is in railroads, an area in which the region has invested very little."[55] Brazil, Colombia, and Peru have specifically suffered due to a lack of ports and roads, making manufacturers reluctant to set up shop in non-urban areas of these countries. Innovation suffers when regional transportation costs are unreasonably high and there is no affordable way to bring your innovation to a large geographic market.

2. An absence of demand

As discussed earlier, innovation is primarily incentivized by the promise of future success and consumption. Without the presence of local demand, there is very little motivation to innovate. To illustrate, Karnani writes,

Half of the world's population on average needs to wear spectacles. But in India the penetration of eyeglasses is dramatically lower at only 7% because the poor do not have access to eyeglasses and/or cannot afford them. It is often concluded from this that there must be a huge business opportunity for a firm to market eyeglasses to the needy. The major flaw in this logic is that an unmet need does not constitute a market. A market exists only to the extent that there are buyers willing and able to pay a price higher than the total costs, including the opportunity cost of capital, of the sellers.[56]

In addition to being unable to pay for products, people in developing countries are often uneducated and unable to perceive value in new innovations. For example, if a scientist were to design a new type of eyeglass lens that could be customized to different types of astigmatisms, most impoverished individuals in India do not have the medical literacy to understand the value of the new innovation. The innovator would need to take on a significant marketing effort to educate the public on ophthalmology, which could quickly become expensive and eliminate any hope at a profit margin. Without an educated public capable of paying a fair price for products, there is little incentive for innovative ventures.

3. Inadequate financial capital

In most poor developing countries, finding wealthy investors to fund innovation is nearly impossible and because the governments are already strained under limited tax revenue, it's difficult for them to provide incentive programs. The UN reports that expenditures on innovation in most developing countries is in a much lower scale than in developed countries. Of course there are a few exceptions such as China, the Republic of Korea, and Singapore. In these Asian countries, innovation is aggressively funded by the government. However, for the rest of the developing countries, it's extremely difficult for aspiring entrepreneurs to find the funding to innovate.

4. Lack of human capital

Access to quality education is also sparse in developing countries. Tertiary or college-level education is very rare in developing countries, where they face a lack of funding, transportation, educational materials, building infrastructure, technological tools, and qualified professors.[57] In addition, local customs and traditions, particularly in the Middle East, prohibit female enrollment. This further limits the educational potential for a large segment of the population. Teaching methods are also often outmoded or the focus is more on theoretical ideas. The students, who are frequently unable to afford a textbook, must then transcribe the notes into a notebook, and those students who regurgitate a credible portion of their notes from memory achieve exam success. These passive approaches to teaching have little value in a world where creativity and flexibility have premium. Creativity, critical thinking, and mental agility are at the heart of all innovation.

Without companies like Uber or Netflix to employ and excite those in developing countries who beat all odds to become skilled and well-educated, "brain drain" tends to occur.

Joseph Stiglitz defines this concept by saying, "Without appropriate jobs, developing countries will lose this much-needed intellectual capital, their brightest children, in whom they have invested enormously through elementary and secondary education and sometimes even through college, to developed countries."[58]

- Promoting innovation has been a proven methodology to gain a competitive advantage, the process of which is a responsibility of Human Resources.
- There are three initiatives Human Resource professionals can adopt to help encourage continuous innovation within their organizations: hiring for innovation, creating a culture of innovation and training, and rewarding for innovation.
- In developing countries, we have identified five Factors of Stagnation which create barriers posed by the local environment: (1) a deficiency of resources, (2) absence of demand, (3) inadequate financial capital, (4) a lack of human capital, and (5) weak legal systems.

At an alarming rate, developing countries are losing their skilled labor to developed countries like the United States and Canada, who accept them under skilled worker Visas. However, in many cases it's hard to blame the migrants. They have a much larger chance at success in their destination countries and are more likely to find other bright thinkers with whom to collaborate and hire as employees. Brain drain benefits developed countries even further.

Ngoma and Ismail write,

> …it was established that brain drain raised the education and income levels of the destination countries at the expense of the source countries… In addition, when labor productivity and wages depends on the average level of human capital, voluntary skilled migration lowers the average level of human capital and productivity performance in the source countries.[59]

It's clear that brain drain negatively affects the innovators in developing countries, along with their potential employees (or employees of their supply chain).

5. Weak legal systems

In developing countries, legal systems that protect innovators often do not exist, are poorly formed, or are not properly enforced. Among others, these systems include property law, contract law, and IP law. It's nearly impossible to incentivize innovation or entrepreneurship when the population is rightfully worried about a neighbor stealing their inventory or a debtor having no legal obligation to repay them. Cooter writes,

> Written contract law in poor countries mostly resembles written contract law in rich countries…The writing is similar, but its application is dissimilar.
>
> Applied law is weakened by high court fees that discourage meritorious suits, low court fees that encourage meritless suits, long delays in trials, formalistic proceedings, the absence of streamlined courts for small claims, judges who are corrupt or politicized, and clumsy procedures to execute court judgments by corrupt officials.[60]

The judges in developing countries are frequently appointed arbitrarily or based on social status, and have no real training of the law. As a result, legal statutes are upheld in an inconsistent, inefficient manner with much bias. High-income countries tend to have shorter legal delays and quicker judgments compared to low-income countries.

Figure 5.16 Google campus
Source: Image by Niharb on flickr

Creative work space

Google is the frontrunner in building whacky workplaces that promote creativity within the company. Stories of Google's pool tables, bowling alleys, free food, gym memberships, and colorful décor are well-known, which means every year, Google gets their thousands of applicants for openings in their offices. Google's Chief Happiness Officer boasts that these creative workplaces keep employees happy, productive, loyal, and motivated, which drives innovation for the company. More and more companies are following Google's lead by engaging employees in creative activities through fun and social breakrooms and through excursions or classes that teach their employees new creative skills (see Figure 5.16).

Source: Coleman (2016)[61]

It's often impossible for impoverished individuals to afford legal counsel or court fees in the first place.[62]

Even if an entrepreneur is able to sue a business partner for breach of contract, the chances of them being "made whole" are slight. Cooter continues,

Collecting damages from poor people is impractical. People in poverty do not have the money to pay damages, or the little money that they have is easily hidden, or they work informally without any records of their earnings, or they have no bank accounts where wages can be garnished, or their property cannot be separated from the property of their relatives.[63]

The legal systems in developing countries are inefficient and impractical when compared to rich countries like the United States where the threat of being sued or prosecuted typically keeps businesses and individuals playing by the rules.

This issue is especially pertinent in the former Soviet nations of Eastern Europe. Transitioning from communist control, these countries had a somewhat developed judicial system with courts and judges, but it had only ever operated in the interest of the state. In other words, there was no precedent of a legal system truly intended to protect individuals or private enterprises.

Development and innovation

Innovation is traditionally considered to be a function of creativity and curiosity to find new or different solutions. Organizations and companies tend to conceive of innovation as a function of their Research and Development (R&D) departments and allocate funding for it. Recently (November 30, 2011) the European Commission allocated 3 percent of their total budget to R&D to kick-start innovation in the Framework for research and innovation called "Horizon 2020".

Innovation results from organizational learning as much as from R&D. It also always involves investment in developing skills and knowledge. Therefore, analyzing a country's total expenditure on R&D as a percentage of its total GDP (R&D intensity) can be a good indicator of its innovation level. Increased investment in R&D may originate from a variety of reasons, for instance, an increasing number of skilled workforces, and the opening up of new-technology enterprises.

Scientists must be free to learn, to speak and to challenge

"You do not mess with something so fundamental, so precious, as science," says Kirsty Duncan, Canada's first Minister of Science. In a heartfelt, inspiring talk about pushing boundaries, she makes the case that researchers must be free to present uncomfortable truths and challenge the thinking of the day – and that we all have a duty to speak up when we see science being stifled or suppressed.

You can check in more details in the full TED Talk in this link: www.ted.com/talks/kirsty_duncan_scientists_must_be_free_to_learn_to_speak_and_to_challenge

Innovation undeniably plays a key role as one of the critical roots that determines the willingness of organizations to spend on R&D. For example, Morocco, Spain and China had higher total expenditure on R&D as a percentage of its total GDP in 2011, at the range from 1.0 percent to 1.9 percent. This indicates that Spain and China have a higher innovation level than Morocco.

Innovation has been a strong indicator for long-term economic growth as it creates opportunities for tomorrow's jobs. Fundamentally speaking, there are two ways to increase output on an economy (see Figure 5.17).

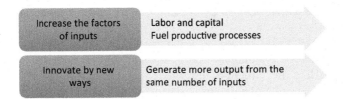

Figure 5.17 Factors of input

The second point is where innovation can play a role in the growth of an economy. In this capacity, technology is one factor of innovation aiding the development of economies.

In order to invest in technology, a culture of innovation is a necessity. Data lies at the heart of appropriate decision-making. The ability to make decisions faster based on relevant information as well as the ability to provide the right messages to the right customers would lead to competitive advantage for the firm. Business processes will evolve by using sensors, and computational power will expand to gather information at every step of the supply chain and evolution and application of artificial intelligence.[64] These technological innovations thus pave the way for development. However, so far, most of the benefits have been gained by educated workforces in developed countries.

In addition to cultural factors, there is also organizational structure that impacts innovation. The first challenge is to reduce economic hardship. With the great need to improve welfare and living conditions of their population, a country needs to balance the allocation of resources aimed at the basic necessities of its citizens against the needs of the newly emerging knowledge workers. Improving the standing of impoverished citizens in developing countries should rightfully take priority. However, lack of opportunity and poor policy choices for those who do have access to higher education has a causal effect on the emigration of the very resources that are able to innovate and effect change.[65]

For a country to be viewed as a competitor in the global economy, innovation should be seen relative to the local context, and capitalize on the unique cultural advantages that the country offers. By identifying strengths and turning them into economic advantages, the country can position itself for success.[66] Each country needs to identify strengths and develop an innovation strategy.

A culture that has some barriers to innovation can be influenced by public policy. Innovation policies have to blend new and old cultural paradigms while still respecting traditional values and ways of doing business. These new cultural patterns should correct some of the more problematic areas while preserving cultural strengths.[67] For example, Morocco does not have formal education or innovation systems in place and faces significant challenges to innovate.

Conclusion

We have presented factors that influence creativity and innovations. The examples of cultural factors in China, Spain, and Morocco that played an important role in the ability to innovate were analyzed. As a developed nation, Spain's focus is on fostering the development and exchange of ideas as a function of corporate process.

As developing nations, China and Morocco are not as far down the path and emphasize creative problem-solving and market development rather than the creation of radically new ideas. There is a clear positive relationship between innovation and economic standing and innovation and culture. Culture comes from its history and form of government. Some culture promotes innovation while others do not. However, economic growth requires innovations of some sort to stay competitive. As discussed earlier, there is an undeniable relationship between the study of Hofstede dimensions and innovations; the four dimensions provide an approximate measurement of innovative level. Nonetheless, this does not conclude that a country or a company has to model its culture differently to promote economic growth. Different companies in the same industry and country may have different cultures and thrive equally.

The definition of innovation is covering a wide range, which includes both improvements in technology and better methods of doing things. It can also manifest in product changes, process changes, new approaches to do business, new forms of distribution, and new conceptions of scope.

However, we know that one size does not fit all. Business innovation is becoming a central research topic in management. Based on the relationship between Hofstede's Cultural Dimensions and innovation, it will help the company to provide an environment for continuous, collaborative "what if" modeling. It will also help the company to increase the ability of adapting to change. To add value in today's rapidly changing, increasingly complex, and global business environment, the management system must be able to quickly adapt to all kinds of change. Such changes include organizational, market, competitive, and regulatory change.

Discussion questions

1. Do culture characteristics impact creativity and innovation in a society?
2. Define creativity and innovation.
3. What are the predominant types of innovation?
4. What are the 4Ps of innovation?
5. Could micro or macro factors impact creativity and innovation?

Case study – continued

Al Capizza: a creative and unique pizza restaurant, São Paulo, Brazil

World pizza market

The world market for pizza is valued at $128 billion as of 2017. Market growth rates for the 2017–2020 period is projected to exceeded the GDP rate in all of the regions that can be verified, whether they be developed markets (the United States, UE) or the emerging markets (Latin America, Africa, Russia, and China).

In the emerging and developing markets, especially, growth is forecast to be in the double digits. Latin America forecast a 45.1 percent increase in market sales (see Figure 5.16). There is a good potential for increase revenues but it is a very

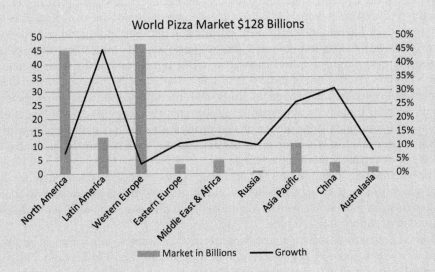

Figure 5.18 Forecast 2017–2020 world pizza market

Source: Euromonitor for pmq.com

competitive market. According to pmq.com, the main players in terms of market share, as of 2014 were: Pizza Hut (14.79 percent), Domino's (9.86 percent), Little Caesars (7.85 percent), and Papa John's (6.45 percent). All together taking over 40 percent of the market among themselves.

Brazil world market share

The Brazilian pizza market is the second largest in the world, coming second only to the United States' pizza market in terms of revenue. With a turnover of more than BRL 20 billion a year, the market remains highly fragmented. The city of São Paulo by itself has over 6,000 pizzerias and consumes about 700,000 pizzas a day. Michael and Sony, realizing the potential and also the absence of "The Big Four" of the world ranking pizzerias, have plans to expand their presence in Brazil. In this context, Sony installed the very first Al Capizza in São Paulo, with the aim of generating a model of franchise (chain).

Customer behavior research

Both Sony and Michael understand the millennials' "technological" demands, and also their love for pizza. Having researched in-depth the trends of consumption, they found that nearly 41 percent of millennials now eat pizza once a week, a big jump from 26 percent in 2017. The following are key findings of the Technomic's 2016 Pizza Consumer Trend Report:

- Pizza is the number 1 favorite comfort food, earning twice as many votes as any other dish. (Take that, chocolate!)
- The pizza industry, in fact, forged ahead in the past year, even with the presence of independents who are bound to decades of proud tradition. Pizza makers are

slow to adopt newer technologies and continued to lag behind other chains in the food industry.

- The signs point to modest growth in this segment, with fast-casual chains leading the charge with the availability of online ordering technology and third-party delivery.
- According to research done by PMQ Pizza Magazine, 63 percent of self-identified "pizza lovers" are women. The average consumer is now health conscious and works out twice a week. This change reflects the broader movement among the population to live a healthier, more balanced lifestyle.
- The 80 million millennials buying pizza are expected to outspend baby boomers by 2017. Not only do they look for the healthier options, they also consider themselves as "foodies" – interested in the experience of eating more than the sustenance. They love custom, build-your-own pizzas with interesting and unique tastes, textures, and ingredients. And they like to talk about their food online.
- Today's consumers have developed a social consciousness towards the brands they connect with. They feel good about supporting establishments that focus on sustainability and natural ingredients. Companies like Pizza Hut have announced a commitment to reduce their energy and water consumption and have begun using more environmentally friendly packaging.

Considering trends for the next five years, in 2016, the brothers Sony and Michael invested $1 million to create the concept of Al Capizza: pizza to be more convenient, healthier, and fairly priced, and aligned to the trends of the world markets. Competition has ceased to be local and has become global. The use of manufacturing and transportation techniques combined with information technologies, especially social networks and mobile ordering software (mobile commerce), became the basis of Al Capizza's business model.

New Case – Innovation for P. 1–3.

The new concept developed by the Corleone brothers does not give up on the quality and freshness of the ingredients, and innovates deeply with ordering procedures (90 percent online) and in the process of assembling the pizza.

The business model

"If the pizza is for delivery, you cannot get to the customer's house dismantled because the cheese went all to one side, leaving the rest of the pizza uncovered", Michael points out.

The family have always insisted on quality as being a differentiating factor of all their pizzerias. And to prove this point the new unit improvised on the traditional L-shaped restaurant to be assembled with clear glass. Now, all customers who pass by the street of the pizzeria can see the workings of the kitchen. This concept was baptized by "Pizza Aquarium" (Fish bowl), something that on the outside sees everything that happens inside. The model store opened in February 2017.

Around 90 percent of orders are generated through digital channels such as WhatsApp, Social Networks, and Third-Party Order Aggregators. Total cumulative revenue is $1.2 million with a monthly net profit margin of 7.5 percent on average. Revenue ramp up more than twice the projection set in the Business Plan (see Figure 5.19). As of July 2017, the financial results of the model store reached the same revenue achieved by the pizzeria in Blumenau in the same July 2017 (which has 16 years of market). Customer satisfaction is measured by the digital ordering channel ranging from 1 to 5. Customers evaluate on four dimensions: delivery time, packaging, food, and price/benefit. There have been 1,600 evaluations so far and the average score for each item is 4.5, so Al Capizza's average rates 4.5 on digital ordering channel. All complaints and suggestions are answered by Michael (one of the partners).

Future plans

The brothers, Sony and Michael, want more. They intend to open 100 units of Al Capizza in Brazil in the next five years. At the same time, in one year they intend to open the first five units in the United States. On the other hand, Domino's announced that it intends to open 500 new Domino's units in Brazil in the next five years. When interviewed, the brothers said that the more Domino's expands, the better it will be for the pizza market as others will need to do their homework. They felt that "The pizza market has invested little in technology. In general, only the large chains of pizzerias have observed the need to innovate both in relation to the customer and in relation to the gastronomy involved." Brothers Sony and Michael intend to invest in R & D, about 5% of their financial revenue to strengthen their digital presence, totem terminals and food technology. It is expected that in 10 years, they will have the same reach as some big four chains, which took 50 years to achieve.

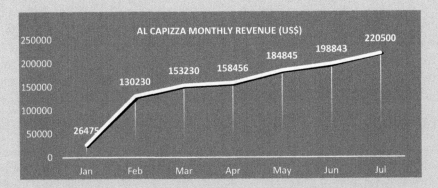

Figure 5.19 Income February/2017 to August/2017

Source: Al Capizza, Brazil/2017

Table 5.2 Key terms

Creativity	Radical, modular and architectural innovation
Prominent theories on creativity	Disruptive innovation
Innovation	Dualism
Knowledge	Intellectual Property (IP)

Questions for discussion

1. What is the creativivity and the innovation of Al Capizza? Do these differentiations provide competitive advantages for them?
2. What is the role of the "Pizza Acquarium" concept in Al Capizza's business model? In your opinion how will the millennials perceive this?
3. What are the roles of information and communication technologies in the success of Al Capizza as a startup?
4. Analyze the arguments about millennials demand for different services.
5. Provide a roadmap of how Al Capizza could compete globally.

Notes

1 Marcus, A., & Gould, E. W. (2000). Crosscurrents: cultural dimensions and global web user-interface design. Interactions ACM, 7(4), 32–46. https://doi.org/10.1145/345190.345238

2 Hollanders, H., & Van Cruysen, A. (2009). Design, creativity and innovation: a scoreboard approach. Pro Inno Europe, Inno Metrics, 26.

3 Whyte, J., Bessant, J. R., & Neely, A. D. (2005). Management of creativity and design within the firm. UK Department of Trade and Industry, 2005.

4 Lee, S. K. (2008, June 7). Optimum Performance Technologies. Retrieved December 16, 2018, from http://optimumperformancetechnologies.blogspot.com/2008/06/organisational-creativity-top-10.html.

5 Amabile, T. M. (1988). A model of creativity and innovation in organizations. Research in Organizational Behavior, 10, 123. Retrieved from http://web.mit.edu/curhan/www/docs/Articles/15341_Readings/Group_Performance/Amabile_A_Model_of_CreativityOrg.Beh_v10_pp123-167.pdf.

6 Puccio, G. J., & Cabra, J. F. (2010). Organizational creativity: a systems approach. The Cambridge Handbook of Creativity (p. 508). Cambridge University Press. https://doi.org/10.1017/CBO9780511763205

7 Kaufman, J. C., & Sternberg, R. J. (2010). The Cambridge handbook of creativity. International Journal (p. 508). Cambridge University Press. https://doi.org/10.1017/CBO9780511763205

8 Woodman, R. W., Sawyer, J. E., & Griffin, R. W. (1993). Toward a theory of organizational creativity. The Academy of Management Review, 18(2), 293. https://doi.org/10.2307/258761

9 Willis, R. (2014, December 17). Creativity vs Innovation! Retrieved December 16, 2018, from www.linkedin.com/pulse/creativity-innovation-robert-willis.

10 Anderson, N., Potočnik, K., & Zhou, J. (2014). Innovation and creativity in organizations. Journal of Management, 40(5), 1297–1333. https://doi.org/10.1177/0149206314527128

11 Amabile, T. M. (1997). Motivating creativity in organizations: on doing what you love and loving what you do. California Management Review, 40(1), 39–58.

12 Puccio, G. J., Cabra, J. F., Fox, J. M., & Cahen, H. (2010, May 1). Creativity on demand: historical approaches and future trends, 24(2), 153–159.

13 Manchester Metropolitan University. (2017). Engage Week timetable of events 3rd–7th July. Retrieved December 16, 2018, from www.mmu.ac.uk/staff/docs/MMU2286_Engage-week-2017-V7.pdf.

14 Anokhin, S., Grichnik, D., & Hisrich, R. D. (2008). The journey from novice to serial entrepreneurship in China and Germany: are the drivers the same? Managing Global Transitions, 6, 117–142.

15 Dejardin, M. (2000). Entrepreneurship and economic growth: an obvious conjunction? The Institute for Development Strategies, (November), 1–14. Retrieved from http://econwpa.repec.org/eps/dev/papers/0110/0110010.pdf.

16 Holcombe, R. (1998). Entrepreneurship and economic growth. The Quarterly Journal of Economics. https://doi.org/10.1177/097135570801700202

17 Gries, T., & Naudé, W. (2009). Entrepreneurship and regional economic growth: towards a general theory of start-ups. Innovation: The European Journal of Social Science Research, 22(3), 309–328. https://doi.org/10.1080/13511610903354877

18 Gries, Thomas & Naude, Wim. (2008). Entrepreneurship and regional economic growth: towards a general theory of start-ups. Innovation The European Journal of Social Science Research, 22. 10.1080/13511610903354877.

19 Fitzgerald, E., Wankerl, A., & Schramm, C. (2011). Inside real innovation: how the right approach can move ideas from R&D to market — and get the economy moving. WORLD SCIENTIFIC. https://doi.org/10.1142/7985

20 Schumpeter, Joseph A. (1911). The Theory of Economic Development, Routledge, https://doi.org/10.4324/9781315135564

21 Rogers, E. M. (2010). Diffusion of innovations. Recorded Books, Inc. Retrieved from www.simonandschuster.com/books/Diffusion-of-Innovations-4th-Edition/Everett-M-Rogers/9781451602470.

22 Henderson, R. M., & Clark, K. B. (1990). Architectural innovation: the reconfiguration of existing product technologies and the failure of established firms. Administrative Science Quarterly, 35(1), 9. https://doi.org/10.2307/2393549

23 Bower, J. L., & Christensen, C. (1995). Disruptive technologies: catching the wave. Harvard Business Review, 73(1), 43–53.

24 Christensen, C. (2013). The Innovator's Dilemma: When New Technologies Cause Great Firms to Fail (Management of Innovation and Change) eBook: Clayton Christensen: Amazon.com.br: Loja Kindle. Harvard Business Review Press.

25 Christensen, C. M. (2006). The ongoing process of building a theory of disruption. Journal of Product Innovation Management, 23(1), 39–55. https://doi.org/10.1111/j.1540-5885.2005.00180.x

26 Christensen, C. M., Bohmer, R., & Kenagy, J. (2000). Will disruptive innovation cure health care? Harvard Business Review, (October), 102–112. https://doi.org/10.1016/0002-9610(92)90118-B

27 Christensen, C. M., Grossman, J. H., & Hwang, J. (2009). The Innovator's Prescription : A Disruptive Solution for Health Care. McGraw-Hill.

28 Christensen, C. M., & Overdorf, M. (2000). Meeting the challenge of disruptive change. Harvard Business Review, March–April), 1–10. https://doi.org/10.1002/rwm3.20019

29 infoDev. (2014). infoDev Annual Report 2012-2013. Retrieved from www.infodev.org/annual-report.

30 Hydroponics Kenya. (n.d.). About Us. Retrieved December 16, 2018, from http://hydroponicskenya.com/about-us/.

31 Christensen, C. (2012, October 23). Disruptive Innovation. Retrieved December 16, 2018, from www.claytonchristensen.com/key-concepts/.

32 Paap, J., & Katz, R. (2004). Anticipating disruptive innovation. Research-Technology Management, 47(5), 13–22. https://doi.org/10.1080/08956308.2004.11671647

33 Paap, J., & Katz, R. (2004). Anticipating disruptive innovation. Research-Technology Management, 47(5), 13–22. https://doi.org/10.1080/08956308.2004.11671647

34 Shaver, E. (2014). The Many Definitions of Innovation. Retrieved from www.ericshaver.com/the-many-definitions-of-innovation/

35 O'Reilly, C. A., & Tushman, M. L. (2004). The ambidextrous organization. Harvard Business Review, 82(4), 74–81, 140. Retrieved from www.ncbi.nlm.nih.gov/pubmed/15077368.

36 Whyte, J., Bessant, J. R., & Neely, A. D. (2005). Management of Creativity and Design within the Firm. UK Department of Trade and Industry.

37 Knight, K. E. (1967). A descriptive model of the intra-firm innovation process. The Journal of Business. The University of Chicago Press. https://doi.org/10.1086/295013

38 Whyte, J., Bessant, J. R., & Neely, A. D. (2005). Management of Creativity and Design Within the Firm. UK Department of Trade and Industry,

39 Hollanders, H., & Vvan Cruysen, A. (2009). Design, creativity and innovation: a scoreboard approach. Pro Inno Europe, Inno Metrics, 26.

40 Lazzeretti, L. (2012). Creative Industries and Innovation in Europe: Concepts, Measures and Comparative Case Studies. Routledge. Retrieved from www.routledge.com/Creative-Industries-and-Innovation-in-Europe-Concepts-Measures-and-Comparative/Lazzeretti/p/book/9780203112571.

41 Dubina, I. N., Carayannis, E. G., & Campbell, D. F. J. (2012). Creativity economy and a crisis of the economy? Coevolution of knowledge, innovation, and creativity, and of the knowledge economy and knowledge society. Journal of the Knowledge Economy, 3(1), 1–24. https://doi.org/10.1007/s13132-011-0042-y

42 Howells, J., & Bessant, J. (2012). Introduction: Innovation and economic geography: a review and analysis. Journal of Economic Geography, 12(5), 929–942. https://doi.org/10.1093/jeg/lbs029

43 Batten, D. F. (1995). Network cities: creative urban agglomerations for the 21st century. Urban Studies, 32(2), 313–327. https://doi.org/10.1080/00420989550013103

44 Krätke, S. (2012). The Creative Capital of Cities: Interactive Knowledge Creation and the Urbanization Economies of Innovation. Wiley.

45 Costa Rica News. (2013, November 27). Costa Rican Entrepreneur Wins Prize Global Competition Clean Energy. Retrieved December 16, 2018, from www.mycostaricanews.com/costa-rican-entrepreneur-wins-prize-global-competition-clean-energy/.

46 Lebel, C., Walker, L., Leemans, A., Phillips, L., & Beaulieu, C. (2008). Microstructural maturation of the human brain from childhood to adulthood. Neuroimage, 1044–1055. Retrieved from www.ncbi.nlm.nih.gov/pubmed/18295509

47 Krugman, P. R., Wells, R., & Graddy, K. J. (2013). Essentials of Economics (3rd ed.). Worth Publishers.

48 Tidd, J., & Bessant, J. R. (2009). Managing Innovation: Integrating Technological, Market and Organizational Change. Wiley.

49 Robischon, N. (2017, October 11). Why Amazon is the World's Most Innovative Company of 2017. Retrieved December 16, 2018, from www.fastcompany.com/3067455/why-amazon-is-the-worlds-most-innovative-company-of-2017.

50 Stanleigh, M. (n.d.). Innovation: A Strategic HR Imperative. Retrieved July 13, 2015, from https://bia.ca/innovation-a-strategic-hr-imperative/.

51 Stanleigh, M. (n.d.). Innovation: A Strategic HR Imperative. Retrieved July 13, 2015, from https://bia.ca/innovation-a-strategic-hr-imperative/.

52 UN News. (2012). Lack of resources threatens water and sanitation supplies in developing countries – UN. Retrieved from https://news.un.org/en/story/2012/04/408532-lack-resources-threatens-water-and-sanitation-supplies-developing-countries-un

53 Field, A. M. (2013). Infrastructure in South America: Fits and Starts. Retrieved from www.joc.com/international-trade-news/infrastructure-news/south-america/infrastructure-south-america-fits-and-starts_20130319.html.

54 UN News. (2012). Lack of resources threatens water and sanitation supplies in developing countries – UN. Retrieved from https://news.un.org/en/story/2012/04/408532-lack-resources-threatens-water-and-sanitation-supplies-developing-countries-un

55 Kotschwar, B. (2012). Transportation and communication infrastructure in Latin America: lessons from Asia. Peterson Institute for International Economics, (April).

56 Karnani, A. (2010). Selling to the poor. World Financial Review, 30–37.

57 World Bank Group. (2017). Education Public Expenditure Review Guidelines. Retrieved from http://documents.worldbank.org/curated/en/155861497609568842/pdf/116334-REVISED-Education-PER-Guidelines.pdf

58 Stiglitz, J. E. (2006). Stability with Growth: Macroeconomics, Liberalization and Development. Oxford University Press.

59 Ngoma, A. L., & Ismail, N. W. (2013). The impact of brain drain on human capital in developing countries. South African Journal of Economics, 81(2), 211–224. https://doi.org/10.1111/saje.12014

60 Cooter, R. (2008). Doing what you say: contracts and economic development. Alabama Law Review, 59(4), 1107–1133.

61 Coleman, A. (2016, February 11). Is Google's model of the creative workplace the future of the office? The Guardian. Retrieved from www.theguardian.com/careers/2016/feb/11/is-googles-model-of-the-creative-workplace-the-future-of-the-office.

62 Cooter, R. (2008). Doing what you say: contracts and economic development. Alabama Law Review, 59(4), 1107–1133.

63 Cooter, R. (2008). Doing what you say: contracts and economic development. Alabama Law Review, 59(4), 1107–1133.

64 Future Work Skills 2020. Retrieved from www.iftf.org/futureworkskills/

65 Djeflat, A. (2005). Innovation Systems and Knowledge Economy in North Africa: New Opportunity for Innovation Take Off? Third GLOBELICS Conference. Pretoria: South Africa: October–November.

66 Aubert, J. E. (2005). Promoting innovation in developing countries: a conceptual framework. World Bank Policy Research Working Paper (3554).

67 Aubert, J. E. (2005). Promoting innovation in developing countries: a conceptual framework. World Bank Policy Research Working Paper (3554).

Part III
The organization

6 Institutions, governance, and strategy

Learning objectives:

1. *Learn the definition of institutions, governance, and strategy*
2. *Understand why appropriate institutions are necessary for nurturing an entrepreneurial ecosystem*
3. *Examine the role of governance for a well-functioning business environment*
4. *Discuss the relationship between corporate governance and institutions*
5. *Analyze why business strategy is necessary for sustainable growth*

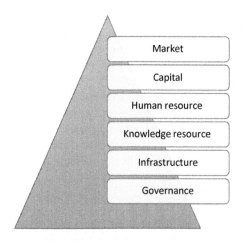

Market

Capital

Human resource

Knowledge resource

Infrastructure

Governance

Figure 6.1 Challenges

Micro and macro startup challenges facing Iran

In this case, many aspects of institutions, governance, and strategy have been highlighted for the country, Iran. In an article by Alireza Jozi, the entrepreneurial and startup ecosystem challenges of Iran are analyzed.[1] In this study of Iran's startup ecosystem, he has identified the challenges into six different categories: Market challenges, Capital challenges, Human Resource challenges, Knowledge resource challenges, Governance challenges, and Infrastructure challenges. These sets of micro, macro, and cultural challenges also exist for most developing countries.

1. **Market challenges**
   a. Startups don't have ambitions to target the international market (though Iran's market is already large)
   b. Sanctions! Meaning no easy and direct way to access the international market
2. **Capital challenges**
   a. Not enough funding in seed-stage startups
3. **Human Resource challenges**
   a. Talent exists, but not the ones startups are looking for
   b. Not enough lawyers experienced in startup legal structures
   c. Huge brain drain rate (talents leaving the country)
4. **Knowledge resource challenges**
   a. Not enough opportunities for private sector involvement in academia
   b. Limited university curriculum in startups and tech entrepreneurship
   c. Not enough investment in R&D

Continued at the end of the chapter…

Introduction

It is important to understand the essential role that institutions and governance play on the development of sustainable growth. Also, it is essential to develop strategies at the micro and macro levels. These are key elements for creating transparent and sustainable organizations which are indispensable for entrepreneurial activities that drive the country's development. The entrepreneurial activities in society will flourish under good governance and having relevant supporting institutions that make the rules and regulations. Regardless of the past and current scenario, having a futuristic strategy is necessary for any country. These strategies are a roadmap containing plan-of-action for reaching a certain outcome. In this chapter, we will present definitions and applications of institutions, governance, and strategy, and their relationship with entrepreneurial activities.

Institution definition

The institution is defined as the rules of the game that shape human interaction. However, institutions are not external to human action; they have a reflexive relationship with human interaction.[2] Clear and transparent rules that are applied equally to all lead to better quality institutions and institutional quality holds the key to prevailing patterns of prosperity around the world.[3]

Developed nations are those where institutions allow investors to feel secure about their property rights, have prevailing laws, and have monetary and fiscal policies that are grounded in solid macroeconomic institutions. They also contain risk mediating policies and the country's citizens have civil liberties and participate in government.[4]

Formal institutions (such as regulations, policies, and sanctions), as well as informal institutions (such as norms and values), need to be considered in development. For example, research in the sociology of culture has documented that communism has left a heavy print on the informal institutions in the transition countries which are not quite conducive to entrepreneurial activity.[5] Baumol was among the first ones to pay due diligence to the idea that institutions could represent an obstacle to entrepreneurial activity.

He further emphasized the importance of the institutional environment on the attitudes and propensities for new business endeavors.[6]

Recently the concept has been examined by a number of economists including McMillan and Woodruff, who found that if an entrepreneur does not have the needed trust in the court's rulings and inability to enforce contracts efficiently, his or her entrepreneurial spirit deteriorates leading to a negative effect on employment growth. Nevertheless, distrust in the judicial institutions of a country could have a degrading effect not only on entrepreneurial activity but also on the business environment overall, leading to a decrease in new investment levels and entrepreneurial confidence.[7,8]

Figure 6.2 Judicial reform
Source: © iStock: jerry2313

In 2002, the Pakistani government implemented a judicial reform that cost $350 million, or 0.1 percent of Pakistan's 2002 GDP. This reform did not involve increased incentives for judges to improve efficiency, but merely provided them with more training. Nonetheless, the reform had dramatic effects on judicial efficiency and consequently on entrepreneurship: judges disposed of a quarter more cases and entry rate of new firms increased by half due to the reform. Using data from the World Bank Group Entrepreneurship Database, estimates suggest that this translates into an increase of Pakistan's GDP by 0.5 percent.

Source: Chemin (2009)[9]

Many authors indicated that Institutional characteristics that are most prescribed to affect the entrepreneurial environment in a country are as follows.[10,11,12] Property rights, as an institutional indicator for entrepreneurial ventures, are essential to the business environment not only because they encompass a certain social security of the status quo, but also because they comprise the "find and keep" component, which is vital for the entrepreneurship aspects associated to discovery, innovation, and creation of new resources, all of which also impacts the entrepreneurial activity in low- and middle-income economies.[13,14] Acemoglu and Johnson (2005), for example, illustrate the direct impact of property rights institutions on investment, financial development, and long-term economic growth, all of which have a considerable impact on the business environment and entrepreneurship.[15]

Political systems and class struggles influence the process of law formulation and, thus, shape institutional order which later on sets the framework for economic activity and entrepreneurship.[16,17] The informal institutions (e.g., social norms and culture) also influence the business environment in a given country to a high extent by shaping the structure of corporate governance on the micro level.[18] Therefore, the interdependency between the micro and macro levels is well-established as they are interconnected and influence each other to a high extent. This is why governmental efficiency and institutions' effectiveness lay the foundations for successful entrepreneurial strategy.

Conditions for entrepreneurial success

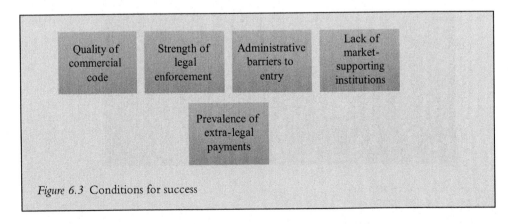

Figure 6.3 Conditions for success

Figure 6.4 Communism
Source: iStock: btgbtg

The communist heritage left a particular legacy of serious institutional weakness, especially with respect to entrepreneurial activity and that could be due to a centrally planned economy controlled by government through production and policies, and incentives and rewards. However, it seems it has been real improvements to entrepreneurial activity, especially in the European Union Accession economies such as Poland in recent years.

Source: Adekoya (2014)[19]

Estrin and Mickiewicz (2011) argue that transitional economies, such as the former Soviet Union and Central and Eastern Europe, have lower rates of entrepreneurial activity and business development due to the legacy of communist planning, which, according to them, needs to be substituted with formal market-supporting institutions.

Furthermore, they claim that even though most of this transition has already occurred, entrepreneurship levels have not increased in some of these countries. According to Estrin and Mickiewicz the main culprit for this is the so-called "lack of institutional memory" due to the prolonged Soviet rule. They argue that the lack of generalized trust in these transition economies also contributes to the low levels of entrepreneurial entry. The phenomenon of "insider entrepreneurship" is observed in transition economies as well.

"Insider entrepreneurship" refers to the idea that new enterprise undertakings are more likely to be started by the ones who have already established themselves in the business world.[20] The generational effect – "the bridge between the influences of the past and the future" – is also worth mentioning as it entails a prolonged period of transition as changes in the norms and culture of the people could be slow-paced. Therefore, it is one of the characteristics of informal institutions.[21]

Figure 6.5 Morocco port
Source: © iStock: SeanPavonePhoto

Meanwhile, institutions can be broadly defined as "A set of humanly devised behavioral rules that govern and shape the interaction of human beings, in part by helping them to form expectations of what other people will do."[22] Or as "…systems of established and prevalent social rules that structure social interactions."[23] This will lead to a higher degree of certainty and expectations of human nature which promote entrepreneurial activities.[24]

As explained earlier, both country governance and institutions are essential sets of cultural and organizational regulations that play an important role in the development, growth, and success of entrepreneurial initiatives. More than that, both institutions and governance, respectively, provide meaning and the rules of social interaction. Therefore, the meaning and way of the entrepreneurial activity itself is a result of institutions and governance structures. For instance, in countries where entrepreneurial activity has more legitimacy, the governance structure itself creates higher entrepreneurial activities.[25]

Macro governance efforts

The Tanger-Med is a brand-new major cargo port located in Tanger, Morocco. The $10 billion project was started by the Moroccan government with the intent of creating jobs and improving the Moroccan economy. About 4,000–5,000 employees work there. The port provides storage and shipping capabilities for Morocco's major export products: phosphates, agricultural items, and fish/sardines. It also includes 29 storage containers for oil, natural gas, and a passenger area. The second phase of the port will take several years to complete, and it is estimated that it will take 9–10 years before the port will become profitable. The port is connected with the newly constructed transportation infrastructure (railway and highway), providing easy access to key distribution channels within the country.

The concept of the port is not inherently innovative, but the business has demonstrated some innovative thinking in its approach to managing government controls and regulation. In order to maximize the speed and efficiency of the building process, the Moroccan government created a dedicated ministry to handle the affairs of the port. This allowed matters, including budgets, permits, and regulations, to be handled within a single organization, avoiding excessively bureaucratic restrictions.

Continued at the end of the chapter…

Having a clear and developed governance structure and strong institutions will positively impact entrepreneurial initiatives. Unfortunately, many developing countries lack viable institutions and governance.

"Institutions can create or destroy incentives for individuals to engage in trade, invest in human and physical capital, and engage innovation."[26] Thus, institutions have always played an essential role in governmental regulation, but their role has grown considerably since the fall of the former Soviet Union and the advent of globalization. In democratic societies, institutions are better developed and are mostly anchored towards good governance. However, in non-democratic societies, institutions are rigid, and the process of incentives for entrepreneurial actions is more selective and more dependent on an alignment with the dominant logic.

Governance definition

Governance is defined as the "processes of interaction and decision-making among the actors in an enterprise".[27] Denis and McConnell define corporate governance as a "set of mechanisms – both institutional and market-based – that induce the self-interested

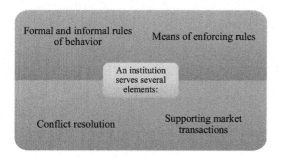

Figure 6.6 Institution elements

Source: https://techcrunch.com/2014/08/02/political-yield/ featured by: BRYCE DURBIN controllers of a company to make decisions that maximize the value of the company to its owners (the suppliers of capital)."[28]

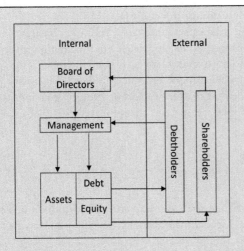

Figure 6.7 Governance

Source: Corporate governance and the balance sheet model of the firm. Adapted from PowerPoint slides accompanying Ross, S. A., Westerfield, R. W., Jaffe, J. (2005). Corporate Finance (7th ed.). New York: McGraw Hill Irwin. And Jensen, M. C. (1993). The modern industrial revolution, exit, and the failure of internal control systems. Journal of Finance, 48, 831–880.

The Board of Directors, at the apex of internal control systems, is charged with advising and monitoring management and has the responsibility to hire, fire, and compensate the senior management team.[29] External governance arises from a firm's need to raise capital. Further, it highlights that in the publicly traded firm, a separation exists between capital providers and those who manage the capital. This separation creates the demand for corporate governance structures.

Country governance, on the other hand, also plays an essential role in the development of an entrepreneurial ecosystem in any given country.[30] Governance refers to all processes of governing that describe rules, laws, norms, and power that is applied by a government, market, family, tribe, and formal or informal organizations.[31]

In the recent past, most governments encourage programs and policies which support the entrepreneurial spirit in the country. This trend is not new; it owes its origins to a report from 1979 by David Birch of MIT called "The Job Generation Process".[32] The most essential of it was the fact that job creation was coming more from small businesses than from large ones. Thus, entrepreneurship was claimed to be a trigger for economic growth and most of the governments worldwide started encouraging it, some sooner and others later.

Nevertheless, creating a sustainable entrepreneurial ecosystem is more complex than it sounds. It demands close attention to a number of factors including the reform of the legal, bureaucratic, and regulatory frameworks. Such reforms require leadership by government institutions such as Ministers who can support small businesses through their public policies. A bottom–up or top–down approach should be undertaken from already existing industries in the different countries. A single model of building a strong and sustainable entrepreneurial system could hardly be applied to a lot of countries, mainly due to their significant differences in culture, governance, and business trends. Therefore, a country's government overall plays an essential role in the growth and stability of a sustainable entrepreneurial ecosystem.

For instance, some of the means for the effective encouragement of entrepreneurship in a country by a government could be helping to sustain small firms, motivating a competitive culture, and alleviating unfair taxation on small firms.[33]

Democracies are traditionally seen as having the best level of governance for promoting development.[34] In The UN System Task Team on the Posts-2015 UN Development Agenda, reference is made to democratic governance as "a process of creating and sustaining an environment for inclusive and responsive political processes and settlements."

The success of governance is defined by the goal, although there isn't a standard or point in which we can say that a country's governance is good; the success of governance is defined by whether the country reaches its desired outcomes.

- The entrepreneurial activities in a society will flourish under good governance and having relevant supporting institutions that make the rules and regulations.
- Institution is defined as the rules of the game that shape human interaction.
- Formal institutions (such as regulations, policies, and sanctions) as well as informal institutions (such as norms and values) need to be considered in development.
- Both country governance and institutions are essential sets of cultural and organizational regulations that play an important role in the development, growth, and success of entrepreneurial initiatives.
- Having a clear and developed governance structure and strong institutions will positively impact entrepreneurial initiatives.
- Governance within an enterprise can be described as the process of interaction and decision-making among key actors.

Governance: a micro perspective

Hufty (2011) describes governance as "the processes of interaction and decision-making among the actors involved in a collective problem solving that lead to the creation, reinforcement, or reproduction of social norms and institutions."[35] Denis and McConnell define corporate governance as a "set of mechanisms – both institutional and market-based – that induce the self-interested controllers of a company to make decisions that maximize the value of the company to its owners (the suppliers of capital)."[36] This definition differentiates between internal and external mechanisms of corporate governance by integrating the economy with the organization to guide the empirical investigation.[37] La Porta et al. (1997) have shown that the legal tradition (home-country conditions and concentration of ownership) of a country impacts corporate governance.[38,39,40] Mallin states that from a global perspective, corporate governance seems to be a twenty-first-century phenomenon which is supported by Stiglitz's view that "economic liberalization has outpaced political globalization and the globalization of our mindsets."[41]

Governance refers to the process of decision-making and implementation (sometimes rejection). Analysis of governance focuses on understanding the formal and informal actors involved in decision-making and implementation of decisions. Governments are just one of the actors in governance; other actors include influential landlords, associations of peasant farmers, cooperatives, NGOs, research institutes, religious leaders, finance institutions, political parties, the military, etc., depending on the circumstances.

Nature and role of economic institutions

Institutions should:

Provide the "rules of the game" in economic life.
Provide the underpinning of a market economy.
Include property rights and supervise contract enforcements.
Work for the improvement of coordination among players.
Restrict coercive, fraudulent, and anti-competitive behavior.
Provide access to opportunities for the broad population.
Constrain the power of elites and manage conflicts.
Be providers of social insurance.
Work towards a predictable macroeconomic stability

Source: Rodrik (2008)[42]

Governance and entrepreneurship: a macro perspective

Governance refers to all processes of governing that are based on rules, laws, norms, and power applied by a government, market, family, tribe, and formal or informal organizations.[43] The impact country governance has on entrepreneurship in the current era of globalization has been explored and discussed in recent years. Nevertheless, some of the research results have shown a negative relationship between a country's level of governance and some have found a positive one. The discrepancy in results between the negative and positive studies on the relationship between country governance efficiency and entrepreneurship is explained by Thai and Turkina.[44,45,46,47] The argument is that on one hand, studies proving negative relationships have used a general level of entrepreneurship data provided by the Global Entrepreneurship Monitor (GEM) which includes both formal and informal entrepreneurship. On the other hand, studies which show the positive relationship between the quality of governance and entrepreneurship are mostly based on variables using the number of registered businesses in a given country. In both cases, however, it could be established that the government plays an essential role in the creation of sustainable entrepreneurship. Therefore, the question becomes what could the government do in practice to encourage the entrepreneurial spirit? For example, Isenberg (2010) insists that governments should emphasize a few key points (illustrated in Table 6.1) in order to successfully encourage sustainable entrepreneurial ecosystems.[48]

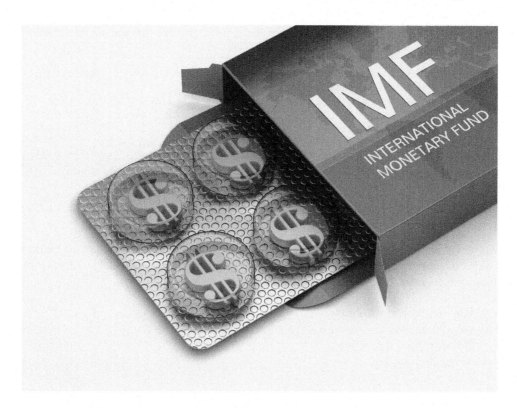

Figure 6.8 Economic institutions
Source: © iStock: adventtr

Economic institution

Furthermore, Isenberg also puts forward recommendations for governments in encouraging the sustainable entrepreneurial ecosystem, which is in Table 6.1.

The main challenge for governments, in this case, would be to support the growing entrepreneurs without intervening too much in the business culture of the country. Contrary to Isenberg (2010)[49], who supports the claim that government efficiency cultivates entrepreneurship, Friedman (2011)[50] denies it. According to Friedman (2011), there is a negative relationship between the perception of government effectiveness and entrepreneurship on a country level. He reaches this conclusion after scrutinizing the six indicators for World Governance, developed by the World Bank Project, the Global Entrepreneurship Monitor (GEM). Using descriptive statistics and Pearson correlations, he analyzes the results of 36 countries across the world and concludes that most of the entrepreneurs in these 36 countries have started their businesses not due to higher perceptions of opportunities offered by the external macro environment, but out of necessity.

Therefore, the macro environment (e.g., government efficiency) did not allure young entrepreneurs through being benevolent, but the nascent entrepreneurship was born as a result of the individual need for economic prosperity. In other words, most of the nascent

Table 6.1 Government recommendations

Do	Do NOT
Use existing industries and build on their foundations, skills, and capabilities.	Assume one model applies to all strategies.
Encourage self-sustainable firms with strong root systems.	Flood the system with "easy money" (e.g., government grants, venture capital, etc.).
Encourage institutional entrepreneurs to act as managers for programs and policies regarding entrepreneurship.	Direct them towards only one specific industry (e.g., high-tech sector) .
Ensure all industry sectors are influenced by the programs.	Treat entrepreneurship the same as small businesses. The policy for the first is "relational" and for the latter, "transactional".

entrepreneurs were motivated by the necessity created by the government or market failure to employ them properly. Friedman (2011) uses data from World Governance Indicators to analyze the impact of the following variables:

- Voice and accountability
- Political stability and absence of violence
- Government effectiveness
- Regulatory quality
- Rule of law.

He concludes that countries with high governance effectiveness have less favorable attitudes towards entrepreneurship when compared to countries with less effective governance.[51] The finding might be due to the fact that countries with a higher GDP per capita had fewer entrepreneurial opportunities. High employment levels and individual job satisfaction could keep people distant from the idea of creating a new business. Also, the market in developed countries is well-saturated in comparison to developing countries.

As a result, the motivation for starting a business in the developed countries would be decreased by the variety of businesses that already exist. Another explanation could be that well-developed countries have higher barriers for entry due to higher regulations and taxes. For instance, Denmark and Finland, which are among the developed countries with high WG scores and heavy taxation, have lower levels of entrepreneurship when compared to countries such as Thailand or China, which have the lowest WG scores in the study but reported higher levels of entrepreneurship due to their decreased level of taxation.

Groşanu et al. (2015) have explored which characteristics of country-level governance most strongly influence the business environment and the entrepreneurship levels from a sample of 132 countries from around the world, using 792 observations in a six-year period from 2007 to 2012. They have found that the government impacts the ease of doing business. The main premise here is that good quality governance in the country stimulates a well-developed and high ranked business environment with more entrepreneurial opportunities.[52]

Essentially, the macro factors most influencing the entrepreneurial framework are as follows:

- A one-point increase in political stability would bring, on average, a 21.3 percent increase in Entrepreneurship (Density);

Table 6.2 Governance on entrepreneurship

Factors	Coefficient	p-value	95% Confidence Interval	
			Lower Limit	Upper Limit
Constant	-4.492	<0.001	-6.073	-2.912
Political Stability	0.213	0.001	0.088	0.337
Regulatory Quality	0.344	0.001	0.142	0.546
Income (log of GNI)	0.518	<0.001	-6.073	-2.912
R2=0.51				

Note: Dependent variable: Entrepreneurship (Density)
Panel data: 95 countries and six years 2007–2012 (GLS estimates)

Source: Groşanu, A., Boţa-Avram, C., Răchişan, P. R., Vesselinov, R., & Tiron-Tudor, A. (2015). The influence of country-level governance on business environment and entrepreneurship: a global perspective. Amfiteatru Economic, 17(38), 60–75.

- A one-point increase in regulatory quality would bring a 34.4 percent increase in Entrepreneurship Density;
- A one-percent increase in income (GNI) per capita would bring about a 0.5 percent increase in Entrepreneurship (Density).

From the earlier study, we can conclude that well-established property rights institutions and market-friendly government policies are an essential framework for the sustainable development of entrepreneurship. A one-point increase in Political stability would bring, on average, a 21.3 percent increase in entrepreneurship and a one-point increase in the Regulatory Quality, bringing a 34.4 percent increase. A one-point increase in income (GNI) per capita would result in about a 0.5 percent increase. Other characteristics that good country governance should have in order to attract new businesses include accountability, transparency, and the rule of law. These are the foundations of good governance and thus, economic growth and entrepreneurial development.[53]

In either case, it is clear that the government's role is essential. In one case, if it is efficient enough it will encourage the sustainable development of entrepreneurship, and in the other case, it will spark it through its own failure. Developing countries would experience more difficulties in sustaining good levels of entrepreneurship if the government is not transparent and fair as investors would be discouraged.

Moreover, entrepreneurs are even more afflicted by high levels of corruption and ineffective regulatory frameworks, as compared to multi-corporations, because of their lack of bargaining power vis-à-vis the bureaucracy. This could explain the reasons for low levels of entrepreneurship in transitioning and developing countries.

Therefore economic development, a stable political environment, and the capacity of governments to promote and implement business-friendly regulations are all macro-factors which are greatly related to a higher level of entrepreneurship and the stimulation and encouragement of the private sector. Therefore entrepreneurship, when measured in terms of new registrations and entry rates, is highly affected and positively correlated with the quality of government and economic growth.[54,55] Scholars Rodrik and Melo stated that numerous links and interdependencies between politics, institutions, and a country's history are highly important to the business environment and entrepreneurial activity.[56,57]

Figure 6.9 Iraqi center
Source: Image by Richie Diesterheft on flickr

3D printed hand at RiTS

Aim of the Iraqi Entrepreneurship Center

In the website "Bite.tech", the CEO of RiTS Aziz Alnassiri talks about reasons for the current economic stagnation in Iraq. Given the lack of funds available, he believes that entrepreneurship is the only means of increasing economic activities. He suggests that a massive number of entrepreneurial projects be initiated, incubated, and supported through a network of organizations dedicated to the cause of successful startups.

He writes about how RiTS, an Iraqi entrepreneurial company, has spent most of 2016 establishing Iraq's first incubator dedicated to the graduates of Al Mansour University College. It has also established Iraq's first Crowdsourcing gathering, which is currently hosted on LinkedIn. It plans shortly to go on the air as an independent self-contained resource that brings together Iraqi entrepreneurs and experienced professionals from around the world to combine their efforts, knowledge, and money to support new startups in Iraq. This initiative has already led to two new ventures being established. A new division within RiTS produces 3D printed mechanical prosthetic hands for Iraqi disabled children. Further, RiTS proposes to take the Iraqi entrepreneurship to the next level by expanding to other areas of technology and also establishing an international presence.

Source: Alnassiri (2017)[58]

Furthermore, the macro perspective of corporate governance has a historical connotation as it originates not from the rational choices and reforms, but is rather a product of historical processes that have occurred in the past in relation to politics, society, law, and economics.[59]

Governance: good and bad

Let's examine what constitutes good and bad governance in order to better understand the operational framework entrepreneurship could exist in transitioning, developing, and developed countries. Every country has to have a set of governing governance to operate regardless of its degree of efficiency and responsiveness. Good governance promotes community, gives confidence to elected members, leads to better decisions, and supports ethical decision-making. But what happens when lax and ineffective governance leads to corruption, cash transfers, and abused power?

This is the case of most of the economically "transitioning" Eastern European countries. They usually have a lower level of entrepreneurship activities than in most developed and developing countries due to the government incompetence and many other issues including corruption.

Even if countries are performing well on the entrepreneurial level, a change in the corruption level could influence them positively or negatively.[60]

Good governance comes with addressing many issues at both macro and micro levels and is concerned with the transparency and long-term well-being of its citizens. Good governance should also be efficient. If it takes too much time and/or funding, the public sector and the citizens may lose interest and sight of the direction the intervention is supposed to be taking the country in. For these reasons, it is crucial that governance finds the crucial balance between good, efficient, and fair.

However, much like ethics, there are some basic principles that successful governance must have. First, it is fundamental to have transparent linkages between the public and private sectors, delivery and ease of access to public services, and the implementation of

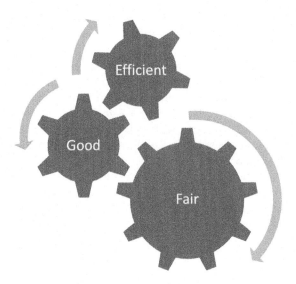

Figure 6.10 Gears

citizens' views when making critical decisions. In addition to this linkage, goals have to be developed in line with the key factors of a developing country which include education, finance, and health. The second basic principle of good, successful governance is its judicial efforts, everything from implementing the law, implementing equality before the law, electoral integrity, and freedom of expression both for the media and citizens among many other democratic concepts. Although democratic governance has some soft and doubtful spots, and despite being seen as the universally superior form of governance, a developing country should strive for a democratic government. This will allow for freedom of expression and decisions and a connection with transparent accountable institutions which support each other and help promote development.

This kind of governance brings success to those in power and politics since resources are priced and allocated to those in politics, and the leader always has to have eyes and ears everywhere due to the probable rise of patrons looking to either revolt or slowly take the leader out of power. Although the allocation of resources for the government is good politics, it is disastrous for the people and the economy of the country since it leaves patrons resourceless, usually in poverty, and basically without the right to anything.

The private sector will mostly be used for services, instead of the public sector, which means the country will not have money to get out of the hole they have been dug into.

The IMF classifies 51 countries as "resource-rich." These are countries which derive at least 20% of exports or 20% of fiscal revenue from nonrenewable natural resources. Common characteristics of 29 of 51 countries include (i) extreme dependence on resource wealth for fiscal revenues, export sales, or both; (ii) low saving rates; (iii) poor growth performance; and (iv) highly volatile resource revenues.

Source: Venables (2016)[61]

Bad governance is created when resources, income, and political power have no correlation and are distributed unfairly. To improve governance, we first must identify the main issue that is the basis of the problem and why these problems slow down development especially in poor, resource-rich countries, often also called "resource-cursed" countries.[62,63] These are the countries that are rich in terms of natural resources but fall short when it comes to standard of living and overall economic level. Thus, bad governance, in this case, leads to poverty, inequality, and deprivation. There are more than twenty countries, especially in the Middle East, that derive a significant amount of their exports from oil and gas and are not real democracies.

Hence, the accountability of the government to its citizens is diminished, leading to increased levels of corruption and an enormous economic discrepancy between the social clusters of society. Instead of taxes and social benefits, the governments of such countries usually tend to facilitate corruption and "patronage networks".

Another factor contributing to the "curse" of rich natural resources is the proclivity to social violence it brings with itself. In combination with bad governance, the consequences and results are highly visible in oil-rich countries.[64] What could be done? Recently, a number of organizations and institutions worldwide started trying to combat the so-called "curse".

For instance, the Extractive Industries Transparency Initiative is trying to improve revenue management in about 30 resource-rich countries. The Open Government Partnership objectives are to fight corruption by securing tangible national plans to fight corruption.[65] Nevertheless, due to the fact that most of them are voluntarily based, no accountability or enforceability is incorporated. On a global level, members of organizations such as the Group of Eight (G8) and the Group of Twenty (G20) meet annually to discuss further remedies for the minimization of corruption and the support of democratic transparency which will contribute to the accountability in business and governance, thus attempting to transform the "curse" to a "blessing".[66] It is not surprising that non-governmental actors are the ones taking over the role of good governance to help these countries.

Nevertheless, instead of completely reforming governance we should focus on the exact problem governance has so it is more effective and the change can occur quicker; for example, if the problem is corruption, an anti-corruption agency might help. Directly and gradually reforming some aspects of governance such as formal institutions – private or public – or property rights could result in dysfunctional, ineffective, and perhaps even counterproductive measures to some countries.

The reforms should be undertaken incrementally and over the long-run in order to be effective. Overall, for a reform change to be effective, changes in institutions need to be complemented by changes in *de facto* political power. Improved governance occurs when the costs and benefits of different stakeholders and the relevant institutions are changed and, therefore, will impact their action. For example, the World Bank intervened in policies and policy making.[67]

Although democracies are seen as the basis of good governance, Scandinavian countries such as Norway and Sweden strive to achieve good governance with a socialist government style, which proves the point that any government style can be effective; all that is necessary is the backing of citizens and the appropriate allocation of resources. The Nordic Model of governance has proved to be effective and efficient for all stakeholders.

On the other hand, dictatorships in South Korea and Taiwan evolved through good governance and democracy. Socialism in Scandinavian countries is also seen as good governance, as it promoted equality for its citizens. As long as the three basic criteria mentioned are met, most systems of government can evolve with good governance which is necessary for sustainable development.

Globalization and governance

Globalization has caused national governments to think and act globally and it is making it hard for some governments to operate under secrecy.[68] Governments need to adjust to a new normal which is a more transparent system of governance. International pressure and the desire of citizens of developing countries to reach the quality and living standards of developed nations are forcing many governments to go through a major transformation.

The national governments are losing their influence and power in decision-making to non-state actors due to innovation in technology and communication. The role of national governments is crucial for development because of its macro position. Some countries in Asia (i.e., Singapore and South Korea) play an active role in advancing the education and evaluation of relevant institutions and governance including the creation of opportunities for entrepreneurial activities. Supporting good governance, rule of law, and transparency is a necessary condition for sustainable development.

Large-scale and accelerated growth has rendered the statist model of governance unviable and encouraged the emergence of polycentric regulations, however the state remains crucial in this new polycentric regulation, because although globalization has led to the empowerment of non-state actors such as multinational corporations, non-governmental organizations and transnational activist network states remain the primary actors for handling social and political externalities created by globalization. Powerful states will use a range of foreign policy substitutes to advance their desired preferences into their desired outcomes. Globalization undercuts state sovereignty and weakening governments' ability to effectively regulate their domestic affairs.

- Governments are just one of the actors in governance; other actors include influential land lords, associations of peasant farmers, cooperatives, NGOs, research institutes, religious leaders, finance institutions, political parties, the military, and so on.
- Well-established property rights institutions and market-friendly government policies are an essential framework for sustainable development of entrepreneurship.
- Entrepreneurs are even more afflicted by high levels of corruption and ineffective regulatory frameworks compared to multi-corporations.
- When performing well on the entrepreneurial level, a change in the corruption level could influence them positively or negatively.
- Good governance comes with addressing many issues at both macro and micro levels and is concerned with the transparency and long-term well-being of its citizens.

As state power has waned, globalization has simultaneously enhanced the power of non-state actors (i.e., multinational corporations – MNCs).[69,70,71] The impact of globalization on national and local governments is clear and the issue of decentralization and evolving institutions has become significantly important. There are different degrees of citizen participation in the political process in most developed and developing countries. It appears that the globalization impact on undemocratic systems of government has been significant; it is questioning the existence of their system of government.

However, in the countries with a democratic system of government, the question concerns the degree of government participation in economic and social issues which essentially deals with reallocation of resources. Finally, given the shifts in the power of national governments, the question is how these decentralized institutions will evolve and are able to operate and serve the interest of citizens.

Globalization has significantly impacted the way that nations are managed. It is becoming harder for countries to set policies without consulting with other nations and being considerate of the impact of its policies. Therefore, some governments have lost their influence in providing a "conventional" model of governance. This is changing the traditional structure of governance and is being distributed in new and different manners. Some scholars argue that in order for us to become more globalized, voters and citizens need to start thinking globally rather than locally.[72] In this process, governance and institutions should converge to some form of similarity. Nevertheless, when local services are not being provided, it may cause citizens to start rejecting the idea of globalization and may resist the move towards globalization. The example of Greece is a unique and obvious one.

The most recent example is the national referendum in Great Britain (Brexit 2016) in which 51.9 percent of the British people have decided that they prefer not to be part of the European Union, the economic and social union of Europe, thus making Great Britain the first country to ever leave the EU in 2019. By breaking its formal relationship with the union, the UK will replace the existing EU laws with UK domestic laws. This is one of the first, bold steps against globalization.

There are three main themes that need to be highlighted regarding the transformation of governance and the role of government in the globalization era: Globalization, Devolution, and the Role of Government. These three themes have transformed the role of government in two ways: (1) it has strained the traditional role of all players and (2) a new era has challenged the capacity of governments and their non-governmental partners to deliver high-quality public services. Globalization has decreased the effectiveness of individual governments' policies and procedures as governments see themselves responsible for their citizens and are considerate of them on an international level. In addition, the creation of international organizations and institutions such as the WTO, the United Nations, and NGOs have also risen to power and have been offering some services better than some local governments. As a result, governments are losing their ability to act alone and have less control in their decision-making.[73]

UK NGOs could miss out on 140 million euros ($150 million) of funding a year from the European Union as a result of Brexit, according to new research by Bond, the UK NGO network.

Source: Edwards (2017)[74]

Figure 6.11 Brexit
Source: © iStock: Ddurrich

When the leaders of a nation, developed or underdeveloped, recognize governance as a possible aid to the struggling economy, it becomes necessary to determine how much is the right amount. With a high level of intervention, there will be ample controls to keep growth on track and remove the threat of corruption in the profitable industries. Good governance can protect those who are less privileged while keeping the playing field level and preventing the wealthiest from suppressing the growth of those beneath them. Nonetheless, it is apparent from the arguments made in previous sections of the chapter that a given level of governance is not only necessary but beneficial for the country as a whole.

Determining what the proper level is comes down to balance, changing traditional approaches, and receiving buy-in.

There is a balance that needs to occur when determining the level of governance for each nation, developed or not, in order to ensure that the internal interests of the nation are preserved. When the nation is attempting to achieve an effective level of governance, it is not uncommon for them to jade their focus towards only the economic and political plights and opportunities within the nation alone. While focusing solely on the needs of one's own nation could yield the quickest results when the level of governance is heightened, it can be extremely difficult to implement that kind of change based solely on the struggles of the developing nation. Simply put, the nation has been struggling for some time economically or politically, so it would be difficult to use solely internal resources to implement a change in governance. For the advancement of globalization, emerging or emerged economies should assist developing countries in this process. This resistance to external help from successful nations, while it will preserve the goals and resources of the nation itself, will make it extremely difficult to foster relationships with foreign institutions that can not only help the developing country but could be an ally when it comes time to trade or expand economically. It is for that reason that some help can go a long way when trying to improve the economic status of an entire nation.

Often times when a developing nation is looking to make significant changes, they turn to a developed nation for assistance. This assistance most often comes from foreign institutions that are designed to help developing nations with this sort of improvement (i.e., WTO, World Bank) or from successful foreign entities.[75] With several benefits to this strategy, including heightened resources, expertise, and information, reaching to developed institutions for help may yield positive outcomes.

The investment logic for sustainability

Sustainability is pretty clearly one of the world's most important goals; but what groups can really make environmental progress in leaps and bounds? Chris McKnett makes the case that it's large institutional investors. He shows how strong financial data isn't enough, and reveals why investors need to look at a company's environmental, social, and governance structures, too.

You can check in more details in the full TED Talk in this link: www.ted.com/talks/kirsty_duncan_scientists_must_be_free_to_learn_to_speak_and_to_challenge

Krasner (2015) recognizes the shortcomings of high levels of governance by noting that leaders seeking rapid economic growth or drastic political intervention often, "have no interest in sustaining accountable governance."[76] The quick fix for governance could yield great payoffs at the onset, but in the long-run, is not invested in sustainable growth of the nation. Respecting the way in which the country operated traditionally and utilizing governance to improve those traditional methods will create the greatest chance for successful change. Additionally, those leaders seeking a quick fix that will exploit the resources of a developing nation are poised to corrupt the political system in the process of growing the economic one. Traditionally countries that focus solely on one system but neglected the other are subject to not only corruption but also an economy that becomes cut throat and relies on the greediness of the haves and the complacency of the have-nots. The economic agenda of a country must align with the political ideals in order for long-term success to be possible and it is the role of governance to bring that alignment into perspective.[77]

Transparency International (TI) has published the Corruption Perceptions Index (CPI) since 1996, annually ranking countries on perceived levels of corruption. The CPI currently ranks 176 countries "on a scale from 100 (very clean) to 0 (highly corrupt)".

Source: Transparency International (2016)[78]

Figure 6.12 Corruption
Source: © iStock: PeopleImages

Newig et al. (2016) describe governance as learning to update beliefs based on evidence, experience, and additional information. They note that participation in the planning for intervention helps to shape the design and eventual effectiveness of the intervention plan. It should be noted that the aforementioned authors specifically discussed the installation of flood risk planning, but the principles and ideology hold true for a larger scale situation.[79]

Borrowing from Newig et al.'s analysis, buy-in is easiest to achieve when those in power are transparent. Transparency around the need for governance within a nation and transparency around the desired results of that governance are what the different groups requiring buy-in will need to be equipped with in order to get on board for the change. Achieving nation-wide buy-in includes having targeted objectives. And with knowledge comes the ability to discuss what will be needed and what can wait for later.

Economic development and entrepreneurship

The economic development of a country is in relation to well-developed institutions that contribute to increased levels of entrepreneurial activity.[80] Porter and his colleagues illustrate competitiveness in accordance with a given country's economic development by differentiating between three specific stages:[81,82]

• Factor–driven stage

Countries in this stage of economic activity have based their competitive advantage at low-cost efficiencies in the production of commodities or low value-added products.

Almost all economies go through this phase where neither innovation knowledge, nor use knowledge is exploited.[83]

• Efficiency-driven stage

Countries in this stage usually increase their production efficiency and, furthermore, educate their workforce labor to be accustomed to applying new technologies and adapting to the globalized environment. In order for competition to exist on this stage, countries must have efficient production and manufacturing practices on large markets thus allowing companies to exploit economies of scale. This economic stage is typically marked by low levels of entrepreneurial activity due to the increasing returns to wage work. Therefore, people are more willing to move from self-employment to wage employment. As when an economy becomes richer, the average firm size usually increases as well, leaving enough room for labor expansion and diminished levels of nascent entrepreneurship. In other words, this stage of the economy encourages individuals to join an already existing profitable business than to create their own. Thus, contrary to conventional wisdom, the more developed the economy becomes, the fewer individuals are pursuing self-employment opportunities.

• Innovation-driven stage

This stage of economic development encompasses an increase in entrepreneurial activity. It is characterized by a decrease in the share of manufacturing in the economy,

Figure 6.13 Asuncion
Source: Image by Tetsumo on flickr

and an increase in technological development and globalization. Technological advancements have directly affected the entrepreneurial environment throughout the world making it both less expensive and less time consuming for geographically and physically separate individuals to exchange information and to be able to work together.

Although most developed countries are in the innovation-driven stage, most developing economies (e.g., Brazil, Russia, India, China) are still in the efficiency-driven stage where manufacturing and exporting is what drives the economy.

Moreover, as innovation is important for competition in foreign markets, developed economies usually are better integrated globally than developing countries. Thus, it is essential for economies to move into the innovation-driven stage in order to develop the necessary environmental conditions conducive to entrepreneurship. For instance, some of the countries who have already achieved this transition include Korea, Ireland, Israel, and Taiwan.[84]

Incubator of companies in the National University of Asunción: INCUNA

In 2009, the companies' incubator called INCUNA was created and managed by the National University of Asunción – UNA, in the Paraguayan capital. The incubator emerged with the need to support university entrepreneurs and undergraduates with the interest to undertake entrepreneurships. Its mission is focused on technology-based ventures, in an attempt to minimize the errors and failures of these ventures. The INCUNA has captured business ideas among university students and supported the formation of innovative technology-based companies, applying management tools to ensure the sustainability of projects. Its main objectives are to create an entrepreneurial culture within the academic environment, promoting development throughout the country, and forming groups and productive chains to improve the regional economy. With the target audience within the university itself, it opens up opportunities for academic jobs if they become successful companies.

A business and entrepreneurial environment is highly determined by the interdependencies between economic development and institutions which could impact other country governmental characteristics as:

- Quality of governance
- Access to capital and other resources
- Perceptions of entrepreneurs.

Thus, institutions could be accepted as critical to the overall setting of economic behavior and transactions as they can impose both direct and indirect effects on the supply as well as the demand of entrepreneurs in a given country. Figure 6.14 illustrates the Nascent Entrepreneurship Rate for 2015, according to the Global Entrepreneurship Monitor.[85]

- Transparent linkages between the public and private sectors, delivery and ease of access to public services, and the implementation of citizens' views when making critical decisions, as well as a principle of good, successful governance in its judicial efforts, are some of the basic principles to have a successful governance.
- Governments need to adjust to a new normal that is a more transparent system of governance.
- The impact of globalization on national and local governments is clear and the issue of decentralization and evolving institutions has become significantly important.
- Globalization has significantly impacted the way that nations are managed.
- There are three main themes that need to be highlighted regarding the transformation of governance and the role of government in the globalization era: Globalization, Devolution, and the Role of Government.

Corporate governance and institutions in developing economies

Development and advancement of governance are necessary conditions for a flourishing entrepreneurial atmosphere. Scholars argued that developing economies are using economic liberalization as their primary engine for economic growth and institutional theory has become the predominant theory for examining management.[86,87] Others have argued that institutions affect organizational routines and help frame the strategic choices facing organizations.[88,89,90,91,92]

In other words, institutions help determine the firm's course of actions and, therefore, determine the outcomes and effectiveness of the organization. The institutions that influence organizational actions in developing economies are not stable and developed, so that will impact the actions of firms.

Additionally, the existing formal institutions often do not promote mutually beneficial impersonal exchanges between economic actors.[93] Therefore, organizations in developing economies are to a greater extent guided by informal institutions.[94] For example, in the case of corporate governance, most developing economies do not have a clear and effective rule of law which, in turn, creates a "weak governance" condition.[95,96]

Most developing economies have laws dealing with corporate governance but those laws are not as clear and enforced as in developed economies. Some developing economies have tried to adopt legal frameworks of developed economies, in particular, those of the Anglo–American system, either as a result of internally driven reforms or as a response to international market demands. In the existing formal institutions, enforcement is either absent, inefficient, or does not operate as intended with laws and regulations regarding accounting requirements, information disclosure, and securities trading.

Therefore, standard corporate governance mechanisms have relatively little institutional support in most developing economies.[97,98] Thus, informal institutions such as family connections, government contracts, and business groups' connections play a greater role in influencing corporate governance. Because of the weak institutional environment in emerging economies, it is common for firms to be under the control of the founding family or retain control through other (often informal) means. As a result, in most developing economies, corporate governance structures frequently resemble those

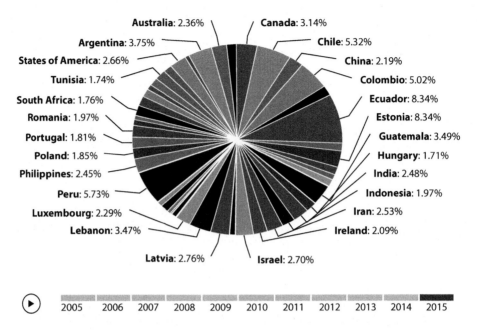

Figure 6.14 Countries percentages

of developed economies in form but not in substance. We can conclude that the development of institutions that support and ensure the implementation of governance is necessary, especially if the aim is to advocate and advance entrepreneurial activities.

Koster and Rai (2008) created a model that predicts that entrepreneurship levels would decrease in the early stages of economic development based on a case study from India. As India has been in a process of rapid economic growth for the last 15 years, they have questioned the assumption that this growth would have an effect on the levels and structure of entrepreneurship. However, empirical data (e.g., GEM) does not support the earlier claim.

Although economic growth has encouraged small and medium-size business development in India, entrepreneurship levels have not had a significant impact on the economy of the country. Nevertheless, they also note that a more formal way of entrepreneurship is not (yet) noticeable in India.[99]

Thus it might actually be true that only high-potential entrepreneurship has a positive impact on economic development for developing countries in an era of globalization.[100] Prieger et al. investigated the effect of entrepreneurship on economic growth, thus concluding that less developed countries have more small businesses than wealthier countries.

This idea is somehow confusing as their empirical evidence also shows that low- and middle-income countries do not have increased levels of entrepreneurship, and there are three possible reasons for this controversy:[101]

• Economic growth in less developed countries might require even more entrepreneurship;

- Other factors might be influencing the impact of entrepreneurship on growth;
- Less developed countries might be encouraging entrepreneurship of a negative kind.

Furthermore, Prieger et al. advise policymakers in less developed countries to be more responsive to the changing roles of entrepreneurs and overall environment; for instance, through the encouragement of a new formation of businesses with high potential and growth.[102]

Strategy

A strategy can be defined as "the creation of a unique and valuable position, involving a different set of activities." And the strategic position arises from "three distinct sources: the work of deciding which target group of customers and needs to serve requires discipline, the ability to set limits, and forthright communication." Of course, strategy and leadership are strongly linked and require making competing choices of what to do and what not to do to have a competitive advantage. Leadership and strategy play an even more important role for an entrepreneur than for a large company. These issues even become more critical in developing countries than in developed countries.[103]

To be able to develop and implement successful strategy it does require viable institutions and good governance. These concepts are established and advanced in most developed countries, thus leading to a higher level of prosperity and transparency in these societies. These sets of micro and macro factors re-enforce each other in creating a well-functioning and transparent advanced society.

Some developing nations are able to revise the rules of the game in the direction of strengthening its governance and institutions which would lead to an increase in its productive capacity.[104] Unfortunately, many developing countries are ending up being led by a strongman, a dynasty, a family, or other non-democratic forms where democratic institutions and values are undermined. The self-interest of the leadership of these countries does not permit the development of quality institutions, transparent governance, and the rule of law.

These issues are essential for the development of entrepreneurial activities that require clear and transparent rules of law – that define rewards and penalties – and its enforcement. The success rates among startups in developing countries are much lower than in developed countries due to the absence of good governance and appropriate institutions. Holding everything constant, there is a continual entrepreneurial brain drain from developing countries (i.e., India, China, and Iran) to developed countries for some of the same reasons. In most developing countries, there are very few successful examples of private companies that have grown to become mature, multinational, and multigenerational. Most large multinational companies from developing countries tend to be supported by their government (i.e., Petrobras, Brazil; Aramco, Saudi Arabia).

- Innovation is important for competition in foreign markets, with developed economies usually better integrated globally than developing countries.
- There are three distinct stages to a given country's economic development: factor-driven stage, efficiency-driven stage, and innovation-driven stage.

- Institutions help determine firm courses of action and therefore determine the outcomes and effectiveness of organizations.
- Development of institutions that support and ensure implementation of governance is necessary, especially if the aim is to advocate and advance entrepreneurial activities.
- In most developing countries, there are very few successful examples of private companies that have grown to become mature, multinational, and multigenerational.

Covi (2016) explores strategies for coping with globalization through an analysis of the "new competitive framework" small and medium-sized enterprises are operating in. He further introduces the concept of "complete productive process" to describe the environmental factors influencing innovation and entrepreneurship in the era of globalization. Moreover, Covi recognizes "local systems" as "cognitive systems" which need to embrace globalization not individually but rather as one comprehensive system.

The main pre-requisite is "collective and cooperative behavior" which is embodied by the concept of "collective local entrepreneurship."[105] A recent Organization for Economic Cooperation and Development (OECD) report concludes that some of the most important factors influencing the creation and sustainability of competitive advantage are as follows:

> "Knowledge networks and innovation are essential features in modern competitive regional economies. This has been recognized over the years and more formal approaches have been developed to encourage the networking and the spread of innovation."[106]

Just as Porter has established, competitive advantage development is highly dependent on the specific details, the "knowhow", and the feeling of belonging to a particular space. As the business environment is affected differently in every country by politics, culture, and legal systems, it is not surprising that different countries would need different strategies for the encouragement of nascent entrepreneurship and small and medium-sized businesses.[107]

Covi further emphasizes the benefit of incremental innovation in comparison to radical innovation, which encompasses the fact that small–medium firms do not have the needed resources to perform a radical innovation. The opposite process has been labeled as "creative destruction" by Schumpeter. Thus, Covi proposes the idea of "Local Collective Entrepreneurship" which would allow for small firms and entrepreneurs to compete in the framework of globalization. Globalization has created an entrepreneurial strategy which is based on the possession of technical and organizational knowledge, well-developed learning ability, and human capital.

Nonaka and Takeuchi (1995) have long concluded that "knowledge is the most important strategic factor of production"; thus, managers should aim at its production, acquisition, movement, retention, and, most of all, application.[108] Arrow (1994) has argued that in the current globalized world, it is more important to possess technical knowledge than to own goods.[109] Covi has furthermore discussed the sources of competitive advantage through the perspective of different schools of thought (see Figure 6.15).

Covi moreover claims that the global economy of the world nowadays is mainly based on different competitive systems and competitive advantages, meaning that there is no one "best way" or strategy to organize the industrial operations in the different countries and economies as their competitive advantages are intangible and significantly marked by their past.

For instance, the rapid technological development of the century has allowed for globalization to offer easier access to new production at the transnational level. However, this is not a strategy for success as it does not contribute towards the decrease of the growth rates among the countries and regional economies. In other words, it does not provide for an equal or same model apply-to-all strategy. Knowledge and skill sets are in the foundation of entrepreneurship; the different levels of local government directly impact entrepreneurial levels in the country. For instance, local, national, regional, and municipal governments impact the learning skills of people on a local level, thus directly contributing or harming the country on a macro level.

Covi (2016) proposes the strategy as shown in Figure 6.15. Case A depicts a situation in which a local system, under the influence of the competitive forces of globalization, has broken its connections to the local supply chain in order to go global. Unless applied to avoid a lock-in situation, this kind of a business action could be regarded as harmful to the sense of identity of the community.

Case B illustrates a situation in which the entrepreneurs had a breakthrough, which has helped them escape Case A. He or she has gained access to an international subcontracting chain and international network.

Case C shows the struggles endured by mature and well-structured local clusters when competing with global markets.

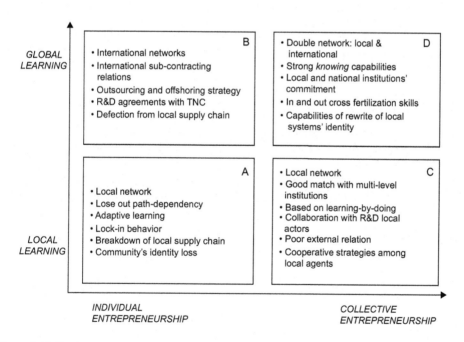

Figure 6.15 Covi strategy

Source: Covi, G. (2016). Local systems' strategies copying with globalization: collective local entrepreneurship. *Journal of the Knowledge Economy*, 7(2), 513–525. https://doi.org/10.1007/s13132-014-0225-4

Case D represents "a short list of ingredients for success" as Covi (2016) calls it (see Figure 6.15). Moreover, he argues that the main purpose here would be to possess the capabilities and the resources to "rewrite the identity" of their territory. Thus, he claims that it is essential for the cluster to provide a double network on a local and international level.

Conclusion

In sum, globalization has had positive effects on the governance and institutions of some developing countries. Traditional forms of governments are no longer effective in light of globalization where there is the higher focus in governance and institutions in theory and practice.[110] Globalization has caused national governments to think and act globally, however it causes these governments to become less effective in providing governance. As a result, institutions and other non-state actors have come to fill in this gap.

The result of this can either help countries to develop further like some Asian countries or fall behind like most Middle Eastern and Latin American countries. What has been effective thus far is a balance between representative governments and the relevant institutions to help deliver good governance. It seems that globalization has had more influences on governance at the micro level such as corporate governance. In some developing economies, corporate governance is evolving more towards the Anglo-American model which is more transparent and generally has good governance.

An important component of rule of law and by-products of good governance has a positive impact on entrepreneurial activities. A combination of good governance and institutions with thoughtful strategies shall lead to sustainable development. A democratic system empowers its citizens to engage in building institutions which enhances development. This allows for the voice of many to be incorporated into the government and governance and thus incorporate stakeholders' interest. Many developing countries' governments need to support and create space so institutions and good governance are developed. Of course, without the active participation of citizens, it will not be achieved.

Discussion questions

1. Why is understanding the definitions of institutions, governance, and strategy important?
2. Why is having appropriate institutions and governance essential for advancing entrepreneurial activities?
3. Is a well-functioning business environment an indication for good institutions?
4. Compare and contrast a few developed and developing countries from the perspective of institutions, governance, and entrepreneurial activities.
5. Compare and contrast strategy of a few enterprises from developed and developing countries.
6. Write a short case that applies at least two important topics in this chapter.

Table 6.3 Key terms

Institution	Factor-driven stage
Governance	Efficiency-driven stage
Global Entrepreneurship Monitor (GEM)	Innovation-driven stage
Resource-cursed countries	

Macro governance efforts

Within the confines of the port area, port-based businesses are given a grace period during which they are exempt from import tariffs, making importation of goods more affordable and enabling businesses to take advantage of the port's services.

Unlike most Moroccan business, which is conducted in French, the "Maritime business is in English". This is an important consideration as the port's strategic geographical location positions it to do business with companies around the world.

In conclusion and based on the earlier case studies, there are several identifiable trends related to innovation. The culture of the countries in which the company resides, the way that employees at the companies are educated, and the innovative processes of the company all greatly influence the way that innovation is realized with the evaluated companies.

Questions

1. What is the degree of public vs private management and ownership of ports and its afflicted organization in developed and developing countries?
2. Does this kind of public ownership lead to sustainable and multi-layered employment?
3. What type, skilled or unskilled, of employment is this?

Case study – continued

Micro and macro startup challenges facing Iran

5. Infrastructure challenges
   a. Slow internet speed
   b. Lack of proper legal framework for startup registrations and investments
   c. Long and lengthy process of company registration
   d. Limited payment options

6. Governance challenges
   a. No proper policy and regulation structure to ease the way of entrepreneurs and encourage them
   b. 24 months mandatory military service for men, and yes that includes entrepreneurs!

Questions

1. Analyze this study and make your argument for and against.
2. Evaluate similar challenges for a set of low- and medium-income countries.
3. Compare and contrast between developed and developing countries for the previously stated challenges.
4. Examine the role of institutions for a set of developed and developing countries.
5. If you are a policymaker, how would you overcome these challenges? What kind of strategy would you propose?

Notes

1 Jozi, A. (2015). 15 challenges of Iran's startup ecosystem. Techrasa. Retrieved from https://techrasa.com/2015/12/25/15-challenges-of-irans-startup-ecosystem/

2 North, D. C. (1990). Institutions, Institutional Change, and Economic Performance. Cambridge University Press.

3 World Trade Organization. (2009). World Trade Report 2004: Governance and Institutions.

4 Rodrik, D. (2007). One economics, many recipes: globalization, institutions, and economic growth. Princeton University Press. Retrieved from https://press.princeton.edu/titles/8494.html

5 Estrin, S., & Mickiewicz, T. (2011). Entrepreneurship in transition economies: the role of institutions and generational change. The Dynamics of Entrepreneurship, 181–208. doi:10.1093/acprof:oso/9780199580866.003.0009

6 Baumol, W. J. (1990). Entrepreneurship: productive, unproductive, and destructive. Journal of Political Economy, 98(1), 893–921. https://doi.org/10.2307/2937617

7 McMillan, J. (1999). Dispute prevention without courts in Vietnam. Journal of Law, Economics, and Organization, 15(3), 637–658. doi:10.1093/jleo/15.3.637

8 McMillan, J., & Woodruff, C. (2002). The central role of entrepreneurs in transition economies. Journal of Economic Perspectives, 16(3), 153–170. doi:10.1257/089533002760278767

9 Chemin, M. (2009). The impact of the judiciary on entrepreneurship: evaluation of Pakistan's "Access to Justice Programme". Journal of Public Economics, 93(1–2), 114–125. doi:10.1016/j.jpubeco.2008.05.005

10 De Soto, H. (2000). The Mystery of Capital. New York: Basic Books

11 Djankov, S., LaPorta, R., Lopez-de-Silanes, F., & Shleifer, A. (2002). The regulation of entry. Quarterly Journal of Economics, 117(1), 1–37.

12 Sobel, R. S. (2008). Entrepreneurship. In D. R. Henderson (Ed.), The Concise Encyclopedia of Economics. Liberty Fund, Indianapolis.

13 Estrin, S., & Mickiewicz, T. (2011). Entrepreneurship in transition economies: the role of institutions and generational change. The Dynamics of Entrepreneurship, 181–208. doi:10.1093/acprof:oso/9780199580866.003.0009

14 Aidis, R., Estrin, S., & Mickiewicz, T. (2009). Entrepreneurial Entry: Which Institutions Matter? CEPR Discussion Paper No. DP7278. Retrieved from https://papers.ssrn.com/sol3/papers.cfm?abstract_id=1405075.

15 Acemoglu, D., & Johnson, S. (2005). Unbundling institutions. Journal of Political Economy, 113(5), 949–995. https://doi.org/10.1086/432166

16 Botero, J., Djankov, S., LaPorta, R., López-de-Silanes, F., & Shleifer, A. (2004). The regulation of labor. Quarterly Journal of Economics, 119(4), 1339–1382.

17 Deeg, R., & Jackson, G. (2007). Towards a more dynamic theory of capitalist variety. Socio-Economic Review, 5(1), 149–180.

18 Melo, L. (2015). Firm-Level Corporate Governance in the Context of Emerging Market Firm Internationalization, Bentley University, Ph. D. Dissertation.

19 Adekoya, R. (2014). How the EU transformed Poland, The Guardian. Retrieved from www.theguardian.com/commentisfree/2014/may/01/eu-poland-10-years-economic

20 Estrin, S., & Mickiewicz, T. (2011). Entrepreneurship in transition economies: the role of institutions and generational change. The Dynamics of Entrepreneurship, 181–208. doi:10.1093/acprof:oso/9780199580866.003.0009

21 Sztompka, P. (1996). Looking back: the year 1989 as a cultural and civilizational break. Communist and Post-Communist Studies, 29(2), 115–129. https://doi.org/10.1016/S0967-067X(96)80001-8

22 Lin, J. Y., & Nugent, J. B. (1995). Institutions and economic development. In J. Behrman, & T. N. Srinivasan (Eds.), Handbook of Development Economics (pp. 2301–2370, Vol. 3A). New York: Elsevier Science, North Holland.

23 Hodgson, G. M. (2006). What are institutions? Journal of Economic Issues, 40(1), 1–25.

24 North, D. C. (1995). The new institutional economics and Third World development. In J. Haapiseva-Hunter, C. M. Lewis, & J. Harriss (Eds.), The New Institutional Economics and Third World Development (p. 360). Routledge.

25 Díez-Martín, F., Blanco-González, A., & Prado-Román, C. (2016). Explaining nation-wide differences in entrepreneurial activity: a legitimacy perspective. International Entrepreneurship and Management Journal, 12(4), 1079–1102. https://doi.org/10.1007/s11365-015-0381-4

26 World Trade Organization. (2009). World Trade Report 2004: Governance and Institutions.

27 www.igi-global.com/dictionary/governance/12372

28 Denis, D. K., & McConnell, J. J. (2003). International corporate governance. The Journal of Financial and Quantitative Analysis, 38(1), 1. https://doi.org/10.2307/4126762

29 Jensen, Michael C. (1993). The modern industrial revolution, exit, and the failure of internal control systems, The Journal of Finance, 48(3), Papers and Proceedings of the Fifty-Third Annual Meeting of the American Finance Association: Anaheim, California January 5–7, 1993.

30 Mazzarol, T. (2014). The role of co-operative enterprise in Australian agribusiness. Enterprise Society: The Conversation, January 19, 2014.

31 Melo, L. (2015). Firm-Level Corporate Governance in the Context of Emerging Market Firm Internationalization, Bentley University, Ph. D. Dissertation.

32 Mazzarol, T. (2014). Does it matter if Australia no longer manufactures things? Enterprise Society: The Conversation, April 11, 2014.

33 Mazzarol, T. (2014). How do Australia's universities engage with entrepreneurship and small business? CEMI Discussion Paper Series, DP 1401, Centre for Entrepreneurial Management and Innovation.

34 Sen, A. (1999). Development as Freedom. Oxford: Oxford University Press.

35 Hufty, M. (2011). "Investigating Policy Processes: The Governance Analytical Framework (GAF). In: Wiesmann, U., Hurni, H., et al. editors. Research for Sustainable Development: Foundations, Experiences, and Perspectives." Bern: Geographica Bernensia: 403–424.)

36 Denis, D., & McConnell, J. (2003). International corporate governance. Journal of Financial and Quantitative Analysis, 38(1)(March), 1–36, p. 5.

37 Melo, L. (2015). Firm-Level Corporate Governance in the Context of Emerging Market Firm Internationalization, Bentley University, Ph. D. Dissertation.

38 La Porta, R., Lopez-de-Silanes, F., Shleifer, A., & Vishny, R. W. (1997). Legal determinants of external finance. The Journal of Finance, 52(3), 1131–1150. https://doi.org/10.1111/j.1540-6261.1997.tb02727.x

39 La Porta, R., Lopez-de-Silanes, F., Shleifer, A., & Vishny, R. W. (1998). Law and finance. Journal of Political Economy, 106(6), 1113–1155. https://doi.org/10.1086/250042

40 La Porta, R., Lopez-De-Silanes, F., & Shleifer, A. (1999). Corporate ownership around the world. The Journal of Finance, 54(2), 471–517. https://doi.org/10.1111/0022-1082.00115

41 Mallin, C., Michelon, G., & Raggi, D. (2013). Monitoring intensity and stakeholders' orientation: how does governance affect social and environmental disclosure? Journal of Business Ethics, 114(1), 29–43. https://doi.org/10.1007/s10551-012-1324-4

42 Rodrik, D. (2008). One Economics Many Recipes: Globalization, Institutions, and Economic Growth. Princeton University Press.

43 Melo, L. (2015). Firm-Level Corporate Governance in the Context of Emerging Market Firm Internationalization, Bentley University, Ph. D. Dissertation.

44 Thai, M. T. T., & Turkina, E. (2014). Macro-level determinants of formal entrepreneurship versus informal entrepreneurship. Journal of Business Venturing, 29(4), 490–510. https://doi.org/10.1016/j.jbusvent.2013.07.005

45 Friedman, B. A. (2011). The relationship between governance effectiveness and entrepreneurship. International Journal of Humanities and Social Science, 1(17), 221–225.

46 Isenberg, D. (2016). The big idea: how to start an entrepreneurial revolution. Harvard Business Review. Harvard Business School Publishing, June 2010. Retrieved from: https://hbr.org/2010/06/the-big-idea-how-to-start-an-entrepreneurial-revolution.

47 Groşanu, A., Boţa-Avram, C., Răchişan, P. R., Vesselinov, R., & Tiron-Tudor, A. (2015). The influence of country-level governance on business environment and entrepreneurship: a global perspective. Amfiteatru Economic, 17(38), 60–75.

48 Isenberg, Daniel. (2010). The big idea: how to start an entrepreneurial revolution. Harvard Business Review. Harvard Business School Publishing, June 2010. Retrieved from: https://hbr.org/2010/06/the-big-idea-how-to-start-an-entrepreneurial-revolution.

49 Isenberg, Daniel. (2010). The big idea: how to start an entrepreneurial revolution. Harvard Business Review. Harvard Business School Publishing, June 2010. Retrieved from: https://hbr.org/2010/06/the-big-idea-how-to-start-an-entrepreneurial-revolution.

50 Friedman, B. A. (2011). The relationship between governance effectiveness and entrepreneurship. International Journal of Humanities and Social Science, 1(17), 221–225.

51 Friedman, B. A. (2011). The relationship between governance effectiveness and entrepreneurship. International Journal of Humanities and Social Science, 1(17), 221–225.

52 Groşanu, A., Boţa-Avram, C., Răchişan, P. R., Vesselinov, R., & Tiron-Tudor, A. (2015). The influence of country-level governance on business environment and entrepreneurship: a global perspective. Amfiteatru Economic, 17(38), 60–75.

53 Rodrik, Dani. One economics many recipes: globalization, institutions, and economic growth, Princeton University Press, 2008; Groşanu, A., Boţa-Avram, C., Răchişan, P. R., Vesselinov, R., & Tiron-Tudor, A. (2015). The influence of country-level governance on business environment and entrepreneurship: a global perspective. Amfiteatru Economic, 17(38), 60–75.

54 Brander, J., Hendricks, K., Amit, R., & Whistler, D. (1998). The engine of growth hypothesis: on the relationship between firm size and employment growth work. University of British Columbia, Department of Economics. Manuscript, July.

55 Klapper, L., & Quesada Delgado, J. M. (2007). Understanding entrepreneurship: influences and consequences of business creation. World Bank Viewpoint.

56 Rodrik, Dani. (2008). One Economics Many Recipes: Globalization, Institutions, and Economic Growth. Princeton University Press.

57 Melo, L. (2015). Firm-Level Corporate Governance in the Context of Emerging Market Firm Internationalization, Bentley University, Ph. D. Dissertation.

58 Alnassiri, A. (2017). Iraqi Entrepreneurship Center. Retrieved from www.bite.tech/news/iraqi-entrepreneurship-center.

59 Morck, R., Shleifer, A., & Vishny, R. W. (1988). Management ownership and market valuation: an empirical analysis. Journal of Financial Economics, 20: 293–315.

60 Avnimelech, G., & Zelekha, Y. (2011). The impact of corruption on entrepreneurship. International Business Ethics and Growth Opportunities. IGI Global, pp. 282–294. Oct. 2008. Web. 3 Oct. 2016. http://link.springer.com/article/10.1007%2Fs11187-008-9135-9.

61 Venables, A. J. (2016, February). Using natural resources for development: why has it proven so difficult? Journal of Economic Perspectives, 30(1), 161–184. doi:10.1257/jep.30.1.161.

62 Stiglitz, J. (2008). The $ 3 trillion war. New Perspectives Quarterly, 25(2), 61–64. https://doi.org/10.1111/j.1540-5842.2008.00980.x

63 Farooqi, H., & Asgary, N. H. (2016). Natural resources and economic development: the case of Afghanistan. Cyrus Chronicle Journal, 1(1), 38–48. https://doi.org/10.21902/2573–5691/2016.v1i1.5

64 Asgary, N. (2016). Role of institutions in sustainable and socially equitable development. Cyrus Chronicle Journal: Contemporary Economic and Management Studies in Asia and Africa, 1(1).

65 Other such institutions include: "The Publish What You Pay" and The World Bank-sponsored Stolen Assets Recovery (StAR) Initiative.

66 Lawson-Remer, T. (2012). Beating the resource curse: global governance strategies for democracy and economic development. Civil Society, Markets, and Democracy Program. Lechner, R. (2009, March 10). The seven pillars of a 'green' corporate strategy. Environmental Leader, n. p. Retrieved November 15, 2014, from www.environmentalleader.com/2009/03/10/the-seven-pillars-of-a-greencorporate-strategy.

67 Baland, J.-M., Moene, K. O., & Robinson, J. A. (2009). Governance and development. In Handbook of Development Economics (Vol. 5, pp. 4597–4656). https://doi.org/10.1016/B978-0-444-52944-2.00007-0

68 Asgary, Nader. (2016). Role of institutions in sustainable and socially equitable development. Cyrus Chronicle Journal: Contemporary Economic and Management Studies in Asia and Africa, MA, Vol. 1, 1.

69 Social Europe (SE). (n.d.). Retrieved December 16, 2018, from www.socialeurope.eu/.

70 Drezner, D. W. (2001). Globalization and Policy Convergence. International Studies Review.

71 Drezner, D. W. (2001). Globalization and Policy Convergence. International Studies Review.

72 Stiglitz, J. E. (2006). Stability With Growth: Macroeconomics, Liberalization and Development. Oxford University Press.

73 Kettl, D. F. (2000). The transformation of governance: globalization, devolution, and the role of government. Public Administration Review.

74 Edwards, S. (2017, April 4). 140 Million Euros of EU Funding a Year at Risk for UK NGOs after Brexit. Retrieved December 16, 2018, from www.devex.com/news/140-million-euros-of-eu-funding-a-year-at-risk-for-uk-ngos-after-brexit-89932.

75 The Nation. (2013, February 22). The World's Political and Economic Landscape is Undergoing Major Adjustments and Changes. Although Some Progress Has Been Made in the Reform of Global Economic Governance, the Financial Crisis is Not Yet behind Us and the Structural Problems Exposed by Th. Thailand Edition ed. China Daily, Asia News Network. Web. Dec. 10, 2015.

76 Krasner, D. (2015). Why We Aren't Winning Wars, www.ohio.com/akron/editorial/stephen-d-krasner-why-we-aren-t-winning-wars.

77 Ragab, A. (2016, September 15). Why Does Corruption Exist? Retrieved December 16, 2018, from www.linkedin.com/pulse/why-does-corruption-exist-alaa-ragab?articleId=6182106880798662656.

78 Transparency International. (2016). Retrieved August 14, 2017, from https://en.wikipedia.org/wiki/Transparency_International.

79 Newig, J., Kochskämper, E., Challies, E., & Jager, N. W. (2016). Exploring governance learning: how policymakers draw on evidence, experience and intuition in designing participatory flood risk planning. Environmental Science & Policy, 55, 353–360. doi:10.1016/j.envsci.2015.07.020

80 Acs, Z. J., Desai, S., & Hessels, J. (2008). Entrepreneurship, economic development and institutions. Small Business Economics, 31(3), 219–234. https://doi.org/10.1007/s11187-008-9135-9

81 Porter M. E. (1990). The Competitive Advantage of Nations. London: Macmillan.

82   Porter, M., Sachs, J., & McArthur, J. (2002). Executive summary: competitiveness and stages of economic development. In M. Porter, J. Sachs, P. K. Cornelius, J. W. McArthur, & K. Schwab (Eds.), The Global Competitiveness Report 2001.

83   Acs, Z. J., Desai, S., & Hessels, J. (2008). Entrepreneurship, economic development, and institutions. Small Business Economics, 31(3), 219–234.

84   Acs, Z. J., & Szerb, L. (2006). Entrepreneurship, economic growth and public policy. Small Business Economics, 28(2–3), 109–122. doi:10.1007/s11187-006-9012-3

85   Nascent phase entrepreneurship levels: Source: Global Entrepreneurship Monitor – Adult Population Survey Measures (2015).

86   Hoskisson, R. E., Eden, L., Lau, C. M., & Wright, M. (2000). Strategy in emerging economies. Academy of Management Journal, 43(3), 249–267. https://doi.org/10.2307/1556394

87   Wright, M., Filatotchev, I., Hoskisson, R. E., & Peng, M. W. (2005). Strategy research in emerging economies: challenging the conventional wisdom – Introduction. Journal of Management Studies, 42(1), 1–33. https://doi.org/DOI 10.1111/j.1467-6486.2005.00487.x

88   Carruthers, B. G., Hollingsworth, J. R., & Boyer, R. (1998). Contemporary capitalism: the embeddedness of institutions. Contemporary Sociology. Cambridge University Press. https://doi.org/10.2307/2655178

89   Feldman, M. S., & Rafaeli, A. (2002). Organizational routines as sources of connections and understandings. Journal of Management Studies, 39(3), 309–331. https://doi.org/10.1111/1467-6486.00294

90   Peng, M. W. (2003). Institutional transitions and strategic choices. Academy of Management Review, 28(2), 275–296. https://doi.org/10.5465/AMR.2003.9416341

91   Peng, M. W., Lee, S. H., & Wang, D. Y. L. (2005, July 1). What determines the scope of the firm over time? A focus on institutional relatedness. Academy of Management Review. Academy of Management. https://doi.org/10.5465/AMR.2005.17293731

92   Powell, W. W. (1991). Expanding the scope of institutional analysis. In The New Institutionalism in Organizational Analysis (pp. 183–203). The University of Chicago Press. Retrieved from http://ci.nii.ac.jp/naid/10030010601/.

93   North, D. C. (1994). Economic performance through time. The American Economic Review, 84(3), 359–368. https://doi.org/10.2307/2118057

94   Peng, M. W., & Heath, P. S. (1996). The growth of the firm in planned economies in transition: institutions, organizations, and strategic choice. Academy of Management Review, 21(2), 492–528. https://doi.org/10.5465/AMR.1996.9605060220

95   Zahra, S. A., Dharwadkar, R., & George, G. (2000, May). Entrepreneurship in multinational subsidiaries: the effects of corporate and local environmental contexts. In Published in Conference Proceedings, Entrepreneurship, Academy of Management, Toronto, Canada, August (Vol. 2130, pp. 4–9).

96   Mitton, T. (2002). A cross-firm analysis of the impact of corporate governance on the East Asian financial crisis. Journal of Financial Economics, 64(2), 215–241. https://doi.org/10.1016/S0304-405X(02)00076-4

97   Peng, M. W. (2004). Institutional transitions and strategic choice (vol. 28, p. 278, 2003). Academy of Management Review, 29(3), 278.

98   Peng, M. W., Buck, T., & Filatotchev, I. (2003). Do outside directors and new managers help improve firm performance? An exploratory study in Russian privatization. Journal of World Business, 38(4), 348–360. https://doi.org/10.1016/j.jwb.2003.08.020

99   Koster, S., & Rai, S. K. (2008). Entrepreneurship and economic development in a developing country: a case study of India. Journal of Entrepreneurship, 17(2), 117–137.

100 Wong, T. A., et al. (2005). Membrane metabolism mediated by Sec14 family members' influences Arf GTPase activating protein activity for transport from the trans-Golgi. Proc Natl Acad Sci USA, 102(36), 12777–12782.

101 Prieger, J. E., Bampoky, C., Blanco, L. R., & Liu, A. (2016). Economic growth and the optimal level of entrepreneurship. World Development, 82, 95–109. doi: 10.1016/j.worlddev.2016.01.013.

102 Prieger, J. E., Bampoky, C., Blanco, L. R., & Liu, A. (2016). Economic growth and the optimal level of entrepreneurship. World Development, 82, 95–109. doi: 10.1016/j.worlddev.2016.01.013.

103 Porter, M. E. (1996). What is Strategy? Published November.

104 Rodrik, D. (2007). One Economics, Many Recipes: Globalization, Institutions, and Economic Growth. Princeton University Press. Retrieved from https://press.princeton.edu/titles/8494.html.

105 Covi, G. (2016). Local systems' strategies copying with globalization: collective local entrepreneurship. Journal of the Knowledge Economy, 7(2), 513–525. https://doi.org/10.1007/s13132-014-0225-4

106 Innovation, Higher Education and Research for Development. (2012). Research Universities: Networking the Knowledge Economy. Retrieved from www.oecd.org/sti/Session%205_Networking%20the%20Knowledge%20Economy.pdf

107 Covi, G. (2016). Local systems' strategies copying with globalization: collective local entrepreneurship. Journal of the Knowledge Economy, 7(2), 513–525. https://doi.org/10.1007/s13132-014-0225-4

108 Nonaka, I., & Takeuchi, H. (1995). The Knowledge-Creating Company: How Japanese Companies Create the Dynamics of Innovation? Oxford University Press.

109 Arrow, K. (1994). Methodological individualism and social knowledge. The American Economic Review, 84(2), 1–9. Retrieved from www.jstor.org/stable/2117792

110 Melo, L. (2015). Firm-Level Corporate Governance in the Context of Emerging Market Firm Internationalization, Bentley University, Ph. D. Dissertation.

7   Ethics and corporate social responsibility

Learning objectives:

1. *Understand the definition of ethics and some of the relevant theories*
2. *Comprehend the stakeholders' theory and corporate social responsibility (CSR)*
3. *Examine the relationship between CSR and human resource management (HRM)*
4. *Evaluate the impact of CSR on entrepreneurship and competitiveness*
5. *Discuss the relationship between CSR, HRM, and strategy.*

Figure 7.1 Wells Fargo

Source: © iStock: wdstock. http://business-ethics.com/2015/05/05/does-corporate-social-responsibility-increase-profits/

Wells Fargo: a case on responsible leadership

Wells Fargo, led by CEO and Chairman John Stumpf, pressured its employees into unethical business practices by conditioning them to go after cross-selling opportunities no matter how detrimental to the customer. By putting such an emphasis on cross-selling and by tying financial performances to unrealistic sales targets, Wells Fargo forced lower-level team members to falsify cross-selling occurrences of their customers so that they could earn bonuses and keep their jobs. This created many negative effects to the customers, including incurring fees for unconsented services, as well as reducing credit scores. To combat negative publicity from these behaviors and the recently fired employees' concerns expressed in the media, Wells Fargo publicly denounced these practices by pointing towards their "Vision, Values, and Code of Ethics" which they hid behind while committing unethical conduct. In addition, they worked quickly to get rid of employees who opposed these practices through a "can the whistleblowers" process by encouraging them to use their ethics hotline and then finding trumped-up charges to fire any employees who utilized it. When all of these problems came to light, Wells Fargo failed at scapegoating individual employees for the falsified cross-selling occurrences and leadership was rightfully forced to shamefully resign.

The key problem in this case is the lack of accountability and responsibility of management and executives for the actions that took place under their control. In 2011, Stumpf knew there was a problem but ignored it until the problem became too large to ignore. Several problems are observable. First, it was the top-down pressure from executives. Second, HR executives were being given tips on how to handle the whistleblowers of the company by completely disregarding the Dispute Resolution Policy of Wells Fargo and finding ways to work around the truth in order to get rid of employees who refused to comply with unethical behaviors. Finally, top management strayed from the Code of Ethics and vision of the company.

Questions for discussion

1. If a new management were to replace the current one, what checks and balances should be adopted to combat any future mishandling of power?
2. How much control should the HR department possess in a business/company? What decision capabilities should the future HR department of Wells Fargo possess?

Introduction

In this chapter, we will define ethics, corporate social responsibility (CSR), and human resource management (HRM), and their implication in the era of globalization for businesses and for entrepreneurial activities. The role of communications and technology in providing the tools that advance transparency and good governance will also be discussed. We will review the connection of CSR to CSE (corporate social entrepreneurship) and analyze their combination, such as the case of hybrid organizations. In addition, we are examining the underlying relationship between CSR and HRM. Finally, we discuss a variety of aspects regarding the efficient managerial implementation of CSR practices, including social entrepreneurship, competitive advantage, and the triple bottom line.

Theories of ethics and their business implications

Ethics is a widely used term and it's synonymous to a moral code, morals, morality, values, rights and wrongs, principles, ideals, standards (of behavior), value systems, virtues, and dictates of conscience. Therefore, it is not easy to define ethics clearly and concisely because they may have different meaning and understanding by different stakeholders, locally and globally. Simply put, ethics is the behavior that is concerned with "ought" and "ought not". It extends above and beyond the standards set forth by the law or those which are commercially profitable.

In literature, the theories on ethics and management have evolved into two parallel streams. Theories of management have been discussed mainly by management scientists, practitioners, economists, and business administrators whose primary concerns remain economic efficiency, organizational effectiveness, and product or service innovation. Some scholars have discussed it in virtual isolation from the ethical implications of management decisions.[1,2] This mechanistic approach expects managers and employees to follow ethics policies and procedures without having a logical justification for why ethical behavior is essential, beneficial, or desirable.

On the other hand, theories of ethics have been studied by social scientists and philosophers explaining ethics in abstract terms such as "axios", "deontos", or "teleos", with little attention to the practical implications for organizations.[3] In other studies, models of ethics have been proposed and key components of ethical behavior were identified for MNCs in isolation from the conceptual foundations of ethics or management.[4]

Theories of ethics such as deontology and utilitarianism have been utilized for performing ethical behavior in organizations.[5,6,7,8] However, these efforts are scattered and have a glaring gap in business ethics literature when considering the relationship between the acclaimed frameworks of ethics and dominant theories of management.

In Table 7.1, we have briefly summarized the main theories of ethics and their implications for business management.[9]

Ethics and business discipline

Business ethics is recognized as a management discipline that has grown from the social responsibility movement of the 1960s. From this movement, the idea of business ethics originated as doing what is right for the company's stakeholders. This is a term commonly referred to as corporate social responsibility (CSR) and is often utilized in defining the ethics.[10,11] CSR – although dealing with categories or levels of economic, legal, and discretionary activities – also refers to ethical values that are expected of business by the society.[12,13]

For several reasons, the demands for social responsibility and ethical behavior of corporations have become substantially stronger. With the growth of American businesses, stakeholders have come to expect more from businesses than was previously demanded. There has also developed a class of new nobility that demands charitable and ethical behavior from individuals (i.e., Gates, Clinton, Omiedyar, Soros, etc.) and corporations that have become powerful and profitable (i.e., Microsoft, Facebook, etc.). The final reason that the demands have increased is that business institutions have become so powerful that their domain has expanded to include some of the areas that were once covered by government agencies. In light of the changes in business and in the American society, it is necessary for companies to make ethical decisions that take into consideration the plethora of social concerns that have become incorporated into the role of businesses.

Table 7.1 Ethic theories

Theory	Definition/characteristics	Implications for businesses
Axiological Ethics "Axiā" (Greek) – "Value"/"Worth"	The science of determining the value of an idea or object for an individual or organization. It differentiates between "instrumental" values or what is good as a means, and "intrinsic" value" which is what is good as an end.	Actions are right or wrong based on their intrinsic goodness regardless of their economic consequences. It emphasizes the inherent happiness of the stakeholders generated from the decisions made by employees or managers.
Teleological Ethics **"Virtue Ethics"** "Teleos"(Greek) – *"brought to its end or purpose"*	Considers an action proper or improper according to the desirability of its outcome. Actions are right and justified if the consequences are good regardless of the intentions and means of achieving the action. Served as basis for the "utilitarianism" of the nineteenth century.	Main objective of ethical action is to achieve an appropriate and advantageous end or goal. Considers an action good if it promotes the greatest happiness possible in economic terms and treats human beings as economic creatures (homo-economics).
Deontological Ethics "Deontos" (Greek) – "that which is obligatory"	Focuses on the obligations and duties that various members of society have towards one another. The Kantian version of deontological ethics dictates that these duties could be determined by a rational process called the "Categorical Imperative" – a universal principle of ethics regardless of individual interests, organizational objectives, or economic consequences.	According to Kantian deontology which subordinates individual interest to higher principles, the ultimate purpose of being for business organizations, becomes the development of rational and moral capabilities of the organization's stakeholders, not the maximization of profits or stockholder's equity.[a]
Perfectionist Ethics	Concerned with the application of principles of moral perfectionism to ethical conduct of individuals and organizations. Expects individuals to live and promote lives that are objectively good.	Dimensions of perfections have been defined, and rationality in decision-making has been identified as one of them.[b]
Utilitarian Ethics "The greatest happiness principle"	Based on the premise that moral worth of an action depends entirely on its contribution to overall perceivable utility for society. Thus, the highest objective of ethical conduct is to maximize the utility of the outcome of an action in terms of happiness, pleasure, or some other satisfaction of desired objectives.	"The greatest good for the greatest number of people." Suitable for business decision-making in that it provides a sound economic basis for testing the efficacy of ethical decisions, clearly identifies the stakeholders, and provides an objective approach to conflict resolution in decision-making.[c]

(continued)

Table 7.1 (Cont.)

Theory	Definition/characteristics	Implications for businesses
Existentialist Ethics	Human freedom is the foundation of the understanding of all motives, reason, morals, and values.[d] Key features include freedom of choice, subjectivity of human experience, and values, which are seen as consequences and not determinants of human moral decisions and choice.[e]	The requirement of individual's awareness of freedom and responsibility to distinguish between choices makes existentialism a highly individualistic ethical doctrine.
Naturalistic Ethics	Based on British empiricism, which implies that all knowledge is derived from experience and sensory perception.	Suggests that true propositions of ethics are derived from objective features of nature independent of any moral judgement, opinions, or subjective values. Highly applicable in tourism and hospitality industries.[f]
Relativistic Ethics	Ethical behavior cannot be defined or prescribed in universally applicable absolute terms. An action can be considered "ethical" in one set of social, cultural, and individual circumstances and "unethical" in a different set of circumstances.	The requirement of giving fair wages while employing fewer workers can be justified on ethical grounds in an economy where there is a better balance between the demand and availability of workers. On the other hand, in countries such as India, where the oversupply of labor is chronic, this choice may not be very ethical.

[a] Gotsis, G., & Kortezi, Z. (2008). Philosophical foundations of workplace spirituality: a critical approach. Journal of Business Ethics, 78(4), 575–600. https://doi.org/10.1007/s10551-007-9369-5

[b] Foot, P. (2003). Natural Goodness. Oxford: Clarendon Press.

[c] Barry, N. P. (1979). Hayek's Social and Economic Philosophy. London: Palgrave Macmillan UK. https://doi.org/10.1007/978-1-349-04268-5

[d] Sartre, J.-P. (1956). Being and Nothingness: An Essay on Phenomenological Ontology, translated by H. E. Barnes. New York: Philosophical Library Inc.

[e] West, A. (2008). Sartrean existentialism and ethical decision-making in business. Journal of Business Ethics, 81(1), 15–25. https://doi.org/10.1007/s10551-007-9477-2

[f] Yaman, H. R. (2003). Skinner's naturalism as a paradigm for teaching business ethics: a discussion from tourism. Teaching Business Ethics, 7(2), 107–122.

While profitability alone often does not show overall performance, in the long-run, good ethics certainly will.

Businesses will engage in ethical practices either because of a desire to be ethical or due to stakeholder concern and at times because of regulations.[14]

For example, Bentley University has sworn to "educate creative, ethical, and socially responsible organizational leaders by creating and disseminating impactful knowledge within and across business and the arts and sciences."[15] Being a member of The Principles for Responsible Management Education (PRME)[16], a UN Global Compact sponsored initiative, Bentley adheres to its mission statement through providing transparency of its

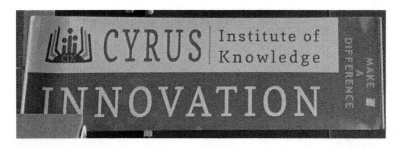

Figure 7.2 CIK logo

CSR-oriented activities through the reports for the UN Global Compact Communication on Engagement.

> CYRUS Institute of Knowledge (CIK) was created in March of 2011 to establish an intellectual atmosphere for scholars and practitioners to engage in the educational activity of generating theoretical and applied knowledge in management sciences, economic development, and sustainable growth, and related disciplines applicable to the Middle East, Central Asia, and North Africa. CIK's vision is "to cultivate the discourse on human capital potentials for better living." CIK's aim is to "Make A Difference" which is highlighted on its logo, website, and marketing documents and it is consistent with its stated values (see weblink). Read more about CIK at www.cyrusik.org/ and analyze it as a non-profit organization.

Bentley's Alliance for Ethics and Social Responsibility (2015) "serves as an umbrella for more than 20 campus initiatives that share resources and ideas to encourage greater internal and external engagement around important issues regarding ethics, social responsibility, civic engagement, and sustainability."[17] Such initiatives should be embraced by all educational and non-educational institutions in order to improve their brand reputation and further enhance their business healthiness in their industry.

The importance of having individuals preserve and enhance their ethical values in combination with recent movement of business ethics and corporate social responsibility should lead to a fair and decent society. Ethical values became the topic of discussion at human-resource meetings, and the outcomes of these discussions affect the surrounding community, thus came to play a role in company decisions.[18]

When companies apply ethical conduct as a seal of their profitability, they measure profit on the scale of ethical integrity, morality, and social contribution.[19,20,21]

Merwe, Pitt, and Berthon (2003) examined what ethics is and how they apply to the business world. They also discussed if it is important to consider the question of why a company should practice ethical behavior.[22] Peters and Waterman's study explored the relationship between corporate ethics and the concept of excellence as defined under the definition of excellence. According to their study, excellence in a company was dependent on eight characteristics.[23] These qualities were then evaluated by self-administered,

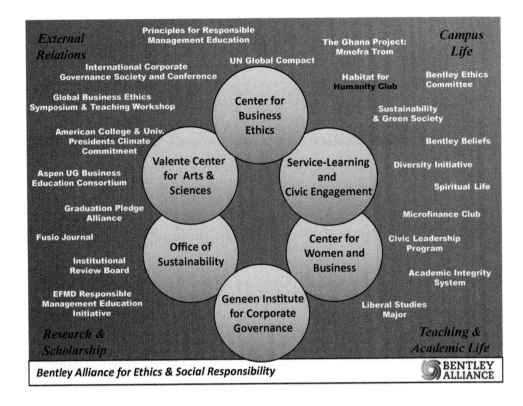

External
Relations

Principles for Responsible
Management Education

UN Global Compact

International Corporate
Governance Society and Conference

Global Business Ethics
Symposium & Teaching Workshop

American College & Univ.
Presidents Climate
Commitment

Aspen UG Business
Education Consortium

Graduation Pledge
Alliance

Fusio Journal

Institutional
Review Board

EFMD Responsible
Management Education
Initiative

**Research &
Scholarship**

The Ghana Project:
Mmofra Trom

Habitat for
Humanity Club

*Campus
Life*

Bentley Ethics
Committee

Sustainability
& Green Society

Bentley Beliefs

Diversity Initiative

Spiritual Life

Microfinance Club

Civic Leadership
Program

Academic Integrity
System

Liberal Studies
Major

*Teaching &
Academic Life*

Center for
Business
Ethics

Valente Center
for Arts &
Sciences

Service-Learning
and
Civic Engagement

Office of
Sustainability

Center for
Women and
Business

Geneen Institute
for Corporate
Governance

Bentley Alliance for Ethics & Social Responsibility

BENTLEY
ALLIANCE

Figure 7.3 Bentley

anonymous questionnaires that were generated from a large commercial database and then sent to a sample of companies operating in industrial markets in the UK. The second component of these self-administered surveys referenced the ethical qualities possessed by the companies. This survey defined ethics as "a set of moral principles or values". The questionnaires were used to assess managerial perceptions of excellence and the perception these chosen managers had regarding the attitudes that their company held to business ethics. The results of this study showed that there was a highly significant correlation between ethics and excellence. It was identified that many of the components of excellence are associated with an ethical culture. It also revealed that many of the excellent companies were also ethical companies.[24] Ahmed et al. (2003) examined ethical beliefs on a global level in an effort to contend that people in different environments shared differed expectations as to what was ethical and acceptable. They used scenarios and surveyed students in business courses in China, Egypt, Finland, Korea, Russia, and the United States. Though all respondents viewed the ethical problems in a similar manner (the basic concepts of right vs wrong and good vs bad), they found that the potential harms resulting from the practices were viewed differently. For instance, when asked whether participating in the unethical behavior would have a negative effect, it was viewed differently across cultures.[25,26]

Figure 7.4 Business ethics

Source: © iStock: tumsasedgars. http://blog.proqc.com/the-quality-social-responsibility-connection/

Pioneering the field of business ethics since 1976

The W. Michael Hoffman Center for Business Ethics (HCBE) at Bentley University is one of the world's leading research and educational institutes in the field of business ethics and was established in 1976. HCBE's mission is to develop leadership in the creation of organizational cultures that align effective business performance with ethical business conduct. It endeavors to do so by the application of expertise, research, education, and a collaborative approach to disseminating best practices.

HCBE strives to: Connect ethical thought and action; Inspire ethical leadership; Enrich ethical knowledge; and Promote ethical collaboration.

Corporate social responsibility definition and implications

The online business dictionary defines CSR as "a company's sense of responsibility towards the community and environment (both ecological and social) in which it operates."[27] Freeman (1984) defined stakeholders as "any group or individual who can affect or is affected by the achievement of the firm's objectives."[28] Others scholars proposed codes of ethics for multinational organizations and discussed voluntary guidelines. The stakeholder's theory maintains that companies should incorporate the interests of the internal (i.e., owners, customers, employees, and suppliers) and the external (i.e., governments, environmentalists, special interest groups, and local community organizations, etc....) constituencies into their business decisions. The main idea of this theory is that the success of an organization depends upon the degree of satisfaction of all stakeholders under consideration.[29,30,31]

Donaldson and Preston make three arguments in support of the stakeholder theory which is descriptive, instrumental, and normative. The descriptive argument is the demonstration of what firms are actually doing. The instrumental argument is that the theory is vital for their business strategy. And it is normative because it is the "right" thing to do – considering everybody that is impacted by it. Therefore, companies that consider the interests of stakeholders will have better success in developing a more sustainable and profitable organization in the long-run.[32]

In the past, companies, organizations, and entrepreneurs were taught that their objective was to make a profit, however, CSR argues that companies should consider their overall impact on their stakeholders. In other words, companies need to understand that all of their activities impact on customers, stockholders, the environment, employees, communities, and all other members of the general public. However, this does not mean that companies cannot make a profit following the CSR strategies. The three most popular reasons for applying CSR are raising profits, benefiting the environment, and bettering the company brand image. By adopting CSR strategies, such as the "seven strategies for delivering profits with principles", revenue-driven CSR participants can integrate their business activities with charitable activities.[33]

- Ethics is the behavior that is concerned with "ought" and "ought not".
- There are eight main theories of ethics that implicate business management.
- Corporate social responsibility (CSR) is often utilized in defining the ethics and is basically doing what is right for the company's stakeholders.
- Preserve and enhanced individual ethical values combined with the recent movement of business ethics and corporate social responsibility should lead to a fair and decent society.
- When companies apply ethical conduct as a seal of their profitability, they measure profit on the scale of ethical integrity, morality, and social contribution.

Therefore, they can make a profit while, at the same time, being responsible for a border community. Figure 7.6 shows that companies with strong CSR will have high efficiency and happiness with their main stakeholders, their employees.

Companies that focus on the environmental effect as their CSR can also make a profit. By using a "green" strategy, the companies can not only reduce their financial burdens/ risks due to environmental blunders but also improve their brand image, as done by Starbucks and Costco. Moreover, since more and more consumers choose a product or service based on the company's CSR record, companies make a profit by bettering their brand image. It is important for companies to apply an appropriate CSR strategy to maximize its positive effects while minimizing negative impacts on its stakeholders.

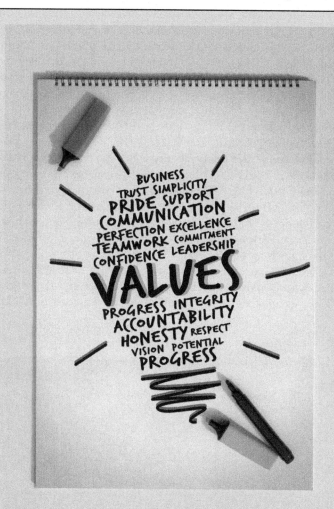

Figure 7.5 Values
Source: © iStock: Devrimb

These days most companies have a "Corporate Responsibility" page which communicates the company's social efforts. It also contains information to educate its customers on the company's ethical policies and standards.

Chevron CSR page[34]

Therefore, companies, organizations, and entrepreneurs individually should consider the following three things: making a frank assessment of their ethos, determining the strategic value that social responsibility activities provides for their firm, and understanding the company's industry and competitive CSR landscape. By making an honest assessment of the firm's ethos, the company can ensure that its actions will not contradict its CSR brand identity. Along with these three considerations, CSR ranking, geography, and the industry type should also be considered. "Corporates' communication of their social efforts could help a company build a reputation that might protect its image against negative publicity or help restore it."[35] All of these fundamentals are applicable to both entrepreneurs and SMEs as well.

Therefore, entrepreneurs who build the foundation of their organization based on ethics and CSR will have higher potential success.

Companies known for a strong CSR brand identity will bring positive media attention for themselves (i.e., Starbucks, Costco, etc.). Negative media coverage can have a material impact on a firm's business bottom line. Additionally, the firm needs to consider whether its CSR related efforts will impact the target audience and to what degree, due to different degrees of authenticity. Besides raising profit, benefiting the environment, and bettering the company brand image, CSR can also help attract labor, retain customers, reduce manufacturing costs, and improve reputation.

Therefore, adopting a CSR strategy can maximize benefits to its stakeholders and at the same time minimize disadvantages in the marketplace. For example, Mark Zuckerberg, co-founder and CEO of Facebook, donated $25 million to the fight against Ebola.[36] This

Figure 7.6 Microsoft offices
Source: © iStock: robertocicchetti

is a perfect example of why the idea of CSR is so important in today's world. Zuckerberg has the means to make a difference via his company and he chose to do so. Furthermore, this donation is the epitome of why companies need to understand CSR so that they are able to follow in his footsteps and give back.

As a child, Bill Gates spent many hours of the day reading reference books like encyclopedias. When he was a young boy, his parents began to become worried that he might be bored and reserved at times. They made the decision to enroll him at Seattle's Lakeside School, where he had outstanding grades in English, drama, math, and science.

Even though his parents were concerned with how Bill Gates acted during his childhood, this did not stop him. He is known for founding the greatest software business, known as Microsoft. His interests and focus were on his business that led him to become one of the leaders of the company. Reviewing codes and assuring that Microsoft advertised its merits were only some of the things Gates took interest in. Not only was Bill Gates a business man, but also a family man. He was known for taking his mother, a well-respected and connected woman, on his tours and business trips.

Bill is a great example of how sometimes you might feel like you don't belong, but you can't let that influence what your goals are. His ambition and hard work show us that you cannot let anyone influence you or make decisions for yourself.

Revenue drove CSR companies to focus on performance that allows for "the better good." Jackson and Nelson state that in order to increase profits while abiding by principles, a company must follow its seven strategies: harness innovation for the public good, put people at the center, spread economic opportunity, engage in new alliances, be performance-driven in all aspects, practice superior governance, and pursue purpose beyond profit.[37]

The pursuit of these seven strategies promotes profitable and competitive activities while focusing on making the world a better place. In order to maximize its profit, a company should measure the success of its processes for these seven strategies through financial and social outcome metrics. A company that is focused on profit should integrate its business activities with charitable activities so that its participation in CSR produces a profit.

Business and charitable activities must be one and the same in order for participation in socially responsible activities to increase company profit.

Figure 7.7 Strategies for I

Source: http://pixr8.com/wp-content/uploads/2015/10/Rohit-Bansal-2-e1446023817609-1170x480.png

Companies that are environmentally conscious in their processes and that participate in activities which benefit the environment make them more competitive, successful, and socially responsible.[38]

Additionally, a "green" corporate strategy bolsters success as it allows for less financial burdens due to environmental blunders (litigation, clean-up costs, etc.) and therefore can be more profitable over the long-run. By adopting a corporate environmental strategy, most firms will advance their company performance.[39] A "green" strategy may make a company more competitive as it can lead to an "improved brand image" in the eye of the company's stockholders.

Companies can use marketing to establish an association between philanthropic efforts and a brand or product. More consumers look for philanthropic or CSR elements when choosing a product or service. However, it is important for these efforts to be sincere as social media allows consumers to see through artificial philanthropic activities that are only used for selfish gains of the company.[40] Companies who choose to generate brand loyalty through sincere philanthropic activities hope to see increases in profit due to this connection between the consumer and their CSR strategy. A company does this through marketing campaigns where it associates itself and its product with a particular cause. An example of this type of marketing campaign is the Dove "Real Beauty" campaign in which Dove attempts to create a new beauty standard, one that does not conform to social standards of beauty. Dove attempted to use emotional reactions (in particular to its 2006 Super Bowl commercial) to advance the reputation between its company and a cause (improved self-esteem through a modern sense of beauty) with an end goal of strengthening its relationship with its consumers and, therefore, increasing profits.

CSR and entrepreneurship

What really motivates people to be honest in business

Each year, one in seven large corporations commits fraud. Why? To find out, Alexander Wagner takes us inside the economics, ethics, and psychology of doing the right thing. Join him for an introspective journey down the slippery slopes of deception as he helps us understand why people behave the way they do.

You can check in more details the full TED Talk in this link: www.ted.com/talks/alexander_wagner_what_really_motivates_people_to_be_honest_in_business

CSR and entrepreneurship have been closely studied recently due to their interconnectedness and impact on the business environment. The technological development of the century has further elevated the impact of the forces of globalization on the market, which has significantly influenced both CSR and entrepreneurship. This has contributed to the recognition of the notion of corporate social entrepreneurship (CSE), which incorporates within itself entrepreneurship, corporate entrepreneurship, and social entrepreneurship.[41,42]

CSE could be regarded as a facilitator of a significant transformation in how the company is operated, where entrepreneurship is considered from the perspectives of an individual founder and a well-established organization.

CSE has been defined as: "the process of extending the firm's domain of competence and corresponding opportunity set through innovative leveraging of resources, both within and outside its direct control, aimed at the simultaneous creation of economic and social value."[43] Austin et al. (2006) state that a successfully implemented CSE consists of three key elements:

- Creating an enabling environment – top management should adopt an entrepreneurial mindset and a commonly shared sense of purpose throughout the organization;
- Fostering the corporate social entrepreneur – mainly change agents. They are distinct from other management roles as they will be the main facilitator of the internal organizational transformation;
- Corporate purpose of a value-based organization – a consistency between words and actions should be prominent in order for the firm to create more value.

Figure 7.8 Starbucks
Source: Image by ishane on flickr

"Aligning self-interest to social responsibility is the most powerful way to sustaining a company's success."
Orin Smith, Former President and CEO of Starbucks Coffee

In order to develop a sustainable CSE, a company must lay the foundations from the highest position of power in any given company. The main focus or goal of CSE is to serve as the basis for a sustainable and robust organizational transformation into a dynamic generator of societal improvement. In other words, more and more companies nowadays could benefit from the creation and maintenance of a balance between gaining "economic wealth" and contributing to the societal quality of life. An organization's vision and

Figure 7.9 Venture capital

Source: Who We Are. (n.d.). Retrieved from www.omidyar.com/who-we-are. Image by Simon Cunningham on flickr

values highly influence a firm's behavior on the market, thus consistent CSR activities could add a wider nonfinancial value. Hence, a potential for strategic and entrepreneurial activities is encouraged. Top-line strategic management is needed for successful incorporation of social causes in a firm's agenda. Other preconditions for the encouragement of entrepreneurial activities across an industry include a conducive regulatory climate and political stability. The external and internal quality of a relationship that an organization maintains is central to building the company's reputation, which later on translates into a direct nonfinancial value added. Therefore, it is essential for an organization to be "responsible while profitable", or in other words, to attempt and address particular societal needs while making a profit. Such organizations are often referred to as "hybrid" organizations. These organizations typically incorporate multiple existing organizational forms and attempt to create and maintain both social and financial wealth. Organizations which aim to create social value independent of financial wealth are typically the not-for-profit and non-governmental organizations. For-profit organizations are on the other side and the hybrid ones are in the middle, combining both sets of values.

Investing in social causes

Omidyar Network is an early seed funding Venture Capital group. The Network primarily invests in entrepreneurs who share their commitment to advancing social good at the pace and scale the world needs today. The company claims to be focused on five key areas they believe are building blocks for prosperous, stable, and open societies: Education, Emerging Tech, Financial Inclusion, Governance & Citizen Engagement, and Property Rights.

Pierre Omidyar experienced this firsthand as the founder of eBay. Just as eBay created the opportunity for millions of people to start their own businesses, the network believes market forces can be a potent driver for positive social change. That's why Omidyar Network invests in both for-profit businesses and non-profit organizations, whose complementary roles can advance entire sectors.

CSR and competitiveness

Scholars have shown that companies such as Costco, Whole Foods, Nestlé, and Starbucks, etc., who were able to clearly identify their companies' shared values with their stakeholders and incorporate CSR within their strategic business decisions, have gained competitive advantages over their competitors.[44,45] Porter and Kramer stated that integrating business and CSR requires adjustments in organization, reporting relationships, and incentives and they need to shift the performance measures to long-term competitiveness from short-term revenue generating. They stated that "the more closely tied a social issue is to a company's business, the greater the opportunity to leverage the firm's resources – and benefit society." [46] Therefore, to achieve a sustainable CSR impact, a company needs to be hands-on and tailor its operational process. Some scholars have presented a list of recommendations which are based on the best CSR practices in various industries.[47,48,49]

Figure 7.10 Nigeria startup
Source: Image by MEAACT on flickr

Developing a positive brand image is one primary driver for firms to develop a CSR strategy which could help a company build a reputation and protect its image. However, there is also evidence that shows managing the company's image is not as straightforward as having a CSR brand identity.

For example, when British Petroleum (BP) was promoting CSR programs, such as "Beyond Petroleum" program, they are more commonly picked up for negative media exposure because of big oil spills in the Gulf of Mexico. When choosing stories to publish, editors consider both the novelty of an event and whether it conforms to widely held beliefs.[50] Companies known for a strong CSR identity that commit an act detrimental to their brand identity will bring media attention to their issue due to the novelty of the event's occurrence. While a firm cannot afford to behave unethically or ignore CSR altogether, there is a risk that accompanies being a CSR leader as the firm takes on a heightened sense of scrutiny from the media.

Connecting minds

Lagos Angel Network helps bring organizations and individuals together who are willing to invest and mentor new technology startups in Nigeria. Tomi Davies, one of the IT consultants and one of the brains of the project, said "something is happening within the investment and technology space in Nigeria." The Lagos Advisory Council launched by the state governor helps different projects like Silicon Lagoon and Lagos Innovation Hotspots Maps.

Iroko is another program created by Lagos Angel Network and has already received more than $10m from Swedish and American investors. Another company named Jumia was able to find funding from the investment bank JP Morgan. This program allows technology companies to find funding and gives them the opportunity to succeed. If you believe that an industry can be developed and can find the funding, don't hesitate to do so.

Source: Angels in Lagos (2012)[51]

For instance, Mark Zuckerberg announced that 99 percent of Facebook shares (worth as much as $45 billion) would be donated for the "advancement of human potential" and the "promotion of equality". In 2010 he donated $100 million to the Newark Public School District. Although it was a generous and benevolent act, intended to serve good, Mark was highly criticized by public officials for it, as such an action was viewed to be inconsistent with his devotion to the "promotion of equality". As a result, he established the Chan Zuckerberg Initiative, which differs from traditional foundations in that it allows funding to help non-profit organizations, make private investments, and participate in political debates. Thus, Mr. Zuckerberg connected his beliefs to his deeds and increased his popularity as a CSR activist.[52]

According to a report by Freshfields Bruckhaus Deringer, more than one-quarter of crises spread to international media within an hour and over two-thirds within 24 hours. Despite six out of ten cases providing days if not months of notice, it still takes an average of 21 hours for companies to respond, leaving them open to "trial by Twitter".

Figure 7.11 Social media
Source: © iStock: rvlsoft

Geography and industry type should also be considered when developing a CSR strategy. Cohn and Wolfe (2014) show that "authenticity" has different meanings for consumers, contingent upon their geographic location and industry sector type.[53] Authenticity here is defined by the individual taking the poll, but was loosely defined as a "company with values and morals and stands by them no matter what challenges are encountered." The study shows industries that have high degrees of authenticity are supermarkets, electric companies, retailers, and coffee shops. See the full report by Freshfields Bruckhaus Deringer (n.d.).[54]

Authentic companies are companies that the consumer sees and experiences on a regular basis with repeated satisfaction. Companies on the bottom end of the authenticity scale are alcohol companies, fast food chains, and social media providers. These authenticity rankings also vary by geographic location. A firm must consider whether its CSR related efforts will impact its target audience and to what degree. In some cases, the firm may be in a sector where CSR strategies may directly support creating a positive, authentic brand identity, generating loyal consumers; or on the other hand, the firm may be in a market where CSR efforts will go relatively unnoticed but morally it has done well.

Most of the discussion about the CSR and competitive advantages are applicable for all organizations and entrepreneurial activities. Because of the sheer size of the MNCs' market share and competitors, they will get more widespread attention about CSR than smaller companies and entrepreneurs. Applying CSR is more critical for survivability for SMEs and entrepreneurs due to resource constraints and limitations. For example, a developing country offering quality products at a reasonable price will bring positive attention to the community. Actually, entrepreneurs who are authentic in applying CSR will get more attention whether they are in the developed or developing country. Perhaps being ethical and authentic stands out more in developed countries than developing because of the advancement in information exchanges.

Human Resources

In general, an entrepreneur who intends to establish an organization has to manage two important sets of challenges: internal and external. Some of the internal factors could be the gathering of creative, innovative, and cooperative staff, a well-developed rewards system, and employee assessment, all of which could contribute to a well-functioning organization. Schmeiter et al. (2013) examined the interrelationships between HRM, organizational climate, and culture factors that impact them.[55] Read more.[56]

Figure 7.12 Responsible drinking
Source: © iStock: Stratol

Leave the driving to Coors

The beer company Molson Coors invests more in responsible drinking education than on alcohol-centered events. Molson reaches out to the community to find ways to spread the message of responsible drinking by putting money behind the TaxiGuy program and covering the cost of free public transit on New Year's Eve around major cities of Canada.

Coors Light®, its American subsidiary, is partnering with Valley Metro and Uber to help residents and visitors ring in the New Year safely. In partnership with Crescent Crown Distributing, Coors Light Free Rides® will be available on all Valley Metro Rail and Bus routes Saturday, December 31, from 7 p.m. until end of regular service.

Molson Coors Canada has used CSR to advance its brand – and is one of the few major corporations to take advantage of CSR on social media. Taking a clue from its sister branch, branches across the continent of America are following suit.

They investigated empirical data from a cross-sectional dataset of 214 knowledge-intensive German SMEs[57] and concluded that "…the strong impact of staff selection, staff development, and training as well as staff rewards on Corporate Governance." This means having a successful team is essential for running the shop.

Overcoming internal challenges of organizational structures and processes leads to appropriate and timely decision-making, which is essential for entrepreneurs.[58] Therefore, entrepreneurs will be able to respond effectively to the external challenges of continuous change on issues such as developing markets, technological evolution, and sophisticated competitors.[59,60] Additionally, entrepreneurs need to evaluate economic, political, and social changes that impact its core business. Nurturing and training entrepreneurs to prepare and recognize these challenges will increase their success rate.

CSR and HRM

Extensive research has been conducted on the relationship between human resource management (HRM) and CSR. Recently researchers started exploring HRM's role in an effective CSR strategy. Voegtlin and Greenwood (2016) have studied and illustrated the variety of publications available on the relationship between HRM and CSR. They have divided it into the following three phases:[61]

*   Early incubation phase (1975–2002) – 7%
*   Incremental growth phase (2003–2008) – 21%
*   Period of rapid growth (2009–2014) – 72%

It is not surprising that we see a significant increase in the interest of researchers on the topic of CSR and HRM.[62] The globalizing business environment has contributed to the rapid change in institutional conditions, organizational forms, and power relations, which have called for a deeper understanding of the implementation of a sustainable long-term CSR program.[63,64]

Nevertheless, applying efficient CSR strategies in managerial practices is considered a challenge.[65,66] A variety of organizations are struggling with the implementation of a viable CSR strategy in managerial practices. This is where effective HRM practices could

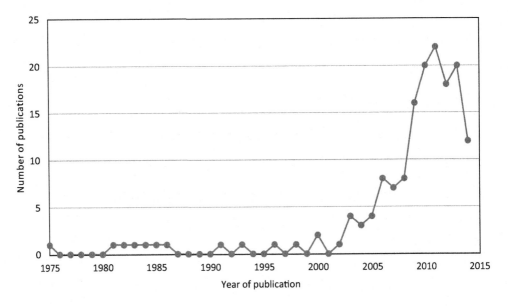

Figure 7.13 CSR publication

prove helpful.[67] A recent study into the field of HRM and CSR has offered different frameworks and theoretical perspectives for the conceptualization of the underlying connection between CSR and HRM.[68,69,70] Both CSR and HRM are highly relevant in the formation of the company's brand image, comprehending the role of the organization, and the sensitive employer-employee relationship. This is why understanding the underlying connection is essential for the success of the company. Moreover, HRM deals with the internal microenvironment of the organization, while CSR is more externally oriented with a focus on the macro environment. Efficient HRM practices could contribute to the understanding, development, and enactment of sustainable and effective CSR application.

CSR and strategy

Despite CSR's rise to seemingly ubiquitous application across many companies due to increased profit, environmental benefit, and improved brand image, developing a CSR program or strategy should not be taken lightly. Poorly executed CSR programs may not only waste valuable resources that could be deployed elsewhere in the firm, but a poorly managed CSR presence can be detrimental to the firm.

In terms of stakeholders, most companies have educated and trained their executives on the importance of CSR and entrepreneurs should make it an important aspect of their vision and mission. For example, organizations need to extend CSR training and education to their suppliers and employees.

- The three most popular reasons for applying CSR are raising profits, benefiting the environment, and bettering the company brand image.
- Entrepreneurs who build the foundation of their organization based on ethics and CSR will have higher potential success.
- Corporate social entrepreneurship (CSE) is a facilitator of a significant transformation in how the company is operated, where entrepreneurship is considered from the perspectives of an individual founder and a well-established organization.
- Austin et al. (2006) state that a successfully implemented CSE consists of three key elements: creating an enabling environment, fostering the corporate social entrepreneur, and corporate purpose of a value-based organization.[71]
- Most of the discussion about the CSR and competitive advantages is applicable for all organizations and entrepreneurial activities. Applying CSR is more critical for survivability for SMEs and entrepreneurs due to resource constraints and limitations.

In terms of decision levels, most companies conclude the importance of CSR on the relationship with the public, but few seem to have found a proper balance between their objectives in CSR and their performance in global supply chains. This has shown that their economic losses can become significant if they are not transparent.[72]

A few key elements to consider when developing an appropriate CSR strategy for the firm to attempt to align CSR efforts with company profits include:

- An honest assessment of the firm's philosophy
- Determining strategic value CSR adds to firm profitability
- Understanding the company's industry and competitive CSR landscape.

Developing a CSR strategy is very important and has more elements than the previous list. However, these are key areas to consider to maximize the potential benefits in developing a CSR strategy while also minimizing negative impacts from implementing an ill-planned CSR strategy.

Applications of CSR: a few examples

Consumers in most countries live in a globalized world with access to information at will, and actions by companies in this environment speak louder than words. Media outlets exist in more forms than ever with an ever-increasing amount of information available for the end-user. In addition to regular media reporting, there are multiple independent CSR rating agencies and self-published CSR reporting by firms (i.e., Transparency International).

In this easily accessible and rich-information environment, firms need to be more careful than ever to align their company ethos with a brand identity and actions that firms take. If not, consumers can easily discover the marketing guise of the CSR branding strategy from the company and see that its actions are not concurring with the claims of CSR principles from the company. Furthermore, consumers will become skeptical of the true intentions of the firm despite its CSR brand identity.

Mali's agriculture sector driven by the Niang brothers

As brothers, Salif Romano Niang and Mohamed Ali Niang have created a social enterprise known as Malô which aims to revolutionize the processing and distribution of rice in Mali. Malô is based on creating a partnership model where rice is purchased from farming cooperatives instead of individual rice farmers to assure that people get a fair price.

When asked about how they believe that their company could advance the agricultural sector in Mali, Salif said:

> It is funny, because our relatives in Mali told us we were crazy when we left the United States to start Malô, and work with rural rice. But Mohamed and I saw a real opportunity in our home country, and it was clear that momentum was being built in the African countries agricultural sector.

These brothers have created a business in which their philosophy was to create a partnership with communities and work to achieve their goals while maintaining the vision of sustainable agricultural growth and food security. The hard work that these young entrepreneurs are doing to establish a business was profitable, but more importantly had a main focus to help the community. This shows that dreams and goals can always be achieved.

Consider examples of social entrepreneurship in your area/state/city. Explain how they have improved the existing strategy/culture to bring in safer/efficient products or services.

Figure 7.14 Mali
Source: Image by CIMMYT on flickr

Companies need to take a careful assessment of their core corporate values to ensure that their actions will not contradict their CSR brand identity. There are examples of companies that have recognized this and changed their behavior. For example, BMW, which promotes sustainability as a core part of its brand identity, stopped racing Formula 1 because it felt this was not aligned with sustainability. This change in behavior was an attempt to align its brand identity with its actions despite the potential loss of branding opportunities through Formula 1 racing.[73] On the other hand, Bank of America is a noted example of a company that has let business strategy conflict with their CSR strategy, thus opening the door to public criticism and negative publicity. According to the Bank of America website (2013), two of their primary CSR missions are "responsible business practices" and creating "strong economies through lending, investing, and giving."[74]

Despite Bank of America stating that their fundamental beliefs revolve around creating a strong economy through lending and investing, Bank of America was a central player in the 2008 financial crisis when they sold financial products backed by risky subprime mortgages. Arguably, Bank of America created a profit for the firm at the expense of the US economy, which is in direct contradiction with Bank of America's stated CSR beliefs. This inconsistency between actions and stated beliefs discounts any believability for their CSR identity by the consumer public.

The conflict between their actions and beliefs is tangibly demonstrated by a Harris Poll where the US consumer listed Bank of America as the number one "worst reputation" firm.[75] This example underscores the need for a company to align corporate actions with the firm's CSR identity to ensure they are not wasting valuable resources on a fruitless endeavor.

Figure 7.15 Project
Source: Image by Robert Couse-Baker on flickr

A well-defined and developed CSR could, on the other hand, highly benefit any institution. By consistently and genuinely following their CSR mission statements, any organization could reach the top of their abilities. This is why it is important that educational institutions provide the necessary tools for the proper preparation of leaders who will be devoted and will contribute to the successful implementation of the company's CSR activities. Read more.[76]

Collaboration between faculty, students, and an institution of higher education

Enlace Project entrepreneurial and development project in Nicaragua has been a successful collaboration between faculty, students, an institution of higher education (State University of New York – Geneseo), and private contributors. This project started in 2005 from a few team research projects in an Economic course and then was supported by the institution and a couple of dedicated entrepreneurial and caring students who built on the initial initiation and accelerated its growth. Examining the impact of this collaborative effort shows the role of some key stakeholders in truly making a big impact in a small town after ten years by advancing education.

CSR and the bottom line

Is a well-developed CSR strategy the same as a business plan to maximize profits? Karnani (2011) discusses the critical views of Milton Friedman's perspective on CSR.[77] Milton Friedman indicates that:

> there is one and only one social responsibility of business—to use its resources and engage in activities designed to increase its profits so long as it stays within the rules of the game, which is to say engages in open and free competition without deception or fraud.[78]

Friedman argues that firms should be focused on activities that drive profitability and would likely view many CSR related activities as ancillary business activities that are not central to the business objective of the firm. This is further supported by Friedman's argument that a business's socially responsible activities are notable for their "analytical looseness and lack of rigor."[79] The lack of a clear correlation between a firm's CSR efforts and profitability is supported by some scholars, which further proves Friedman's point of focusing on profit generation.[80] The argument is that it is difficult to quantify CSR efforts and a firm's financial performance. Therefore, it is important to develop a CSR strategy that displays potential profit opportunity for a company rather than deploying firm resources to assist activities without clear lines of strategic firm opportunity.

Some companies choose not to focus on CSR as a core practice due to the lack of alignment of their business strategy and are doing well! Apple is one example as it experienced some of its most lucrative earnings while managing manufacturing plants like Foxconn in immoral labor conditions, which included explosions leading to death, underage employment, and suicides.[81]

CSR strategy continues to grow with increasing importance in today's media-rich environment, but it may be a strategy at the margin. That is to say that all companies should concern themselves with developing a social strategy but careful consideration should be given to how and to what degree. The firm needs to commit to resources dedicated to supporting CSR activities while also supporting the core business objectives of the firm. In some instances, a company's core business objective simultaneously supports both the social welfare and the economic benefit of the firm. In this case, there is a positive relationship between CSR investment and the profitability of the firm.[82]

- Having a successful team is essential for organizations.
- Nurturing and training entrepreneurs to prepare and recognize these challenges will increase their success rate.
- HRM deals with the internal microenvironment of the organization, while CSR is more externally oriented with a focus on the macro environment.
- Developing a CSR program or strategy shouldn't be taken lightly, as poorly executed CSR programs can be detrimental to the firm.
- The firm needs to dedicate resources to supporting CSR activities while also supporting the core business objectives of the firm.

Karnani (2011) calls this the "Zone of Opportunity", and argues that investment spending in this zone is just good business practice, as it allows the firm to take advantage of all market opportunities. In order to maximize profits, businesses should carefully ensure their CSR strategy is contained within their business strategy, focusing on synergetic alignments between profit generation and social responsibility.

Conclusion

This chapter discussed three important topics – ethics, CSR, and HRM – which are deeply linked concepts with clear implications. Their influences on entrepreneurial and business reputations and outcomes were highlighted. The definition and theories of ethics, CSR, HRM, and their implication for entrepreneurial activities and development have been examined. The role of communications and technology as tools for transparency and good governance are analyzed. Finally, we have provided some real-world examples related to the subjects. While all three main topics that were discussed in this chapter are very important, unfortunately, due to the limitation of space, we had to combine them into one chapter with a brief summary of each.

Discussion questions

1. What is the definition of ethics and its relationship to entrepreneurship?
2. What ethical theories are relevant to the discussion of this chapter?
3. What is the relationship between stakeholders' theory, CSR, and entrepreneurship?
4. How are CSR and human resource management issues applicable to entrepreneurial activity?

Table 7.2 Key terms

Axiological ethics	Utilitarian ethics	Corporate social responsibility (CSR)
Teleological ethics	Existentialist ethics	Corporate social entrepreneurship (CSE)
Deontological ethics	Naturalistic ethics	Zone of Opportunity
Perfectionist ethics	Relativistic ethics	

5. Provide a few examples of entrepreneurial activities that have applied ethics and CSR.
6. Write a short case that applies at least two important topics in this chapter.

Notes

1 Taylor, F. W. (1911). The Principles of Scientific Management. New York: Harper & Brothers, Print.
2 Van Buren, H. J. (2008). Fairness and the main management theories of the twentieth century: a historical review, 1900–1965. Journal of Business Ethics, 82(3), 633–644.
3 Foot, P. (2003). Natural Goodness. Oxford: Oxford University Press; Guyer, P. (2002). Ends of reason and ends of nature: the place of teleology in Kant's ethics. Journal of Value Inquiry, 36, 161; Jackson, K. (2005). Towards authenticity: a Sartrean perspective on business ethics. Journal of Business Ethics, 58, 307–325.
4 Asgary, N., & Mitschow, M. (2002). Towards a model for international business ethics. Journal of Business Ethics, 36(3), 239–247.
5 Garofalo, C. (2003). Toward a global ethic. International Journal of Public Sector Management, 16(7), 490–501. https://doi.org/10.1108/09513550310500373
6 Yaman, H. R. (2003). Skinner's naturalism as a paradigm for teaching business ethics: a discussion from tourism. Teaching Business Ethics, 7(2), 107–122. https://doi.org/10.1023/A:1022636929914
7 Tännsjö, T. (2007). Against sexual discrimination in sports. Ethics in Sport, (Ed.2), 347–358. Retrieved from www.cabdirect.org/cabdirect/abstract/20073163457.
8 Van Buren, H. J. (2008). Fairness and the main management theories of the twentieth century: a historical review, 1900–1965. Journal of Business Ethics, 82(3), 633–644.
9 Asgary, N., Walle, A., and Saraswat, S. P. (2014). "Ethical Foundations and Managerial Challenges: The Strategic Implications of Moral Standards", Journal of Leadership, Accountability and Ethics, Vol. 11, 2.
10 Joyner, B., & Payne, D. (2002). Evolution and implementation: a study of values, business ethics and corporate responsibility. Journal of Business Ethics, 41(3), 297–311.
11 Lawrence, A., & Weber, J. (2011). Business and Society: Stakeholders, Ethics, Public Policy (13th ed.). McGraw-Hill Irwin.
12 Joyner, B., & Payne, D. (2002). Evolution and implementation: a study of values, business ethics and corporate responsibility. Journal of Business Ethics, 41(3), 297–311.
13 Lawrence, A., & Weber, J. (2011). Business and Society: Stakeholders, Ethics, Public Policy (13th ed.). McGraw-Hill Irwin.
14 Joyner, B., & Payne, D. (2002). Evolution and implementation: a study of values, business ethics and corporate responsibility. Journal of Business Ethics, 41(3), 297–311.
15 Bentley University. (n.d.). Alliance for Ethics & Social Responsibility. Retrieved December 16, 2018, from www.bentley.edu/centers/alliance.

16 PRME—Principles for Responsible Management Education. (n.d.). Retrieved from www. unprme.org/.
17 www.bentley.edu/centers/alliance
18 Badaracco, Jr. J. L. (1995). Business Ethics Roles and Responsibilities. Chicago: Irwin.
19 Joyner, B., & Payne, D. (2002). Evolution and implementation: a study of values, business ethics and corporate responsibility. Journal of Business Ethics, 41(3), 297–311.
20 Asgary, N., & Walle, A. H. (2002). The cultural impact of globalisation: economic activity and social change. Cross Cultural Management: An International Journal, 9(3), 58–75. doi:10.1108/13527600210797433
21 Asgary, N., & Li, G. (2016). Corporate social responsibility: its economic impact and link to the bullwhip effect. Journal of Business Ethics, 135(4), 665–681. https://doi.org/10.1007/s10551-014-2492-1
22 van der Merwe, R., Pitt, L., & Berthon, P. (2003). Are excellent companies ethical? Evidence from an industrial setting. Corporate Reputation Review, 5(4), 343–355. https://doi.org/10.1057/palgrave.crr.1540183
23 Peters, T., & Waterman, R. (1988). In Search of Excellence: Lessons from America's Best-Run Companies. New York: Harper Collins Publishers.
24 van der Merwe, R., Pitt, L., & Berthon, P. (2003). Are excellent companies ethical? Evidence from an industrial setting. Corporate Reputation Review, 5(4), 343–355. https://doi.org/10.1057/palgrave.crr.1540183
25 Ahmed, M. M., Chung, K. Y., & Eichenseher, J. W. (2003). Business students' perception of ethics and moral judgment: a cross-cultural study. Journal of Business Ethics, 43(1/2), 89.
26 Gowing, M., & Islam, M. (2003). Some empirical evidence of Chinese accounting system and business management practices from an ethical perspective. Journal of Business Ethics, 42(4), 353–378.
27 www.businessdictionary.com/definition/social-responsibility.html
28 Freeman, R. E. (1984). Strategic Management: A Stakeholder Approach. Boston: Pitman.
29 Adam M., et al. (2001). H2A.Z is required for global chromatin integrity and for recruitment of RNA polymerase II under specific conditions. Mol Cell Biol, 21(18), 6270–6279.
30 Asgary, N., & Mitschow, M. (2002). Towards a model for international business ethics. Journal of Business Ethics, 36(3), 239–247.
31 Sethi, S. P. (2003). Globalization and the good corporation: a need for proactive coexistence. Journal of Business Ethics, 43(2), 21–31.
32 Donaldson, T., & Preston, L. E. (1995). The stakeholder theory of the corporation: concepts, evidence, and implications. Academy of Management Review, 20(1), 65–91.
33 Jackson, I., & Nelson, J. (2004). Values-Based Performance: Seven Strategies for Delivering Profits with Principles. Corporate Social Responsibility Initiative Working Paper No.7. Cambridge, MA: John F.Kennedy School of Government, Harvard University.
34 Chevron Policy. (2018, October 11). Corporate Responsibility. Retrieved December 16, 2018, from www.chevron.com/corporate-responsibility.
35 Vanhamme, J., & Grobben, B. (2008). "Too good to be true!": the effectiveness of CSR history in countering negative publicity. Journal of Business Ethics, 85(S2), 273–283. doi:10.1007/s10551-008-9731-2, p. 276.
36 Phillip, A. (2014). Facebook's Mark Zuckerberg and wife Priscilla Chan donate $25 million to Ebola fight. The Washington Post. Retrieved from www.washingtonpost.com/news/to-your-health/wp/2014/10/14/facebooks-mark-zuckerberg-and-priscilla-chan-donate-25-million-to-ebola-fight/?utm_term=.1a85e74b14bc.
37 Jackson, I., & Nelson, J. (2004). Values-Based Performance: Seven Strategies for Delivering Profits with Principles. Corporate Social Responsibility Initiative Working Paper No.7. Cambridge, MA; John F.Kennedy School of Government, Harvard University.

38 Wunsch, C., & Lechner, M. (2008). What did all the money do? On the general ineffectiveness of recent West German labour market programmes. Kyklos, 61(1), 134–174.

39 Curcio, R. J., & Wolf, F. M. (1996). Corporate environmental strategy: impact upon firm value. Journal of Financial and Strategic Decisions, 9(2), 21–31.

40 Vallaster, C., Lindgreen, A., & Maon, F. (2012). Strategically leveraging corporate social responsibility to the benefit of company and society: a corporate branding perspective. California Management Review, 54(3), 34–60. (ISSN 0008-1256)

41 Zahra, S. A. (2015). Corporate entrepreneurship as knowledge creation and conversion: the role of entrepreneurial hubs. Small Business Economics, 44(4), 727–735. https://doi.org/10.1007/s11187-015-9650-4

42 Austin, J., & Reficco, E. (2008). Corporate social entrepreneurship. Int'l J. Not-for-Profit L., 11, 86.

43 Austin, J. E., Leonard, H., Reficco, E., & Wei-Skillern, J. (2006). Social entrepreneurship: it's for corporations too. Social Entrepreneurship: New Models of Sustainable Social Change, 169–180, p. 175.

44 Porter, E., & Kramer, M. R. (2006). Estrategia y sociedad. Harvard Business Review, 3–15.

45 Kiran, R., & Sharma, A. (2011). Corporate social responsibility and management education: changing perception and perspectives. Global Journal of Management and Business Research, 11(6). Retrieved from https://journalofbusiness.org/index.php/GJMBR/article/view/517.

46 Porter, M. E., & Kramer, M. R. (2006). Strategy and society. Harvard Business Review, 84(12), 78–92, p. 88.

47 Gonzalez, M. C., & Martinez, C. V. (2004). Fostering corporate social responsibility through public initiative: from the EU to the Spanish case. Journal of Business Ethics, 55(3), 275–293. Harris, P. (20120. Apple hit by boycott call over worker abuses in China. The Guardian. Retrieved from www.guardian.co.uk/technology/2012/jan/29/apple-faces-boycott-worker-abuses.

48 Perez-Aleman, P., & Sandilands, M. (2008). Building value at the top and the bottom of the global supply chain: MNC-NGO partnerships. California Management Review, 51(1), 24–49.

49 Asgary, N., & Li, G. (2016). Corporate social responsibility: its economic impact and link to the bullwhip effect. Journal of Business Ethics, 135(4), 665–681.

50 Luo, W., Li, Y., Tang, C. H., Abruzzi, K. C., Rodriguez, J., Pescatore, S., & Rosbash, M. (2012). CLOCK deubiquitylation by USP8 inhibits CLK/CYC transcription in Drosophila. Genes Dev, 26(22), 2536–2549.

51 Angels in Lagos. (2012, October 28). Retrieved December 16, 2018, from www.economist.com/baobab/2012/10/28/angels-in-lagos.

52 Byruch, G. (2016). Corporate social responsibility: Mark Zuckerberg makes a statement. Medium, Dec. 7, 2015. Web. Nov. 8.

53 BCW. (n.d.). BCW. Retrieved from https://bcw-global.com/.

54 Freshfields Bruckhaus Deringer. (n.d.). Containing a Crisis: Dealing with Corporate Disasters in the Digital Age [PDF].

55 Schneider, B., Ehrhart, M. G., & Macey, W. H. (2013). Organizational climate and culture. Annual Review of Psychology, 64, 361–388.

56 Nguyen, H. (2016, October 17). CSR and when to come to marketing strategy. Retrieved from www.linkedin.com/pulse/csr-when-come-marketing-strategy-lee-nguyen.

57 Schneider, B., Hanges, P. J., Smith, D. B., & Salvaggio, A. N. (2003). Which comes first: employee attitudes or organizational financial and market performance? Journal of Applied Psychology, 88(5), 836.

58 Hammer, M., Champy, J., & Künzel, P. (1994). Business Reengineering: Die Radikalkur für Das Unternehmen (p. 120). Frankfurt: Campus.

59 Kemelgor, B. H. (2002). A Comparative Analysis of Corporate Entrepreneurial Orientation between Selected Firms in the Netherlands and the U.S.A. Taylor & Francis, pp. 67–86.

60 Kuratko, D. F., Hornsby, J. S., & Goldsby, M. G. (2004). Sustaining corporate entrepreneurship. International Journal of Entrepreneurship and Innovation, 5(2), 77–89.

61 Voegtlin, C., & Greenwood, M. (2016). Corporate social responsibility and human resource management: a systematic review and conceptual analysis. Human Resource Management Review, 26(3), 181–197. doi:10.1016/j.hrmr.2015.12.003

62 DeNisi A. S., Wilson M. S., & Biteman J. (2014). Research and practice in HRM: a historical perspective. Human Resource Management Review, 24, 219–231.

63 Hagiwara N., Wessel J. L., & Ryan A. M. (2012). Race and gender acknowledgment in the presidential election 2008: when did stigma acknowledgment hurt or benefit the candidates? Journal of Applied Social Psychology, 42, 2191–2212.

64 Stone, D. L., & Deadrick, D. L. (2015). Challenges and opportunities affecting the future of human resource management. Human Resource Management Review, 25(2), 139–145.

65 Matten D., & Moon, J. (2008). "Implicit" and "explicit" CSR: a conceptual framework for a comparative understanding of corporate social responsibility. Academy of Management Review, 33, 404–424.

66 Jamali, D., & El Dirani, A. (2013). CSR and HRM for workplace integrity: advancing the business ethics agenda. In W. Amann, & A. Stachowicz-Stanusch (Eds.), Integrity in Organizations: Building the Foundations for Humanistic Management (pp. 439–456). London: Palgrave Macmillan.

67 Jamali, D. R., Dirani, A. M., & Harwood, I. A. (2014). Exploring human resource management roles in corporate social responsibility: the CSR-HRM co-creation model. Business Ethics: A European Review, 24(2), 125–143. doi:10.1111/beer.12085

68 Voegtlin, C., & Greenwood, M. (2016). Corporate social responsibility and human resource management: a systematic review and conceptual analysis. Human Resource Management Review, 26(3), 181–197. doi:10.1016/j.hrmr.2015.12.003

69 Jamali, D. R., Dirani, A. M., & Harwood, I. A. (2014). Exploring human resource management roles in corporate social responsibility: the CSR-HRM co-creation model. Business Ethics: A European Review, 24(2), 125–143. doi:10.1111/beer.12085

70 Gond, J.-P., Igalens, J., Swaen, V., & El Akremi, A. (2011). The human resources contribution to responsible leadership: an exploration of the CSR–HR interface. Journal of Business Ethics, 98(S1), 115–132. https://doi.org/10.1007/s10551-011-1028-1

71 Austin, J. E., Leonard, H., Reficco, E., & Wei-Skillern, J. (2006). Social entrepreneurship: it's for corporations too. Social Entrepreneurship: New Models of Sustainable Social Change, 169–180.

72 Asgary, N., & Li, G. (2016). Corporate social responsibility: its economic impact and link to the bullwhip effect. Journal of Business Ethics, 135(4), 665–681.

73 Vallaster, C., Lindgreen, A., & Maon, F. (2012). Strategically leveraging Corporate social responsibility: a corporate branding perspective. California Management Review, 54(3), 34–60. https://doi.org/10.1525/cmr.2012.54.3.34

74 Bank of America (2013). Corporate Social Responsibility 2013 Report. Retrieved from https://about.bankofamerica.com/assets/pdf/Bank-of-America-2013-Corporate-Social-Responsibility-Report.pdf

75 Reputation Quotient. (n.d.). Retrieved from https://theharrispoll.com/reputation-quotient/.

76 Enlace Project. (n.d.). Retrieved from www.enlaceproject.org/; and SUNY Geneseo. (n.d.). Retrieved from www.geneseo.edu/.

77 Karnani A. (2011). "Doing well by doing good": the grand illusion. California Management Review, 53(2), 69–86.

78 Friedman, M. (1970). The social responsibility of business is to increase its profits. New York Times Magazine, September 13, 32–33, 122–124.

79 Karnani, A. (2011). "Doing well by doing good": the grand illusion. California Management Review, 53(2), 69–86.

80 Aupperle, K. E., Carroll, A. B., & Hatfield, J. D. (1985). An empirical examination of the relationship between corporate social responsibility and profitability. Academy of Management Journal, 28(2), 446–463.

81 Duhigg, C., & Barboza, D. (2012, Jan. 26). In China, the human costs that are built into an iPad. The New York Times, A1.

82 Karnani, A. (2011). "Doing well by doing good": the grand illusion. California Management Review, 53(2), 69–86.

Part IV

Process

8 Marketing, technology, and entrepreneurship

Learning objectives:

1. *Define marketing and describe its characteristics for developed and developing countries*
2. *Analyze marketing mix – 4Ps*
3. *Comprehend the notion of entrepreneurial marketing*
4. *Effectively apply the steps from the marketing timeline*
5. *Evaluate the impact of marketing, triggered by technology, and its overall effect on entrepreneurship.*

A born marketer

Figure 8.1 Philips
Source: Image by John Georgiou on flickr

A tale of two brothers: Philips & Co.

Gerard Philips founded Philips & Co. in 1891, in Eindhoven, Netherlands. With financial support from his father, he set up a factory and began the production of carbon-filament lamps. However, despite his technical knowledge in identifying a business opportunity in the newly emerging electricity field, he was unable to leverage profitability out of his idea, due to the lack of a strategic entrepreneurial expertise. In 1895, the Philips Company was on the verge of bankruptcy. At this stage, Gerard Philips' younger brother, Anton Philips, entered the family business. Anton had experience working at a brokerage firm. An engineer by education, Anton Philips started working as a sales representative for the Philips Company. Anton was a very good salesman. Gerard could focus on what he knew he did best: the R&D side and the production process. Anton, on the other hand, would never have sold as many light bulbs without the continuous quality improvements his brother guaranteed. He began contributing a series of important business ideas, which led to expansion and evolved into an electronics multinational.

Questions

1. Could it be that the real driver of progress and innovation is collaboration between people?
2. A variety of backgrounds (education; character; culture …) can make a company more adaptable to its ever changing environment. Healthy debates can lead to better decisions. We all know many reasons why diversity in teams and in the boardroom is important. But do we really choose diversity over like-mindedness when confronted with a business challenge?

Introduction

In the era of globalization and fierce competition, marketing is essential to survive and succeed. Expanding tools for marketing in this era seem to have created a flat space to advertise a product or services. This chapter focuses on the knowhow and tools for entrepreneurs, particularly those in developing countries, to successfully market their products or services. We will present marketing concepts and their application for entrepreneurs, in order to advance their objectives. Furthermore, topics on the background information on the role of marketing for business success, characteristics of marketing, and marketing by entrepreneurs in developing countries will be discussed. We will also assess how enterprises could identify their business and clients in order to better construct their marketing positioning and branding placement. Nowadays, technological developments and globalization have radicalized the way marketing is done and seen inside and outside an organization. Digitalization has completely transformed the company's focus.[1] Thus, entrepreneurs should now concentrate on engaging consumers more than on their products. How does marketing play a role? It is the "persuasion tool" which companies use to further their brands.[2]

In addition, we will examine the marketing mix (price, place, and promotion) and discuss a few customer loyalty programs suitable for new enterprises. Many challenges relating to marketing for entrepreneurs and small and medium-sized firms are somewhat similar. As we discussed in the previous chapters, entrepreneurship is a process with an end goal of becoming an enterprise in the form of a small, medium, or large enterprise.

Entrepreneurs contribute significantly to the national economic development in both developed and developing countries. Entrepreneurs have contributed by generating a vibrant manufacturing sector (i.e., China), emergent regional economy, winning the global market through increased exports, and providing employment opportunities. OECD 2013 Report indicates that the important role of entrepreneurs for sustainable growth is due to their effectiveness in promoting innovation and providing employment opportunities. The challenge, however, is the availability of adequate financing to fund the inception and progressive growth of a business owing to the specific characteristics and challenges faced by new enterprises. The sophisticated marketing theories and formal marketing models and practices may not be appropriate and applicable to some of them. However, it is important to understand how entrepreneurs in developing countries could use marketing to reach their customers and increase their market share.

Definition of marketing

According to the American Marketing Association, marketing is the "Activity set of institutions and processes for creating, communicating, delivering, and exchanging offerings that have value to customers, clients, partners, and society at large."[3]

Marketing plays a central role in business success; most aspects of a business depend on a successful marketing campaign.[4] According to Peter Drucker, the aim of good marketing is to make selling unnecessary.[5] Marketing that is customer-oriented has a higher success rate than marketing that is product-oriented. The seller's aim should be to sell what they make and the marketer's objective is to make what they can sell. Without marketing, an entrepreneur may not be able to be successful in expanding and prospering. By producing dimensions in one or more of the marketing mix, companies can sell more to an existing customer or expand the number of customers, particularly for low budget entrepreneurs, whose marketing resources and planning process are limited. In addition, a marketing plan is essential in building an organization's reputation and product awareness.

Marketing efforts such as effective communication and offering quality products and services can build a business's reputation and expand market share and therefore increase sales and revenue. A successful marketing plan for an entrepreneur is essential. Generally, entrepreneurs have many more challenges in marketing their product or service because they do not have a record to stand on compared to developed companies.

Characteristics of marketing in developed and developing countries

Most entrepreneurs have an idea or a product/service and may have partners or a few employees, therefore, making them independent. Their enterprise may be managed by (co) owners in a personalized way, especially in a developing country. They generally have a lack of expertise in the field and other resources. Resources include finances, facilities, technology, specialists, and knowledge. One of the main reasons for high failure rates among entrepreneurs is their operational mediocrity, which is due to the lack of stated resources.

These challenges are much greater in developing countries because many tools of marketing may not be available and therefore make it difficult to expand.

The potential success of a new enterprise (or any enterprise), depends upon the formulation and implementation of a strategy.[6,7] A strategy typically consists of short- and

Main aim of marketing

Changing trend in marketing

Figure 8.2 Marketing

long-term acknowledgment and response to any challenges or opportunities coming from the given business environment or industry.[8] For example, the strategy could be the set of decisions for resource acquisition and allocation. Strategies relating to the marketing function are thus highly essential for any new enterprise. To build customers' trust and to the position, the brand for the right segment of the market shall lead to marketing success for brand reputation and consequently higher profits.

Networking and positive word of mouth is the first stage and most efficient for an entrepreneur or an SME. Many other channels of marketing are informative and useful in attracting the attention of the potential customer. However, they are not persuasive forms of marketing. The word of mouth has a greater influence on an individual level rather than the other traditional channels of marketing.

Entrepreneurs could use inexpensive social media to stay in touch with their customers in countries where technology and communication are available, is low cost, and is user-friendly. For example, being present on social media websites such as Facebook, Twitter, LinkedIn, and online blogs is highly efficient as the target market can stay interested and they can voice their opinion about the product/services the company offers, thus completely transforming the flow of information between customers and suppliers and giving them the opportunity of an instant interaction. This can also help make the company more "customer-centric". Of course, it is easier to sell a product that meets the demand of the customers rather than persuading the customers to buy a product a company might find the most profitable.

**Major reasons for high failure
rates among new enterprises**

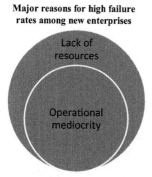

Figure 8.3 Failure reasons

By catering to the demands of the customers, the company might make relatively less profit per unit of the product sold. However, the product will have repetitive and rapid growth in sales. Entrepreneurs can be more innovative by taking the views and opinions of customers into consideration and making a product that has greater acceptability and higher demand on the market. For an entrepreneur, the objective is to achieve profits through thoughtful positioning and branding and ensuring its customers are satisfied.

The thoughtful product branding and positioning could be embodied in alignment between the company's mission statement, CSR, and actual activities, as reported by the media. Customer satisfaction and awareness are essential and necessary conditions for marketing strategies to be successful.

However, even if some marketing approaches and strategies are implemented, for most entrepreneurs and enterprises, an absence of proper and formal marketing practices exists. A strong focus on customer care, reliance on intuition, and consciousness of the environment is essential. For entrepreneurs and SMEs, there is no formal organizational function to deal with marketing activities, which is often replaced by a single person or a few individuals who are reluctant to work with external experts and make decisions relying on intuition and energy. The likelihood of having the expertise in the field is very low. Therefore, most of the marketing practices in that context are executed in an inconsistent way.

In addition to those generic features, enterprises face other threats. First, they are affected by both the external and internal environment. Due to globalization and internationalization of the marketplace, they may be forced to compete domestically and internationally. Second, most entrepreneurs acknowledge that they need to gain more, faster, and better marketing knowledge and information but they lack access to resources or are reluctant to pursue these needs. Any entrepreneur should be able to clearly articulate the fundamental issues that follow, which are essential for a successful marketing strategy.

Marketing mix – 4Ps

The Economic Times defines the marketing mix as a set of actions or tactics a company uses to establish its products, services, and brand on the market. Decisions about the Product, Place, Price, and Promotion of a brand are essential and must be taken prior to any marketing activity is set in motion. In a way, your marketing mix is the general plan or template for your marketing strategy, as it encompasses analysis of both internal and external strategic decisions.

Products and services

A definition of the primary products and services is also needed for the successful execution of any strategy. Offering multiple products or services increases the chance of attracting a larger customer target market. However, enterprises need to focus on marketing the most profitable or most frequently sold product or service, because it is part of the internal factors of an organization's operations, so the entrepreneur in charge has control over it. Now it is important to understand the competitive landscape. Knowledge about the difference between the enterprise and its competitors is essential for marketing the enterprise products more effectively and finding the one characteristic which differentiates your product from all other competitors on the market.

An entrepreneur must thoroughly analyze the given industry and compare price, quality, product offering, and marketing strategy to ensure his/her business is keeping up with potential competitors. This effort may also assist in finding out the sources of differentiation. The need to track their competitors' advertising spending, couponing, promotional activity, social marketing, websites, and packaging is necessary.

While an entrepreneur may lack the finance to hire specified servers to do the tracking and compiling, the rapid technology development of the century allows the enterprise to do this without spending a lot of money or time on it.

- Marketing plays a central role for business success: most aspects of a business depend on a successful marketing campaign.
- One of the main reasons for high failure rates among entrepreneurs is their operational mediocrity and a lack of stated resources.
- The potential success of a new enterprise (or any enterprise) depends upon the formulation and implementation of a strategy.
- To build customers' trust and to position the brand in the right segment of the market, targeting the right people from this segment and increasing the brand reputation are major objectives of a marketing strategy.
- The trend in marketing efforts are moving towards "customer centric" positions from the previous product and sales centric positions.
- Networking and positive word of mouth is the first stage and most efficient for an entrepreneur or an SME.
- Social media completely transforms the flow of information between customers and companies by giving them the opportunity to react quickly to changing customer needs.

Place

Although figures vary widely from product to product, roughly one-fifth of the cost of a product goes on delivering it to the customer. Place is concerned with various methods of transporting and storing goods and then making them available for the customer. Delivering the right product to the right place at the right time involves a well-designed distribution system. It might be more efficient for some manufacturers to sell to wholesalers who then sell to retailers, while others prefer to sell directly to retailers or customers.

Distribution is important because it is the channel to get the product or service to the target audience.[9] The two common channel options are direct and indirect channels. Entrepreneurs could choose to sell directly to their customers without the involvement of any intermediary. The examples include direct sales force, mail, and online store. They may also select one or more intermediaries like an agent, broker, dealer, distributor, wholesaler, or retailer to reach their customers. Evolution of new technology, communication, and means of transportation impact where an entrepreneur will locate, online or in store. Please see Table 8.4 in the Appendix.

The online store normally contains product descriptions, prices, images, contact details, company logo, and a general business description. Apart from that, businesses need to create a merchant account and select the acceptable payment method (e.g., Visa, Master, and PayPal), decide the shipping carriers, and set shipping rates. The e-commerce platform is widely used in developed countries and is slowly evolving in some developing countries (i.e., China).

A major disadvantage of e-commerce is that it is less effective than personal selling in discovering and satisfying customers' emotional needs and wants.[10] Also, customer service and after-sales service is difficult to maintain compared to physical stores.

Figure 8.4 Customer
Source: © iStock: tumsasedgars

Everything revolves around your customer

It's been proven in a number of consumer studies that a vast majority of consumers will pay for better service. Since a great experience is a known cause for increased brand loyalty and word of mouth referrals, you'll also be happy to hear that Nielsen reported personal recommendations as far more trustworthy (and effective) than ads from a consumer standpoint.

If you can't go toe-to-toe with the big guys on price, amazing service should be your winning proposition.

E-store, therefore, needs to be carefully designed to meet customers' particular demand and incorporate that service dimension. The most essential point for an e-store site's design is navigability, which refers to the ability for users to use the site easily and fast.[11] The site layout should be simple and clear so that the customer can have a user-friendly experience. Also, an e-store site's important feature is interactivity between the user and the site itself. Businesses need to have a frequently asked question (FAQ) section to handle the questions that might be normally asked by the customer. In addition, the web atmosphere is fundamental in changing shoppers' mood and creating a pleasant emotional experience. Music, visuals such as 3-D displays, and downloadable video clips are usually used to make an online storefront visually compelling.[12] A majority of the customers prefer a quick and accurate display of information about product and price. In many developing countries these methods of marketing and sales are used.

Apart from web store design, Martin notes that businesses need to ensure a reliable supply source of goods.[13] Many e-commerce site owners usually face the situation where their source goes out of business or runs out of merchandise. Businesses, therefore, need to have the backup plan to prepare for the situation. In addition, choosing a dependable web host is crucial for the success of the web store. There are a great number of e-commerce sites in the form of hosted services and subscription-based web applications where businesses could choose from.

Some e-commerce sites that are frequently used by small businesses include BigCommerce, SmallBusiness Yahoo!, eBay, Amazon, Alibaba, etc. There are different price ranges in each site depending on the different level of service: many of them have released a free 15-day trial, traffic-driving tools, as well as mobile and social commerce options that could be integrated to social media sites. The criteria for choosing channels include the customer, the product, the environment, and the business objectives. Enterprises need to know all aspects of their potential customer, who they are, where they come from, and when and how they usually shop to determine the best-suited way to target them.[14]

It is clear that the physical appeal of a product and its presentation is very important for customers. Although signaling and in-store marketing do brand your business, they are comparatively less effective in bringing in new customers. A common strategy is to first release sufficient (though not high-budget) marketing and advertising in order to induce people to observe the product inside the business and then to advertise and promote heavily there.

Pricing

Compared to the other three elements of the marketing mix – product, promotion, and place – which impact the costs of marketing, pricing is the key determinant of profitability; having a pricing strategy is a crucial task for a business. Setting the right price is a challenging decision and should be carefully assessed. Pricing too high will drive away customers while pricing too low may lead to customers' perception of poor quality of the product.[15] Price is tied to the cost of inputs. By analyzing the cost of each good and service, prices can be set to maximize profits and reduce unprofitable goods or services.[16] Businesses need to assess the material, labor, and overhead costs of all components to derive their overall costs.

When an enterprise is mainly serving customers who are price-sensitive or when it enjoys a reduction in production and marketing costs, with an increase in volume, it can charge a low initial price. If the target audiences have a strong desire for the products and can afford to pay higher prices, the enterprise can afford a higher ceiling on price.[17] Of course, the enterprise should not be under competitive pressure.

Another strategy of pricing is discovering what your competitors are charging the customers. This provides an enterprise with a range within which they could set a price. When conducting the competitive analysis, the enterprise should assess not just the pricing, but also the whole package that includes the targeted customers, and other value-added services your competitor offers.

Small businesses are commonly believed to underprice. It is largely because they don't exert the operational efficiency larger players normally have, thus have an incorrect analysis of their costs. Therefore, rather than comparing the product/service price of large competitors, small businesses could add other differentiators that add value and justify higher prices.

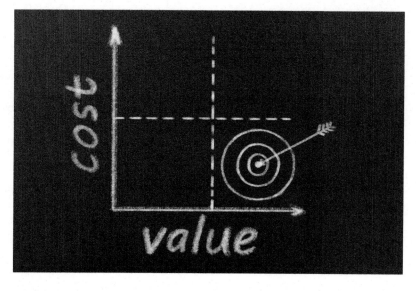

Figure 8.5 Price
Source: © iStock: marrio31

When the price is right

Selecting the right entry pricing strategy is critical for a new business or product launch. Pricing is a primary marketing component, and what you enter the market with dictates your customers' initial reaction.

Penetrative

Penetration pricing is aptly named, as it's a strategy specific to market entry. The premise is to offer very low up-front prices to attract customers from competitors or in the open market.

Skimming

Price skimming is a common contrasting approach to penetration. You start with premium price points to optimize short-term profit from the most aggressive customers.

Premium

Premium pricing is a specific approach to launch high early prices you intend to maintain. This coincides with a high-end product and service offering that you believe has a large enough market to sustain your business over time.

Competitive

When companies are more concerned about entering the market with competitive prices, they build meaningful relationships based on "non-price" factors such as product quality, service, patented features, environmental and civic involvement, and distinct benefits.
    Read more: http://smallbusiness.chron.com/entry-pricing-strategy-61428.html

For example, they could increase the product's value proposition by enhancing its exclusivity, locating the product at the point of sale such as in a convenience store, additionally providing helpful, knowledgeable, friendly customer service.[18]

According to Crane, it is easier to set a higher initial price and lower the price over time than the reverse way.[19] To raise the price, enterprises should communicate with customers the uniqueness and value of their products and services.[20,21] A useful alternative is to offer the customer a variety of choices such as off-peak pricing or tiered pricing, where the prices vary depending on attachments to the product.

The price should not be set in isolation; it should be integrated with product, promotion, and place to form a coherent mix that provides superior customer value. For example, for businesses that want to adopt low-end competitive pricing, the strategy needs to focus on reducing the costs. Entrepreneurs need to bargain to get the best possible price for the merchandise, locate the business in an inexpensive location, closely control inventory to minimize storage cost, limit product lines to best-selling items, and produce advertising to focus on "price specials".[22]

Price deals

Price deals are usually intended to promote trial use of a new product or line extensions, to attract new buyers for a mature product, or to persuade existing customers to increase their purchases and accelerate their use. Price deals work most effectively when the price is the consumer's primary consideration or when brand loyalty either does not exist or is very low. Holding everything else constant, generally, low price products indicate low quality.

Buyers may learn about price discounts either at the point of sale or through advertising. At the point of sale, price reductions may be posted on the package, on signs near the product, or in storefront windows. Many forms of advertisements can be used to inform consumers of upcoming discounts, including radios, newspaper, and social media. Existing customers treat discounts as rewards and often respond by buying in larger quantities. Price discounts alone, however, usually do not appeal to first-time buyers.

The main types of price deals include discounts, bonus pack deals, refunds or rebates, and coupons. Price discounts offer direct value to customers and therefore create an unambiguous incentive for consumers to purchase. However, price reductions can easily be matched by the competition and, if used frequently, can devaluate brand image.

- Customer satisfaction and awareness are essential and necessary goals of every marketing strategy that is conducted.
- Enterprises face threats from both the external and the internal environment. Most entrepreneurs acknowledge that they need to gain more, faster, and better marketing knowledge and information to stay ahead of the competition.
- Decisions about the Product, Place, Price, and Promotion of a brand are essential and must be taken prior to any marketing activity being set in motion.
- An entrepreneur must compare and thoroughly analyze the given industry and compare price, quality, product offer, and marketing strategy to ensure his/her business is keeping up with potential competitors.
- Evolution of new technology, communication, and means of transportation impacts where an entrepreneur can be located, either online or in a physical store.
- Enterprise may be serving customers, who are price-sensitive or are in need of a product. For businesses that want to adopt a low-end competitive pricing, the strategy needs to focus on reducing the costs

Promotion

The traditional marketing mix is composed of four mixed facets, known as the 4Ps: Price, Product, Placement, and Promotion. There are different theories about where social media fits into this model. It could lay in the promotional sector with PR and advertising, or in a fifth category all on its own: consumers. Nowadays, as more and more businesses have become consumer-centric, it is not surprising that buyers' power has increased dramatically. These days customers are more informed, connected, and thus are empowered more than ever before. Therefore, understanding this trend and embracing it in their marketing

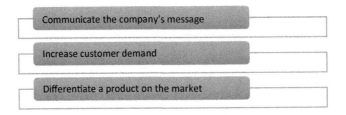

Communicate the company's message

Increase customer demand

Differentiate a product on the market

Figure 8.6 Marketing strategy

strategy is essential. Thus, it is important for entrepreneurs to understand that a marketing strategy does not comprise of promotion. Promotion is simply the means of raising customers' awareness of the product or service the company offers. Nevertheless, the company needs to formulate a viable marketing strategy which could be communicated to the customer through the means of promotion. The result of establishing a marketing strategy is a well-defined company mission statement which is communicated to consumers through promotion. The strategy typically has three main objectives as shown in Figure 8.6.

Promotion is also part of the promotional mix or plan, which also constitutes advertising, direct marketing, sales promotion, and publicity.

Others have identified a marketing communication mix, where: "Marketing communications is the means by which firms attempt to inform, persuade, and remind consumers—directly, or indirectly—about the products and brands that they sell."[23]

The marketing communication mix consists of eight major types of communication, mainly divided between personal and nonperson channels. The personal channels could have three major sources: company (advocate), an independent third party (expert), or as simple as social contact, for instance, your neighbor. On the other hand, the nonperson communication channels comprise of media, atmospheres, and events.[24]

- Media channels: print, broadcast, display (billboards, posters, symbols), and electronic media.
- The atmosphere is in regard to the office environment a company portrays systematically in front of potential customers or stakeholders (website).
- Events – events have become the mainstay of small-business marketing attempts.

To make itself visible, gain attention, and mainly communicate its message to the market, a company might take advantage of the promotional tools displayed in Table 8.1.

Despite which channel a company wishes to utilize, it is essential for the company message to be consistent and well integrated with the company's strategy.[25]

Advertising

Advertising is essential for any business, especially for entrepreneurs. Giorgi and Rahman state that a firm's informality is pervasive in developing countries; low benefits and high indirect costs are the main barriers to formality.[26]

Table 8.1 Promotional tools

Advertising	Public mode of communication. Advantage of concurrency.
Sales promotion	Coupons, contests, premiums, etc. Gain attention through calling the consumer to act.
Events and experiences	Sponsorships of sports, arts, entertainment, or cause events.
Public relations and publicity	News stories are typically viewed as more reliable and authentic to consumers.
Direct marketing	Email, direct marketing, and telemarketing. Usually customizable as addressed to a specific individual.
Interactive marketing	A company which supports the two-way communication between its customers and itself.
Word-of-mouth marketing	Still one of the most utilized and beneficial channels of a company seeding its message in customers' minds.
Personal selling	Requires a live, immediate, and interactive relationship between individuals. Personal selling leads to relationships.

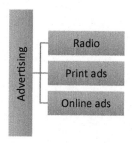

Figure 8.7 Advertising

Advertising's high barrier to entry reinforces exclusivity and brand prestige, makes the competition a lot easier, and makes acquiring market share easier.[27]

Entrepreneurial marketing

It is important for marketers to differentiate between marketing strategies being used in entrepreneurship activities (starting a business for instance), and entrepreneurship activities used in marketing strategies by already established companies. This chapter and the book overall focuses on entrepreneurship in regard to the creation of new businesses. Nevertheless, it is important to understand the concept of *entrepreneurial marketing (EM)* as well: "EM draws on the work of both marketing and entrepreneurship scholars by focusing on how individuals and management teams accept the risk to innovatively and proactively leverage resources to create value in the marketplace."[28]

Figure 8.8 Low price
Source: Image by Andy Roberts on flickr

Psychological pricing

Lisa Hephner shares key statistics on purchase habits of Americans during the holiday months of November and December. It is well known to every retailer (online and offline) the importance of these two months. Lisa writes about promotional ideas for SMEs. While large retailers have the money to advertise, hold billboards, and hand out flyers, small retailers can compete using creative ideas.

<u>Number 9</u>: Ever wonder why you see so many prices, and particularly sale prices, that end in 9? The simplistic theory is that most people suffer from a "left digit effect" in which they give more weight to the left most number in a price such that $59.99 is thought of as $50 and is processed by the brain as significantly lower cost than an item priced at $60 would be.

<u>Anchoring, Framing, and Relative Pricing</u>: In terms of marketing, anchoring is commonly leveraged by displaying very high "regular" prices that are crossed out or otherwise replaced by significantly lower sale prices.

<u>Innumeracy</u> (Your Customers Won't Do Math): In short, customers immediately perceive the value of "buy one get one free" offers, but struggle with the value of "half off" or "50% off" promotions. (Yes, the latter two are the same.)

<u>Strategic Coupon Use</u>: Even more than sale prices, people love coupons! According to a Forrester research study on coupons, 60 percent of respondents agreed that they "Love to Receive Digital Coupons" and 50 percent report being more likely to visit a store if they receive a coupon.

Read more: https://paysimple.com/blog/the-small-business-guide-to-holiday-sales-and-promotions/.

Table 8.2 Entrepreneurial marketing

Locus	Role of EM	Area of focus	Illustrative example
Vertical	As strategy	EM as a disposition of the top management team. EM fundamentally must reflect both the needs of the customer and the entrepreneur. EM as strategy making heuristic.	P&G's incoming CEO in the late 1990s forced the product managers to "burn the boats", give away IP, and stop supporting the big brands to become more innovative.
Horizontal	As culture and process	EM residing across functional areas and business units. EM being across the organization as culture.	41 below Vodka's social media and CRM strategy for marketing.
Temporal	As response	As a strategic response to environmental turbulence.	Walmart's entry into health, organic, and now locally produced food.

Source: Adapted from Wales, William, Monsen, Erik, & McKelvie, Alexander. (2011). The organizational pervasiveness of entrepreneurial orientation. Eentrepreneurship Theory and Practice, 35(5), 895–923.

In Table 8.2 you can find a framework which categorizes EM according to its main locus – *vertical* (as a strategy, coming from top management); *horizontal* (culture and process – when it is across the organization, and *temporal* (as a response to an environmental macro factor).

Marketing timeline

Prior to delivering its mission statement and company message to the market, a company must define its own business and conduct research on the business environment it wishes to operate, including industry, major stakeholders, and competitors. Consequently, an analysis of the customers the company aspires to offer its products or services to is needed; in other words, an identification of the *target market*. To best analyze the business environment, an enterprise might use a variety of tools (PESTEL, RBV, 4Ps, 5Ps, etc.).

Due to globalization, geographical boundaries have been blurred and in combination with the rapid technological development of the century, these tools have become easily available online, thus decreasing the barriers to entry in some industries where marketing and differentiation could bring a lot of profit.[29] This is particularly beneficial to entrepreneurs as it gives them almost equal access to information, the utilization of which is essential for the success of the business as marketing knowledge could be a source of competitive advantage.[30,31] After the analysis has been conducted, the new company will possess valuable information on how to proceed further with positioning its brand on the market. However, this is not the last step. If the company has done all the steps previously mentioned, it will be able to position itself on the market in the most profitable way through organizing a marketing campaign. However, the marketing campaign needs to correspond to the position that the company wants to take in customers' minds. Hence, it is highly important for the company to conduct this prior research to better comprehend where the highest need for the certain product or service is and how to best position itself

Figure 8.9 iPhone
Source: Image by Josh Hallett on flickr

in people's minds to gain the most profit. Once the marketing campaign is in motion, marketers must closely follow customers' responses to the product or service or both, and provide the company with feedback on customers' feedback and further positioning strategies. Even after the campaign is over, the company must take the necessary measures to establish the Return on Investment on Marketing (ROMI), as *"you cannot manage what you cannot measure"* (Peter Drucker) and gain valuable insights on how it should continue its marketing efforts in the future, which channels were most successful, etc.[32]

Step 1: Defining your mission – "what Business are we in?"

Defining your business niche is the most critical but overlooked aspect of building a successful marketing campaign. This is important because developing through their products and/or services, an enterprise creates effective and realistic marketing. However, they must be clear and fully understand the need that the product or service satisfies. This is particularly important for entrepreneurs since most of them have limited marketing budgets and resources.

An entire generation's very first iPhone

The best product strategy that Apple employs is coming up with very good products. They call it the "great product" strategy. By continuing to hold on to high standards of quality, Apple refuses to get on the bandwagon that most other device makers are using, and for years opted to stick to offering the most expensive products that have a lot more, and better, things to offer.

Starting with their first generation on iPhone, the subsequent years saw the release of iPhone 3G, iPhone 4, and iPhone 5. All the releases were focused on a "luxury" segment of the mobile industry; that is until September of 2013, when Apple released for the very first time the cheapest version of iPhone, the iPhone 5C. The iPhone 5C was sold at a discounted price point in comparison to the 5S. It started at $99 on-contract and over $500 without a contract.

One possible theory would be that Apple is trying to offer devices that it believes can entice a younger audience. According to Jason Hiner of ZDNet, there's an entire generation of youth who've grown up on the iPod, migrated to the iPod Touch, and are now coming of age to make the transition to a smartphone – hopefully an iPhone 5c. Hiner argues, "From that perspective, the carnival of colors available for the iPhone 5c and its colorful silicone cases make perfect sense. They've got 'youthful self-expression' written all over them."[33]

Through careful market research and a very good understanding of their "future" market, Apple has identified the opportunity to sell early to teenagers who in the coming years are Apple's core target segment.

Identifying the target market and product type are essential because they will influence other aspects of the marketing strategy and the business overall. If an enterprise's target market consists of people with a high level of income, then it does not need to put a lower price tag on its products. If the enterprise wants to have a high volume–low price business, the price might be the key criterion for advertising. These enterprises should

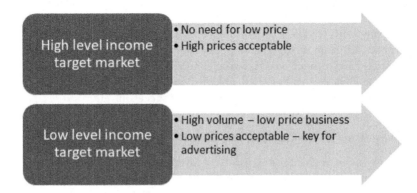

Figure 8.10 Target market

target a wider customer pool, nevertheless, no matter the business focus; the enterprise needs to conceive a proper balance between price and quality.

Both types of strategies have their advantages and disadvantages. Entrepreneurs must identify the best fit, the design needs, and their respective marketing campaigns to attract the right kind of customers.

Step 2: Identifying the client (target market)

After having an overview of your business, it is important to delve deeper into identifying the ideal target market. By identifying and understating an ideal client, an enterprise can design a marketing strategy and customize it to fit consumer needs. Demographic and psychographic information is often used to identify the target market. Generally, people with similar demographic backgrounds tend to behave similarly and companies can benefit from this similarity. For example, teenagers may use a different information search channel compared to middle-aged people; demographics information could direct an enterprise when choosing marketing mediums.

Customer profiles and characteristics assist in understanding the potential market. The important attributes to analyze include those listed in Table 8.3.

Different methods shall be used to acquire this information.[34,35]

After knowing the rational dimension of customers, it is also critical to know the emotional side, which indicates the psychographics about customers. Psychographics segmentation illustrates a group's attitudes and behaviors and gives ideas on how customers are likely to make decisions based on who they might like and trust.[36] By adding the psychographics of customers, an enterprise can target customers more accurately and gain a deeper understanding of their needs. An enterprise can get to know how customers feel and act by knowing their hobbies and interests. This kind of information is often obtained through open-ended questions in surveys and observations of sales.

Also, social media sites like Facebook are helpful in gaining both demographics and psychographic information. An enterprise can learn about web analytics related to the types of customers and their opinions/comments.

Table 8.3 Customer profile

Demographic segmentation	Psychographics segmentation
Age and Gender	Personality and Values
Email address, Phone number, Zip Code	Interests
Education and Income levels	Lifestyle
Occupation and Ethnic background	Behavior

An important point to pay attention to is that an enterprise should not waste efforts in attracting all types of customers. This is not a successful client acquisition strategy. An enterprise target market should be specific enough so that the enterprise can produce products and services tailored to the targeted customers' unique needs. Also, specific markets are easier for an enterprise to reach. Since there are many trade associations, publications, and mailing lists available for a certain market, it is easy for a business to customize their marketing efforts according to the client's needs and wants.[37]

It is essential to understand and differentiate a prime customer's base. *Typical* customers are those who frequently purchase from a given business.[38] *Prime* customers tend to have fewer transactions, but make up a larger portion of your profit. One easy way to differentiate a customer is to track the purchase history and generated revenues of your existing customers' bases.[39]

Step 3: Analyze the environment

The Marketing Mix 4Ps: Product, Place, Promotion, and Price.

Product

Product expansion is critical for an enterprise that wants to expand its market share. Product expansion takes different forms including upgrading existing products, adding new products to the product line, expanding new product lines, and selling products in new markets.[40] Having multiple product lines is beneficial because it contributes to diversifying the risks. The more products in a product line, the more the company is likely to attract customers with different preferences, which would result in higher profits. A higher degree of product lines will lead to diversification and minimization of the risk. However, this may take away the company's focus from utilizing its strengths effectively,

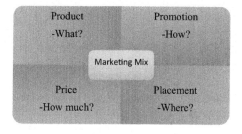

Figure 8.11 Marketing mix

which may lead to dilution of its quality and services. Therefore, clearly defining the boundaries between core business and diversification is essential. Expanding product lines improves customer base and loyalty as they may purchase more products and engage more with the companies.[41] This is true, especially if products and services are complementary to each other.

However, product expansion may have its downside in cannibalizing sales revenue of the existing products assuming they are not complements to each other. It is also generally believed to be time consuming and expensive to diversify. Therefore, expansion of products or services would make more sense when an enterprise has a certain degree of maturity. A strategic expansion is the acquisition of growth opportunities relative to competitors and that is dependent upon the favorability of market conditions.[42,43]

There are several steps enterprises need to follow to safely expand their product lines. First, businesses should discover the specific needs of their customers and the best method is to conduct a competitive analysis.[44] They can track their competitors' brochures and other marketing materials to find out what they are currently offering.[45] A useful guide is to rethink the psychographics such as attitudes and fears and also the demographics such as age, gender, household income, education, and buying habits of your target market, then analyze companies which have reached the same group. The blue ocean strategy is another strategy that the firm can use. The blue ocean strategy makes it conceivable for entrepreneurs to raise the chances and level of success. The blue ocean would utilize strategies such as offering insights on innovative positioning of new ventures, such as extension of the product line and the tools to make it possible. Another approach in identifying demand for a product is similar to what Apple computer did. They foresaw the future application of technology in communication and entertainment and created the iPhone with its unique characteristics, thus creating and satisfying customers' needs. Many of the new apps, social media, etc. that entrepreneurs have been creating are done without in-depth old-fashioned marketing research.

Walter Isaacson; The Innovators: how a group of hackers, geniuses, and geeks created the digital revolution

Following his blockbuster biography of Steve Jobs, The Innovators is Walter Isaacson's revealing story of the people who created the computer and the internet. According to the author, the computer and the internet are among the most important innovations of our era, but few people know who created them. The author shows that most of the innovations of the digital age were done collaboratively. There were a lot of fascinating people involved, some ingenious and a few even geniuses. This is the story of how their minds worked and what made them so inventive. It's also a narrative of how their ability to collaborate and master the art of teamwork made them even more creative.

Walter Isaacson was born on May 20, 1952; he is an American writer and journalist. He is the President and CEO of the Aspen Institute and the University Professor of History at Tulane University. He has been the chairman and CEO of Cable News Network (CNN) and the Managing Editor of Time. He has written biographies of Leonardo da Vinci, Steve Jobs, Benjamin Franklin, Albert Einstein, and Henry Kissinger.

Figure 8.12 Bio
Source: Wikipedia and Goodreads. © iStock: marekuliasz

Linton believes that observing customers' feedback on social media sites generates helpful insights into customers' needs and preferences. Significant comments favoring certain product features provide a useful guide for any businesses in product expansion.[46] Also, businesses could invite customers to collaborate or contribute to product development. Covel suggests that businesses talking directly to customers in a casual, authentic atmosphere can help them discover features of the product they like and the items that might be convenient to have in addition to what they are buying.[47]

Moreover, companies could offer incentives like discounts for purchase to encourage more consumers to participate. Generally, it is better if a third party is in charge of conducting information interviews to ensure more objective and accurate information. Lastly, it is essential that businesses also use market research data and continuously improve upon their relationship with suppliers, distributors, and pretty much every stakeholder in the value chain.

For instance, Nornberg believes that distributors are valuable in offering information on what competitors are doing.[48] Also, they could enable an enterprise to assess the best distribution channels for selling its products to new markets.

- Price deals are usually intended to attract new buyers or to persuade existing customers to increase their purchases.

- The main types of price deals include discounts, bonus pack deals, refunds or rebates, and coupons.
- These days customers are more informed, connected, and thus are empowered than ever before.
- Marketing communications is the means by which firms attempt to inform, persuade, and remind consumers about the products and brands that they sell.
- Today's technological tools have decreased the barriers to entry in some industries, where marketing and differentiation could bring a lot of profit.
- Once the marketing campaign is in motion, marketers must closely follow customers.
- SME resources should be focused on identifying target markets and product types that will influence other aspects of the marketing strategy and the business overall.
- Demographic and psychographic information is often used to identify the target market. Customer profile and characteristics also assist in understanding the potential market.
- Expanding product lines improves the customer base and loyalty as they may purchase more products and engage more with the companies.
- It is essential that businesses also use market research data and continuously improve upon their relationship with suppliers, distributors, and pretty much every stakeholder in the value chain.

Branding or the "brand myopia"

The technological revolution has provided a two-way connection between brands and consumers. Therefore, an effective branding strategy could provide a company with a competitive advantage in a highly competitive market. Typically, branding has been defined as: "The promotion of a particular product or company by means of advertising and distinctive design…" (Oxford Dictionary).

However, nowadays, a more precise definition is presented by the online business dictionary, which defines branding as:

> The process involved in creating a unique name and image for a product in the consumers' mind, mainly through advertising campaigns with a consistent theme. Branding aims to establish a significant and differentiated presence in the market that attracts and retains loyal customers.[49]

The underlying difference in the two definitions is the fact that while the first centers on *promotion* as a branding strategy, the latter focuses on consumers. In other words, it outlines promotion as simply the way a company communicates its previously established image ("brand") in consumers' minds. This should be the definition of branding that all entrepreneurs understand to further build and develop it according to other internal and external factors.

Nevertheless, branding should not be perceived as an end in itself or merely a management tool, which if managed successfully could assist in the achievement of organizational objectives. This managerial fault has lately been coined as "Branding Myopia", where brands are viewed as an end in themselves.

In their core, brands are symbols around which a company's stakeholders (e.g., consumers, competitors, and suppliers) construct identities for certain products.[50] Entrepreneurs should also consider the external (macro) environment. Currently, major anti-branding movements and anti-globalization activities have illustrated people's antipathy of large corporations. This could be highly beneficial for entrepreneurs who understand and utilize it to their advantage through an effective branding strategy.

Imagine if market characteristics were divided between order winners and order qualifiers, where the winners would get the most beneficial market characteristics, and qualifiers would be the requirements. In such a scenario, having a brand is no longer seen as an order winner. Technology and globalization have transformed it to an order qualifier, as having a brand is no longer enough. Therefore, it is important for any company to know how to gain more brand equity.

Now, brands are embodied by products but enacted by customers. Moreover, as brands nowadays have multiple dimensions, their meaning varies with the passage of time and in accordance with the many stakeholders. In the branding process, the initial steps are of crucial importance as they are key to successful management of a brand evolution, which requires that "the brand does not lose its roots in the past."[51]

Technology and marketing

Social networking: online and real life

Many social networking platforms are available and many more are evolving. An entrepreneur shall be forward-looking and identify where social networking will be in the future and how it can be used efficiently.[52] The question is where to commit and allocate our time and resources.

Social networking has always been a vital part of promoting businesses for SMEs since it is an effective way of making your mark.

> **"What physics taught me about marketing"**
>
> Physics and marketing don't seem to have much in common, but Dan Cobley is passionate about both. He brings these unlikely bedfellows together using Newton's second law, Heisenberg's uncertainty principle, the scientific method, and the second law of thermodynamics to explain the fundamental theories of branding.
>
> You can check in more details in the full TED Talk in this link: www.ted.com/talks/dan_cobley_what_physics_taught_me_about_marketing#t-439298

People quite simply prefer doing business with people they know and like, so cementing a relationship in person can translate an unenthusiastic relationship into a long-term and mutually beneficial one.

Social network will drive value. The principal benefit of new social platforms is that today's knowledge workers have connected to each other and consumers. Social media platforms such as Facebook and Twitter accounts provide abandoned opportunities for marketing online. The beauty of online marketing is that it will level the playing field between a Fortune 500 company and a small business, holding everything else constant.

As social media has increased in importance, many businesses have been forced to assign social networking tasks to current staff. This leads to inconsistencies between organizations as one company may have an administrator, another business owner, and another member of the marketing staff handling updates.[53] With the rise of social media, it has been much easier and helps to enhance communication. Entrepreneurs could use free tools to keep customers updated about their business, communicate and build a relationship with customers, and make customers "know, like, and trust" their business.[54] Social Media Marketing is also the resource of word-of-mouth promotions. When prospects obtain the positive responses from satisfied customers through social media, word of mouth has already been proliferated.

Whether a video, a blog post, or a status update, content is the engine of the social web; if an enterprise produces and shares useful content, your community will be more likely to become customers, and this would result in repeat customers for the enterprise. To be able to create appropriate and effective content, an enterprise needs to understand the needs and mindsets of its customers. One useful way to do this is using social media sites to monitor what people are discussing about your enterprise, in terms of product and quality when compared to competitors. In addition, businesses need to frequently produce content using social media platforms to educate customers, satisfy customers' informational needs, solve their issues and problems, engage them, and entertain them.[55,56]

By participating in community activities, the enterprise will increase visibility and reputation. This shows to the customers that the enterprise cares about them and thus helps the enterprise to become the opinion leader in that respective area. To increase the visibility of the enterprise, it should also build relationships with the person or businesses which write about the industry, company, and products.[57] This is applicable because many of them are willing to connect with the organization. However, the enterprise should not expect them to directly advertise like posting corporate materials. Instated, the enterprise could offer them the critical information that complements their current work. Due to the fast dissemination of information, entrepreneurs should pay special attention to the negative comments on social platforms. The enterprise should investigate what really happened, explain to the customers, apologize, and make efforts to improve their reputation.

With social media, entrepreneurs and SMEs are able to use free and low-cost social tools to help increase word-of-mouth advertising while decreasing the need for more expensive outbound advertising platforms like the yellow pages, cable television ads, etc.[58] The popular social media sites used by entrepreneurs include Facebook, Twitter, Pinterest, Instagram, LinkedIn, and Google+. However, they still require a major time commitment from the enterprise to work properly.

Companies should therefore not try to be active in every platform, instead focusing time and resources on the social media channels that generate the highest return on investment for the business. To identify the sites that are most effective for an enterprise, it needs to experiment with different sites and track which sites offer the highest return in traffic.[59] Also, different social networking sites require users to operate in different ways. For example, an enterprise may use Pinterest to share their product's image but use Twitter to share industry news as well as employment opportunities.[60] When an enterprise has a presence on multiple social networking sites, it is useful to use third-party tools like HootSuite.com and tweet deck that can operate multiple social media platforms at once.[61]

How do you measure an intangible object such as brand equity?

When the customer experience provided by the brand is measured over numerous iterations and it endures over time, it results in the creation of brand loyalty. Today, customers can – and do – easily communicate the strength of their brand attitude to others via customer reviews and social sharing.

Brand recognition is hugely responsible for a customer to recognize a psychological feeling of what it stands for.

Example: When we hear Apple we instantly recognize its superiority in design and technology. Similarly brands such as Mercedes and Bentley bring a feeling of prestige and luxury while not all companies compete for the same recognition. Toyota stands for durability, BMW for performance, Samsung for its technology, and Spirit Airlines for its affordability.

While measuring a company's brand equity, the company has to answer questions such as:

- How much more will a consumer pay for a product or service that is branded over a product or service that is unbranded?

The company also has to look at strategies such as how to:

- Conduct market research that focuses on tracking comparison among competitive brands or products against a benchmark.
- Conduct both qualitative and quantitative surveys to ensure that customers recognize the brand for its stated vision and promises.
- Product/Service differentiation is a lynchpin for brand loyalty.

Social media marketing takes new skills and most of us can acquire skills to manage it. By definition, it is accessible.[62] Investment in social media will become a necessity, not a luxury. Businesses are already coming to terms with the need to integrate their social media efforts with their content strategy, and are seeing the impact of social media in terms of lead generation, referral traffic, and revenue.[63]

Businesses need to be aware that it can take a long time to build up a social network, expand customer base, and generate enough leads to keep in business. Business should therefore not rely on them as a sole source of doing business. In addition, entrepreneurs need to extract information and data from social media to drive business strategy.[64]

It is feasible to analyze and measure the business environment as technology has been advancing almost exponentially every two years, in accordance with Moore's law.[65] Terms such as *big data and business analytics* have attracted worldwide attention due to the benefits their utilization bring to the company.[66] Some have even called it the "Big Data Revolution", which has irrevocably transformed how marketing is done and seen.[67] For about two decades now, search engines have proliferated (Google being in the center) and revolutionized online research. In an era in which libraries are primarily used for the Wi-Fi signal rather than the books they offer, technology has certainly taken its turn. Thus, conducting a business environment analysis has become easier than ever which contributes to the simplification of creating a marketing strategy (a comprehensive marketing plan) which is created based on the prior analysis of the business environment and with a focus on the marketing mix.

As far as branding is concerned, technology has now made it possible for companies to precisely analyze the impact of its potential branding strategy on the sales volume through a recently presented approach, called the centrality-distinctiveness (C-D) map. For the first time companies are offered a direct physical measurement of how their brand is perceived on the market. The successful utilization of this tool might bring better insights into the desired market position, resource allocation, and overall brand strategy.

- Branding should not be perceived as an end in itself or merely a management tool, which if managed successfully could assist in the achievement of organizational objectives.
- It is important for any company to know how to gain more brand equity.
- Social networking has always been a vital part of promoting businesses for SMEs since it is an effective way of making your mark.
- To be able to create appropriate and effective content, an enterprise needs to understand the needs and mindsets of its customers.
- An enterprise could offer its customers critical information that complements their current products and the company's vision.
- With social media, entrepreneurs and SMEs are able to use free and low cost social tools over the more expensive outbound advertising platforms.

Source: DeVault (2018)[68]

After choosing a geographic market and a customer segment, a company must conduct a "survey on consumers' perception of the brand's centrality and distinctiveness."[69]

- Unconventional brands – possess unique characteristics (ex. Tesla). Mainly a niche strategy.
- Peripheral brands – *"Me too"* strategy; inadequate distinction, thus not a top choice (ex. Kia, Mitsubishi), still quite profitable.
- Aspirational brands – wide appeal and high differentiation (ex. For beer – 62 percent of unit sales).
- Mainstream brands –first to mind in a category but still indistinctive, thus lacking pricing power. Nevertheless, still popular and bought by consumers (ex. Ford, Chevrolet).

Increased centrality is usually considered as a sales booster, while the distinctiveness of a brand is associated with the higher end niche brands, thus sales volume is lower. Nevertheless, distinctiveness is important as it has the price advantage in the long term.

For further examples of how different companies perform on the C–D map, please visit: https://hbr.org/2015/06/a-better-way-to-map-brand-strategy.

Search Engine Optimization (SEO)

Building a website is like building a house. When built properly, they both combine interdependent components into a functional and attractive whole. In a house, the components are things like plumbing and ventilation; in a website, they're things like Search Engine Optimization (SEO) and navigational structure.[70] SEO has evolved over the past few years with a greater emphasis on the quality of the actual content.[71] Good SEO is essential for building credibility and positioning your company as an industry leader.[72] SEO is the process of affecting the visibility of a website or a web page in a search engine's "natural" or un-paid ("organic") search results. Businesses need to have an SEO plan to increase organic searches via blogs, web content, etc. Basically, this can be applied to any business model. In general, the earlier (or higher ranked on the search results page) and more frequently a site appears in the search results list, the more visitors it will receive from the search engine's users. Figure 8.13 shows the process of SEO.

Therefore, businesses need to consider how search engines work, what people search for, the actual search terms or keywords typed into search engines, and which search engines are preferred by their targeted audience through social media. Optimizing a website may involve editing its content to contain various social networks, HTML, and associated coding to both increase its relevance to specific keywords and to remove barriers to the indexing activities of search engines. Promoting a site to increase the number of backlinks or inbound links is another SEO tactic.[73]

Figure 8.13 SEO

Before summarizing, we would like to discuss how entrepreneurs could use the marketing advice and suggestions provided in this chapter to increase their market share. While some people use the terms "entrepreneur" and "small business owner" synonymously, there are still differences between the entrepreneurial venture and the small business. First, entrepreneur is a person. Small business is an organization/entity which is created by an entrepreneur. Therefore, small businesses generally are larger in size and have higher access to resources than entrepreneurs. In addition, small businesses may have different objectives and views than entrepreneurs. Therefore, entrepreneurs need to choose the right combination of strategies based on their own capabilities and goals.

Conclusion

Considering the key role played by marketing in business success and the special characteristics of entrepreneurs, it becomes imperative to produce a detailed marketing plan focusing on technology and marketing strategy. To understand their business, entrepreneurs need to determine their product focus (quality vs quantity), what are their primary products and services, and analyze the competitive landscape. To identify their customers, entrepreneurs need to collect the demographic information and psychographic attributes and differentiate their typical customers from prime customers. In terms of product expansion, entrepreneurs can consider the alternatives such as upgrading existing products, adding new products to their product line, expanding into new product lines, offering new-to-the-world products, and selling products in new markets. In terms of the choices in distribution channels, entrepreneurs could choose to set up an online store, a physical store or both.

- Enterprises need to identify the sites that are most return of investment (ROI); initially they need to experiment with different sites and track which sites offer highest return in traffic.
- Investment in social media will become a necessity, not a luxury.
- For about two decades now, search engines have proliferated (Google being in the center) and revolutionized online research.
- The centrality-distinctiveness (C-D) map can offer companies with a direct physical measurement of how their brand is perceived in the market. The successful utilization of this tool can bring better insights on the desired market position, resource allocation, and overall brand strategy.
- Good SEO is essential for building credibility and positioning your company as an industry leader.
- Businesses need to have an SEO plan to increase organic searches via blogs, web content.
- HTML and associated coding are required to both increase SEO's relevance to specific keywords and to remove barriers to the indexing activities of search engines.

Either way, entrepreneurs need to design the store content to attract customers and enhance their shopping experiences. In terms of promotion, entrepreneurs could advertise on the radio, the newspaper, and the web.

Also, they could use direct mail, social media, and promotion at events to directly reach their customers. Moreover, entrepreneurs could use sales promotions like price deals, bonus pack coupon publications, continuity programs, and sampling to stimulate customers' purchases. To design an effective pricing strategy, entrepreneurs need to assess the cost structure, understand their position strategy, and competitors' pricing. In addition, entrepreneurs could design tiered customer loyalty programs by offering different types of rewards to attract and retain customers. To create an effective marketing strategy, entrepreneurs need to integrate each part to produce a consistent message.

Discussion questions

1. What is the definition of marketing and how has it changed over time?
2. Did you find marketing theories relevant in this chapter?
3. What is the relationship between marketing, technology, and entrepreneurship?
4. Describe the first two steps a company must undertake prior to formulating a marketing strategy.
5. Provide a few examples of how technology has transformed marketing.
6. Write a short case that illustrates at least two important topics from this case.

Appendix

Table 8.4 Online store

Online Store	• Online transactions for many products, growing exponentially.
	• Customers are attracted to online shopping because they can easily conduct an information search and price comparison.[a]
	• Having an online store is attractive to businesses because it allows the enterprise to reach a wider range of customers both in the country and internationally.
	• Provides convenience for your customers since they can access the enterprise's website 24/7 at any place as long as an online connection is given. It is also believed to be cost-effective because the reduction in costs of face-to-face sales force and premise.
	• Intuit indicates that physical stores usually have limited space for storing products, thus, by having online stores, businesses could choose to store the products in warehouses, thereby offering a wider range of products and keeping costs down. A complement to the warehouse model could be showrooms in selected high traffic locations.[b]

[a] Juon, C., Greiling, D., & Buerkle, C. (2011). Internet Marketing From Start to Finish: Drive Measurable, Repeatable Online Sales with Search Marketing, Usability, CRM, and Analytics. Indianapolis, IN: Que Pub.
[b] Intuit. (2013) Why Ecommerce Solutions? [Online] Retrieved March 1, 2013, from www.intuit.com/ecommerce/create-your-online-store/.

Table 8.5 Key terms

Marketing	Price deals
Target market	Brand myopia
Strategy	Marketing communications
Return on Investment on Marketing (ROMI)	Big-data and business analytics
Marketing mix	Entrepreneurial marketing
Psychographics segmentation	Search Engine Optimization (SEO)

Notes

1 Kumar, V., & Gupta, S. (2016). Conceptualizing the evolution and future of advertising. Journal of Advertising, 45(3), 302–317. doi:10.1080/00913367.2016.1199335

2 Kozielski, R. (2016). Determinants of business success – theoretical model and empirical verification. Folia Oeconomica Stetinensia, 16(1), 274–285. doi:10.1515/foli-2016-0018

3 www.ama.org/

4 Lorette, K. (2013). The Importance of Marketing for the Success of a Business [Online]. Retrieved March 20, 2013, from http://smallbusiness.chron.com/importance-marketing-success-business-589.html.

5 Swaim, R. (2013). Peter Drucker on Sales and Marketing. PEX. Process Excellence Network. Retrieved from www.processexcellencenetwork.com/organizational-strategies-for-innovation-continuou/columns/peter-drucker-on-sales-and-marketing/.

6 Miles, R. & Snow, C. (1978). Organizational Strategy, Structure, and Process. New York: McGraw-Hill.

7 Porter, M. E. (1980). Competitive Strategy. New York: The Free Press.

8 Knight, G. (2000). Entrepreneurship and marketing strategy: the SME under globalization. Journal of International Marketing, 8(2), June, 12–32. EBSCOhost, search.ebscohost.com/login.aspx?direct=true&db=bth&AN=3225341&site=ehost-live.

9 Jobber, D. (2010). Principles and Practice of Marketing (6th ed.). New York: McGraw-Hill.

10 Dennis, C., Fenech, T., & Merrilees, B. (2004). E-retailing. New York: Routledge.

11 Dennis, C., Fenech, T., & Merrilees, B. (2004). E-retailing. New York: Routledge.

12 McCue, T. J. (2010). BigCommerce Review: Building a Small Business Online Storefront [Online]. Retrieved March 20, 2013, from http://smallbiztrends.com/2010/08/bigcommerce-review-building-a-small-business-online-storefront.html.

13 Martin, S. (2012). For Your Small Business: Opening an Online Store [Online] Retrieved March 20, 2013, from www.expand2web.com/blog/for-your-small-business-opening-an-online-store/.

14 Crane, F. G. (2010). Marketing for Entrepreneurs: Concepts and Applications for New Ventures. California: SAGE Publications, Inc.

15 Crane, F. G. (2010). Marketing for Entrepreneurs: Concepts and Applications for New Ventures. California: SAGE Publications, Inc.

16 Beesley, C. (2012). How to Price Your Small Business' Products and Services [Online]. Retrieved February 10, 2013, from www.sba.gov/community/blogs/how-price-your-small-business%E2%80%99-products-and-services.

17 Zahorsky, D. (2013). Pricing Strategies for Small Business [Online]. Retrieved March 20, 2013, from http://sbinformation.about.com/cs/bestpractices/a/aa112402a.htm.

18 Zahorsky, D. (2013). Pricing Strategies for Small Business [Online]. Retrieved March 20, 2013, from http://sbinformation.about.com/cs/bestpractices/a/aa112402a.htm.

19 Crane, F. G. (2010). Marketing for Entrepreneurs: Concepts and Applications for New Ventures. California: SAGE Publications, Inc.

20 Berthon, P., Holbrook, M. B., Hulbert, J. M., & Pitt, L. (2007, January 1). Viewing Brands in Multiple Dimensions. Retrieved from https://sloanreview.mit.edu/article/viewing-brands-in-multiple-dimensions/.

21 Kozielski, R. (2016). Determinants of business success – theoretical model and empirical verification. Folia Oeconomica Stetinensia, 16(1), 274–285. doi:10.1515/foli-2016-0018

22 Beesley, C. (2012). How to Price Your Small Business' Products and Services [Online]. Retrieved February 10, 2013, from www.sba.gov/community/blogs/how-price-your-small-business%E2%80%99-products-and-services.

23 Rao, N. (2014, June 9). Marketing Communication: Channels and Promotion Tools. Retrieved from http://nraomtr.blogspot.com/2011/12/marketing-communication-channels-and.html.

24 Kotler, P. (2014). Kotler On Marketing (1st ed.). [Place of publication not identified]: Free Press, Print.

25 Batra, R., & Keller, K. L. (2016). Integrating marketing communications: new findings, new lessons, and new ideas. Journal of Marketing, 80(6), 122–145. EBSCOhost, doi:10.1509/jm.15.0419.

26 Giorgi, G., & Rahman, A. (2013, September). SME's Registration: Evidence from an RCT in Bangladesh. Elsevier Science Ltd. http://search.proquest.com/abicomplete/docview/1417004268/141BD3756D63D43EA7D/35?accountid=8576.

27 Stone, K. E. (2012, September 18). Why traditional marketing trumps social media, and what to do about it. Forbes. Retrieved from www.forbes.com/sites/yec/2012/09/18/why-traditional-marketing-trumps-social-media-and-what-to-do-about-it.

28 Miles, M., Gilmore, A., Harrigan, P., Lewis, G., & Sethna, Z. (2014). Exploring entrepreneurial marketing. Journal of Strategic Marketing, 23(2), 94–111. doi:10.1080/0965254x.2014.914069

29 Kumar, V., & Gupta, S. (2016). Conceptualizing the evolution and future of advertising. Journal of Advertising, 45(3), 302–317. doi:10.1080/00913367.2016.1199335

30 Polanyi, M. (1966). The logic of tacit inference. Philosophy, XLI(155), 1–18. https://doi.org/10.1017/S0031819100066110

31 Kozielski, R. (2016). Determinants of business success – theoretical model and empirical verification. Folia Oeconomica Stetinensia, 16(1), 274–285. doi:10.1515/foli-2016-0018

32 Drucker, P. (2012). Management Challenges for the 21st Century. Routledge.

33 Hiner, J. (2013). Two factors reveal Apple's real mission with iPhone 5c. Between the Lines. Retrieved from Zdnet: www.zdnet.com/article/two-factors-reveal-apples-real-mission-with-iphone-5c/

34 Hoxie, M. (2011). 90 days to success marketing and advertising your small business. Course Technology, Cengage Learning.

35 Joseph, J. (2012) The Experience Effect for Small Business: Big Brand Results with Small Business Resources. [Books24x7 version] Retrieved February 1, 2013, from http://common.books24x7.com.ezp.bentley.edu/toc.aspx?bookid=45346.

36 Joseph, J. (2012) The Experience Effect for Small Business: Big Brand Results with Small Business Resources. [Books24x7 version] Retrieved February 1, 2013, from http://common.books24x7.com.ezp.bentley.edu/toc.aspx?bookid=45346.

37 Jantsch, J. (2006). Duct Tape Marketing: The World's Most Practical Small Business Marketing Guide. [Books24x7 version] Retrieved January 22, 2013, from http://common.books24x7.com.ezp.bentley.edu/toc.aspx?bookid=37673.

38 Hoxie, M. (2011). 90 days to success marketing and advertising your small business. Course Technology, Cengage Learning.

39 Jantsch, J. (2006). Duct Tape Marketing: The World's Most Practical Small Business Marketing Guide. [Books24x7 version] Retrieved January 22, 2013, from http://common.books24x7.com.ezp.bentley.edu/toc.aspx?bookid=37673.

40 Jobber, D. (2010). Principles and Practice of Marketing (6th ed.). New York: McGraw-Hill.

41 Linton, I. (2013). Four Reasons to Expand a Product Line [Online] Retrieved March 15, 2013, from http://smallbusiness.chron.com/four-reasons-expand-product-line-55242.html.

42 Kulatilaka, N., & Perotti, E. C. (1998). Strategic growth option. Management Science, 44, 1021–1031. http://dx.doi.org/10.1287/mnsc.44.8.1021

43 Sharifi, H., Ismail, H. S., Qiu, J., & Tavani, S. N. (2013). Supply chain strategy and its impacts on product and market growth strategies: a case study of SMEs. International Journal of Production Economics, 145(1), 397–408. doi:10.1016/j.ijpe.2013.05.005

44 Gordon, K. T. (2004). Pros and Cons of Expanding Your Product Line [Online] Retrieved February 20, 2013, from www.entrepreneur.com/article/71094.

45 DeLeon & Stang. (2009). Four Tips for Expanding the Product Line Develop a Logical Plan for New Launches [Online] Retrieved March 1, 2013, from www.deleonandstang.com/news-articles/managers-edge-article/four-tips-for-expanding-the-product-line/.

46 Linton, I. (2013). Four Reasons to Expand a Product Line [Online] Retrieved March 15, 2013, from http://smallbusiness.chron.com/four-reasons-expand-product-line-55242.html.

47 Covel. S. (2008). Tips: How to Expand Your Product Line [Online] Retrieved February 21, 2013, from http://online.wsj.com/article/SB121927283771758259.html.

48 Nornberg, V. M. (2013). 3 Sure-Fire Ways to Expand Your Product Line [Online] Retrieved March 15, 2013, from www.inc.com/vanessa-merit-nornberg/growth-strategies-sure-fire-ways-to-expand-your-product-line.html.

49 http://robinsoncreativeinc.com/branding/

50 Berthon, P., Holbrook, M. B., Hulbert, J. M., & Pitt, L. (2007, January 1). Viewing Brands in Multiple Dimensions. Retrieved from https://sloanreview.mit.edu/article/viewing-brands-in-multiple-dimensions/.

51 Berthon, P., Holbrook, M. B., Hulbert, J. M., & Pitt, L. (2007, January 1). Viewing Brands in Multiple Dimensions. Retrieved from https://sloanreview.mit.edu/article/viewing-brands-in-multiple-dimensions/.

52 DeMers, J. (2013, September 24). The top 7 social media marketing tips that will dominate 2014. Forbes. Retrieved from www.forbes.com/sites/jaysondemers/2013/09/24/the-top-7-social-media-marketing-trends-that-will-dominate-2014/.

53 Hendricks, D. (2013, October 16). How social media campaigns will change in 2014. Forbes. Retrieved from www.forbes.com/sites/drewhendricks/2013/10/16/how-social-media-campaigns-will-change-in-2014/.

54 Roeder, L. (2013). Social Media Marketing: A Small Business Primer [Online] Retrieved February 20, 2013, from http://lkrsocialmedia.com/social-media-marketing/.

55 Bodnar, K. (2013). Generating Small Business Customers with Social Media Marketing: Small Business Case Studies [Online] Retrieved February 20, 2013, from www.hubspot.com/Portals/53/docs/small-business-social-media-ebook-hubspot.pdf.

56 Hartman, D. (2013). Operations Strategy for Product Expansion [Online] Retrieved February 16, 2013, from http://smallbusiness.chron.com/operations-strategy-product-expansion-25609.html.

57 Scott, D. M. (2011). The New Rules of Marketing and PR. New Jersey: John Wiley & Sons, Inc.

58 Juon, C., Greiling, D., & Buerkle, C. (2011). Internet Marketing From Start to Finish: Drive Measurable, Repeatable Online Sales with Search Marketing, Usability, CRM, and Analytics. Indianapolis, IN: Que Publishing.

59 Roeder, L. (2013). Social Media Marketing: A Small Business Primer [Online] Retrieved February 20, 2013, from http://lkrsocialmedia.com/social-media-marketing/.

60 Hartman, D. (2013). Operations Strategy for Product Expansion [Online] Retrieved February 16, 2013, from http://smallbusiness.chron.com/operations-strategy-product-expansion-25609.html.

61 Roeder, L. (2013). Social Media Marketing: A Small Business Primer [Online] Retrieved February 20, 2013, from http://lkrsocialmedia.com/social-media-marketing/.

62 Shaughnessy, H. (2012, April 12). Marketing 2015: be prepared to be surprised. Very surprised. Forbes. Retrieved from www.forbes.com/sites/haydnshaughnessy/2012/04/12/marketing-2015-be-surprised-be-very-surprised/.

63 DeMers, J. (2013, September 24). The top 7 social media marketing tips that will dominate 2014. Forbes. Retrieved from www.forbes.com/sites/jaysondemers/2013/09/24/the-top-7-social-media-marketing-trends-that-will-dominate-2014/.

64 Hoxie, M. (2011). 90 days to success marketing and advertising your small business. Course Technology, Cengage Learning.

65 Friedman, T. (2016). Thank You For Being Late (1st ed.). New York: Farrar, Straus and Giroux.

66 Wedel, M., & Kannan, P. (2016). Marketing analytics for data-rich environments. Journal of Marketing, 80(6), 97–121. doi:10.1509/jm.15.0413

67 Kumar, V., & Gupta, S. (2016). Conceptualizing the evolution and future of advertising. Journal of Advertising, 45(3), 302–317. doi:10.1080/00913367.2016.1199335

68 DeVault, G. (2018, September 04). Measuring Brand Equity. Retrieved from www.thebalancesmb.com/how-to-measure-brand-equity-2296827.

69 Bagga, C. K., & Dawar, N. (2015). A better way to map brand strategy. Harvard Business Review, 90–97. Print.

70 Shorr, B. (2013, June 26). 10 ways companies screw up their websites. Forbes. Retrieved from www.forbes.com/sites/allbusiness/2013/06/26/10-ways-companies-screw-up-their-websites.

71 Simon, D. (2013, May 09). 10 SEO tips for 2013. Forbes. Retrieved from www.forbes.com/sites/dansimon/2013/05/09/10-seo-tips-for-2013/.

72 Hall, J. (2013, September 04). What every leader needs to know about SEO. Forbes. Retrieved from www.forbes.com/sites/johnhall/2013/04/09/what-every-leader-needs-to-know-about-seo/.

73 In basic link terminology, a backlink is any link received by a web node (web page, directory, website, or top level domain) from another web node. The terms backlinks, incoming links, inbound links, inlinks, and inward links present incoming links to a website or web page.

9 Financing opportunities and challenges

Learning objectives:

1. *Understand the necessity of funding for entrepreneurs*
2. *Comprehend the potential sources of funding*
3. *Evaluate the financing life cycle*
4. *Examine financial barriers and entrepreneurial growth*
5. *Discuss the role of government as the source of funding for entrepreneurship.*

Figure 9.1 Bank logo
Source: © iStock: kgtoh

Banking reimagined through microfinancing

Dr. Muhammad Yunus is a Bangladeshi social entrepreneur, banker, economist and civil society leader who was awarded the Nobel Peace Prize for founding the Grameen Bank that pioneers the concepts of microcredit and microfinance. Grameen Bank was founded in 1976 in Dhaka, Bangladesh, with the main aim to provide credit to the poorest of the poor in rural Bangladesh without any collateral. From its origins as an action-research project in 1976, Grameen Bank has grown to provide collateral-free loans to 7.5 million clients in more than 82,072 villages in Bangladesh and 97 percent of whom are women.

Introduction

Development of infrastructure, agribusiness, legal systems, financial systems, regulatory bodies, and sophisticated economic/social policies are all integral parts of any country. While the general business environment has an immense indirect impact on every business and on an entrepreneur who operates in such an environment, this chapter specifically focuses on those that have a direct measurable impact on entrepreneurial growth: access to finance.

This chapter discusses opportunities, obstacles, and constraints facing entrepreneurs in their pursuit to obtain finance. It emphasizes the importance of obtaining financing for entrepreneurial growth. From an economic perspective, a distinction is made between micro constraints and macro constraints (i.e., direct vs indirect constraints). From a scale perspective, differentiation is made between startup entrepreneurs vs large enterprises in their quest for securing financing. From a global perspective, the discussion should analyze in the context of a developing country. While developed countries are discussed for reference, the assumption is that the reader understands the general business environment in a developed country and can comprehend the unique, systemic problems in developing countries.[1] Finally, the interplay between the macro (i.e., indirect) and micro (i.e., direct) constraints will be analyzed along with the conduciveness of a business environment to illustrate that entrepreneurial credit access is a systemic and circular problem.

There will be discussions later in the chapter on all of the points mentioned earlier that may be helpful to provide an example to illustrate each point. Imagine an entrepreneur who is trying to obtain financing for his business venture. He/she goes to the bank and applies for a loan. In developed countries (e.g., the United States), the only credit constraints for entrepreneurs are direct constraints (e.g., credit score). Assume the entrepreneur has good credit. The bank runs his/her credit and sees if they are creditworthy. After a review of the business plan, a loan is granted based on the credit information.

Now, assume the same scenario for an entrepreneur in a developing country (i.e., Ethiopia) who has bad credit. The entrepreneur goes to the bank but they have no way to assess their creditworthiness (due to the fact that there is no central credit bureau and information-sharing between banks is limited). The bank, therefore, asks them to pledge their house as collateral for the loan. Now, if he/she agrees to the loan and then goes bankrupt a few months later, the bank tries to sell the entrepreneur's house to repay the loan, but it turns out they are not the legal owner of the house and falsely pledged it to obtain the loan. The bank now has no collateral and must recognize the loan transaction as a loss. There are many different positive or negative scenarios that can happen. Would you think the banks in the second scenario will lend to small entrepreneurs with no

Figure 9.2 Entrepreneurship in China

Source: Image by Ken Lund on flickr. Full article: Tse, E. (2016, April 05). The rise of entrepreneurship in China. Forbes. Retrieved from www.forbes.com/sites/tseedward/2016/04/05/the-rise-of-entrepreneurship-in-china/#6271e2623efc.

collateral again? Probably not. However, in this fact pattern, the problem has become systemic. There is no accurate way for the bank to properly assess risk due to the poor legal system, property rights, and lack of credit information sharing in developing countries. Therefore, in these countries, indirect constraints have a significant impact on the overall access to finance for entrepreneurs.

While these examples are extreme, they serve to illustrate the variety of factors that can potentially cause credit constraints. In developed countries, well-established legal systems, clearly defined property rights, and central credit bureaus direct constraints (e.g., credit score). These are the most significant influencers in the lending decision (see Table 9.1). However, in developing countries, indirect constraints (e.g., an underdeveloped legal system, poor property rights, lack of information sharing) have a much louder voice in influencing the lending decision.[2]

While many constraints are considered circular (e.g., a developed legal system is needed in order for financiers to lend money with confidence), the scope of this chapter will be limited to the direct constraints of obtaining finance while touching upon the indirect effects of other constraints (e.g., an underdeveloped legal system, ineffective government policy, etc.).[3] Beck (2014) argues that financial systems play a critical function in an economy's growth and therefore allocating savings towards this use would be a good use of funds.[4]

Table 9.1 Well-established, versatile business environment

Characteristics of a well-established, versatile business environment is defined as an environment that has:

- Well-established legal and regulatory bodies;
- Well-defined property rights;
- Effective contract enforcement;
- Competitive markets (product, labor, and capital);
- Legal framework that allows for relatively easy entry and exit of enterprises.[a]

---

[a] Beck, T., & Levine, R. (2005). Legal institutions and financial development. In Handbook of New Institutional Economics (pp. 251–278). Boston, MA: Springer.

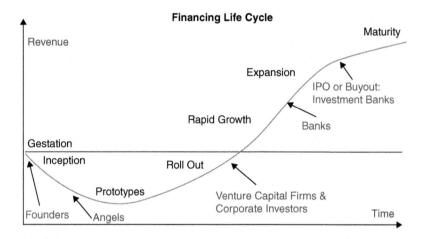

Figure 9.3 Financing life cycle

Financing life cycle

In the United States and most developed countries, there are multiple sources of funding available for entrepreneurs. Figure 9.3 represents the life cycle of financing which links revenue and stages of the products or services. The initial funding has to come from the wealth and income of funders and immediate family and friends. Of course, angel investors and crowd or community funding are other options. As the product or services move further towards the output stage, other sources of funding from angel investors and venture capital will become available. When the product or services are reaching what is called "roll out" stage, then additional sources of funding such as banks and IPO will become available. In most developing countries the primary sources of funding are family, friends, and banking institutions. In some countries, governments may provide some initial seed funding. In the following sections we will discuss intuitional, regulatory, and cultural constraints that exist in the developing countries and suggest solutions.

Entrepreneurial growth and a country's economic development

The general perception is that entrepreneurs drive growth and innovation and help move a developing country towards economic equality. Big businesses are often portrayed as corrupt and a representation of those in power, thus losing the average person's trust, while entrepreneurs are seen as the white knights who attempt at balancing equality and driving growth.

Lobbyists, interest groups, and policymakers alike will often preach that entrepreneurs are the engines of development. There have been some micro-studies and cross-country research is done, where most conclusions illustrate a positive correlation between the growth percentage of entrepreneurs and the growth rate of a country; this means a higher percentage of entrepreneurs positively correlates to higher growth rates, suggesting entrepreneurs drive growth and development.[5] While little research suggests that entrepreneurs are a significant contributor to growth, it is far from conclusive especially given a slew of other variables that could account for the correlation.[6]

However, research has found that a better indicator of development and growth is an overall positive environment conducive to doing business. In other words, the number of entrepreneurs is not as strong an indicator of development and growth as is a well-established and versatile business environment.

When an environment conducive to doing business is in place, both entrepreneurs and large enterprises flourish. Therefore, perhaps more important than ensuring a level playing field for entrepreneurs (e.g., through the use of entrepreneurial special subsidies) is ensuring the proper framework is established to conduct business (e.g., an established legal system, competitive regulations, etc.). Policies focused on overall business improvement are aimed to better serve entrepreneurs than are policies directly focused on subsidizing certain market demographics. Additionally, overall business improvement is more sustainable and requires less administration by policymakers. To emphasize the importance of conducive business and financial environments, it may be helpful to review a few examples which illustrate why it is quintessential.

Example: Registration Costs

Although the breadth of a good business environment is sprawling, of particular note to an overall conducive business environment is the ease of entrance and exit of enterprises. This may be of particular interest to active entrepreneurs and inexperienced entrepreneurs looking to break into a market. If the business environment has higher barriers to entry, it will be less conducive for new entrepreneurs to enter the market. From this perspective, it is important for policy to keep barriers to entry low (e.g., through regulation of low registration costs, etc.) rather than subsidizing those barriers for certain groups (e.g., subsidizing registration costs for entrepreneurs). A subsidy is not sustainable and will only temporarily fix the problem. However, regulating registration costs so they remain low across the board is sustainable. The market has a way of self-correcting when proper regulations are in place.

Taking the regulation of registration costs as an example, Italy and the UK provide us with real-life examples of how two different regulatory strategies can provide very different results for both entrepreneurial growth and overall economic growth. It can be reasoned that high registration costs hurt competition and hinder the growth of entrepreneurs. That is, a high cost of doing business provides little incentive to enter a market. Low registration costs, on the other hand, would make for a more conducive business environment and make a market more attractive for a potential entrant. The countries provide a glaring example of how critical regulatory influence and a conducive business environment are to shaping economic growth and development.[7] Italy has taken the approach to make registration costs high. Conversely, the UK has taken the approach to keep registration costs low.[8] What results from the two approaches are inefficient and slow-growing entrepreneurs in Italy and rapid entrepreneurial growth in the UK. This suggests that market-enabling policies, such as low registration costs, encourage entrepreneurial growth which has translated to overall economic growth in the UK. Many developing countries have a long, bureaucratic, and time-consuming process.

- Access to finance has a direct measurable impact on entrepreneurial growth.
- Entrepreneurs face opportunities, obstacles, and constraints in their pursuit to obtain finance.
- Entrepreneurial credit access is a systemic and circular problem, giving indirect constraints with significant impact on the overall access to finance for entrepreneurs, primarily in developing countries.
- In most developing countries, the primary sources of funding are family, friends, and banking institutions.
- Policies focused on overall business improvement are aimed to better serve entrepreneurs than are policies directly focused on subsidizing certain market demographics. Additionally, overall business improvement is more sustainable and requires less administration by policymakers.
- A well-established and versatile business environment is a stronger indicator of development and growth than the number of entrepreneurs.

While unintended, these barriers (i.e., registration costs) have a disproportionately negative effect on entrepreneurs when compared to larger enterprises which have the infrastructure in place to absorb such high costs. Therefore, even if the UK were to subsidize registration costs for entrepreneurs (e.g., through tax incentives, etc.) a better approach to the problem is to implement regulations that foster the overall business environment without giving certain groups any special incentives.

Legal framework and property rights

Legal framework and property rights are related to the financial constraints of entrepreneurs; the different aspects are so intertwined that they are nearly inseparable. Imagine a small business needing a loan to buy a business facility. The entrepreneur has a 25 percent cash down payment but needs a loan to finance the rest of the purchase of the facility. The small business goes to a bank to acquire a loan. The bank will require a laundry list of items such as audited financial statements of the business to ensure the business can service the debt (i.e., pay the note to the mortgage). Additionally, the small business owner is expected to put a hefty down payment on the property and will be asked to provide references of good character and credit since many developing countries lack centralized credit bureaus that share credit information. After all the due diligence is completed and the legal documents are signed, the mortgage note serves as legal proof of the bank's ownership in the property. The business owner will pay back the note and, upon final payment, receive the title to the property.

Women entrepreneurs finance initiative

UNDP is the United Nations' global development agency. It works in nearly 170 countries to provide knowledge, experience, and resources to help create country-owned solutions to global and national challenges. UNDP manages the UN development system, ensuring greater UN coherence at the country level. Funded entirely through voluntary contributions, UNDP manages an annual budget of some US$5 billion, including roughly US$1 billion of core resources that support basic program activities, technical expertise, and the global country networks needed to deliver worldwide programming.

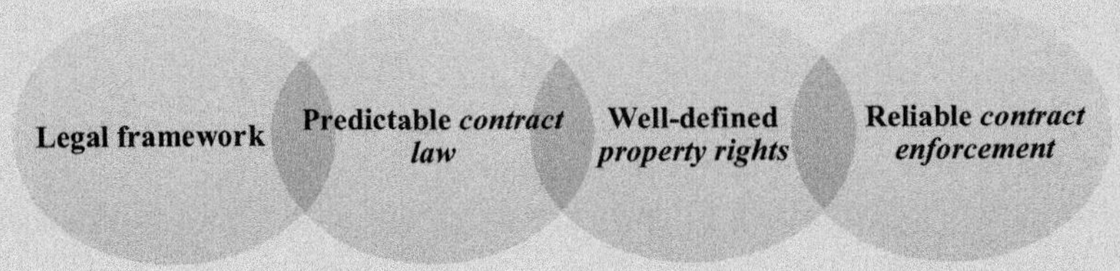

Legal framework   Predictable *contract law*   Well-defined *property rights*   Reliable *contract enforcement*

Figure 9.4 Strong mix for good business environment

However, the entire process described means nothing without the following (see Figure 9.5):

The financial institution relies on the court and the legal system for recourse should the borrower default on his loan. Without the necessary framework, the bank has no recourse should the borrower default on the loan. This creates a significant exposure for the lender.[9] Therefore, from the lender's perspective, it is highly risky to lend to the entrepreneurs in an environment that lacks the necessary legal framework. So why would a lender provide financing to entrepreneurs? Often times, they will not.

Proper legal infrastructure is more than important to lenders in the context of loaning capital to entrepreneurs; it is essential. Although this is not a problem unique to them, entrepreneurs receive a disproportionate benefit (with regards to financing) by having a strong legal framework in place. This is because lenders are more likely to make concessions for larger enterprises – even if the legal framework is not in place – whereas they would not do so for entrepreneurs. This is a function of the size of the transactions (i.e., the amount of profit the bank stands to make) as well as enterprise transparency and reputation (large corporations are more likely to be established and comply with lending requirements).

- Well-defined property rights

- Sound legal framework

- Effective contract enforcement

Figure 9.5 Necessary variables

A similar concept can be applied to the registration costs previously discussed. Although high registration costs affect entrepreneurs and large enterprises alike, the effects are far more profound for entrepreneurs than they are for large enterprises. This is because large enterprises are in a better position to absorb the impact of the high cost.

Conversely, high registration costs could make or break entrepreneurs when deciding whether or not to enter a market.

The previously discussed points illustrate that an overall conducive business environment benefits growth and development significantly, and entrepreneurs stand to gain a disproportionately larger benefit from an overall conducive business environment.

Financial barriers and entrepreneurial growth

This section serves to expand on the entrepreneurial trends and constraints that were alluded to in previous sections and provide additional insight into the issues. Enterprises and entrepreneurs have consistently ranked "financing" as the biggest obstacle preventing growth. Specifically, the cost of financing is rated by over 35 percent of entrepreneurs as the single biggest obstacle hindering growth. (It should be noted that most entrepreneurs surveyed in this study were from developing countries, rather than developed.) This is of particular importance for two reasons (see Table 9.2).

Therefore, the lack of financing availability has a higher negative impact on startup entrepreneurs than on large companies. Studies have shown that financing obstacles tend to affect entrepreneurs more profoundly than large firms. This is consistent with other findings noted earlier (i.e., the impact of registration costs and legal framework on entrepreneurs). In other words, the availability of financing is more likely to be extended to larger enterprises rather than smaller ones; however, the lack of finance is exponentially worse for entrepreneurs as opposed to large enterprises. The lack of financing availability

Table 9.2 Financing preventing growth

First:	Second:
Financing costs rank highest and therefore are considered to be of prime importance to entrepreneurs.	There is a direct relationship between the availability of finance and entrepreneurial growth. The two have a positive correlation which is directly measurable. Therefore, not being able to obtain financing will have a direct negative impact on entrepreneurial growth. Since finance is directly correlated to entrepreneurial growth, it provides empirical evidence for policymakers and financial institutions. This is much different than trying to measure the indirect effects of something.
Corruption, legal issues, regulation, high taxes, technological barriers, or any other noteworthy constraints simply hail in comparison to financing in terms of growth constraints.	
This is not to say that any of these issues are not in and of themselves constraining. However, when 35 percent of surveyed respondents rank the cost financing as the single most constraining element they face, it shows the magnitude of importance of the issue.	For example, if one was trying to measure the result on entrepreneurial growth due to the reduction in corruption, it would be very hard to make direct attributes. This is because there are many confounding variables in the equation, all of which may be the dependent variable.

has nearly twice the constraining effect on the growth of entrepreneurs as it does on the growth of large enterprises.

As a result of the unavailability of finance, smaller firms tend to finance less through traditional financing sources and rely more on internal equity or capital contributions from entrepreneurs' friends and families. In developing countries, entrepreneurs tend to finance less than 10 percent of their needs through bank finance, as opposed to larger institutions which finance upwards of 20 percent.[10] This is partially due to the cost of financing (i.e., fixed transaction costs are too expensive for smaller firms) and partially due to credit availability (i.e., institutions are reluctant to lend to entrepreneurs). They also find that government has an important role to play in "funding and management, but less so in risk assessment and recovery."

With respect to credit availability, entrepreneurs tend to struggle with financing obstacles such as collateral requirements, bank paperwork, interest rate payments, and the need for audited financial statements. We can call these types of obstacles "red tape". As a result of this red tape, banks are not able to service entrepreneurs. The bank views entrepreneurs as highly risky and the return on investment simply is not there from the lender's perspective.

The circular problem

The ironic part of this "red tape" problem is that it is somewhat circular. Entrepreneurs need loans to buy assets, yet they need assets for collateral in order to get a loan. In this sense, the problem can be viewed as institutional or systemic. Lack of financing leaves many entrepreneurs credit constrained.

When credit constrained, entrepreneurs' growth is not constrained by lack of sales, market conditions, or competition. Instead, growth is constrained by their inability to obtain financing.

A study in the developing country, India, analyzed the detailed loan information for over 250 entrepreneurs. The loans were issued in connection to a subsidized lending program aimed to extend credit to Indian entrepreneurs. What the analysis of the detailed loan information found was that the growth of these entrepreneurs was constrained solely by credit.[11] In other words, if financing was available, their firm would be able to grow. However, since financing was not available, the entrepreneurs were not able to grow. In this sense, the only thing impeding growth was the availability of capital.

The effect the infused capital (i.e., the loan) had on each business was tracked and the results were surprising. The analysis showed that sales increased proportionately to the amount of credit received, thus proving the credit constraints facing these companies was truly preventing growth.[12] While the results of this study showed that these Indian firms were indeed credit constrained, it should be noted that subsidized credit is not necessarily the solution to alleviate this problem. A more detailed discussion surrounding this policy will be presented in future sections.

Lender perspective, environment, and the role of government

So far we have discussed how capital markets affect entrepreneurs. However, to better understand the credit market, it is important to look at how lenders are affected by entrepreneurs. By analyzing the reverse relationship (i.e., entrepreneurs' effect on the lenders), the stage will be set for a discussion on policy. From a lender perspective, banks

Figure 9.6 Thailand
Source: © iStock: MongkolChuewong

are typically risk-averse. High risk requires a higher rate of return on their investment. Therefore, a loan for an entrepreneur will innately have a higher interest rate than that of a large developed enterprise. This is due both to the size of the loan (the absolute return on investment amount) as well as the interest rate on the loan (the rate of return for the bank).

Thailand; the best country to start a business

Deidre McPhillips (March 7, 2017), a writer for USA Today, discusses the top places in the world to start a business in 2017. Many might instantly think it could be America because it has the highest GDP (Gross Domestic Product) or the "world's best economy" but you would be wrong. McPhillips gives us a ranking where she gives and explains the top countries and why.

In 2017, Thailand was ranked the best place to start a company for the second year in a row. For instance, in Thailand it only takes about 26 days to start and run a company. Also, starting a company only costs 6.6 percent of the average income per capita in Thailand. This means that if you assume you are making about average income in Thailand it will only cost about 6 percent of your yearly income to create and run a business.

Following Thailand, the best countries to start a company in descending order to five consist of China, Malaysia, India, and Indonesia. It's interesting when reviewing the next four because in somewhere like Malaysia (3rd best) it only takes 18 days to start a company. Although this is much faster than Thailand, there are many other factors about Thailand that makes it better than all of the rest.

Radu (2018)[13]

The relationship between interest rates and risk is not necessarily linear. A linear relationship would result in interest rates skyrocketing for riskier entrepreneurs. Finance access would be extended to virtually every entrepreneur and the interest rates for the riskiest entrepreneurs would be absurdly high. At this point, the lender would prefer not to lend. This is because there is a pinnacle where (1) the selection risk (that is, the risk that the lender will select an unworthy borrower), and (2) the default risk become so high that the lender would prefer not to lend. Unfortunately, when this approach is applied by lenders, it means that some qualified borrowers will be left out. This is an opportunity cost which lenders are willing to take. Simply put, there is a maximum number of entrepreneurs that a financial institution will be able to naturally serve given the number of funds available. We can extend the concept of Production-Possibility Frontier (PPF) from economics to finance and define an Access Possibility Frontier.[14] Lenders are looking to maximize their lending opportunities. The Access Possibility Frontier for entrepreneurs is defined as the maximum share of viable loan applicants that could be served by any financial institution prudently given all other existing variables.

By defining the maximum number of loan applicants that can be served by financial institutions, the environment can better be analyzed in order to determine systemic problems in the credit market.[15] No two markets are identical. Therefore, to pose a blanket solution for all credit markets is not appropriate. The following sections describe the three basic types of policies that affect capital markets. Each policy has been generalized and each market will require a customized approach and multi-faceted solution to solve a host of challenges.

However, generalizations can be made to classify policies into three categories: (1) market developing, (2) market enabling, and (3) market harnessing.[16] A discussion about each type of policy, examples of solutions, and the problems each policy aims to address are detailed in the following.

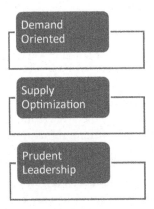

Figure 9.7 Three categories of policies

Figure 9.8 Needs cycle

Capital market developing policies

Every developing country needs a market developing policy. In this sense, the breadth of these types of policies is seen as the baseline for the sound financial capital market framework (see Figure 9.8). Market developing policies are the baseline for lending. These types of policies are the framework for all lending and are designed to provide significant depth and breadth. An environment where access to finance is limited or altogether unavailable would require a significant overhaul of rules, regulations, and policies that affect the credit market.[17]

For example, a non-existent credit market is likely a result of weak contract law, information asymmetry, and an ineffective legal system. Therefore, the appropriate market developing policies would focus on:

1. Improving contract law so that lenders could more easily enforce collateral rights and reduce the administrative burden of collateralizing loans.
2. Establishing a centralized credit bureau to make due diligence and lending decisions more streamlined. This would enhance visibility into individuals and organizations and also increase competition among lenders.
3. Strengthening the legal system and contractual enforcement. As previously discussed, an efficient legal system and contractual enforcement methods give lenders confidence and is an essential part of the development of capital markets.
4. In this process, the rights and recourse for borrowers are defined and described.

Capital market enabling policies

Capital market-enabling policies foster the breadth of access to finance. Therefore, the application of such policies would be applicable to environments where there is (1) capital demand-originated problems, (2) supply sub-optimization, or (3) prudent lending by credit suppliers. In the following is a discussion of each environment and the appropriate policies to address such environments.

Capital demand-originated problems

The environment

An environment has a demand-originated problem when there is not enough demand for capital lending. This is often the result of self-exclusion by entrepreneurs. Self-exclusion

Figure 9.9 UNDP

Source: © iStock: mizoula. Read more: UNDP About us. (n.d.). Retrieved from www.undp.org/content/undp/en/home/about-us.html

happens when entrepreneurs do not apply for lending due to a self-perception that obtaining financing is impossible.

This is a complex problem where both cultural and social perceptions (among other perceptions) influence the entrepreneur's self-image. For different reasons, it is hard to acquire funding from financial institutions and private venture capital in the early stage for entrepreneurs. Due to institutional barriers and financial constraints in developing countries, it is much more challenging for entrepreneurs to acquire funding. In general, the initial sources of funding for entrepreneurs are immediate family members and friends.[18] Due to the underdeveloped financial markets and related private and public institutions in the developing countries, the immediate family members and friends play a more crucial role in funding for entrepreneurs. Overall, there is a disadvantage for entrepreneurs in developing countries compared to developed countries because of weak or non-existent contract laws that define the role of demanders and suppliers of funds.

Therefore, holding everything else constant, potential success rates in acquiring sustainable funding is lower for entrepreneurs in developing countries compared to developed countries.

Financial illiteracy is also another major problem of self-exclusion. For example, many entrepreneurs do not keep books and records. Therefore, financial transparency does not exist and there is an information asymmetry between the entrepreneur and the lender. In such a situation, the financial illiteracy of the entrepreneur causes opaqueness of the business entity and therefore the lender is unable to properly assess the entity's creditworthiness.[19] This type of problem creates low demand for capital lending because financially illiterate candidates often self-exclude themselves from the market.

Supply sub-optimization

An environment experiences supply sub-optimization when creditors are not effectively servicing a large enough portion of the market. In this sense, creditors are operating below the Access Possibility Frontier and not fully exploring all market possibilities. There are various causes of supply sub-optimization such as stringent regulatory policies, which make it burdensome for lenders to fully pursue and exploit entrepreneurial lending opportunities. This type of environment requires market-enabling policies to be implemented in order to develop the credit markets.[20]

For example, to combat supply sub-optimization, regulatory bodies could lower interest rates. The availability of cheap capital would allow lenders to explore lending options to non-traditional ventures such as lending to entrepreneurs. Additionally, the low cost of capital would make it financially "worth it" for the banks. Another example of a policy which, if implemented by the regulatory bodies, would combat supply sub-optimization would be to lower the capital reserve requirements of banks. The amount of cash a bank must keep on hand is regulated.

If a market is experiencing sub-supply-optimization, high capital reserve requirements will only fuel the problem. Lowering the capital reserve requirements, on the other hand, infuses cash into the economy and into the hands of entrepreneurs. However, if capital requirements are lowered, regulatory bodies must ensure that the excess capital is fairly distributed to both entrepreneurs and large enterprises. In other words, there must be controls in place to ensure the regulator's objectives are accomplished. A simple control would be to allocate X percentage of capital to finance entrepreneurs.

Lending policies

Similar to the supply sub-optimization discussed earlier, prudent lending by creditors will lead to an underserviced capital market. The cause, however, is often a result of a weak economy, high cost of lending, instability in the currency and the government, and/or rapid inflation.[21] This type of environment calls for stability in the economy, government, and market-enabling policy implementation.

The policies

The three capital market environments discussed earlier all call for market-enabling policies in order for capital markets and the entrepreneurs they serve to develop, grow, and prosper. Although each policy will be tailored to suit each specific environment, all policies will have the same underlying objective: to develop the credit markets and enable access to finance. Policies aimed to combat demand-originated problems would focus on public awareness, changing cultural trends, and encouraging financial literacy.

Policies of this nature could include free financial literacy courses and continuing education classes aimed to educate entrepreneurs. Through these policies and programs, the environment will begin to change and develop, thus reducing self-exclusion levels among entrepreneurs.

Policies addressing supply sub-optimization and prudent lending are generally more robust. More robust policies are partially a result of these problems (i.e., prudent lending

Figure 9.10 Entrepreneurship train

Source: © iStock: oops7. Full article: Bradsher, K., & Wines, M. (2011, November 07). China's businesses find loans are harder to get. The New York Times. Retrieved from www.nytimes.com/2011/11/08/business/global/chinas-businesses-find-loans-are-harder-to-get.html

and supply sub-optimization) being a larger hindrance to market growth and partially a result of policy effectiveness in these areas. From a policy perspective, effective policy is more easily implemented in combating prudent lending than it is in combating demand-oriented problems, as demand-oriented problems have significant cultural and social obstacles that mitigate the effectiveness of the policy (see Figure 9.7).

The examples of market-enabling policies that are effective in addressing supply sub-optimization and prudent lending are largely in the areas of informational frameworks. For example, creating a centralized credit registry would allow better information flow between lenders and effectively increase competition among lenders. Increased competition would enable more entrepreneurs to be serviced by lenders. Another regulatory framework could include leasing and factoring. Policies in these areas are good examples of how entrepreneurs receive a disproportionate benefit relative to large enterprises. In other words, although the policy does not provide specific benefits or incentives to entrepreneurs, entrepreneurs would be the primary beneficiaries of such policies. This is because leasing and factoring benefit less established companies. Factoring is a financial transaction where a company sells its receivables, at a discount, to a third party.[22] The third party benefits by capitalizing on the margin between the discount (the amount they paid) and the value of the receivables (the amount they collect). The SME benefits by reducing collection costs and receiving the money up front, rather than waiting three to six months to collect the cash.

- The problem of acquiring loans can be viewed as institutional or systemic: Entrepreneurs need loans to buy assets, yet they need assets for collateral in order to get a loan.
- Sales increase proportionately to the amount of credit received.
- Banks are typically risk averse; a loan for an entrepreneur will innately have a higher interest rate than that of a large developed enterprise.
- The Access Possibility Frontier for entrepreneurs is defined as the maximum share of viable loan applicants that could be served by any financial institution prudently given all other existing variables.
- There are three basic types of policies that affect capital markets: Market developing policies that serve as a baseline for lending; Capital market enabling policies that foster the breadth of access to finance; and Market harnessing policies where lending standards are not prudent enough.
- An environment has a demand-originated problem when there is not enough demand for capital lending.
- Potential success rates in acquiring sustainable funding is lower for entrepreneurs in developing countries compared to developed countries.

Policies that enable factoring and allow for transparent information flow directly benefit entrepreneurs. Larger enterprises often have less of a need to factor receivables because the organization is large enough to absorb the waiting time during collection.

Entrepreneurs, on the other hand, are often times credit constrained and need to collect receivables quickly in order to meet their cash flow obligations (i.e., working capital requirements, accounts payable, debt service, etc.).[23]

Similarly, policies enabling leasing greatly benefit entrepreneurs. Leasing is a way to obtain necessary business assets while minimizing upfront costs. For example, if an SME needs a piece of machinery, it has two basic options: buy or lease. Buying the asset would require a large initial investment and potentially financing. Additionally, it commits the business to ownership where ownership may not be required or desired (e.g., long-term technology assets that may be rendered obsolete).[24] Alternatively, leasing provides lower initial costs, flexible repayment structure (often times tailored to the cash flow of the asset), fixed or variable interest rates, and some accounting/tax benefits depending on the SME's situation. Leasing typically makes more sense for credit-constrained entrepreneurs. However, if the necessary policies are not in a place that allows for leasing, entrepreneurs will not be able to reap the benefits.

Capital market harnessing policies

The environment

Environments in need of market harnessing policies are those where lending standards are not prudent enough. In this environment of excess access, lenders grant loans to a larger

Figure 9.11 Nicaragua entrepreneurship

Source: Image by Francesco Volpi on flickr. Full article: News. (n.d.). Retrieved from https://site.jaamericas.org/new-blog/

share of applicants above the warranted interest rates, risk premiums, and other economic variables.

These types of environments can be risky because it can over-extend financial institutions and their insurers, and have a devastating effect on the overall health of credit markets. "[…] Costly regulations hamper the creation of new firms, especially in industries that should naturally have high entry."[25]

The most recent example of such excess access is the credit market associated with the subprime mortgage crisis in the United States. Lenders did not exercise reasonably prudent standards and granted loans to applicants that were not creditworthy. The problem was further compounded by mortgage securitization, corporate entity-level independence issues, and valuation problems. However, at the heart of the problem was excessive access to credit.

The policies

Government policy is especially important when it comes to market harnessing strategies. These policies have to balance market enablement, which allows for growth and prosperity, with harnessing corporate greed and risk. If left unregulated, lenders would be pushed towards an unsustainable equilibrium and eventually to collapse. A typical policy that would harness risk in the credit market would focus on raising the necessary cash required to be held on deposit. Higher deposit amounts mean a bank cannot lend as much and is more likely to exhibit diligence in lending, thus lending to only the best candidates. Other policies include adjusting interest rates, regulating new entrants, and revising the foreign policy.

The role of government in policy making

All of the policies discussed previously require government intervention. It is the government that makes policy and enforces them. It is important that a government has the necessary infrastructure to make and enforce the policy. But how much intervention is required? Opinions on the government's role in the business world encapsulate a variety of political, ideological, and theoretical views/opinions. However, in the context of entrepreneurship finance, the role of government needs to strike a balance between enabling credit and funding markets without unduly shifting the risks onto the government itself.

Nevertheless, in the developing countries, the role of government in terms of providing financial incentives and appropriate regulations that result in expansion of entrepreneurial activities is essential.

Conclusion

This chapter has presented fundamental ideas in the area of entrepreneurial finance in developing countries, discussed credit constraints and obstacles that entrepreneurs face, analyzed various market environments and policies that create such environments, and opined upon regulatory solutions to each market. The common themes throughout this chapter include entrepreneurs being disproportionately hurt by the lack of financing availability, leading to the conclusion that entrepreneurial growth is largely dependent on access to finance (i.e., entrepreneurs in developing countries are credit constrained), and necessary regulatory intervention is needed for the overall credit market rather than subsidized point solutions. Entrepreneurs, therefore, must have a clear understanding of the environment and its surrounding bank and governmental policies in order to be able to fully benefit from it. An assessment of the potential for credit availability is needed and financial books of new firms must be regularly updated in order to decrease the so-called "self-exclusion" process. This should be a priority to any business as an increased self-exclusion typically leads to missed opportunities and lost profit.

Discussion questions

1. Discuss funding challenges that entrepreneurs are facing.
2. State potential sources of funding and their mission.
3. Examine the financial life cycle.
4. Provide some examples of successes and failures of entrepreneurs due to funding.
5. Discuss the role of governments as a potential source of funding for entrepreneurship in most countries, especially developing countries.

Table 9.3 Key terms

Financing life cycle	Property rights
Barriers to entry	Access Possibility Frontier
Legal framework	Demand-originated problem

Notes

1 Adasme, O., Majnoni, G., & Uribe, M. (2006). Access and risk—friends or foes? Lessons from Chile. Policy Research Working Papers. doi:10.1596/1813-9450-4003

2 Aghion, P., Fally, T., & Scarpetta, S. (n.d.). Credit Constraints as a Barrier to the Entry and Post-Entry Growth of Firms. Economic Policy. WileyCentre for Economic Policy Research Center for Economic Studies, CESifo Group Maison des Sciences de l'Homme. https://doi.org/10.2307/4502214

3 Banerjee, A. V., & Duflo, E. (2014). Do firms want to borrow more? Testing credit constraints using a directed lending program. The Review of Economic Studies, 81(2), 572–607. doi:10.1093/restud/rdt046

4 Beck, T. (2014). Finance, growth, and stability: lessons from the crisis. Journal of Financial Stability, 10, 1–6. doi:10.1016/j.jfs.2013.12.006

5 Beck, T., & Demirguc-Kunt, A. (2006). Small and medium-size enterprises: access to finance as a growth constraint. Journal of Banking & Finance, 30(11), 2931–2943. doi:10.1016/j.jbankfin.2006.05.009

6 Beck, T., & Torre, A. D. (2006). The basic analytics of access to financial services. Policy Research Working Papers. doi:10.1596/1813-9450-4026

7 Beck, T., Demirgüç-Kunt, A., & Martinez Peria, M. S. (2007). Barriers to SME Lending around the World. World Bank mimeo.

8 Beck, T., Demirguckunt, A., & Maksimovic, V. (2008). Financing patterns around the world: are small firms different? Journal of Financial Economics, 89(3), 467–487. doi:10.1016/j.jfineco.2007.10.005

9 Beck, T., & Demirguc-Kunt, A. (2006). Small and medium-size enterprises: access to finance as a growth constraint. Journal of Banking & Finance, 30(11), 2931–2943. doi:10.1016/j.jbankfin.2006.05.009

10 Beck, T., Klapper, L. F., & Mendoza, J. C. (2010). The typology of partial credit guarantee funds around the world. Journal of Financial Stability, 6(1), 10–25. doi:10.1016/j.jfs.2008.12.003

11 Benavente, J. M., Galetovic, A., & Sanhueza, R. (2006). Fogape: an economic analysis. Working Papers. Retrieved from https://ideas.repec.org/p/udc/wpaper/wp222.html.

12 Berger, A. N., & Udell, G. F. (1998). The economics of small business finance: the roles of private equity and debt markets in the financial growth cycle. Journal of Banking & Finance, 22(6–8), 613–673. doi:10.1016/s0378-4266(98)00038-7

13 Radu, S. (2018, January 23). These Are the Top 5 Countries to Start a Business. Retrieved from www.usnews.com/news/best-countries/best-start-a-business.

14 Cetorelli, N., & Strahan, P. E. (2006). Finance as a barrier to entry: bank competition and industry structure in local U.S. markets. The Journal of Finance, 61(1), 437–461. doi:10.1111/j.1540-6261.2006.00841.x

15 Cole, S. (2004). Fixing Market Failures or Fixing Elections? Agricultural Credit in India. MIT mimeo.

16 Allen, F., & Gale, D. (2004). Competition and access to finance: international evidence. Journal of Money, Credit and Banking, 36(3), 453–480.

17 De la Torre, A., Soledad Martinez Peria, M., & Schmukler, S. L. (2008). Bank involvement with SMES: beyond relationship lending. The World Bank. https://doi.org/10.1596/1813-9450-4649

18 El Jadidi, J., Asgary, N., & Weiss, J. (2017). Cultural and institutional barriers for western educated entrepreneurs in Morocco. Cyrus Chronicle Journal: Contemporary Economic and Management Studies in Asia and Africa, 61–75.

19 Dinc, I. (2005). Politicians and banks: political influences on government-owned banks in emerging markets. Journal of Financial Economics, 77(2), 453–479. Web.

20 Frame, W. S., & Woosley, L. (2004). Credit scoring and the availability of small business credit in low- and moderate-income areas. The Financial Review, 39(1), 35–54. Web.

21 Frame, W. S., Srinivasan, A., & Woosley, L. (2001). The effect of credit scoring on small-business lending. Journal of Money, Credit and Banking, 33(3), 813. Web.

22 Gormley, T. A. (2005). Banking competition in developing countries: does foreign bank entry improve credit access? Department of Economics, MIT.

23 Hallberg, K. (2001). A Market-Oriented Strategy for Small and Medium Scale Enterprises. IFC Discussion Paper 48.

24 Khwaja, A. I., & Mian, A. (2005). Do lenders favor politically connected firms? Rent provision in an emerging financial market. The Quarterly Journal of Economics, 120(4), 1371–1411. Web.

25 Klapper, L., Laeven, L., & Rajan, R. (2006). Entry regulation as a barrier to entrepreneurship. Journal of Financial Economics, 82(3), 591–629. https://doi.org/10.1016/j.jfineco.2005.09.006

10 Essentials of bookkeeping

Learning objectives:

1. *Learn essentials of bookkeeping*
2. *Understand why entrepreneurs must keep financial records*
3. *Comprehend how to calculate fixed, variable, and total costs*
4. *Understand how to calculate profit*
5. *Examine budgeting and financial spreadsheets.*

Figure 10.1 MNA
Source: © iStock: rpellicer

Developing an accounting and auditing architecture in the MNA region

Countries in middle and North Africa are working with the World Bank to strengthen their international and national financial architecture. The World Bank Group wants to help create an environment in which commercial business can thrive in these nations. Thus, Financial Management (FM) has been founded with its key components being to ensure development process, accountability, and efficiency in the management of public resources and promoting private investment and growth. Middle and North Africa (MNA) FM's focus on engaging with MNA countries' systems and working closely with counterparts and other partners to build in-country capacity as they work to ensure the financial integrity of their operations. Since conditions in one country can affect the financial environment of a region or even the world, the World Bank works to strengthen the international and national financial architecture.

These key partnerships have been working towards creating a Strong Financial Architecture by bringing in corporate financial reporting to defined standards. Tapping into its broad and detailed knowledge in accounting, financial management, and auditing, World Bank hopes to improve financial reporting and bring international standards into practice. It also has both Accounting and Auditing resources to analyze the country's strengths and weaknesses in financial reporting, compare national accounting and auditing standards with international standards, examine compliance with national standards, and evaluate the strength of enforcement mechanisms. This analysis will help to address gaps and also includes policy recommendations.

Since investors and lenders need reliable financial information to make sound decisions about financing, Word Bank hopes good corporate financial reporting will help promote investment, develop markets, and improve access to credit.

Questions

1. What initiatives could small business owners make to ensure good corporate financial reporting procedures are followed in their company?
2. List reports that an investor might review before taking the decision to invest in any venture.

Read more: Msadek (2009)[1]

Introduction

An entrepreneur who has an idea and passion to bring his/her product or service to the market needs to have some basic knowledge of accounting to be able to identify the bottom line which is critical information for moving forward. An entrepreneur must make many decisions including identifying target customers, finding the best suppliers for raw materials, deciding how to get the product or service to market, and how products should be priced. Some of these decisions seem very intuitive, but it is very difficult to evaluate them without being able to measure how they affect the amount of money the business is generating. To do this, they must keep records of revenue and carefully identify

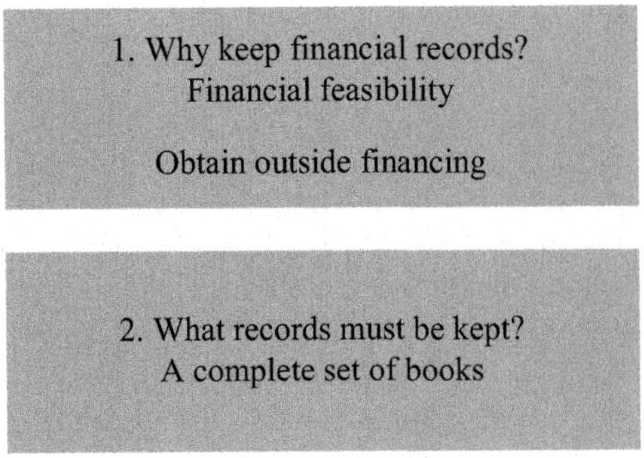

> 1. Why keep financial records?
> Financial feasibility
>
> Obtain outside financing

> 2. What records must be kept?
> A complete set of books

Figure 10.2 Records

and track expenses. A budget is one of the most important documents an entrepreneur must create, and it depends heavily on detailed records of expenditures and revenues (See Figure 10.2). It seems that bookkeeping is more intimidating to many entrepreneurs or small businesses than other aspects of running a business. In developing economies, entrepreneurs and small businesses often operate in the informal sector, avoiding the need to keep financial records for tax purposes. According to World Bank estimates, the informal sector represents 10 to 20 percent of the GNP in developed countries and more than 30 percent in developing ones.[2] This can discourage bookkeeping for those who do not understand the necessity of financial records for the success of any business.

This chapter will address two important questions related to bookkeeping for an entrepreneur. First, why must an entrepreneur keep financial records? Without the knowledge of financial feasibility of the business, it is hard to acquire support for growth. When we look at developed economies, the most important motivating factors for entrepreneurs is the need to obtain outside financing and reporting requirements from tax authorities.

In an environment lacking these objectives, entrepreneurs may think that bookkeeping will add unnecessary complexity to running their business. We will explain many benefits of keeping complete and accurate account books and also the risks a business faces having no clear financial picture gleaned from accurate records.

The second question to be addressed is: What records must be kept? In other words, what comprises the minimum for a complete set of books? We will provide information for bookkeeping by clearly explaining the simple records that will provide the information needed to reap the benefits outlined.

Why is bookkeeping important?

Why does every entrepreneur need to have financial information about revenue and costs of the business and keep a complete and accurate set of books? Financial records tell the story of what is really happening in business as a whole. As a business owner, "Without a complete set of books, you find yourself trying to evaluate your business by looking at isolated areas, such as cash and inventory – these being the most observable, and also the most misleading."[3]

An example of how this can be a problem is the common practice entrepreneurs and SMEs takes to base their prices on the cost of materials plus an arbitrary markup, without factoring in many costs that are harder to identify. Without tracking explicit costs (i.e., rent, utilities, insurance) and the implicit costs (opportunity cost of an entrepreneur), the prices can be settled below an appropriate profit margin – sometimes even at a loss – without knowing it.

In other words, an entrepreneur can overestimate a business's profit. Therefore, knowing the cost of producing a unit of a product or service is essential. The *explicit cost* is a cost that is the source of the cash outflow for business activities to which the expense is recognized. These explicit costs are wage expenses, rent or lease costs, and the materials cost that are directly paid. An *implicit cost* is the opportunity cost to what an entrepreneur must give up to do this job. Total cost is explicit plus implicit costs which are defined as an opportunity cost in economics (see Figure 10.3).[4]

There are many reasons that bookkeeping is crucial beyond proper pricing. Keeping complete and accurate financial records allows a business owner to complete the tasks outlined in Figure 10.4.

Generally, a business plan serves as a kind of "roadmap" for an entrepreneur. Financial records serve as a dashboard that shows financial viability and the adjustment of his/her practices and strategies as necessary. If outside financing is an option, financial records will almost certainly be required. Many entrepreneurs have to exploit outside initial funding. In this case, more detailed records increase the chances of securing a loan or persuading an investor. Also, for formal or registered businesses, financial records will be necessary for tax reporting. Another good reason to keep financial records is the possibility to apply for governmental incentives for innovation, including R&D, capital expansion, energy sustainability, employment, and training.[5] The nature of these records will depend on the tax jurisdiction and form of business. This chapter does not intend to address the financial records necessary for tax purposes.

Figure 10.3 Total costs

Figure 10.4 Record benefits

Figure 10.5 Contribution margin

Setting prices

One of the most important reasons for an entrepreneur to keep careful financial records is to be able to set prices for goods or services at a level to make an appropriate profit. When determining what price will be charged, many variables need to be considered (such as competitors' prices, the willingness of customers to pay, what differentiating factors may justify a higher price, and what signals the prices are sending). The details of this process was presented in Chapter 8 on marketing. For now, it is important for an entrepreneur to know how much it costs to produce each item and identify how much profit is made per unit, known as the *contribution margin* when making these decisions. Contribution margin is defined as the selling price per unit minus the variable cost per unit (see Figure 10.5).

It does represent the portion of sales revenue that is not paid for variable costs and therefore contributes to the payment for fixed costs. Correctly calculating the cost of the product is important for setting an appropriate price that will cover all of the costs and provide enough revenue for reinvestment and growth. The amount of variable costs is also known as "Cost of Goods Sold" (COGS).

In addition to direct material and direct labor represented in the COGS, entrepreneurs also have to understand the *indirect costs*, which are other expenses that must be paid to produce the product or services. This includes costs such as maintenance for the equipment, business trips, communication expenses, marketing campaigns, administrative work, the time spent researching new designs, among others.

While these costs cannot be attributed to an individual product, they contribute to a line of production; therefore, the costs should be an estimate per period and divided among the units of the products that are produced in a given timeframe.[6] Therefore, an entrepreneur has to know all costs, explicit and implicit, and incorporate them into setting their pricing mechanism.

Environmental accounting for sustainable development

Scholars at the World Bank examined environment and resource management concerns in the economic decision-making process.[7] They explore the linkages between development and environment with the understanding that when environment is concerned, someone will eventually have to bear the "external costs" of the current production and consumption activities. They feel that their approach will more accurately represent the true income of a country while the GDP fails to account for the negative effects on the environment.

Reading through the book, one can understand the overview of a variety of approaches, from constructing of environmental and resource accounts for developing countries, measurement of development using the sustainable social net national product approach, practical solutions towards correcting national income measures by taking into account the environmental losses, and much more.

Budgeting

Once an entrepreneur has done a careful analysis of the expenses, then it will be possible to create an annual budget. A budget is one of the most important documents an entrepreneur can create, and it depends heavily on detailed records of expenditures and revenues. The budget needs to underline the financial viability. In its most basic form, a budget is a documentation of how much money a business owner plans to spend (expenses) and make (revenues) over a given period of time. In the case of the annual budget, the timeframe would be a year. But such a simple description conceals its true power. For a carefully prepared budget, the process of determining the proper numbers needed to calculate the final expense figures can be quite illuminating. Additionally, an entrepreneur must carefully analyze the business and its market to work out a useful sales forecast.

At the end of a year, the budget serves as a concrete way to measure performance against goals and can be even more useful when it is used to compare progress to incremental targets throughout the year. By comparing monthly or quarterly figures to budgeted amounts, a business owner can see when things are not going as planned and take action to correct the course of action.[8]

Tracking expenses and revenue

To create a budget, an entrepreneur must project how much he will spend in the coming year and what volume would be expected to sell and at what price. This entails taking a closer look at previous years' budgets to determine how much it costs to run the business and carefully analyze past sales.

Everything in the expenses should be included, from the cost of materials to wages that have been paid in the previous year(s). In order to do this, an entrepreneur needs a detailed record of previous years' expenses. Being able to calculate break-even for the year is essential. Break-even is the output level in which total revenue minus total cost (explicit plus implicit) is equal to zero (Figure 10.6).

An entrepreneur cannot operate in the long-run if only the accounting cost is being covered; they may do it only in the short-run. While preparing the budget, it is important

Figure 10.6 Break-even

that the entrepreneur recognizes that not all costs are the same. Some have to be paid no matter how many products or services are produced, such as purchasing a new machine or renting a place – these expenses are known as *fixed costs*. Ohers, known as *variable costs*, depend completely on how many products are made. Variable costs include things such as the cost of raw materials or hourly wages for employees. Not every cost fits clearly into one category or another, which we will discuss in more detail later.

Entrepreneurs should first determine the total amount of fixed costs and based on the sales forecasts determine the total variable cost and therefore total cost. By going through this analysis, entrepreneurs can determine if the price that is set for the product is providing enough profit margin. Identifying areas for saving money and cutting costs represents the organization's long-term budget goals. For example, if by learning a new technique of production, time decreases from an hour to 45 minutes, money will be saved. This continuous improvement process is known as *kaizen budgeting* and was developed by Japanese companies to reflect the practice of improvement.[9]

Monitoring performance

In creating a budget, entrepreneurs have to set financial goals of the business. As the year progresses, he/she can compare the actual performance to the set targets. Many business owners will choose a regular schedule on which to go back to their budget, compare results, and adjust it if necessary. Most will go through this process at the end of each month, although the timing will depend on the cost of such analysis and the responsiveness of the business. Prior to the creation of a budget, the questions outlined in Figure 10.7 need to be answered by the entrepreneur.

Having accurate records helps to answer these questions to the best estimate. Ideally, an entrepreneur shall be able to go beyond the regular "yes" or "no" answers and will be further able to analyze the reasons for any unexpected results. It may also be helpful to compare the results, month to month. Developing a proforma is essential for an entrepreneur.

For example, an entrepreneur can analyze and decide under different pricing scenarios what would be break-even, positive or negative profit. Entrepreneurs should take note of which costs are having the most impact on profitability and identify any possible ways to keep these down and watch for any particular expenses that are rising. It may be useful also to compare the costs of the current period to the same period in previous years.

When analyzing sales, it can be useful to take note of trends which can be potential opportunities for growth or even threats to profitability. By tracking the sales of

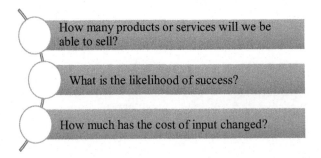

Figure 10.7 Questions to answer

each type of product over the course of the year, entrepreneurs may notice that some are becoming more popular while others are selling less. These types of observations become most useful if entrepreneurs can identify possible reasons behind the patterns. For example, consider a business selling small clutches; if the sales of these small clutches started increasing in April, right around the time that a popular actress was seen with a similar style, the entrepreneur should consider producing more in order to capitalize on its current trendiness. Conversely, if sales of a previously popular style have been dropping off, it may be time for the entrepreneur to try a new design more in line with what is becoming fashionable.

Outside financing

Banks and other sources of financing will usually require detailed financial records in order to determine whether or not to extend a loan to business and terms of the loan depend on the financial performance of the business. Lack of these records is a major barrier to growth for many small businesses in developing economies.[10] Entrepreneurs may decide that to grow more quickly, a new machine is needed as soon as possible. To do this, the entrepreneur would have to ask for a loan from a bank. The bank will want to see documentation of the company's previous period's financial performance to decide how big of a risk they are taking by lending the money. The more evidence the organization shows that it's being profitable, the more likely it is for the bank to provide funds.

Figure 10.8 Accountant
Source: Image by Simon Cunningham on flickr

Accountant with an entrepreneurial bug

Accountants have the skills, experience, and knowledge necessary to provide services to a variety of individuals and organizations. Even though accountants are seen as well-paid professionals, many of them are venturing into side businesses in order to make additional income. According to Statista, "In 2011, the revenue of accounting, tax preparation, bookkeeping, and payroll services in the U.S. ranged at approximately 120.44 billion U.S. dollars."[11] This number is expected to increase to the $160 billion range by 2018.

While a large portion of revenue is generated by top accounting firms, such as Deloitte and Pricewaterhouse Coopers, smaller operations are in a position to achieve great success as well.

According to MyTopBusinessideas.com here are Top 10 Small Business ideas for Accountants & Auditors to peruse:

Bookkeeping
Payroll service
Tax preparation service
Blogging
Freelance writing
Tutoring
Consulting / financial advisor service
Selling accounting software
Microfinance
E-commerce[12]

Simply by having these records, entrepreneurs also demonstrate that their organization is mature enough and the people in charge are competent leaders of business with adequate financial controls in place. Lack of these factors could be a major concern for many banks and support agencies when dealing with entrepreneurs and small businesses in developing economies.[13]

- An entrepreneur needs to have some basic knowledge of accounting to be able to identify the bottom line, which is critical information for moving forward.
- Financial records tell the story of what is really happening in a business as a whole.
- Total cost is explicit plus implicit costs, which is defined as opportunity cost in economics.
- Financial records serve as a dashboard that show financial viability and to adjust his/her practices and strategies as necessary. They enable the entrepreneur to set prices for goods or services at a level to make an appropriate profit.
- The budget needs to underline the financial viability and it's a documentation of how much money a business owner plans to spend (expenses) and make (revenues) over a given period of time.

Decision-making

By keeping accurate financial records, entrepreneurs are able to make informed decisions. When deciding which items to produce more or less of, entrepreneurs are better off to have hard numbers instead of a general idea. Entrepreneurs can better anticipate when the company should have more inventory available for sale, or when it will be better to produce at lower volumes. Entrepreneurs can set realistic goals and create feasible plans for expanding or investing in new equipment. When entrepreneurs need a loan or want to approach an investor, the documentation needed will be readily available.

What records should be kept?

Now that entrepreneurs are convinced that a complete and accurate set of books must be kept, the following sections explain the advantages of being precise. What records comprise of the minimum needed to provide an accurate picture of the business's financial position? Answering this question as simply as possible should make an entrepreneur feel that bookkeeping is a manageable task. This section will attempt to outline the basic records needed for an enterprise as it starts growing.

Like businesses everywhere, the exact records needed, and the structure of the business in a developing economy, will depend on the type of business, as well as its size and complexity.[14] There are standards for accounting, usually defined per country, that are defined by organizations such as US GAAP (United States Generally Accepted Accounting Principles), AASB (Australian Accounting Standards Board), ICAI (Institute of Chartered Accountants of India), and also the IFRS (International Financial Reporting Standards) whose standards provide a common ground for accounting comparison among different countries.[15]

Many startups in developed economies can invest in simple software such as QuickBooks that will walk them through setting up a basic chart of accounts and automate the double-entry process, but this may not be an option for entrepreneurs in developing economies. Without the aid of software, double-entry accounting may be unnecessarily complex to fill the needs of a small business. Most businesses will find that they need to track a few key categories of information (see Figure 10.9).

While this information is easier to collect for established businesses, for a startup business, this data may not be as accurate. Accounts payable and receivables and cash on hand can be kept as simple journals. For simple businesses, expenses and revenues can be tracked in a single multi-column journal. Larger businesses with higher expenses and revenue categories may want to keep the two separately. Before creating the journal(s) to record this information, a business owner must take a careful look at the business and

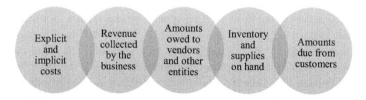

Figure 10.9 Categories of info

determine what expenses are incurred regularly. These must be broken into fixed costs (overhead) and variable costs that change with production levels. Inventory may be the most complex topic to tackle budgeting.

Many business owners may find that determining the expense categories is more difficult than maintaining their books over time and that learning the concepts behind inventory valuation is a challenge. However, taking the time to set up the records properly, in the beginning, will make the information they contain more useful.

Once an entrepreneur has learned some of these basic concepts related to bookkeeping and has set up the books, the entrepreneur will benefit from learning to compile the information into a basic income statement, also known as a profit and loss statement. This will allow entrepreneurs to use financial information in the books to evaluate the profitability of the business.

"The beauty of data visualization"

David McCandless turns complex data sets (like worldwide military spending, media buzz, Facebook status updates) into beautiful, simple diagrams that tease out unseen patterns and connections. Good design, he suggests, is the best way to navigate information glut and it may just change the way we see the world.

You can check in more details in the full TED Talk in this link: www.ted.com/talks/david_mccandless_the_beauty_of_data_visualization#t-1077985

Basics of bookkeeping: journal of revenues and expenses

Large businesses, particularly those that are traded on an exchange, may have strict requirements as to the form and content of the financial records they must keep, but smaller businesses have much greater leeway in making these decisions. However, no matter the size of the business, the primary question that a business owner must answer is "Which alternative provides the most useful information for decision-making purposes?" To help determine this, it is useful to consider two constraints, *cost-benefit* and *materiality*.[16]

There is always a price associated with collecting and storing information which must be weighed against the benefit of the information itself. For a large corporation, this will come in the form of elaborate enterprise resource planning systems, entire departments of additional employees, storage space, and independent auditors. An entrepreneur or a small business owner may invest in a software package to help keep track of finances or may choose to use paper journals, but the most important cost will frequently turn out to be time and effort. An entrepreneur needs to realize the importance of opportunity cost of the extra effort put into using paper journals.

When deciding how to structure the bookkeeping system, entrepreneurs should realize the benefit of adding an extra detail against the amount of time it will take to track it. If the additional information will not add enough value to justify the extra time, then it may be better off with a simpler system. Entrepreneurs can also weigh the value of the time against the cost of paying a bookkeeper to help track the finances. Advantages of hiring a bookkeeper would be avoiding unnecessary time waste in analyzing laws and procedures that do not belong to the daily activities of the entrepreneur. Some small business owners may even be able to find a bookkeeper that is willing to take payment-*in-kind*. For example, an entrepreneur could trade a purse or sewing lessons for the services of a bookkeeper. Nevertheless, even hiring a bookkeeper, the entrepreneur should have a basic knowledge of accounting to be able to understand the reports and make the best use of them.

- Break-even is the output level in which total revenue minus total cost (explicit plus implicit) is equal to zero.
- It is important that the entrepreneur recognizes that not all costs are the same: there are fixed and variable costs.
- Ideally, with proper records, an entrepreneur shall be able to go beyond the regular "yes" or "no" answers and will be further able to analyze the reasons for any unexpected results.
- Banks and other sources of financing will usually require detailed financial records and depend on the financial performance of the business.
- By keeping accurate financial records, entrepreneurs are enabled to make informed decisions; with this information, entrepreneurs can set realistic goals, and create feasible plans for expanding or investing in new equipment.

An entrepreneur must also consider the impact that a transaction will have on the overall financial state of the business. This is known as *materiality*. For an entrepreneur or a small business, most transactions may be material, as each purchase or sale represents a larger percentage of activity than it does for a larger business. This is especially true for small expenses that are incurred with some frequency. For example, this is easy to see with the materials used to make the products: each clasp may cost only a few cents, but it needs to be included in the cost of each purse. However, the same is true for the bus fare an entrepreneur pays when shopping for the clasps; while each trip may only be a small amount, this will add up over the course of a month or a year. In particular, for an entrepreneur or a small business that plans to grow, it is important to record even the small transactions as they add up eventually. This will allow the entrepreneur to see which expenses are growing fastest as the business becomes larger, as well as which sources of revenue are doing most to fuel the growth.

While larger businesses may benefit from a method known as *double-entry bookkeeping*, this practice would create more complications than it would be worth for most small businesses. For a startup, *single-entry bookkeeping* will allow an entrepreneur to capture all of the information needed to reap the benefits described in the previous section.[17]

At the heart of the single-entry bookkeeping system is the revenue and expense journal, in which entrepreneurs will record the details of all of the business transactions. Every time the business receives money from a customer or pays money to a vendor, it must be recorded in this journal. The revenue and expense journal should be structured in a way that is most useful, capturing all the material information at a level of detail that best informs the decision-making. The entrepreneur needs to decide whether to use a single journal for both revenues and expenses, or if it is better to keep two separate journals. This will be discussed in more detail in the following.

Figure 10.10 Hiring
Source: © iStock: pinkomelet

Hiring an accountant

The financial implications of business ownership are extensive, yet critical to a company's success. Having a dependable, efficient accounting system can free up your time to focus on the things you love about your business.

Though one can outsource accounting, one has to explore accounting solutions that fit their needs and budget. Consider the following questions that will give you an understanding of your company's needs and help choose the best option:

- What is the size of my company? Small businesses generally have fewer than 20 employees.
- What technology is available to me and my employees?
- Is my understanding of basic accounting up to the task?
- Does my cash flow allow for accounting expenditures on a monthly or annual basis?
- How comfortable am I handing over sensitive business data to an individual or accounting service?
- Is daily data entry something that I or one of my staff can reasonably accomplish?
- Does my company operate in a complex tax environment that may be subject to audit?
- Do my competitors in the industry find a particular method to be most useful?
- Are there compatibility factors to consider with other technological processes that regularly occur, like payroll?

Figure 10.11 Journal

Table 10.1 Spreadsheet

Number	Date	Description	Revenue	Expense	Sales Rev.	Class Rev.
516	1/3/2015	Jana Silva	$275	–	$150	$125

Note that the transactions entered in this journal do not include any instance when an entrepreneur withdraws money for personal use, as this is not an expense of running the business. Identifying revenue and expenses can present several difficulties for entrepreneurs in developing economies, many of whom operate in the informal sector. One of the biggest problems is identifying the expenses associated with the business and separating these from the business owner's cost of living, as the line is not always clear. This makes it even more important that an entrepreneur keeps careful records, beginning with the revenue and expense journal.

The journal can be either a book or an electronic spreadsheet. Traditionally, many small business owners have used a 12-column journal. See Figure 10.11 for what the first five columns should be.

The remaining columns should consist of categories of the expenses and revenues. Table 10.1 is a sample of the spreadsheet. At the end of each month, the entrepreneur will add-up each revenue and expense category and record the results. Entering each revenue and expense twice provides a way to double check the accuracy of the entered amount. The sum of the revenue subcategories should equal the total revenue for the month and likewise for the expenses. It is important that entrepreneurs also keep all of the receipts to be able to review, if needed, and also for tax purposes.

An example of a basic revenue and expense journal is provided in Table 10.2.

If entrepreneurs find the need to track revenues and expenses in more detail, then the business needs to use more subcategories than a single revenue and expense journal can provide. In this case, the entrepreneur will set up a separate revenue and expense journal, each with as many subcategories as required. It is important to remember that the purpose of keeping financial records is to provide a business owner with the information required to analyze and evaluate the business performance and to make informed decisions. Entrepreneurs must determine the precise form that will best serve their specific needs of the business and can adjust the system as required. As changes occur, entrepreneurs must take care of the financial records by incorporating the added complexity.[18]

Expenses

In the previous sections, we described many reasons why an entrepreneur needs to have detailed records of the expenses that have been incurred while running the business. We

Table 10.2 Spreadsheet example

Company X

No.	Date	Description	Type		Revenue			Expenses				
			Revenue	Expense	Retail Sales	Classes	Custom Orders	Materials	Wages	Supplies & Equip.	Travel	Misc.
	12/02/2015	Balance Fwd	2150,00	1810,00	1200,00	250,00	700,00	870,00	400,00	480,00	60,00	55,00
	12/02/2015	Sara	180,00		180,00							
417	14/02/2015	NI Fabric Co.		200,00				200,00				
Cash	15/02/2015	Bus Fare		5,60							5,60	
	18/02/2015	José Renato	60,00		60,00							
418	20/02/2015	J&J Supplies		90,00				70,00		20,00		
	21/02/2015	Marah Ferreira	250,00		125,00	125,00						
	21/02/2015	Isadora Silva	180,00		80,00	100,00						
	21/02/2015	Jana Santos	120,00		120,00							
419	22/02/2015	Martha Harte		100,00					100,00			
TOTAL			2940,00	2205,60	1765,00	475,00	700,00	1140,00	500,00	500,00	65,60	55,00

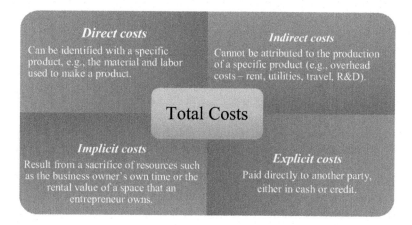

Figure 10.12 Total costs

also describe the categories into which costs can be divided too. Entrepreneurs can use this information to set prices, create budgets, and analyze the financial status of the business.

While the implicit costs do not affect cash flow, they still must be included in any financial analysis to represent the true cost of running the business (see Figure 10.12). Another distinction that warrants a slightly more detailed explanation is that of *fixed* versus *variable* costs.

Fixed and variable costs

Fixed costs are those which entrepreneurs will have to pay no matter how many units of product or services they are making. This includes the cost of production space (land) and its utilities or any insurance costs, among others. The fixed costs are the costs that do not change with the output and entrepreneurs should cover them before producing anything. *Variable costs* are those that will increase with the level of production, usually on a per–unit basis.

Note that if an entrepreneur increases production enough, he/she must move to a larger space and, thus, increase its rental expenses; however, rent is not considered a variable cost because it does not increase with each unit increase in production. With large enough increases in production and a long enough timeline, almost any cost will go up, so we may only consider whether a cost is fixed in the short term. Any direct materials and direct wage labor will be variable costs for the same reason. In the long-run, theoretically, there is no fixed cost for businesses.

Some costs may not be either fixed or variable but have properties of both. Consider electricity. Whether a business produces any product or services, the entrepreneur will have to pay a base amount to the utility company. The more product or services produced, the longer the lights need to be kept on, and the more equipment is kept running, the bills will go up proportionally, holding everything else constant.

Sales and revenue

While it is crucial that entrepreneurs track expenses carefully, it is just as important to keep detailed records of revenue. Many of the points of analysis discussed in previous sections require information relating to sales and revenue: tracking overall trends such as seasonality, comparing different methods or locations of sales, or analyzing the popularity and profitability of various products and services.

- There are standards for accounting, usually defined country by country.
- Most businesses will find that they need to track a few key categories of information: explicit and implicit costs; revenue collected by the business; amounts owed to vendors and other entities; inventory and supplies on hand; and amounts due from customers.
- A profit and loss statement will allow entrepreneurs to use the financial information in the books to evaluate the profitability of the business.
- There is always a price associated with collecting and storing information that must be weighed against the benefit of the information itself.
- Entrepreneurs must determine the precise form that will best serve their specific needs of the business and can adjust the system as required.
- There are four categories into which costs can be divided: direct costs; indirect costs; implicit costs; explicit costs.

Exactly which comparisons will be most useful will depend on the specific business, thus each entrepreneur must determine revenues and keep detailed records. As mentioned before, an entrepreneur can choose whether to include revenue collections in a single journal with expenses or to capture enough detail about the sources of income in a separate journal. While there are specific rules governing what needs to be reported as income for tax purposes, entrepreneurs should realize that there is an infinite amount of flexibility in the records they keep for themselves. If an entrepreneur feels the need to know both types of revenue the business is collecting (sales, service, etc.) and its sources (markets, fairs, online, etc.), he/she can create a journal that allows the tracking of both, simply by including both sets of subcategories and entering each transaction three times instead of two.

Along with information on how much is collected from the customers, entrepreneurs may want to take time to record information about *who* their customers are. While this is not a purely financial record, it can also help to analyze sales and identify purchasing trends according to customer categories. By tracking demographic information, the entrepreneur can learn more about the characteristics of people buying his/her products: their age, where they live, where they heard about the products, etc. Entrepreneurs can use this information to try to target future sales to similar kinds of people. These records can also help to identify who their regular customers are or if certain customers are helping to spread the word about the company, enabling entrepreneurs to send targeted messages to these key supporters.

Entrepreneurs may want to contact and let regular customers know when a business has a new product they might like or send them a birthday card with a discount coupon to show gratitude.

Accounts payable

In addition to cash transactions, many entrepreneurs and small businesses take advantage of credit extended by vendors or will invoice customers and allow payment within a set

Figure 10.13 Account problem
Source: © iStock: izusek

timeframe. Businesses that use these extended payment terms must keep records of these transactions separately from the journal of revenue and expense.

A cleaning products trading company started its service operation in late 2015 in Brazil. After about six months of being in operation, the entrepreneur saw that his earnings did not accompany its increasing sales. Due to the lack of planning, the entrepreneur had difficulty understanding whether he was actually making any profit. Therefore, he had to reach out to a specialist. Through help from a consultant, the company identified that the profit is in one of its 12 services. This outcome was due to its high variable costs, mainly by the entrepreneur. In order to address this problem, two solutions were proposed: either just market one service and increase its prices and sales (which is very unlikely) or cut its variable cost. This short summary highlights the high importance of understanding the details of accounting.

Additionally, if there are barter exchanges in their business, then that should be included in the spreadsheet.

An enterprise may have multiple vendors, therefore they should create a record for each vendor that allows paying on the account. This should include all relevant information about the vendor, such as the name of the company, address, and phone number. Along with information about the vendor, an entrepreneur should create a chart to record the details of each credit transaction and include the following information:

Table 10.3 Accounts payable

Accounts Payable: Account Record						
Vendor: Que Beleza Fabric				**Contact:** Sandra		
Address:				**Phone:** (21) 9999		
Trans. Date	Invoice No.	Amount	Date Due	Date Paid	Amount Paid	Account Balance
2/19/2015	56	$ 600.00	3/19/2015	3/15/2015	$ 600.00	$ –
3/20/2015	68	$ 625.00	4/20/2015	4/10/2015	$ 625.00	$ –
4/15/2015	82	$ 900.00	5/15/2015	5/15/2015	$ 600.00	$ 300.00

- Transaction or invoice date
- Invoice number (if applicable)
- Amount of the transaction
- Due date or transaction terms
- Date paid.

For an account that pays down incrementally, entrepreneurs will also want to include columns for amount paid and account balance. An example of an account record for accounts payable follows the structure shown in Table 10.3. It is important that the entrepreneur tracks the accounts payable carefully and remembers to incorporate them in the planning process. If the accounts payable are growing faster than the revenue stream, it may mean that business is trying to grow faster than the customer base can support it.

Managing accounts payable well is crucial for maintaining good relationships with suppliers.

Accounts receivable

It is defined as the amounts a business needs to receive because it has sold its goods or services on credit to a customer (down payment). In this case, businesses will create a record for each customer who pays on an account and will track the amount that is due and how long it takes to collect it. The record will look very similar to that created for accounts payable and an example is shown in Table 10.4.

When extending credit to a customer, it is important that the business makes clear the expected timeframe for repayment and monitors when payments are not coming in as expected.

Inventory

In the process of making a product or a service, an entrepreneur purchases and stores the materials that will be used to create them. To track the costs of a product, businesses

Table 10.4 Accounts receivable

Accounts Receivable: Account Record						
Customer: *Marisa Monte*			**Phone:**	*(21) 9999999*		
Address:						
Trans. Date	Invoice No.	Amount	Date Due	Date Paid	Amount Paid	Account Balance
5/3/2015	150	$ 125.00	6/3/2015	5/28/2015	$ 125.00	$ –
11/15/2015	215	$ 150.00	12/15/2015	12/17/2015	$ 150.00	$ –
3/12/2016	232	$ 100.00	4/12/2016			$ 100.00

must first track the costs of these materials. Additionally, a business must keep a record of the finished products that are available for sale. Inventories can be divided into three types: raw material, work in progress material, and finished goods which are not sold yet.[19] For a business that purchases finished products and resells them, their inventory will consist of *merchandise* available for sale. Some businesses may be required to track the value of their inventory for tax purposes, but it is important for an entrepreneur to track this information for its own use as well.

While the systems used to value inventory in large companies can be very complex, a small business will generally use one of two methods: *specific identification* and *first-in-first-out (FIFO)*. Specific identification can be used for items such as the product or services that an entrepreneur makes, or any one of a kind, easily tracked product. FIFO is used for items that are bought in larger quantities and may not be traced easily. FIFO costing assumes that the first item to be placed into inventory is the first item to be used or sold.

Conclusion

The importance of keeping complete and accurate financial records for any business, large or small, cannot be overstated. These records provide a way to analyze past performance and serve as a basis for future planning and forecasting. Without carefully tracking expenses, a business cannot set prices to identify its profitability. Sales records allow a business to be most responsive to the customers' needs and to tailor offerings to the market's needs. Additionally, good bookkeeping may allow an entrepreneur to access additional sources of capital, through outside investors or bank loans.

Although bookkeeping may be one of the most intimidating aspects of running a business for many entrepreneurs and SMEs, it does not need to be daunting. The basic records necessary to capture the activity of business are simple to keep, so long as they are set up properly in the beginning. Set-up should not be difficult once the business owner understands how the records will be used; the careful examination of the business during this process can be useful in and of itself.

Table 10.5 Key terms

Explicit cost	Cost-benefit and materiality
Implicit cost	Materiality
Contribution margin	Double-entry bookkeeping
Cost of Goods Sold (COGS)	Direct costs
Break-even	Indirect costs
Fixed costs	Accounts receivable
Variable costs	Inventories
Kaizen budgeting	First-in first-out (FIFO)

- Keeping detailed records of revenue is important to track overall trends such as seasonality, comparing different methods or locations of sales, or analyzing the popularity and profitability of various products and services.
- There is an infinite amount of flexibility in the records kept for themselves, besides those reported as income for tax purposes.
- Accounts payable are transactions that take advantage of credit extended by vendors or will invoice customers and allow payment within a set timeframe. Managing them well is crucial for maintaining good relationships with suppliers.
- Accounts receivable are the amounts a business needs to receive because it has sold its goods or services on credit to a customer (down payment).
- Inventories can be divided into three types: raw material, work in progress material, and finished goods which were not sold yet.

Discussion questions

1. Why is learning bookkeeping required?
2. Select a small or medium size firm and analyze its budget.
3. What is the explicit and implicit cost?
4. Describe economic and accounting costs and analyze their implications for entrepreneurship.
5. Are there differences in terms of the application of these issues for developed and developing countries?

Notes

1 Msadek, S. (2009, March). Accounting and Auditing Practices & Development Effectiveness. MENA Knowledge and Learning Quick Notes Series; No. 4. World Bank, Washington, DC. Retrieved from https://openknowledge.worldbank.org/bitstream/handle/10986/10993/517920BRI0MENA10Box342050B01PUBLIC1.pdf?sequence=1&isAllowed=y.
2 Benjamin, N. (2014). Informal economy and the World Bank. World Bank, May. Retrieved 25 May, 2017. Web. http://documents.worldbank.org/curated/en/416741468332060156/pdf/WPS6888.pdf

3 Kamoroff, B. (2008). Small Business Operator: How to Start Your Own Business, Keep Your Books, Pay Your Taxes and Stay out of Trouble. Laytonville, CA: Bell Springs Pub., Print.

4 Gwartney, J. D., Stroup, R. L., Sobel, R. S., & Macpherson, D. (2008). Economics: Private and Public Choice. South-Western College Pub., Print.

5 Survey of Global Investment and Innovation Incentives. (2017, March). Retrieved May 25, 2007, from: www2.deloitte.com/global/en/pages/tax/articles/global-investment-and-innovation-incentives-survey.html.

6 Newman, P. (2006, September 15). Setting Competitive and Profitable Prices. Retrieved April 9, 2009, from www.entrepreneur.com/article/167198.

7 Ahnad, Y. J., & Lutz, E. (1989). Environmental accounting for sustainable development. In The World Bank Symposium/The World Bank.–1989.–118 p.

8 Horngren, C. T., Datar, S. M., Rajan, M. V., & Foster, G. (2008). Cost Accounting: A Managerial Emphasis. Prentice Hall. 221. Print.

9 Horngren, C. T., Datar, S. M., Rajan, M. V., & Foster, G. (2008). Cost Accounting: A Managerial Emphasis. Prentice Hall. 221. Print.

10 Bartlett, W., Bateman, M., & Vehovec, M. (2002). Small Enterprise Development in South-East Europe: Policies for Sustainable Growth. Boston: Kluwer Academic. Print.

11 Statista. (2014). Revenue of accounting, tax preparation, bookkeeping, and payroll services (NAICS 5412) in the United States from 2008 to 2018 (in million U.S. dollars). Statista Research Department. Retrieved from www.statista.com/forecasts/311178/us-accounting-tax-preparation-bookkeeping-and-payroll-services-revenue-forecast-naics-5412

12 Top 10 Small Business ideas for Accountants & Auditors 2018. (n.d.). Retrieved from www.profitableventure.com/accountants-and-auditors/.

13 Diaz-Briquets, S., & Weintraub S. (1991). Migration, Remittances, and Small Business Development: Mexico and Caribbean Basin Countries. Boulder: Westview. Print.

14 Lawrence, S. (1996). Accounting problems of developing countries. In International Accounting (p. 421). Cengage Learning Business Press.

15 International Financial Reporting Standards. (2017, May 18). In Wikipedia, The Free Encyclopedia. https://en.wikipedia.org/w/index.php?title=International_Financial_Reporting_Standards&oldid=78101246.

16 Kieso, D. E., Weygandt, J. J., & Warfield, T. D. (2010). Intermediate Accounting. Hoboken, NJ: John Wiley & Sons. Print.

17 Fox, J. (1994). Accounting and Recordkeeping Made Easy for the Self-employed. New York: John Wiley. Print.

18 Pinson, L. (2007). Keeping the Books. Chicago: Dearborn. Print.

19 Brigham, E. F., & Houston, J. F. (2012). Fundamentals of Financial Management. Cengage Learning.

Index